Shakers

From Neo-Christianity
to Presocialism

The University of Massachusetts Press, Amherst 1971

The American Shakers

From Neo-Christianity to Presocialism

HENRI DESROCHE

Translated from the French and
edited by John K. Savacool

Originally published in 1955 as *Les Shakers américains:*
D'un néo-Christianisme a un pre-socialisme?
Copyright 1955 by les Éditions de Minuit

Translation and new matter copyright © 1971
by The Shaker Community, Inc.

Library of Congress Catalog Card Number 78–123537
Set in Bell and Linofilm Baskerville types and
printed in the United States of America by
Kingsport Press Incorporated

Published with the support and cooperation of
The Shaker Community, Incorporated

Publisher's Acknowledgments

THE University of Massachusetts Press takes great pleasure in presenting M. Henri Desroche's work on the American Shakers to the English-language community and wishes to acknowledge the following individuals and organizations:

We appreciate the monumental task Professor Savacool faced in not only translating the French text but also checking sources and quotations in English while on a sabbatical in Paris far from the libraries and reference works most convenient to such a chore. We thank him for labors far beyond the duty of an ordinary translator.

Professor Norman Birnbaum of Amherst College (M. Desroche's American representative) read through the typescript and made numerous helpful recommendations. Mary L. Richmond of the Shaker Bibliographic Project double-checked all the citations in the notes and offered many emendations to the text as well—her work greatly enriched the book and eased the publisher's task considerably. Mr. Eugene Merrick Dodd, curator of the Hancock Shaker Village, read the typescript and made a number of suggestions. June Guicharnaud did a scrupulously meticulous job of copy-editing.

Last, the Press is grateful to Mrs. Laurence K. Miller and the Shaker Community, Incorporated, of Pittsfield, Massachusetts, for the generous subvention and moral support which made the translation and publication of this volume possible.

Contents

List of Charts

The American Shakers

From Neo-Christianity to Presocialism

Introduction

Shakerism has a double claim on our interest, for its story comes to us as one of the last chapters in the history of sectarian Christianity and as one of the first chapters in the prehistory of modern socialism.

It derived from the millenarian obsession of the Cevenole prophets in southern France during the religious persecutions of the first decade of the eighteenth century. A few survivors fled to London, where they were referred to as the "French Prophets" when they revived the trances and deliria that had so excited the imaginations of the insurgent mountaineers and weavers of the Cévennes. They were soon joined by a group of "English Prophets," and subsequently, in 1742, in the more or less clearly defined wake of the movement, there appeared a strange subgroup of convulsionaries whom the public called "Shakers"—and the name was to stick. This small, exhilarated band began to gnaw away at the membership of the Quakers and the Methodists, especially among the population of Lancaster, which had already been upset by the emergence of the first textile mills. Up to this point the Shaker story still belongs to what is rightly called the history of religious sects.

But at the same time it already belongs to the prehistory of socialism. For this vague movement had crystallized in the primitive social consciousness of a British proletariat still in its Luddite phase. Ann Lee, the founder, was a Manchester factory girl at a time when columns of striking workers were smashing the machines they blamed for their misery.

Having thus been on the edges of the workers' movement, at its very beginning, Shakerism would continue to follow a path parallel to that of American socialism. It preceded, by several decades, the great wave of Owenites, Fourierites, and Cabetists in North America; and when these societies appeared, the Shakers either inspired them or became their rival. They recruited, among the disillusioned members of these societies, those who had nevertheless not given up; and the movement influenced (perhaps) Bellamy, supported Henry George, and undertook a mission to convert far-off Tolstoi. At any rate, and despite its varying fortunes, despite the cruel decline that gnawed away at its numbers after the Civil War, it remains in retrospect — considering its duration, size, and success — at the top of the list of organizations of communities in America.

The period of serious religious differences within Christianity seemed to have passed: the most recent, Methodism, was appreciably anterior to the first Shaker expansion. The period of serious doctrinal differences within socialism was yet to come: the first of these, represented by the Owenites and the Fourierites, would appear several decades after the Shaker movement was founded. Between these two periods the Shakers tried their luck, and success looked so certain that they thought they had introduced a new era, the age of the "Millennial Church," which they envisioned as a dual creation, achieving a pristine Christianity in a definitive form of socialism.

It was only a dream which was later to be filed away in the company of other "Utopias" that have fallen victim to the harsh facts of reality. Although this judgment of Shakerism is undoubtedly valid, it does not diminish the sociological importance of the event. And, perhaps, considering recent interest in developing a sociology of Utopia, one should even protest and say "on the contrary, not valid at all."[1]

By virtue of its double claim, as a religion and as an early form of socialism, Shakerism has been the subject of regular articles not only in encyclopedias, dictionaries, and histories of religious sects,[2] but also in the inventories and sociological descriptions of the nineteenth-century American "communities."[3] One could add to this list (for they sometimes include interesting interviews) the numerous accounts of the trips made to nineteenth-century America.[4] On the whole, in these travel books the subject is popularized to meet a reader's taste for the picturesque, and the accounts are tiresomely repetitious. Of course, there are exceptions (such as certain chapters of Nordhoff and Hinds), which have often been used as source material, sometimes only half acknowledged.[5]

A second level of information has been furnished by the more detailed and solid accounts written either by partisans or dissenters, the first being facile apologists, and the second, inevitably, gross exaggerators. *A Portraiture of Shakerism* by Mary Dyer is an important example of the second type, if only by virtue of the care taken by the author to include material from previous pamphlets.[6] *Shakerism, Its Meaning and Message* by Anna White and Leila Taylor is the most recent example of partisan account. J. Prudhommeaux, who visited the Shakers when this work was being written, thought that it would replace all others on the subject.[7] Thus in the story of Shakerism there are the dark views and the bright views that interweave and are often in dialogue with each other.

A third level of information — and the most important — is formed by the large body of publications in which the life of the "sect" was directly expressed without any intermediary: legends of their heroes and saints,[8] theological treatises and exegeses,[9] reports of trials,[10] hymnals,[11] manuals of decorum,[12] catalogues,[13] collected correspondences,[14] speeches and sermons,[15] brochures of apologetic or polemic disputes,[16] and so on. The basic material is plentiful.

Finally, there are the unpublished records in the archives. Their location and contents were the subject of two bibliographic notes.[17] They have been partially exploited in several excellent studies that have appeared in America since the beginning of the century. Foremost among these are certainly the comprehensive work of MacLean[18] and the three books by Edward Deming Andrews.[19]

It is not the purpose of the present work to add anything new to the history of the Shakers. One of the more recent overall historical studies is that by Marguerite Melcher.[20] It has been superseded by Andrews in a recently published work which cannot be consulted too often.[21]

The documents presently available[22] may be considered sufficient for undertaking a sociological analysis of this socioreligious dissent represented for almost 200 years by the Shaker movement, with its thousands of members, its nineteen communities, its ambition to bring to a successful conclusion the traditional stand of free churches against the world of church establishments,[23] its hour of pride in beating American socialism on the ground of "true Christianity,"[24] and also its end result, which seems to have earned the Shaker movement a place among vanished species in the annals of sociogenesis.[25] Such is the analysis that will be undertaken here.

This analysis will revolve largely around what must be called the Shaker "communities." The ideological double-talk that periodically lurks in the word "community" and "communistic" has been rightly exposed.[26] The Shakers themselves did not use the word systematically: the small-scale group, based on property-production and consumption in common, the group which formed the mother-cell of their social organization, was usually referred to in their literature as a "Family." Indeed, sociologically, this group would be nearer to the "big family" (such as the Serbian "zadruga" or family-in-common)[27] than to the "village community" if the "Family" ties as the Shakers conceived them were not purely spiritual and did not systematically exclude all ties of flesh and blood.[28] American authors, however, commonly use the term "community" to designate what the Shakers created.[29] A. E. Bestor recently tried to justify the general use of this term and to define its limits.[30] When applied to the Shakers the term becomes doubly equivocal, since it has often been used to designate two distinct elements in the Shaker social structure: the "Family" and the "Society."[31] But the word does have certain advantages, if only that of being widely used in the literature of the subject. And while respecting the reservations just made, we shall continue to use it in this study.

Rather than continue prejudging the various meanings of the word, I shall simply point out how the "community" experiment of the Shakers occurred historically at the point of intersection of two historical realities: the "sect" and the "cooperative."

When E. Troeltsch describes "sect" in the language of "community" his description matches Shaker typology detail for detail:

Lay Christianity, the moral and religious development of the person, absolute loyalty both to the group and to individual friends, religious equality and fraternal love, indifference to the authority of the State and the ruling classes, hatred of the courts and of taking oaths, dissociation of religious and economic life by means of an ideal of poverty and frugality or, circumstantially, of *mutual dependence on the religious level turning into practical communism,* frankness in religious debate, criticism of the offical guides and theologians, an appeal to the New Testament and to the early Church.[32]

And again: "Contrary to the institutional principal of an objective organism, the sect is a *voluntary community* whose members have freely joined together. . . . One is not born into a sect; one enters it on the basis of a conscious conversion." Troeltsch's remarks suggest a positive interpretation of the "Sect Type" (*Sektentypus*), which he associates with voluntary church membership for believers, in contrast to the pejorative interpretation that dominates the church establishment (*Kirchentypus*), with its obligatory membership for the masses.[33] His description ties in easily with the "type" of religious association that the Shakers held as a model. Troeltsch's perfectly uniform, brotherly, egalitarian, and libertarian environment, which would be both antichurch and antiworld, is precisely what the Shakers wanted to establish. This resemblance between Troeltsch's "Sect Type" and the Shaker ideal is brought out all the more sharply by the fact that Troeltsch does not seem to recognize the full significance of this dissident movement.[34]

"Mutual dependence which, by force of circumstances, creates a practical communism." Under the Shakers this circumstantial transformation became the goal of a systematic development. In the Shakers' "voluntary community" the religious fact engendered an economic fact.

Moreover, although the Shaker communities still correspond to Troeltsch's description of a communist brotherhood that has been created, circumstantially, by a "sect," they also correspond to, and anticipate, what several sociologists have defined as a fully developed cooperative. This is what J. Prudhommeaux in his lectures on "Experimental Communism in the New World" called a "communist society" as distinguished from "copartnership" or "joint-stock company,"[35] what Charles Gide called "complete cooperation" in the Collège de France lectures in which he endeavored to define the stages leading to its realization,[36] what Henri Lasserre also called "complete cooperating,"[37] what Martin Buber called *vollgenossenschaft* when referring to the analyses of Buchez and W. King;[38] lastly, it is what Henrik Infield called "all-inclusive cooperation" as distinguished from "segmented cooperation."[39]

In all these approaches to the subject the ideal cooperative community is defined as:

1. Property held in common and joint ownership of the means of production, particularly of land
2. Community organization of production
3. The tendency for goods to be consumed by the same people who produce them
4. Collective consumption
5. Unaminous support of the social ideal that the community advocates, practices, and eventually preaches to the outside world.

Each of these features is, of course, an ideal and thus subject to variations and degrees of realization. The Shakers went a long way toward realizing them:

1. Shaker property was held in common and there was joint ownership for all members of the "Church Order."[40]
2. The Shakers organized their work by groups, with a system of alternation in which some observers believe they can detect the influence of Fourier.
3. In these Shaker farm communities food was consumed by those who produced it; there were small autonomous workshops for the production of consumer goods (clothing, furniture, housekeeping machines, lodging, etc.).
4. The Shakers were organized for collective consumption (dwellings, meals, schools, etc.).
5. There was a unanimity of faith among the "True Believers." Theirs was a practical faith implying indifference to the personal ideologies of group members (this permitted a certain pluralism), but also implying a break with the "Churches" (antisacramentalism) and with the "world" (the principle of conscientious objection).

The details and the complexities of these Shaker traits will appear in the course of this study.

A first step toward clarification of this typology comes when the Shakers are compared to similar communities that grew and blossomed on the American scene at a particularly rapid rate during the eighteenth and nineteenth centuries.

During recent decades there have been successive attempts to enumerate and classify these community enterprises. One of the most pertinent of these, the study by Deets, maintains that it is possible to approximate with a high degree of accuracy the dates of the founding and the breaking up of 130 Utopian community systems in North America, representing 244 separate communities. Among these there were 35 systems representing 125 admittedly religious communities and 95 systems representing 119 nonreligious communities."[41] (See Table I.1.).

TABLE I.1
Utopian Community Systems

	BASIS OF ORGANIZATION	
	Religious	*Nonreligious*
Systems (or networks) of communities	35	95
Separate communities	125	119
Average number of communities per network	2.71	1.25

The systems based on religion seem to have proliferated at twice the rate of the systems *not* based on religion. And in this first group the Shaker movement was well ahead of the average. The same religious consciousness and the same organizational structure was found in the nineteen Shaker communities or, more precisely, in the nineteen societies, each of which usually comprised several Families; and the size of a Family often grew to a number beyond anything found in the nonreligion-based groups, these often being limited to the size of a Shaker subgroup.

The religious communities also seem to have enjoyed a longer life, as is indicated by Deet's résumé when one translates his results into percentages, as in Table I.2.

TABLE I.2
Survivors in Utopian Systems (by percent)

SYSTEMS	BASIS OF ORGANIZATION	
Survivors at the end of:	*Religious*	*Nonreligious*
one year	90%	50%
25 years	50%	3%
100 years	several	none

These comparisons are useless as the basis for making a value judgment. Classification of communities as religious or nonreligious types remains relative. The same relativity that clouded classification of types in studies of the Russian dissensions growing out of Raskol[42] makes it difficult to classify the "American communities." If an Owenite like Frederick Evans was drawn to the Shakers, who were a maximum religious type, it was precisely because he found in them the kind of struggle against organized religion that Robert Owen had taught him to look for. Brook Farm, that "Port-Royal of American Fourierism," remained transcendentalist at the same time that it became Fourierist. The road traveled by one of its founders, George Ripley, is quite suggestive in this respect. And in what category should Oneida be placed, with its half-scientific, half-religious emphasis on eugenics? Since the logic implicit in the organization of all these experiments implied a measure of ambiguity, it would be difficult not to include Oneida with the others.

One can, however, affirm categorically that as far as longevity is concerned, the Shakers are well ahead of all the other groups of communities—nearly 200 years ahead. This lifespan is exceeded only by the Hutterites, and then only if one counts the European phase of their history.

It is very difficult to obtain any precise information on dates and sizes. Some of these are furnished by J. Eaton and S. Katz[43] in an inventory that integrates the results of previous research. Clark's book on the small sects[44] furnishes additional information. But it is just as if the community experiments had wanted to conceal from themselves the disproportion between the habitual narrowness of their practical program and the fullness of their ambition.

If, while taking into account the fact of inevitable approximations, one examines the list—set up in terms of size and longevity—of the communities classified as religious (see Chart no. 2), one is led to make several observations:

1. The great period of American community experi-

ments (based on religion) occurred before 1850. After that period, if the Hutterite immigration had not brought in an important new phenomenon, there would have been nothing left for us to count except a few whimsical, small-scale, fumbling subgroups. If it is to be complete, the analysis should include a complementary table listing all the communities called nonreligious. On this list the socialist experiments (Owenites, Fourierists, and Cabetists), although ephemeral, would appear particularly important, and later there would appear the more indigenous networks of the Ruskinian and Georgist communities.

2. Taken as a whole, the religious communities founded during the period before 1850 have a common origin, and recognition of this is fundamental to an understanding of their nature. They all appear on the scene as part of the European exodus, with its common motivation, which was to flee the Churches and the European governments with which those churches were in collusion. A Shaker will go so far as to speak of the European "God" who had been defeated in the War of Independence. Nor was this motive alien to the first English migration. The Puritans, for example, before becoming intolerant of the Quakers in New England had emigrated to the New World in order to flee religious intolerance in the homeland.[45] It is also known that this first migration, having had the same common cause, also had, at least temporarily, the same effect: the first contingents to debark in the new land organized themselves into "communities."[46] The fact remains that American communities (based on religion) in the eighteenth and nineteenth centuries, whether they had emigrated from Holland,[47] Germany,[48] Sweden,[49] Bohemia,[50] or England, were above all motivated less by a clear idea of what they wanted than by a certainty of what they did not want, and what they did not want was the coalition of church and state, which had been making life impossible for them in Europe. A free land where they could freely live their faith — fundamentally, that is what they were asking for, obsessed as they were with their duty to move out of a world they so easily

conceived to be in the hands of the Antichrist. Analogous reasons would later determine the emigration of the Doukhobors, who were guided and protected by Leo Tolstoi, and the exodus of the Hutterites, who, ultimately, were joined by the Brüderhofe.

3. All of these migrations belonged to the post-Reformation period. Similar nonconformist movements had appeared within the medieval church, but the possibilities for migration at that time had remained restricted to a Mediterranean world that was more or less a closed circle. For lack of a way out, the medieval solution was extermination, asphyxiation, reconversion, or survival in the mountains. For several centuries that was how the Waldenses held on to what one is tempted to call their *maquis*. It is also possible that the existence of religious orders offered a partial, temporary outlet and even, for certain nonconformisms, a kind of ecclesiastic solution. It will be seen that, under similar conditions, certain Shakers were going to try to assure the survival of their movement by becoming a chartered order in the framework of American Protestantism. At any rate, after the emergence of the great Protestant orientations (the Lutherans, the Anglicans, and the Presbyterians), it seems that here and there appear examples of a lay religious movement that is not only non-Papist but also non-Episcopalian and even non-Presbyterian, and which (a) claimed a certain primacy of the "inner light" and the Holy Ghost, not only over church tradition but also over the Holy Scriptures themselves;[51] (b) preached that revelation is never-ending and that therefore a new age, the age of the spirit, required and provided new prophets; and (c) intended at last to live their church life as a world within the world, their refusal to honor the ties between established churches and constituted authority having, as a corollary, the obligation of *their* church to evolve in a milieu of economic and political self-sufficiency. Anabaptism was the first manifestation of the type, and, as everyone knows, the debacle at Münster was far from exhausting that movement.[52]

To groups with these tendencies the discovery of a new world in America offered an alternative to the *maquis*. Their migration took on the appearance of a sacred exodus. Accelerated by the Reformation and by the steady disintegration of authoritarian religion, to the extent that they found no means of expression within the reform movement itself, these religious libertarians would henceforth seek, in accordance with their belief in new heavens, the vital living space of a new land. No wonder the Quaker William Penn, newly endowed with a piece of the new continent, would find such an abundance of candidates for the promised land[53] when he made the rounds of dissident Europe.

4. In the European background of the American religious communities of this first period, one more analogy can be seen: their distant place of origin ties almost all of them to the socioreligious revolutions in Europe between the fifteenth and the eighteenth centuries. The great turmoils caused by the fifteenth-century war against the Hussites, by the sixteenth-century Peasants' Revolt in Germany, and by the seventeenth-century political revolution in England, these all endowed America of the eighteenth and nineteenth centuries with communities whose members descended from the veterans of those revolutions. And it should be stressed that these members formed or preformed their communities during the pacifist phase that regularly seems to follow the bellicose phases of such movements. Bethlehem can be traced back (through Herrnhut) to Hunwald (1457), the pacifist community which brought the Bohemian monks together after the military defeat of the Taborite group at Lipan in 1434.[54] The Hutterites, a branch of pacifist Anabaptism, grew rapidly after the massacre of the peasants and the disappearance of Thomas Münzer in Frankenhausen in 1525. The German pietist communities flourished during the same phase and were in direct contact with the stampeding prophets of the Cévennes, both pietists and Cevenoles having known Zinzendorf and, through him, probably, the Moravian tradition.[55] The Shakers themselves were linked

not only to the Cevenole prophets in exile but also, through the Quakers, to the wave of pacifism which followed the political liquidation of the Levellers during the English revolution and the failure of the Diggers communities which had tried to establish squatters' rights on private property.[56]

Everything happened just as if the social drives and the religious motives brought together by these historic movements were, after failing in a trial of force, trying out a technique of flexibility and disengagement by starting all over again to make a new world in miniature which would compensate for having failed to remake the old one on a grand scale. This hope was all the less likely to be realized since the world of here-and-now, the only one that exists, was becoming less elastic. American society could provisionally offer these groups of immigrants a surface on which they could settle and organize their communities. But the density of America's scientific culture and technological civilization would soon alter their modes of cohesion and witness their decline—a decline that could be avoided only by new emigration, as in the case of the Hutterites. Moreover, depending on the nature of one's optimism or pessimism, this decline can be interpreted as indicating either the perishableness of the community formulas in the hands of those outsiders or the deadliness of the ideological and technological environments in which men tried to make these formulas live and survive.

These few coordinates in time and space should be sufficient to situate the general nature of Shakerism and to introduce our study.

CHAPTER ONE

Cevenole Prophesying

THE TWO great Shaker classics are the *Testimony*[1] and the *Millennial Church*.[2] In each of them Cevenole prophesying is mentioned as the direct source of the movement.

The account in *Testimony* is quite brief.[3] The *Millennial Church* on the other hand, presents a detailed report of the Cevenole message:

They testified that *the end of things drew nigh*, and admonished the people to *repent and amend their lives*. They gave warning of *the near approach of the Kingdom of God, the acceptable year of the Lord;* and in many prophetic messages, declared to the world that those numerous scripture prophecies concerning *the new heavens and the new earth; the kingdom of the Messiah; the marriage of the Lamb; the first resurrection,* and *the new Jerusalem descending from above, were near at hand,* and would shortly be accomplished.[4]

About the year 1706, a few of them went over to England, where they renewed their testimony; and through the ministration of the same spirit to others, many were united to them. . . . And though the greater part, after having finished their testimony, soon died away; yet many of them maintained their confidence through life, and a portion of them, who still retained the power of their testimony, in a greater or lesser degree, and having full faith in its accomplishment, stood as living witnesses of God, and, like faithful watchmen of the night, waited the approaching dawn.

About the year 1747, a small number who were endowed with the spirit of these witnesses, were led by influence of the Divine Spirit to unite themselves into a small society, in the neighborhood of Manchester, under the ministry of James and Jane Wardley. These were both sincerely devoted to the cause of God, and were blest with great manifestations of divine light. . . . They boldly testified, *that the second appearing of Christ was at hand; and that the Church was rising in her full and transcendant glory, which would effect the final downfall of Antichrist.* They affirmed that the world of *the great day of God* was then commencing, and would increase until every promise of God should be fulfilled.[5]

From this account come two dates that are sacrosanct in Shaker annals: 1706, the arrival of the French Prophets in England, and 1747, the revival led by James and Jane Wardley. These two dates delimit a period that requires a few supplementary details.

In the many accounts of their own history the Shakers are usually satisfied to treat this period by reproducing or summarizing part of the *Millennial Church.* It is in an unfriendly pamphlet by Mary Dyer[6] that the Shakers are portrayed as wanting to know more about their antecedents than what is revealed in their official text. It is true that this text does cautiously stipulate:

And probably too, as often happens in times of great outpourings of the divine Spirit, there were individuals found among them [these French Prophets] into whose hearts Satan found means to infuse a false testimony of faithful witnesses, by associating with it the dictates of his own lying spirit. Unbelievers who slight every manifestation of true light, will often take occasion by the false predictions of such individuals, to reject and misrepresent the whole as unworthy of credit.[7]

But Shaker prudence does not seem to have wanted to venture any further in a more explicit examination of events in this overvenerated or insufficiently illuminated past.

Mary Dyer, on the other hand, was soon going to examine this question and use it to satisfy the needs of her churlish nature. She found what she was looking for. She reread the polemicists of the period[8] and unearthed enough from them to cover the Shakers' forefathers with ridicule; hence, the famous story of the abortive resurrection of Docteur Eames.[9] She also unearthed the name of John Lacy, linking James and Jane Wardley, whose appearance on the scene in

1747 is noted in the chronicle, with the French Prophets who debarked in London in 1706: Elie Marion, Jean Cavalier, and Durand Fage.[10]

The odyssey of these emigrated prophets is now well known,[11] and we also know that when these refugees from religious persecution in the Cévennes came to London, they were soon again in conflict with ecclesiastic and civil authority. Moreover, they took pains to tell everyone about their quarrels with the conservative French ministry in the Church of Savoy (in Westminster).[12] When the Bishop of London became concerned, the pastors of the French colony summoned the prophets to a hearing, and after a series of five interviews (from October to November), the Church of Savoy dissociated itself from the prophets' activities. The Consistory Act, read aloud in London's three French churches on 5 January 1707, condemned the behavior of these would-be prophets and judged their acts to be the result of willful practices completely unworthy of the wisdom of God, and their pronouncements to be replete with offensive contradictions, obvious lies, predictions that had already been proved false, and blasphemies very dangerous to religion. The resistance in France had ended in a deadlock and driven these Cevenoles to England. Their proselytizing within the émigré colony of London resulted in another deadlock, and this one would lead them to sink roots deep into English society itself.[13]

One of their first and most turbulent recruits was John Lacy. It was he who, in April 1707, translated the *Théâtre sacré des Cévennes* into English under the title *A Cry from the Desert, or Testimonials of the Miraculous Things Lately Come to Pass in the Cévennes verified upon Oath and by Other Proofs* (London, 1707). It was also he who, in July of that year, published at his own expense *The Prophetical Warnings*, a work that was inspired by and, according to Vesson, plagiarized from *Avertissements* by Elie Marion, which had been published three months earlier.[14] Another book by the same John Lacy was soon forthcoming: *Warnings of the Eternal Spirit by the Mouth of His servant John, Sirnam'd Lacy. The*

Second (and Third) Part (London, 1707). Perhaps, as G. Ascoli points out, there was an element of competition in this prolixity of John Lacy.[15]

But whatever may have been the motives of these men, their excitement seems to have been great, judging by the abundance of attacks and arguments that went back and forth during the years 1707–1708, of which an impressive list has been established.[16] Another occasion of public unrest came on 28 November 1707 when a suit was brought against Marion, Daudé, and Fatio. The three "prophets" were sentenced to the pillory and ordered to make a public condemnation of Elie Marion's tract *Advertissement*. Finally, one month later came the death of Thomas Emes, the follower whose name Mary Dyer would spell "Eames." A series of ill-advised prophecies announced his resurrection for the month of May 1708. John Lacy used public disturbances and the likelihood of police intervention as a pretext to cancel the miracle and explain to the people, whom it was useless to hold in check: "We have preferred public peace and security of the government to our own interest and our reputation."[17] The disappointment – if there was any – did not seem to have halted the progress of the movement on the English scene, since a good number of English names figure on the roll book which was started in 1708–1709 and organized according to a scheme that Elie Marion and the prophetess Jeanne Roux had borrowed from the twelve tribes of Israel. In the handwritten letter to Flotard in which Portalès transcribed this inventory, out of 150 members, all equipped with their new biblical names, 90 are English.[18]

In subsequent years the English naturalization of the movement was facilitated and accelerated by the departure to the continent of the French Prophets. From June to September 1711 several of them (including Elie Marion) made a four-month trip to Germany and Holland. This trip produced a new collection of prophecies.[19] Then, from 1712 to 1714, came the long and complicated journey to Germany, Sweden, Poland, Bohemia-Moravia, Hungary, and Constantinople, with a return via Italy. This was the journey during which Elie Marion met his death on 29 November 1713. Naturally, the others brought a new book of prophecies back with them.[20]

During this time the English branch revealed its persistent vitality in a series of manifestations in which one can see some elements that are significant for the subsequent history of the Shakers:

(a) *A rash of "prophecies":* Inspired souls were prophesying all over the country, and they carefully collected the "Warnings" as they came in from Bristol, Edinburgh, Glasgow, and Birmingham.[21]

These prophecies of the "English Prophets" were sometimes combined with those of the "French Prophets." The messages collected by the latter during their long trip of 1712–1714 were published in Amsterdam with a foreword (in French) entitled "Warnings from the Holy Spirit, Message Delivered in English in Edinburgh on Sunday 10 February 1714 from the Mouth of James Cunninghame." Cunninghame had been spreading the word in England since 1710.

Did the early Shakers know about this series of collected warnings? It is not impossible, at any rate, that they were referring to one or the other of these collections when they wrote that the spirit of the French Prophets continued to act "in a greater or lesser degree"[22] and that doubtful testimonies might well have been joined to the true testimonies.[23]

(b) *Evangelical journeys:* "From 1708 to 1710, regular meetings were held in the center of London. But although Lacy and Potter more willingly stayed in London, others went out to Cambridge, Oxford, Coventry, Worcester, Bristol, deep into Wales, Ireland, Scotland. . . ."[24]

Around 1711, according to Ascoli, the Spirit forbade the prophets to assemble for any more meetings.[25] Nevertheless, they started to meet again around 1739 and in a manner that was virulent enough to cause the Methodists formally to take a stand. At any rate, they never ceased to proselytize, since (a precedent to remember) fifty-eight years before Ann Lee set sail for the New World, an English prophetess, Mary

Keimer, crossed the Atlantic expressly to spread the new faith in Pennsylvania.[26] Note that in doing this she was taking up again the feminist tradition of evangelizing that had been inaugurated in the New World a century earlier by the Quakers.[27]

(c) *Crises within the movement:* Two of these should be noted since their themes more or less directly announce the themes of the Shakers. The first was opened in 1710 by Abraham Whitrow. In accordance with a logic that has been repeated many times in religious history, this man started to pour all the fire of his prophetic talents into a campaign for social reform: "In his mouth the Spirit began to speak a language that was clear and precise. He preached a social leveling, total communism, the obligation of the rich to share all their wealth with the poor."[28] At this point, as so often happens, the prophet won the support of a prominent person, in this case Sir Richard Bulkeley. John Lacy spent useless time and ink in an effort to dissuade him from following this new line, but Bulkeley accompanied Whitrow on trips through England and Ireland, writing down his messages. These became the subject of a book: *Warnings of the Eternal Spirit as Pronounced by the Mouth of God's Servant, Abraham Whitrow.*[29] In his preface Bulkeley insisted on calling Whitrow's text the purest and most certain expression of the Gospel as it had been before deluding commentaries had corrupted the holy word.[30] If the Shakers knew of this conflict, they must have sided with Whitrow's language against John Lacy's hesitation; moreover, another reason would soon prejudice them against Lacy.

A supplementary discussion had indeed been opened by John Lacy and his new theory of marriage. Is it possible that on this subject Lacy showed the influence of a tendency already central to Cevenole prophesying? It is difficult to say.[31] The fact remains that he left his wife in 1711, claiming the right and the duty to take a prophetess into his bed; all this he justified in his "Letter from John Lacy to Thomas Dutton or Reasons Why the First-named Left His Wife and Took into His Bed Elizabeth Gray, a Prophetess" (1711). "Failure of marriage," the Shakers were to cry. But they would give their slogan a meaning quite the opposite of John Lacy's and would pass over his name in silence when they established an inventory of their predecessors. Lacy nevertheless remained a leader among the English Prophets. This we know, since in 1720 and 1725 two important tracts on prophecy were signed with his name.[32]

By insisting on the difference between themselves and the French Prophets, the English prophetic movement probably remained subject to numerous internal differences of its own. Unfortunately it is difficult to discover onto exactly what branch James Wardley grafted the group which, according to Shaker accounts, he formed into a society in 1747. Daryl Chase is inclined to believe that Shaker writers overstated their relationship with the French Prophets in order to play down their ties with the Quakers. Indeed, some historians think that as a phenomenon the French Prophets had almost completely disappeared around 1740.[33] Moreover, their disappearance would tally with the image suggested by *Millennial Church* of "a few faithful watchmen in the night." However, in 1742 the subject of prophecy again inspired an Anglican to write a "history of the French Prophets, of their convulsions, their ecstasies, their inspirations" entitled *Strange Tale, or Faithful History* (Glasgow, 1742).[34] At about the same time, John Wesley was in conflict with prophetic gatherings, and not just in Manchester.[35] Survival, then, was not limited to Lancashire, where the Wardley group had appeared. Morever, the phenomenon of religious trances was not limited to the surviving circles of prophecy. Similar convulsions were observed in Wesley's first meetings. Perhaps, to explain this similarity one could find, here and there, some connection between the extravagant hopes of apocalyptic evangelism and the illiteracy of men besieged by failure and despair. It remains to point out that Wesley and Whitefield addressed themselves to mass audiences of the industrial proletariat. The English Prophets, on the other hand, seemed to have remained in small groups.[36] It is possible that the Wardley revival, as amplified by Ann Lee in America, represented a return to the custom of preaching to the multitudes, something that had been impractical for the French Prophets in exile and unpracticed by their English followers. Thus one can say that Ann Lee reached back over the forty-year span (1707–1747) made famous by John Lacy and joined hands with the great tradition of Cevenole prophesying from which the Shakers would later claim to have descended, although they were to remain silent on the subject of events during the intervening forty years.

If this be so, what traits of the Cevenole ancestors constituted the distant beginnings of traits later found in their Shaker grandsons? We shall limit our answer to a simple enumeration.

1. *Religious experience as a state of ecstasy, a characteristic of revivals.* Quite apart from the effusions of ignorant fanatics, Cevenole prophesying from the very beginning was characterized by "seizures," "trances," and "holy rolling." As early as 1689 Jurieu was using the word "Shakers" when speaking of the prophets in the "wilderness": "*nos Trembleurs*" (15 June 1689). The dramatic changes and modalities of their convulsions have already been described.[37] According to the Shakers, this extraordinary behavior could be attributed to no cause other than "the power of almighty God." On this point Cevenole apologetics read like Shaker literature, and descriptions of the Shaker trances are strikingly similar to descriptions of the Cevenole ecstasies.[38]

2. *Millennialism.* Jurieu's prophecies and computations are well known, as are their repercussions on the psychological states of the Cevenole fighters.[39] The most famous of these is certainly the one of 1686 in which he predicted the fall of "Babylon" for 1689—*within three years.* The Shakers learned about this later and, far from being disconcerted by the subsequent events, went to work to give it a godly interpretation: "The candid believer will readily discern between truth and falsehood, and pay that respect to the true manifestations of the Spirit of God which their importance deserves."[40] This passage of *Millennial Church* is followed by a computation[41]

which postpones for almost a thousand years the long-term events that were apt to validate Jurieu's predictions of 1686–1698.[42]

3. *The role of women*. The importance among the Cevenoles of the woman-prophet and her religious functions has often been pointed out.[43] Very early in England women could also be seen occupying important positions in the movement. We have already mentioned how Mary Keimer departed for Pennsylvania on an evangelizing mission. At the heart of the English group there were many prophetesses: "The principal roles had fallen to Lacy, Potter, Glover, and to some young English girls: Betty Gray, Mary Beer, Mary Keimer, Mary Turner, Anna Watts, and Anna Maria King."[44]

Was this religious upgrading of women accompanied, as so often happens in similar dissents, by a basic revalution of her social role and by calling into question the institution of marriage? A long manuscript-pamphlet in the library of Nîmes tries to prove that this was the case and that the prophetesses of the Cévennes were really all latter-day Héloïses.[45] If this was true, then John Lacy's libel in 1711 must have had some precedents. That there was a general questioning of marriage as an institution is certain, but it is difficult to know whether it was being revaluated from an ascetic, a "courtly," or a licentious point of view, as the history of parallel movements such as the medieval dualists and the Russian Khlysti[46] have shown. The Shakers, who quite deliberately chose to call into question the institution of marriage from an ascetic point of view, were not immune to accusations of license. In any case, it is clear that the Wardleys had decided in favor of "spiritual" marriage,[47] whether or not this option had been favored by their prophet-predecessors.

4. *The working-class character of the dissent*. The popular base of the Cevenole dissent has been pointed out time and again. The recruiting was done largely from among the peasants, journeymen, artisans, and weavers.[48] The reasons for this (presence of the people, absence of the ruling and the middle class) have been meticulously examined and discussed. The strictly political exploitation of this uprising does indeed look

like an extraneous operation or something that has been tacked on after the event. And, moreover, the movement does not present the traits of a *jacquerie* with precise demands for social reform.[49] At first it would seem to be a refusal of the people to submit to the "sacrilegious" coalition of civil power and the church establishment. The prophetic utterances provoked by this refusal lent a theocratic and anti-ecclesiastic note to the crude organization of the Cevenole bands, and at the same time, after much splitting of hairs, they spread doubts on the legitimacy of civil authority, in this case the authority of the royal crown. "Every nation that seats a king on the throne reserves the right to unseat him when he goes beyond the limits of his duties." This declaration comes from *Soupirs de la France esclave qui aspire après la liberté,* a book published in Holland in 1689. It is significant that this book was republished in France a hundred years later (1788).[50] Does this mean that in France, associated with Protestant resistance, one can see the first signs of a new political consciousness leading to a conception of popular sovereignty? The thesis has been defended.

The Shakers also were to derive from a popular environment and from a milieu of artisans and weavers. We shall see that they were as wildly republican *ad extra* as they were theocratic *ad intra.*[51]

5. *Antiecclesiastic attitude, or secularism* ad extra. About the time when the Raskol's revolt against the Russian Orthodox hierarchy had deprived that movement of its parish priests and forced it to develop the extreme congregationist formulas of the "bezpopovtsi" (popeless ones), the Protestant pastors of France faced a series of official harassments, followed by the brutal revocation of the Edict of Nantes, which forced them to choose between exile, prison, or recantation. The French Protestant Church came out of this period decapitated, and with the majority of its pastors in exile, it too began to operate as a system of pastorless congregations.[52]

A gap was created between the ministers and their flocks. This gap was increased by the fact that laymen were performing the function first of preachers and later, after investiture by the assemblies, of ministers. Jurieu approved this spontaneous move.[53] Even women were not excluded from these improvised responsibilities: "The shepherds were far from their flocks; what did it matter whether the comforters were men or women?"[54] Brousson, in his summons to the ministers who had fled to the Protestant states, constantly reiterates this fact: "Has not God already given the call and is He not still calling on laymen to preach to your flocks the truth that you no longer preach to them?"[55] The appearance on the scene of the *pasteurs du désert* followed by the mission of Antoine Court represented an attempt to repair the breach between the people and their ministers, but the leadership of this "Church in the Wilderness" remained in lay hands and was controlled by the elders.[56]

Both the ministry and the congregations continued to evolve, but each in its own way and without influencing one another. Thus, in 1706, when the French Prophets arrived in London, a conflict quickly developed between these voices out of the "wilderness" and the French pastors in the Savoy Church. Since in a dispute like this the French pastors of London could expect no help from the English Church, the conflict served to accelerate the secularization of the prophetic movement. Thirty-four years later John Wesley, for very different reasons, inaugurated a system of lay preachers in order to meet the demands of his evangelizing program in England.

The movement was soon marked by resentment against the established churches and their collusion with the civil powers of the land. In 1714 the French Prophets published a book in which the text was introduced by a symbolic engraving: "In this engraving the Church is portrayed by the figure of a woman stripped to the waist and tied by four ropes whose ends are being pulled by four churchmen belonging to different Christian denominations: Roman, Greek, Lutheran, and Calvinist. Brandishing their swords, four armed kings threaten to attack the woman whose clothes lie in a heap at the feet of the churchmen. Obviously, the prophets had declared war on all the different clergies and were making no exceptions."[57] Elsewhere, almost the very same idea was to lead to the legend of the Grand Inquisitor.

The Shakers meant to push this demand for complete secularization to the extreme. After a decision similar to the one made by dissident groups of the Raskol,[58] they were led to proclaim the universal priesthood of laymen and to call themselves priests "in the order of Melchisedeck."[59]

6. *Pacificism or holy crusade?* A mixture of both tendencies was basic to the prophetic movement in the Cévennes. Under all circumstances the best of the Cevenoles deplored violence. Even so, the tendency to armed resistance had been given theological justification in Jurieu's *Pastoral Letter* of 12 January 1689: "An Inquiry into the question of whether or not it is permitted to defend one's religion by force of arms."[60] Jurieu's positive position prevailed. Other pastors remained faithful to pacifist principles. One of these was Daniel Raoul, who is cited for his protests against the use of arms.[61] This same Daniel Raoul is referred to as the spiritual forefather of a religious group called the *Inspirés de la Vaunage,* sometimes known as the "Trembleurs,"[62] a group which the English Quakers of 1786 recognized as one of their own. The *Trembleurs* ("Shakers" or "Quakers") were, among other things, profoundly pacifist. They are now considered to be the seed of French Quakerism. Their history has been written.[63]

This encounter on French soil of the English Quakers and the French *Inspirés* or Prophets, which took place in 1785 and ended with the assimilation of the *Inspires* by the Quakers had a lesser known counterpart: the encounter that took place in England during the years 1740–1750, which also produced a pacifist movement and which ended with the dissident Quakers being assimilated by the French Prophets or at least by their successors. Indeed, James and Jane Wardley are both said to have started off as Quakers. The fruit of this cross-fertilization came to be known as the "Shaking Quakers" or Shakers.

CHAPTER TWO

Religious Evolution, Industrial Revolution & Disintegration of the Family in 18th-Century England

THE SECOND phase of Shaker prehistory extends from the founding of the Wardley society in 1747 to Ann Lee's embarkation for America in 1774. For this phase the two fullest accounts are also found in the texts of *Testimony*[1] and the *Millennial Church.*[2] From their twice-told tale one can draw the following facts.

At an unspecified date James Wardley (a tailor) and his wife, who worked at the same trade, were "endowed with the spirit of these witnesses" (the French Prophets). The Wardleys seem to have dropped out of the Quaker society to which they belonged, and for several years, without any denominational ties, they bore witness to the imminent fall of Antichrist and the Second Coming of Christ. Their mission had its beginnings in the town of Bolton.

In 1747 they moved to Manchester and founded a small society of thirty members, who held their meetings somewhere on Cannon Street, where the principal merchants of the city had their homes. In fact, the meeting place of the Wardley society was the house of a certain John Townley, a wealthy masonry contractor.[3] There they revived the trances of the old French Prophets,[4] earning for themselves the name of "Shakers." As so often happens, this epithet which had been imposed on them in derision was subsequently adopted by the group as a gesture in defiance of outside opinion.[5] The movement soon spread from Manchester into the surrounding region.

In 1758 Ann Lee joined the society. The only thing we know with certainty about her background is that she was twenty-two years old and had had a wretched childhood and adolescence. The Shaker narratives substantiate the fact that at the time Ann Lee entered the Wardley society she had already been married for six years to a blacksmith named Stanley, by whom she had had four children, three of whom died in infancy, and the other of whom, a girl, was to die at the age of six.

In 1770 Ann was imprisoned on charges of "profaning the Sabbath." It was during this imprisonment that she had the great revelation which gave her "a full and clear view of the mystery of iniquity, of the root and foundation of human depravity, and of the very act of transgression committed by the first man and woman in the garden of Eden."[6] From that day on, she testified in a clear and precise manner that "no soul could follow Christ in the regeneration, while living in the works of natural generation, or in any of the gratifications of lust."[7] This principle was to become the basic tenet of Shakerism. After Ann Lee was released from prison, by virtue of the light she had received she replaced the Wardleys as the leader of the little society.

In 1773, although the group did not grow in numbers, "the faith and substance of the gospel continued to increase in the hearts of the faithful,"[8] and, as the Shaker texts point out, they ceased all public testimony at that time.

In 1774 Ann Lee had another revelation. She was warned that she would have to seek refuge in America and "at the same time she received a divine promise that the work of God would greatly increase, and the millennial church would be established in that country."[9] Permission to accompany her was given to "all those of the society . . . who were able, and who felt any special impressions on their own minds so to do."[10] Thus, accompanied by eight men and women, she boarded ship on 19 May 1774, and after the wondrous adventures customary during that kind of ocean voyage, they disembarked in New York City on 6 August of the same year.

As one might expect, there have been attempts to explain the sociology of the founding by a psychological analysis of the founder. In a study that errs in basing its conclusions exclusively on sources hostile to the Shakers (the pamphlets), Theo Schroeder has brought to light the following details, which could serve as a psychoanalytic explanation: James Wardley's reputation for polygamy, Ann Lee's need to dominate, her inferiority complex due to low birth and illiteracy, the undeniable existence of a father complex,[11] inhibited erotic desires subsequently sublimated in an exaggerated form of mysticism, and sexual obsessions indicated by certain acts of exhibitionism and sadism described by outsiders condemning those first Shaker meetings.[12] The author is not frank about his working hypothesis, which is that all mystic exaltation is a means of neutralizing an inferiority complex based on erotic emotional disturbances. He believes that morbid depressions and emotion-charged self-centeredness are different aspects of the same personality disturbance, and he supports this generalization with evidence amassed during a broad investigation of this type of problem.[13] Whatever truth there may be in Schroeder's hypothesis and whatever its relevance to the case of Ann Lee (a twofold discussion that goes beyond the scope of the present study), one can at least maintain that a psychoanalytic explanation does not exclude others. A sociological analysis can and should bring to light other coordinates and behavior patterns which in Shaker accounts seem quite probable but which, alas, no historical research on the subject has ever succeeded in making really clear.

I. The Religious Coordinates

The first to consider are the Quaker antecedents. Forerunners James and Jane Wardley are mentioned as having once belonged to the Society of Friends. In a later chapter we shall examine the long delayed attitude, half-hostile, half-friendly, that the Shakers assumed toward Quakerism. It is difficult to determine exactly the nature of their relations during these years 1740–1750. Daryl Chase surmises that the Quaker filiation has been systematically minimized by the later Shaker chroniclers. Research in the Quaker archives at Bolton and Manchester has to date uncovered no mention of the Wardley's defection from the Society of Friends. Yet the fact of this dissent must have been recorded. This seems all the more likely in view of the number of times that Ann Lee's disciples identified themselves as "Shaking Quakers," and in view of the fact that Quaker-baiting polemicists had tried to associate the Shakers with the Society of Friends in a single reproof. Ascoli blames this confusion of the two societies on a pamphleteer named Keith, who, "after preparing a lengthy brochure attacking the Quakers, immediately added a preface, a supplementary exposition, and an expanded conclusion to show that the Camisards deserved to be condemned for the same reasons as the *Trembleurs*."[14]

"Trembleurs"? He was, of course, referring to the Friends, whose trances, at least during the early period of their history, had earned them the name of "quakers" or men who quake (in French, *trembleur*). Similar trances would earn a similar name for the descendants of the French Prophets, who had been gathered into a group shepherded by the Wardleys. And the second group, like the first, was to debate the significance of the name.[15] Later Shaker apologists would point to this similarity of phenomena and names bridging more than a hundred years, as proof that "the power of God" had been withdrawn from their predecessors, henceforth associated with established order, and passed onto the United Believers, who were continuing the struggle against Antichrist and his empire. Indeed, it is true that, after a century of persecution and anxiety, the Quakers were being treated with tolerance. This new sense of security could have made them even more anxious to stay aloof from these ambiguous innovations. A pamphlet such as the one by Keith made it imperative for them to maintain the distinction between the two groups. Indeed, at the beginning of the eighteenth century there appeared a Quaker pamphlet condemning the sham miracles of John Lacy and the French Prophets.[16] Despite this display of hostility, the Quakers did not succeed in preventing the new movement from infiltrating their ranks. We know that on 9 June 1714 a certain Henry Pickworth was repudiated by the Quaker Quarterly Meeting at Lincoln because, among other acts meriting reproach, he had been attending the meetings of those called "French Prophets."[17] The Wardleys had committed the same offense. Were they the subjects of a similar repudiation? That is what the Quaker archives should tell us. After all, it is possible that since the Wardleys were small fry in the movement, their defection did not have the same repercussions as the breaking away of a writer like Pickworth and was thus either officially unnoticed or passed over in silence.

At any rate, several facts seem to prove that there was a similarity in the behavior of the seventeenth-century Quakers and the eighteenth-century Shakers. Ecstatic trances were to be seen during the earliest meetings of both groups.[18] Both decried biblical literalism and appealed to the Inner Light and a revival of the prophetic spirit.[19] Both groups had their eccentrics. The "ranting" so deplored by William Penn had its equivalent in the vulgar language and excessive behavior that marked the first American meetings of the Millennial Church.[20] And, finally, both groups were in competition with established religion and intended to make life difficult for the other churches, which they deemed to be practicing liturgies of Antichrist. We know that when the Quakers suppressed the ministry within the structure of their own society, they initiated a campaign outside the church and harassed pastors exercising their functions at the altar or in the pulpit. They interrupted services, peremptorily summoned preachers to answer their questions, and even addressed the congregation after the regular services. It was this attitude, among other things, that was responsible for the persecutions during the second half of the seventeenth century, when thousands of Quakers were thrown into prison, some of them to die there.

Now at a relatively late date in the history of religious strife the same tactics were used by the French Prophets; only, this time the Quakers were included among the adversaries. Elie Halévy mentions the tumultuous entrance made by two of the lady prophets during the silent prayer of a Quaker meeting in Bristol. That particular intervention caused a public disturbance, and the sheriff had to call for soldiers to disperse the crowd.

In the light of this double heritage it is not surprising that the Shakers revealed a similar attitude toward those outside their society. On the subject of Ann Lee's imprisonment around 1770, the Shaker chronicle discretely notes: "under a pretense of her having profaned the Sabbath."[21] Other reports of the event are more explicit. They explain that this profanation of the Sabbath probably meant that the Shakers were doing their sacred dances and that the *mob* considered this a sacrilegious act on Sunday.[22] But the violence was probably not one-sided. Andrews notes at least three brawls followed by arrests. Daryl Chase found a clipping from the *Manchester Mercury* dated 20 July 1773, stating that "Saturday last ended the Quarter Sessions, when John Townley, John Jackson, Betty Lees, and Ann Lees (Shakers), for going into Christ Church, in Manchester, and there willfully and contemptuously, in the time of Divine service, disturbing the congregation then assembled at morning prayers in the said church, were severally fined twenty pounds each."[23] That was the year during which the Shakers ceased holding meetings open to the public.[24] It is not surprising that this incident was passed over in silence by the writers of the Shaker annals. At the time the annals were composed, early Shaker agressiveness had been replaced by a pacifist attitude which, at least in interchurch affairs, was only too glad to offer (and demand) tolerance in return for tolerance. This evolution suggests one more similarity to the history of the Quakers.

Nor is it surprising that shortly afterward Ann Lee had a revelation telling her to seek in America a refuge for herself and a field for her mission. This is yet another trait marking a similarity to the Quakers. After just about one century, Ann Lee was embarking on an adventure exactly like the one of the Quaker Mary Fisher in 1656. Formerly a serving girl in a Yorkshire inn, she had become a preacher after her conversion to Quakerism, was imprisoned a first time in 1652 for having risen to speak after the official religious service in a place of worship, and was punished a second time three years later for a similar offense. Finally, she had a "call" summoning her to the West Indies and, accordingly, in 1656 she boarded a ship and set sail for America.[25] We also know that the second part of Ann Lee's revelation, the command to establish a church in the New World, had become almost traditional. A similar hope had been nourished not only by the first Quakers in New England and the later ones in Pennsylvania but also, at a more recent date, by certain English prophetesses;[26] and long before all of these, it was nourished by the first Puritan fathers who aspired to break all contact with existing European states in order to establish a pure church that would be unspoiled by things human and offer a system of civil government free of all the arbitrary institutions found in the Old World.[27]

When they arrived in the New World, the Shakers had happier relations with the Quakers than the members of that older sect had experienced with their own predecessors. In the history of these two sects there are numerous moments at which they acted in concert.[28] Certain of these have already been noted, and there will be others. Many years later Elder Frederick Evans was to sum up the Shaker-Quaker relation in a few incisive sentences:

True, I could say to you that we are shaking Quakers—that we include all the elements and principles of the Quaker order. Those which the Quakers hold in common with Presbyterians and Swedenborgians—the marrying and giving in marriage—we drop; but that which constitutes them Quakers—the peace principles, the no poverty principle, the plainness of dress and of language, and the inflexible adherence to principle, the spiritual religious life that they are called to live—these are all included in the Shaker order.[29]

By 1871, when Elder Frederick Evans was writing, the Shakers were pointing out similarities; a hundred years before, they would have thought it more normal to underscore the differences.

A second religious coordinate to be noted among the early Shakers is their link with the Methodists. It is explicitly recognized by Ann Lee in a passage of the *Testimonies* which cites her as saying: "When Whitefield first set out, he had great power and gifts of God. I was one of his hearers in England, but after he came to America he was persecuted for his testimony. He then returned to England, and took protection under the King; by which means he lost the power of God, and became formal, like other professors."[30]

Another of the Shaker forefathers was John Hocknell, an ex-Methodist who deserves special attention in any study of the society's early years. The *Testimony* notes that he had first joined a Methodist society but that in the end he had left this group to become a member of the Wardley circle. Like his relative John Townley, whose home in Manchester served as a meetinghouse for the Shakers, this man John Hocknell was rich. Can it be that he was alienated by the early Methodists' policy of recruiting new members from the working class?[31] At any rate, he became the patron of the new group. According to the story as it is invariably retold in Shaker books, it was John Hocknell who paid for the emigrants' ocean passage, and he who bought the land at Niskeyuna in America and who probably donated his fortune for the development of the various Shaker societies as they appeared in the New World.[32] Perhaps Hocknell had been prepared for this role of benefactor by his experience with the Methodists or at least by a tendency in the early Methodist Church.. Before adopting the philanthropic doctrine that the redistribution of surplus goods is, at once, obligatory and a matter of individual conscience, the first Methodists had explicitly tried to imitate the early Christian communities—as would the Shakers many years later. One of the oldest Methodist documents, distributed to their local societies around 1744, decreed that, "until it becomes possible to own all things in common, each member should bring to the common holdings all that he can spare."[33] And, according to Elie Halévy, even before this, one could observe an influence of Moravian communitarianism on certain of John Wesley's disciples. Nevertheless, the idea of a community founded on common ownership of goods and property could not have been the determining motive of Hocknell's decision to subsidize the Shakers, since this ideal (which quickly disappeared from the horizon of Methodist thought) did not become firmly established on the Shaker horizon until after their first decade in America. Therefore the explanation for John Hocknell's shift from the Methodists to the Shakers does not lie entirely in the attractiveness of the communal ideal. Perhaps he was simply attracted by the exuberant spontaneity of the Shaker meetings, something that Wesley, the master organizer, would never cease to dread.

In Wesley's journal there are several indications of disputes with the "French Prophets." As early as January 1739, the founder of Methodism visited one of the prophetesses. He went to call on her in the company of three or four friends, proclaiming that he had come in order to determine whether or not this spirit was of God. The prophetess spoke profusely about the fulfillment of the prophecies, about the imminence of Christ's return to earth, and about the spreading of the Gospel throughout the world. Reasoned talk was interspersed with trances. When the session was over, the prophetess begged her listeners not to judge her too hastily, but to wait and pray, to take up their cross, and to remain firm in the presence of God. Then Wesley added: "Two or three of our company were much affected, and believed she spoke by the Spirit of God. But this was in no wise clear to me. The motion might be either hysterical or artificial. And the same words any person of a good understanding and well versed in the Scriptures might have spoken. But I let the matter alone; knowing that this, 'if it be not of God, it will come to naught.'"[34]

This reserve on the part of Wesley did not last. In June 1739, in an allusion to the French Prophets, he wrote: "'Woe to those,' said the Lord, 'who prophesy in my name and whom I have not sent to do so.'"[35] He was all the more alarmed in that his own preaching had, at one time, aroused in his listeners manifestations identical to what he had observed in the "Prophets." Wesley himself made note of this similarity: "Just as do the French Prophets."[36] In 1760 his position was categorical. When asked if he approved of the Quakers, the answer was: "Yes, in certain matters." When then asked if the same were true for the French Prophets, the answer was: "No."[37] It was during the same year of 1760 that John Hocknell left the Methodist Church to join the Wardley group.

Historically there was, however, one thing that the Methodists unquestionably held in common with the Shakers: both were accused of Catholicism. In the case of the Methodists this is well known; it is less evident in the story of Shaker development. In both societies there was an opposition to the reformed churches, a return to auricular confession, an appeal for support of church charities, a penchant for achieving perfection through asceticism, and a newly created semimonastic organization—all of which furnished ample evidence to anyone wishing to accuse them of a return to Romanism. An English gentlemen who had known the Shakers in Manchester made a brisk comment on this assimilation of papistry:

This peculiar sect, if they belong to any known religious denomination, are a species of the Roman Catholic. Like the papal church, they have their popes, their extraordinary saints, their auricular confessions, absolutions, exorcisms, and purgatories; like them the decrees of their church are binding on the consciences of men; their elders have power to forgive sins; and like the papal church they forbid to marry—pretend to miraculous gifts, and hold to invocations of departed saints. Their likeness to the Roman church the Shakers are sensible of, and say the papal is the only true church on earth established on the gospel plan; but that its spirit was lost, and hath revived in the Shakers. —Hence that they are now the only true church on earth.[38]

In the turbulence of England's eighteenth-century religious revival, distinctions between the different sects were slow to appear.[39] During the first years of the movement the French Prophets sent delegates to Count Zinzendorf and expressed a desire to join forces with the Moravian brothers,[40] a step that Wesley also considered very seriously. Likewise, Wesley tried the American adventure as a possible solution. A posteriori, it is obviously easy to point out striking differences between the two cults; Wesley's concern with economic reform, his loyalty to the crown, his genius for organizing the lower classes, the waverings in his theology of marriage, all contrast with the communitarian radicalism of the Shakers, their support of American republicanism, their never-ending inability to launch a movement among the lower classes, and their intransigent neo-Manichaeism. But in the beginning, behind their common nonconformism (just as behind the Anglican evangelizing during the same century) there was an identical religious awakening to the imperative demands of the first industrial proletariat, then in formation.[41]

It is in the context of this social problem that the sharpest differences between the two sects will appear, taking into account, of course, the fact that the two religious groups were very different in size. Both Methodists and Shakers went beyond the old solution of paternalism and mystification which had called for patience from the poor and generosity from the rich. Those sacrifices, affording the haves and the have-nots an equal claim to eternal salvation, had been exacted on the basis of a theological position that carried double weight at the beginning of the eighteenth century, since it supported an economic argument whose conclusions could not be criticized.[42] And this line of thought was to crop up again in certain later Methodist documents.[43] Unlike the Shakers, Wesley had no trace of dualism in his theological thinking; for him there was nothing intrinsically evil in society except what evil men had put there, and he believed that what ill will had introduced could be replaced by good will or rather, the will to do good. It was enough for men to want to do good. This position led the Methodists to the gigantic job of giving the free economy a moral basis, in the principle of self-government, a task that could be accomplished only by undertaking the equally gigantic job of giving English workers an effective human, social, and religious education.[44] The Shakers, on the other hand, believed in a radical dualism of good and evil, and this led them to refuse all compromises with the "world"—a world in which there was a coalition of church and state. This refusal to compromise with the world as it existed led them to conclude that it was necessary to remake society on the basis of a new type of human relationship. For the Shakers there was a corollary to this conclusion and it was decisive: since the economic evils were based on "biological" evils, only a new kind of biological relation would make it possible for them to refashion society and its economic structure.

Wesley's program enabled the Methodists to reach the English lower classes; but it soon became, or pretended to be, reformist rather than revolutionary and thus tended to resemble more and more a middle-class ideology. The Shaker program, on the other hand, was to be radical; but by virtue of its premises, it was never to appeal to the working classes in either England or America. Bit by bit it would lead the Shakers to justify their down-to-earth mysticism by way of a Malthusian theology.

Perhaps John Hocknell was embarrassed by his wealth and found that joining the Shaker Church was a way to salve an unhappy or even guilty conscience. According to the annals, he lived long enough to see the communities he had subsidized flourishing in "things temporal and spiritual." Indeed, he had, in a world that was still relatively elastic, provided a solution for the eight English travelers who set sail with him for America. But behind them they left the industrial proletariat, which, as it came to self-consciousness, would have to look elsewhere for a solution that was available to all.

II. The Socio-Economic Coordinates

Concerning their relationships with this English working class during the second half of the eighteenth century, the Shakers tell us little more than the trades of the principal people involved. We know specifically that James and Jane Wardley were tailors in Bolton. We also know that Ann Lee was the daughter of a blacksmith from Manchester, and that she was married to Abraham Stanley, who was also a blacksmith. We know that before her marriage, she, like most of the children of her class, had not been able to attend school, and that at an early age she had earned her living, first as a worker in a cotton mill, then as a cutter of hatters' fur, and finally as a cook in a hospital. She is supposed to have distinguished herself in this last job by her punctuality, cautiousness, and frugality.

From these meager details one major fact stands out. Between 1740 and 1770 the founder of the Shaker Church had been a Manchester factory girl. The dates, the job, and the town are decisive elements in this early account.

In his study of the industrial revolution in eighteenth-century England, Paul Mantoux points out the unrivaled importance of the city of Manchester.[45] Just as the textile industry was, chronologically, the first of the great industries in England, Manchester was the first city to experiment with industrialization and consequently with a proletarianization, in the modern sense of the word. During the period of Ann Lee's childhood this experiment was well under way.

It is not difficult to assess the demographic development of the region and the technical effects of industrialization. Nor is it difficult to determine the place occupied by the small, developing Shaker group in the history of this ensemble. The growth of Bolton is important. This is the town from which came James and Jane Wardley. They had been tailors in that town and consequently were well placed in the textile trade, an industry that has always supplied religious and social revolutions with their avant-garde. In 1753 Bolton was probably still much the way the Wardleys had known it (if one accepts the hypothesis that they had already made a definive break with that city): a place where weavers from the countryside would come into town toting their merchandise in a sack slung over one shoulder, while on the other arm they would carry a basket of fresh butter.[46] The sack of newly woven cloth and the basket of fresh butter bear eloquent testimony to an alternation of labors which, in the preindustrial age, assured the economic equilibrium of the countryside in England as in other nations. But this city was already entering another phase of industrial development. It was in Bolton that, in 1750, Arkwright set up shop as a barber and thought through the problems that led to his invention of the spinning frame. It was also in Bolton that, between the years 1774 and 1779, Samuel Crompton would be working on the construction of the spinning mule. The whole region was undergoing intense demographic and technological fermentation.

There was social fermentation as well. Manchester became a center of Luddite agitation. If the first law for the supression of Luddism was passed in 1769, then the first agitations must have been prior to that year. And the Luddite phenomenon must have been spreading through this part of the country, since ten years later it reached its paroxysm in Bolton and Lancashire County. The travelers' reports quoted by Paul Mantoux evoke a picture of impressive parades in which groups of hundreds, sometimes thousands, of Luddites marched against the factories to destroy the machines.[47]

The slow despair responsible for the Luddite explosion was undoubtedly similar to the state of mind of young Ann Lee as she faced the problem of earning her living. James and Jane Wardley belonged to an older generation. Ann Lee, who as a youngster had been thrown into the maw of a Manchester cotton factory, belonged to a social species of a new type: the child laborer of the Manchester factories. Mantoux says that the workers were reluctant, and rightfully so, to send their children into the factories. For a long time it was considered a shameful thing to do.[48] There is every reason to suppose that Ann Lee's father, the blacksmith, was tormented by such feelings of shame when he had to make the dreadful decision and send his daughter into the factory to work: "Their children, as was common with poor people in manufacturing towns, were brought up to work instead of being sent to school."[49] The workday in Manchester averaged fourteen hours, and children were hired from the age of four up. Working conditions involved a strict discipline, sometimes enforced by bad treatment and generally carried out in an atmosphere that was both physically and morally debilitating. "Due to this mixture of depravity and suffering, cruelty and contempt, the factory offered the puritan conscience its perfect image of Hell."[50]

No other conclusion was possible to the mind of a girl like Ann Lee, unless it be the corollary that, since the Kingdom of God is the opposite of hell, it must be sought in a world that is antipodal to the one she knew. The world she lived in seemed to be turning at an accelerated rate in two different rhythms: production and reproduction. The Luddite mobs were attempting to halt production through physical violence. Ann Lee would attempt to halt reproduction by violence on a spiritual plane. It is reasonable to assume that she had encountered physical violence during her days in the factory, although we have no precise knowledge of the dates or length of time involved in this experience. But it is certain that she knew spiritual violence and that it came to her through the ominous demographic equilibrium in the nascent proletariat: "Many births, many deaths."[51] Many births: she had learned the economic consequences of this from the family in which she was born. Many deaths: she had ample biological proof of this when she considered the fate of the four children in the family she had tried to found. The millenarian vision of the French Prophets inspired her with a kind of metaphysical Luddism that went away and beyond the scope of Methodist zeal for reform; remaining untouched by the first bumbling attempts to organize among the proletariat,[52] Ann Lee was simply going to ask the world to stop turning so that she could pursue her dream. And it was a powerful dream, articulate, rich with somnambulistic information, a dream in which she lived rather than one which lived in her. This dream demanded to be transformed, first into words—and they came to her from an unknown source[53]—and then into decisions, acts, and organizations, into something that would endure. The mystical side of Ann Lee's personality never lessened the real-world demands of this willful master builder. "Put your hands to work and your hearts to God" was Ann Lee's motto. It was to become the motto of the Families and retain its force until the day when an evolved industrial reality would render even the violence of their dream inefficient and useless.

III. The Family Coordinates

First of all, of course, there was the family into which Ann Lee was born. It was a large family: five sons and three daughters, the second of which was Ann Lee. The Shaker chroniclers tell us that her father was "respectable in character, moral in principle, honest and punctual in his dealings, and industrious in business."[54] Her mother was esteemed to be "a religious and very pious woman." Thus the home atmosphere was not spiritually degrading, like the atmosphere in the factory. There was probably nothing but household lack of privacy (inevitable on Toad Lane[55]) to provoke the kind of precocious reactions inplied in an allusion in the *Testimonies*: "It is remarkable that, in early youth, she had a great abhorrence of the fleshly cohabitation of the sexes, and so great was her sense of its impurity, that she often admonished her mother against it, which, coming to her father's ears, he threatened, and actually attempted to whip her; upon which she threw herself into her mother's arms, and clung around her to escape his strokes." The way this story is told leads one to think that the scene might well have occurred several times. Although this particular incident was not mentioned by Theo Schroeder in the psychological analysis outlined in his study of Shaker celibacy,[56] it could have corroborated his thesis.

The social reasons for this childhood response are clarified by another anecdote recorded in the *Testimonies*. It actually sums up what was later to be the theology of the new church. After Ann Lee had become "Mother Ann," she received a visit from a certain Beulah Rude, who came from a very poor family. When Mother Ann asked Beulah how many children she had and Beulah replied, "Five," Mother Ann exclaimed, "Five! When you had one, why did you not wait and see if you were able to bring up that as you ought before you had another? And when you had two, why did you not stop then? But now you have five! Are you not ashamed to live in the filthy works of the flesh? You must go and take up your cross,[57] and put your hands to work, and be faithful in your business; clothe your children, and keep them clean and decent; and clean up your house, and keep that in order."[58] It is obvious that in this admonition Mother Ann was asking Beulah to give her children the very satisfactions that had been denied the little girl on Toad Lane. This seems all the more probable when we read in the *Testimony* that Ann's mother died while Ann was still young.[59] Since the mother no doubt died in childbirth, hostility to the works of the flesh would have been aroused in the young adolescent. In Ann's later visions her mother appeared as someone doomed to perdition and whose face was veiled in darkness! After her death one can imagine what the blacksmith's house was like when the child or young adolescent Ann Lee, forced by poverty to perform her fourteen hours of work a day, returned in the evening—or in the morning— to this motherless home. Elsewhere we shall see that the Shaker case against procreation is based on the fact that the imperious demands of the flesh lead us to procreate "unseasonably." The misery of the children thus produced must have been unquestionable proof for Ann Lee. At any rate, this painful firsthand experience of a disproportion between a prolific birth rate and limited resources had marked the life of the founder long before her future learned disciples attempted to structure this motif into Malthusian concepts. Moreover, neither Ann Lee's behavior nor the crude motivations that, indirectly, she used to explain it, are without precedent in the history of neo-Manichaean behavior.[60]

Did the family that Ann Lee founded with Abraham Stanley confirm her observations on the family into which she was born? The Shaker texts have a tendency to make the husband, Abraham Stanley, into a veritable scapegoat. White and Taylor, in the last of the great Shaker texts, describe Abraham Stanley as a decent man who liked his beef and his beer, his corner by the fireplace, and his chair at the tavern. This was the man who, after following Ann all the way to America, left her and went off to live with someone else—"with a prostitute," add the writers of the Shaker chronicles with an ill temper that makes one doubt their sincerity.[61] Indeed, Stanley's attitude seems to have been much more an effect than a cause. His entrance into the Lee household had probably enabled him to attain "a comfortable standard of living." The cause of their disagreement is stated clearly in the *Testimonies* by Ann Lee herself: "The man to whom I was married, was very kind, according to nature; he would have been willing to pass through a flaming fire for my sake, if I would but live in the flesh with him, which I refused to do."[62] Subsequently, Shaker writers were to emphasize Stanley's ingratitude to Ann, who had cared for him during the long illness contracted after their arrival in New York. Moreover, they accused him of using his convalescence to enjoy himself in New York's bawdy houses, and treated his departure with another woman as an apostasy. But Stanley's decision to leave his wife came at least five years after Ann Lee's resolution to have no more sexual relations with her husband.[63] The drama of their respectively untenable positions was often to recur in the early history of American Shakerism. Discontented husbands and wives would be testifying in court that they could no longer live harmoniously with each other.

And the Shakers were led to defend their church's attitude in the American courts of law with a complete exegesis based on the well-known passages in the Epistle to the Corinthians, texts from which canon law had drawn the traditional Christian attitudes toward marriage and celibacy.

The exact nature of Ann Lee's life before her marriage remains uncertain. The obviously labored text of the *Millennial Church* stipulates: "But not having attained that knowledge of God which she early desired, and finding no one to strengthen and assist her in the pursuit of that true holiness which she sought after, nor even to encourage her to withstand the powerful example of a lost world . . . she grew up in the same fallen nature with the rest of mankind, and *through the importunities of her relations*, was married to Abraham Stanley, a blacksmith by trade."[64] The obvious sense of the passage is that at the insistence of her family, Ann Lee plunged into the common degradation of marriage. Could this insistence on the part of the family have had quite another purpose: to win her away from people like the Wardleys (the Andrews hypothesis)? Was it an attempt to pull her out of a psychological depression, or could it have been intended to bring to an end a phase of loose living of the sort that she would later be accused of in the pamphlets?[65] We do not have enough information to answer these questions, and the story of Ann's childhood and adolescence remains hazy.

We are equally in the dark about the relation between Ann Lee's "revelation" and what was being taught by the Wardleys. The title of precursor attributed to this couple in the official Shaker texts fails to conceal the rupture which certainly took place at the moment of emigration to America. Most likely, members of the group were given a choice: "Permission was given for all those of the society to accompany her, who were able, and who felt any special impression on their own minds to do so."[66] In this same passage of the *Millennial Church* it is specifically stated that Ann Lee's revelation was confirmed "by signs, visions and extraordinary manifestations to many individual members."[67] Perhaps this separation was friendly in order to avoid an open dispute. If so, it was facilitated by the fact that, of the two patrons, one decided to stay (John Townley) and the other decided to leave (John Hocknell). Had there been disputes prior to this departure? Certainly, and Ann Lee's celebrated "revelation" was what caused the disagreements. The fawning style of the Shaker chronicles leaves no room for doubt about this. The *Millennial Church* records that "those of the society who received and obeyed her testimony, found a great increase in the power and gifts of God; while on the other hand, those who rejected it, lost all their former light and power and fell back into a state of darkness, and into the common course of the world."[68]

The ideological basis of this rupture has never been made clear. According to a passage in the *Testimonies,* when differences arose between Ann Lee and her husband, he consulted the official church and she sought the advice of Jane Wardley.[69] The church must have tried in vain to persuade Ann that she should give up some of Jane's ideas. Here is the story as told by Ann Lee in the *Testimonies:* "Some time after I set out to live up to the light of God manifested to me through James and Jane Wardley, I fell under heavy trials and tribulation on account of lodging with my husband and as I looked to them for help and counsel, I opened my trials to Jane; she said: *'James and I lodge together but we do not touch each other any more than two babes.* You may return and do likewise.'" This anecdote from the *Testimonies* suggests that a

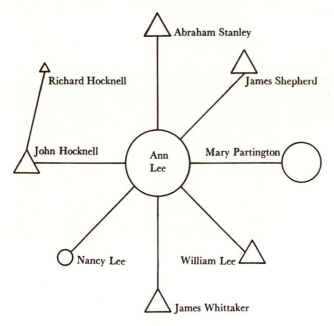

CHART 1a. *Sociogram of the Shaker Group Which Accompanied Ann Lee to America*

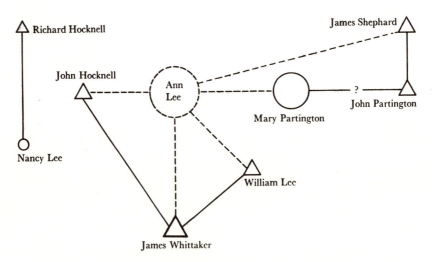

CHART 1b. *Sociogram of the Shaker Group at the Death of Ann Lee*

48 * Eighteenth-Century England

special conjugal "arrangement" (frequently found in this type of religious dissidence) was a secret practice in the Wardley group as early as 1760. Ann Lee, a new convert, recognized that she was not able to practice continence in secret, and because of this inability she was tormented by guilt.[70] This led her to propose to the Wardleys that the *secret* continence become an *open* principle of the society, and it was this proposal that became the source of conflict between Ann Lee and the rest of the group. In a sort of chain reaction this need for an avowed policy of celibacy was to lead her and her disciples to a further need: That of developing a social structure which would provide modes of "lodging" and "lodging together" in a way that would peacefully generate a new type of relation between men and women. This structure was to be the Shaker *Family*. The history of mixed monastic orders in dualistic religions reminds us that this part of Ann Lee's program was also not without precedent.[71] The *social* structure would, in turn, tend to create an *economic* system, and, after ten years of groping for an economic solution, Ann Lee was to find one in the communal ownership of property.[72]

There remains to be examined one last document from this period during which the original Family was formed: the roster of the group that embarked for America in 1774. The nine original members were listed in the following order: Ann Lee, Abraham Stanley, William Lee, James Whittaker, John Hocknell, Richard Hocknell, James Shepherd, Mary Partington, Nancy Lee.

Using the scant information available on each of these names from Shaker and non-Shaker sources, the following particulars were obtained. Of the nine who left England, four belonged to the Lee family: Ann and her husband Stanley, Ann's youngest brother William, and her niece Nancy Lee (who, moreover, was not William Lee's daughter, since he had had but one child, a son). No information is available on Nancy's parents. Abraham Stanley has already been discussed. William Lee will be discussed later.

On the other hand, of the nine in the original group it is

probable that there were five defections. The first to defect was Stanley. His motives have already been indicated. Next to go was John Hocknell's son Richard, who married Ann Lee's niece Nancy and, naturally, left the movement.[73] Finally, the names of Partington and Shepherd call to mind two further defections, although their identities are not entirely clear. A year after the group arrived in New York, a certain John Partington had joined them "with his family." He may have been the husband or the brother of Mary Partington, who was part of the original band. Their exact relationship is not recorded, nor is it recorded whether or not he took Mary with him when he left. What we know is that after the death of the founding mother in September 1784, James Whittaker acceded to the position of power, and that this change of regime caused two veterans, one of them from the original group, to defect: James Sheperd and John Partington. Comment on their defection was appropriately brief: "They lost all relations with God."[74]

The three remaining loyal members were then: John Hocknell, William Lee, and James Whittaker. The first, as we have already indicated, was the patron of the movement and official treasurer for Mother Ann. The second was her bodyguard. The *Millennial Church* tells us that William Lee was a former blacksmith and soldier, and mentions his strong, clear, and sonorous voice as well as his robust constitution.[75] "He was very remarkable for his strength, both of body and mind." Several times the Shaker text affirms that "he feared not the face of man"; indeed, one finds him regularly in the center of the picture every time there was a skirmish with a hostile mob. It was he who constituted an avant-garde in the solitary forest of Niskeyuna, where, surrounded by Indians, he occupied the land while waiting to be joined by the rest of the band a few months later. According to the believers, he was feared by all sinners "who could not but tremble at the sound of his voice."[76] It is not unlikely that on occasions of physical penance such as the first converts were wont to impose on themselves, Elder William Lee's contribution was not limited to mere intimidation. As a supplement to John Hocknell's treasury, William's musculature provided Mother Ann with all that was needed in the way of a secular arm. The Shakers were grateful, and their gratitude naturally led them to see a halo of virtues around these faces and attribute to them all the spiritual gifts later found in their portraits by the official chroniclers.

The third remaining member is more interesting, if only because his role was more important. It was he who in 1784 was chosen to succeed Ann Lee as leader, in preference to John Hocknell (who did not die until 1799) and to the other two Englishmen who were about to defect from the society. The importance of his new role was in dramatic contrast with his youthful years. James Whittaker was born in 1751, when Ann Lee was sixteen; therefore he was twenty-three years old at the time of the exodus and thirty-three years old when he assumed the succession after Ann Lee's death. He remained at the head of the movement for only three years and died at the age of thirty-six in 1787. The central importance of his role is evident from the careful record of details in the Shaker chronicles. By trade he, too, was a weaver. From the few allusions to his family, one gathers that his father was Jonathan Whittaker of Oldham, near Manchester, and that the name of his mother was Ann Lee—"probably a distant relation of Mother Ann," surmise the Shaker texts, repeating it regularly and offhandedly from decade to decade. This was not in the least unusual; the name of Lee or Lees seems to have been widespread in that part of the country. What was unusual was the nature of the tie between the Whittaker family and the movement. For an understanding of this, there are two series of basic data and they do not seem to tally: first, there are the facts as presented in the traditional Shaker texts; then, there is James Whittaker's correspondence with his parents, which, of course, predates the chronicles by many years.

As to the first part, Ann Whittaker (born Ann Lee) was a member of the Wardley society and was a "faithful Believer." She used to bring young James to their meetings, and it is there that Ann Lee (Mrs. Stanley) must have met him.[77] According to the Shaker texts, Jonathan Whittaker, his father, "stood in opposition for a while; but was afterwards convinced and embraced the gospel, and had an anxious feeling to come to America with his son, but was not able;[78] he died in the faith."[79]

It is difficult to reconcile this retrospective optimism of the Shaker chroniclers with the irritated tone assumed by James when answering the touching letters sent him by his parents back in England. In a letter dated 7 May 1775, a full year after the emigration, we read:

This comes from thy loving Father and Mother, hoping to find thee in good health both body and soul. Thy Father is very poorly and not likely to live very long. Thy Mother is in rather a better state of health, but poorly. . . . If thou finds any liberty from the Lord with a desire to come to England, if thou have no money to pay thy passage, We'll pay when thou comes to England. . . . Fear not coming to England, for thy loving Father and Mother will clear thy passage.[80]

James's reply to this letter reflects an exultation that approaches fanaticism:

I am weaned from all terrestial connexions; and in lieu thereof, I have joined the host of heaven. . . . I hate your fleshly lives, and your fleshly generation . . . as I hate the smoke of the bottomless pit. . . . Stay in England till you go down into your graves as long as you are for following natural generation. . . . Away with your looking towards me for help. . . .[81]

In view of the fact that both of Whittaker's parents belonged to the Wardley group, this letter may be considered as evidence of a schism which either led to the American emigration or was caused by it. If old Jonathan Whittaker was not able to make this voyage with the first group, it was not for lack of the material means to pay for the crossing, since a year later he offered to pay for his son's passage home. Moreover, Hocknell in any case would have given him the funds to make the trip, just as he had done for the others. No, if old Jonathan Whittaker did not make the trip across the Atlantic it must have been because he was reluctant to break up his home in order to follow Mother Ann. Most likely, it was his wife (the *other* Ann Lee) who refused to make the voyage, despite her previous assiduous attendance at the meetings of the Wardley group. This, it would seem, was the cause of James Whittaker's grievance against his parents.

It is still difficult to conceive how, during a brief period of religious training,[82] the twenty-three-year-old Ann Lee[83] managed to replace the real mother in the affections of seven-year-old James Whittaker, something all the more difficult to imagine when one considers that James's real mother was also a faithful attender of the Wardley services. One gets lost in a maze of conjecture as to what happened during that period of religious initiation, except on one point: James, son born of the flesh to Ann Lee (Mrs. Whittaker), became the son born of the soul of another Ann Lee (Mrs. Stanley). Indeed, Mother Ann came to consider James as her "adopted son." Mother in the flesh of four children, all of whom died young, she had become mother in spirit of a child who seemed to promise great things. And when she later went alone into the wilds of Niskeyuna, like the biblical Woman of the Wilderness, to whom her disciples loved to compare her, it now seems only natural that she should have pushed the scriptural comparison to the extreme: "and the dragon stood before the woman which was ready to be de-livered, for to devour her child as soon as it was born. And she brought forth a man-child, who was to rule all nations with a rod of iron: and her child was caught up unto God, and *to* his throne. And the woman fled into the wilder-ness where she hath a place prepared of God" (Revelation 12:4–6). The letter from the Whittaker parents reached their son James just at the moment when the project of with-drawing into the wilds of Niskeyuna was about to be realized. "I have joined the heavenly hosts," he wrote. This certitude dates from his first "visions" in England[84] and from the time when Mother Ann promised him the "Bishoprick"[85] or re-gency over a church whose spiritual sway would be coextensive with all the nations of the world. The great day was coming. Was it not incumbent on him to consider England, where lived his "natural relations," as the shores of hell, since he, himself, had crossed the seas to reach to gates of paradise?[86] ·

The details of this inner drama will help us formulate a brief and clear statement of Ann Lee's vocation, its principles, and their implications. On one level it may be valid to interpret a vocation like hers as the sublimation of a personality complex into a socio-Utopian mysticism. Yet even this interpretation rests on a recognition of the fact that Ann's vocation grew out of a basic pattern of family disintegration and that this was the direct result of living conditions among the working class under the Manchester brand of capitalism. It was these living conditions that threatened Ann Lee's very right to "be" and made her determined to assert her freedom.[87] Ann Lee could have given up at twenty. She did not give up, but her decision to free herself from the determining forces resulted in a victory that was hollow and unrealistic, since, by avoiding contact with the stream of economic forces, she was losing all chance to use them to serve her own purposes. Thus the atrophy that Ann Lee represents on the social and historical scene was a function of the hypertrophy of her self-esteem. The world became so much of a "nothing" that Ann Lee became "all" and could think of herself as emanating from the godhead.[88]

Foremost among those determining forces were the social conditions to which Ann Lee had to submit. They are relatively easy to know. One has only to examine the official and unofficial reports written since 1740 or read the special analysis of those conditions in two famous studies: one by Friedrich Engels on the predicament of the English working classes; the other, of a later date, written by Karl Marx in the historical section of his book on capitalism.

What about the numerous progeny of the Lee family and the disproportion between this abundance in population and the scarcity of their resources? The Lees were an example of proletarian fecundity, a reality so flagrant that in Lancashire, twenty-eight years after Ann Lee's "revelation," the same fateful view of determining social forces brought about the same protests and led Malthus to write his first essay.[89]

What about the lack of privacy in her father's house? From the Health Department reports of 1866–1867, Marx would later cite a series of examples of this promiscuity and quote the judgment of a doctor who said: "For children raised in these wretched surroundings, it is a baptism in infamy."[90]

What about the working conditions of child labor? Engels studied certain sectors of the garment industry firsthand and reported: "These numerous girls, like slaves living under a mortal fear of losing their jobs, are driven to perform work so unflagging and demanding that a grown man, to say nothing of a delicate girl of fourteen to twenty, would not be able to bear up under the strain."[91]

Engels cites an observer who reported that in Manchester three-fourths of the working girls between fourteen and twenty had been "deflowered."[92] Perhaps it is in this context that the following passage from *Millennial Church* is to be understood: "Ann Lee . . . finding no one to encourage her to withstand the powerful example of a lost world . . . grew up in the same fallen nature with the rest of mankind."[93]

What about Ann Lee's four children, all of whom died at such an early age? The Public Health report of 1866 designated Manchester as the city with the highest rate of infant mortality. Moreover, Ann experienced death in two different contexts: first, in the property context of the family workshop, she lost her mother; then, in the production context of the factory, she lost her four children. Family life was decidedly untenable. "Thus did the social order make family life almost impossible for the workers," wrote Engels before concluding that "when one forces people into a situation suited only for a beast, they have the choice of revolting or succumbing to bestiality."[94]

The slow elimination of the members of Ann Lee's family, one after another, did not exactly correspond to the brutal alternative that Engels has described. The religious atmosphere, first in her immediate family circle and later in the

Wardley house, was too morally austere for her to renounce the family outright. Moreover, feelings in this atmosphere were too self-involved to provide any revolutionary perspective based on an understanding of economic structures and techniques still in their formative stage. It is very possible that, as Ann Lee's thought evolved in the direction of her "Family" (which would be the mother cell of the Shaker structure), she hesitated between the idea of a libertarian community such as would later appear in French people's societies in the years preceding 1848 (for example, the "Club de la Chopinette"[95]) and the idea of an ascetic community organized according to a formula which was an unconscious resurrection of the small group meetings of the old dualistic Freemasons. The first led to what Marx called "a crude communism" based on "prostitution for everybody."[96] The second would lead Ann Lee to a communism that was equally "crude" in its resistance to culture and human progress, but this time based on universal celibacy. This idea, too, was not completely new. The millenarian Joachim of Floris had suggested it during the Middle Ages. At any rate, Europe's fading millenarian vision, which had its last blaze in the Cévennes, would soon receive new life from an unexpected encounter with another millenarian movement, this one in full bloom: American millenarianism.

CHAPTER THREE
American Millenarianism

IN ITS broadest sense the term "millenarian" implies a view
of the world as seen by those who stand at the end of time,
this end having been brought about by the victory of good
over evil, of God over Satan, of Christ over the Antichrist.
According to postmillenarians, this victory is to be slowly
and progressively achieved by the labors of mankind. According to premillenarians this victory is to be brutal and
catastrophic.[1]

In its narrowest sense the term "millenarian" is generally
used to paraphrase chapter 20 of the Revelation of Saint
John the Divine, and in this case it designates the time that
must pass between the first and second Resurrections of
Christ as foretold by the holy writer. According to the text
of Revelations this period will last a thousand years, during
which Satan is to be kept enchained; and during this en-
chainment those who have not worshiped the Beast will reign
at the side of Christ. "They shall be priests of God and of
Christ, and shall reign with him a thousand years."[2]

In both the broad and the narrow sense the term "millenarianism" implies a period during which the reign of God
is realized *on earth*. In its broadest sense the millenarian
vision predates the Christian era and has origins in the
ancient Persian dualisms. It is even perfectly possible that
its roots go back to the Babylonian myths that influenced
Jewish thought either during the captivity or after the return
to Palestine (see Ezekiel and Daniel). At any rate, it appears
that this millenarian strain flourished during the darkest

years of Jewish history, particularly during the Hellenic persecutions, just as it would later appear during a dark hour of the Christian era (John's vision of the Apocalypse occurred at the time of persecutions under Nero and Domitian).

Were the early Christians millenarians? It is an indisputable and rarely discussed fact that a large proportion of these early Christians, including some of the most notable of the church fathers (Papias, Irene, Justin, Tertullian, Lactantius) lived in the expectation of Christ's return to earth. It is generally admitted that the dimming of the millenarian vision in the Christian Church coincided with the appearance of Augustine's great critique. The fact that this waning of millenary expectations likewise coincided with the rise of the church to a position of dominance after three centuries, during which its growth was rooted in its tribulations, has given rise to divergent explanations.[3]

How did this millenarian movement, after being almost completely extinguished in the fourth century, manage to rise again fifteen hundred years later in, among others, the Shaker dissidence? One can discern the broad outlines of what happened.

I. European Millenarianism

Saint Augustine is said to have dealt the mortal blow to millenarianism. After him, the millenarian vision grew more and more feeble until it expired in certain extravagent doctrines that appeared during the Protestant Reformation.[4] Is this an accurate assessment of its history? Do not a few supplementary observations call for a more complex analysis?

In the first place, one must not fail to account for the persistent recurrence of a series of phenomena bearing the marks of the old Iranian dualism, transferred and transformed. Its stages were complicated and its causes baffling, but century after century the old oriental dualism has infiltrated the Occident. It produced the Manichaeans, the Messalians, the Paulicians, the Bogomils, the Patarines, and the Albigenses; and all of these religious outcroppings were more or less intertwined with socio-political upheavals and carried with them a horror of the Antichrist; also, each in its own way preached the hope for a millennium which would be realized by a final separation of Light from Darkness. In the last chapter of the present study we shall see how heavily this dualism weighed on the Shakers in their efforts toward self-justification.[5]

From the beginning of the twelfth century on, through the great religious controversies and simultaneously in the great social conflicts, we can see, in disparate forms but with extraordinary continuity, a rebirth of millenarian nostalgia.

The name of Joachim of Floris seems to dominate all the others. Without going into the details of his complex message, one may grasp in broad outline the doctrine that emerges. This is the theory of the "Third Age" or "Age of the Spirit." The history of the world, according to Joachim, unrolls in the rhythm of a three-phase movement: the age of the Father, the age of the Son, and the age of the Spirit. These ages overlap, and often there are no clear distinctions between them. In the first age men live the life of the flesh; in the second, the life of the flesh and the Spirit; in the third, the life of the Spirit alone. The first is the age of servitude; the second, the age of obedience; the third, the age of freedom. From this base Joachim proceeds to multiply his trios: faith, hope, and charity; slaves, freedom, and friends; winter, spring, and summer; nettles, roses, and lilies; and so on. The first age was one of married couples; the second was the age of clergy; the third will be the age of monks. According to Joachim, the future of the world does indeed lie in a universal monasticism.

Joachim synchronized this tableau of the world's past and future with a complicated chronology in terms of which the Third Age was supposed to start in 1260. He made this prediction near the end of the twelfth century.[6] A few decades later a fervent Joachimite, Gherado da Borgo San Donnino, was to publish his *Introductorius in Evangelium Aeternum,* in which he reminded his readers that the day of reckoning was imminent. The creation of the mendicant orders at this time, particularly the one founded by Saint Francis, seemed to be the first sign of the Event that the Joachimites were expecting. The year 1260 itself was not barren of signs for Joachim's disciples. About that time one notices not only a proliferation of the flagellants throughout Italy, the appearance of the Guillemites (those Medieval brothers of the Shakers) in Milan, and the founding of the Apostolics with Segharelli's first sermons, but also, on a broader front, an acceleration of the current carrying the left-wing Franciscans to revolt against Rome, and an alliance with the Piedmont peasants in the uprising during the first decade of the fourteenth century — a dissidence that K. Kautsky would characterize as the "first communist revolution in the Western world."[7] Millenarian religion was leading the way to social reform. It was not to be the last time that this would happen.

One indirect result of the great Franciscan unrest was the presence, if not of Wycliffe, at least of certain Wycliffite ideas in the Great Revolt of 1381. A few years later, this time directly influenced by Wycliffe's doctrines, came the Hussite uprising in Bohemia, a movement that was bursting at the seams with millenarian nostalgia.[8] The hussites pointed out that a certain Martin Hanska had announced the imminent end of the world and that Militz de Kromeriz, a precursor of John Hus, had set the date between 1365 and 1367.[9] During the Hussite war the Bohemians were expecting the Second Coming to occur at any moment. The Taborites had even designated five towns which were to be spared destruction in the general conflagration, and large groups of people gathered there to set up communist societies.[10]

A century later there was another great upheaval, and it too was covertly related to the doctrines of Joachim of Floris.[11] This was the Peasants' Revolt in Germany. Its leader, Thomas Münzer, had been brought up on Joachim and is quite

possibly one of the key links between the mystical millenarianism of the Middle Ages and the social millenarianism that
would later take root in nineteenth-century socialism. That
is why Münzer attracted the admiring attention of Friedrich
Engels in his book on the Peasants' Revolt.[12] The disaster at
Frankenhausen in 1525 failed to put an end to the people's
expectations. Passing over the case of Melchior Hoffman,
who, ten years later, fanaticized Münster by claiming to be
one of the witnesses referred to in the Apocalypse (Revelation 11:3), we note a refugee from Frankenhausen, Hans
Hut, who, only a year later in Nikolsburg, was fending off
the attacks of Balthasar Hubmaïer by announcing the end of
the world for 15 May 1527, the second anniversary of the
Frankenhausen debacle. When Hut subsequently advanced
this date to 1529, the delay did not seem to discourage his
numerous disciples, who had sold their goods, abandoned
their homes, and were wandering around aimlessly waiting
for the Second Coming.[13] In all known details those people
acted like the 1,600 Canadian Doukhobors who went through
the same performace and experienced the same disappointment 400 years later, in 1902.[14] Nevertheless, the Turks did
invade Hungary, just as Hans Hut had predicted,[15] although
the consequences of this conquest were not what he had expected.

Thus we can distinguish a first historical strain of millenarianism, and it is quite possible to say that, through the
Zinzendorfian descendents of the Moravians and through
the French Prophets in London, the Shakers were, if only
vaguely, in touch with it.

A second millenarian strain is the one linking the Shakers
to France, and as we have already pointed out, the Shakers
were clearly aware of this one. The daily despair of the
Cevenole Protestants lent substance to their millenarian
doctrine. Pierre Jurieu's reckonings supplied the form. In
making his calculations the Protestant theologian was not
without antecedents. In 1648 he referred to a certain Dra-
bitius, who, together with Kotterius and Comenius, had had
a reputation as a seer during the Christians' struggle against

the Turks in Hungary.[16] At the beginning of the seventeenth century Jurieu's own grandfather, Pierre du Moulin, had also written a "Fulfillment of the Prophecies," concluding that persecution by the Catholic Church would end in 1689.[17] But it was Jurieu who made millenarianism the central theological question. According to him, those who did not want to see the thousand-year reign were either "those who, in general, do not want the Church to reign on earth or those who believe that persecution will continue until the end of Time because Christ's reign will occur only in the glory of heaven."[18] His bold affirmation of the millenarian principle did not prevent Jurieu from being cautious in its application. Time and again he stated that "this is no more than a hope or a conjecture." Likewise, his affirmations became more and more qualified: "I think it would be difficult," he wrote, "to indicate the year precisely, because God has not worked out his timetable that closely. A few years more or less mean nothing to Him."[19] But this did not prevent Jurieu from speculating and although his method of calculation was quite different, he concluded, as had his grandfather before him, that 1689 was to ring in the hour of deliverance. "I have come to believe," he wrote, "that the three and a half days (Revelation 11:3–11) are three and a half years. If this is so, counting three and a half years from the revocation of the Edict of Nantes in October 1685, the deliverance of the Church will come in the year 1689."[20] This prediction was made on 16 March 1686.

A year later Jurieu made another prediction: "I would not dare say for sure that the revocation of the Edict of Nantes is to be understood as indicating the death of the witnesses (Revelation 11:7) and that we should start counting time at that date, although I am much inclined to think so. This is why I look for something big to happen in the year 1689."[21]

In his pastoral letter of 2 July 1689 Jurieu deemed the day of reckoning to be uncertain, but this did not prevent him from asserting it. First he presented his calculations as probabilities. Then he remarked that fulfillment was already under way. Had not James II "protector of Babylon," been crowned in May 1685 and had not the Edict of Nantes been revoked in October of the same year? The predicted time span ended in 1689. This was the very year that William of Orange set foot on English soil and was crowned king in London. We know that this prophecy of Jurieu had considerable political repercussions on the course of the war in the Cévennes. As for its religious consequences, they are to be found in the French Prophets of London, then in the English Prophets, and finally, although transformed, in the early Shakers.[22]

Mention must be made of a third channel of European millenarianism—the English strain. It goes off in several different directions during the seventeenth-century revolution. There was the mystic millenarianism of the Mechanic Preachers, with their conception of predestined poverty.[23] There was also the political millenarianism of the victorious revolutionary wing. In 1652 John Owen told the House of Commons that the wars then raging were the kind which would soon pave the way for the Kingdom.[24] Even Cromwell did not escape this glorious awareness of the great day at hand.[25] There was also the social millenarianism of the Levellers and, after them, of the Diggers. In 1649 Gerald Winstanley, like Thomas Münzer in 1525, maintained that God's Kingdom was intended for life on earth and would soon be seen in the communal brotherhood of workers, who until that time had been held in contempt. Such, he said, would be the reign of God and since such was the will of God, such would be the reign of Christ.[26] Then, finally, there is conspiratorial millenarianism, similar to the doctrine of Wilhelm Weitling, which later caused disturbances in Germany. This strain appeared among the "Men of the Fifth Monarchy," a group which took its name from a passage in the seventh chapter of Daniel and which had enjoyed a certain notoriety a hundred years earlier in Münster. Its prophet was Thomas Venner; its doctrine was a belief that Christ's reign on earth would be the definitive monarchy after those Assyria, Persia, Greece, and Rome.[27] Its goal was to overthrow Cromwell; its means, insurrection. Its prophetess, or one of its prophetesses, was most likely Anna Trapnel, whose vaticinations have been collected in an enormous volume. The date of the great event was to be 1657. The date, as had so often happened, was postponed to 1661. And, as had so often happened, the postponed date was no more successful than the first.[28] The list is incomplete, but even from this enumeration (which is more of a sampling than an inventory) it should be evident that the French Prophets did not sow their oracular pronouncements on absolutely fallow ground.

Thus, even during the pre-American phase of their history, the Shakers were in a position to be directly or indirectly affected by one or another aspect of this European millenarianism and could draw from it what they needed to illuminate their own reading of the Holy Scriptures. Moreover, during the early years of the movement, their lives were sufficiently embittered for them to deem the predicament of the proletariat in Lancashire during the years 1740–1780 to be no less hopeless than the fate of the Jews during their Babylonian captivity, or the oppression under Antiochus Epiphanes, or the Christians during Nero's persecutions, or the Bohemians encircled by the Crusaders, or the German peasants asserting their rights in the face of a hostile aristocracy, or the English under Cromwell. The similarity of these hopeless situations made up for what they lacked in historical continuity of tradition. At any rate, as far as continuity was concerned, the Shakers were going to find it, or something like it, in the land they had selected for their exodus.

II. American Millenarianism

In their long manual of Shaker history White and Taylor relate that during a journey to Philadelphia "Elder Calvin [Green] visited the descendants of a small band of German people known as Pilgrims, who, about a hundred years before, had emigrated to America for the sake of freedom to live according to their faith." Elder Green's description of these people led the two Shaker historians to see so many analogies that they treated the Pilgrims' doctrine as a veritable premonition of Shakerism. "Having received a special illumination from the Spirit of God, they [the Germans] adopted the virgin life believing it to be necessary that they might follow Christ." Then White and Taylor mention another detail, important for identifying the Philadelphia experiment: "Numbering only about forty and not trying to propagate their beliefs, the society, who lived true to their tenets, dwindled away by death until the last one disappeared—the name of the site of their settlement, Germantown, and a small printed book of their beliefs and revelations being the sole relics of the heroic little community." The account concludes with the statement that "Elder Calvin [Green] speaks of this movement as one of the many that for half a century before the rise of the Shakers were continually springing up in different countries, whose beliefs and revelations correspond very closely with those of Mother Ann Lee. 'These all form a cloud of witnesses,' says the Elder, 'of the work among Shakers—all testified that the appearance of Christ was drawing nigh.'"[29] We shall soon see how important this view of the past and its "cloud of witnesses" was to the development of the Shakers' own millenarian doctrine.

This reference in White and Taylor is so precise and so symptomatic that it deserves to be examined more closely. The group that Calvin Green described, except for a few approximations in the text, can be identified with certainty.[30] There is no doubt that this is the community founded by Meister Johannes Kelpius, a Rosacrucian scholar reputed to have been passionately interested in Talès, Tauler, and Jacob Boehme, as well as the Church fathers, notably Tertullian, Ambrose, Augustine, and Cyprian. Kelpius had succeeded Jacob Zimmermann as the leader of a group of German pietists. Zimmermann, after predicting the end of the world for autumn 1694, had decided to lead his flock into a wilderness in accordance with the celebrated twelfth

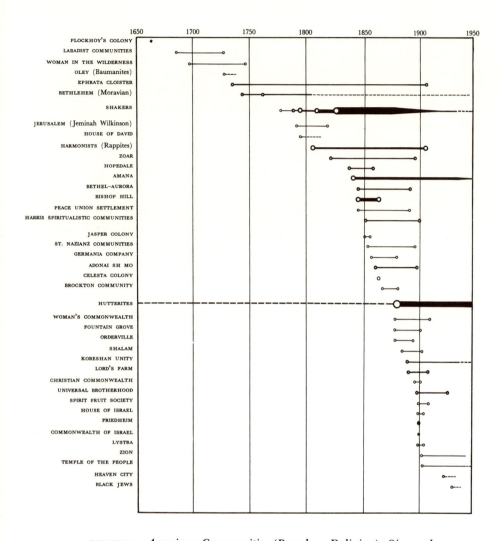

CHART 2. *American Communities (Based on Religion): Size and Longevity*

chapter of Revelation, which had already influenced and would again influence so many real events. But Zimmermann died in 1694, in Rotterdam, on the very day that they were to set sail for the New World. Johannes Kelpius assumed the responsibilities of leadership and led the expedition to a successful conclusion. Immediately after their arrival in America, they organized a religious revival, much to the satisfaction of the colonists in Philadelphia. Then they began construction of their tabernacle, a wooden building forty feet square, containing a meeting room, classrooms, and cells for forty brethren. Indeed, forty was, for them, a mystic number. Green cited it in his report, and it is this figure, thus quoted, that confirms identification of the Germantown sect. Kelpius and his disciples had really come there to prepare themselves for the end of the world. Even after the fateful autumn of 1694 had passed, they clung to their conviction and continued to await the great event. Telescopes were brought in. Kelpius had them installed on the roof of the tabernacle, and he spent long nights searching the heavens for signs announcing the Event. As so often in such cases, the Kelpius community was completely communistic and based on a strict celibacy. If such doctrines seemed to have been conceived to delight the Shakers, how much more pleased the Shakers would have been had they learned the name later given to Kelpius's community. Members of the Germantown sect had first decided to call themselves something like "Philotheists," but the other German colonists in the area imposed a different name, and it is this appellation which remained in use and which Shaker imaginations must have seen lighted up in letters of gold if, indeed, they ever learned of it. The local German residents called them *Das Weib in der Wuste* or "The Woman in the Wilderness."

The long wait was interminable and the community started to disintegrate, especially after the death of Kelpius, who, as he grew older, seemed to have become increasingly preoccupied with his life as a hermit. The experiment broke up completely in 1748.[31]

This effort to make a millenarian prophecy the basis of community life was not the first that the New World had seen. According to S. J. Case in *The Millenial Hope*,[32] the Plymouth fathers did not specify any date, but if someone had told those first settlers that after three quarters of a century the church would still be on this earth, they probably would have smiled, partly out of pity, partly out of disapproval, but mostly out of disbelief.

Nor was the Kelpius experiment the last of the line. It led directly to another phenomenon never mentioned explicitly in the Shaker annals, but which belongs in any discussion of their theory that a "cloud of witnesses" had preceded them. This was the Ephrata community, which had its roots in the myth of the "Woman in the Wilderness."

During the years 1719–1720 groups of pietist origin arrived in Germantown from Germany. They formed a small congregation of Baptists and took the name of Dunkards (from the German *dunken*: to baptize). Rousselot de Surgy had compiled a number of descriptions throwing light on the religious ferment in the Pennsylvania colony at that time.[33] From them we learn that in 1720 there arrived a new group of Germans who had come with the express intention of joining Kelpius's "Woman of the Wilderness" community. Among them was a certain Conrad Beissel, who, after a dispute, left the Dunkards to found a new community called Ephrata. Without going into the details of this story here,[34] we should mention a few of the more interesting traits of Beissel's group. Ephrata was also millenarian, sometimes with an extraordinary fervor. The faithful of his group seem to have made themselves special gowns to wear at the moment of their ascension to heaven; one of them is reported to have been seen climbing to the rooftop of his house, already dressed in these robes and prepared for the great moment of transfiguration. In general, however, these millenarians were calmer folk. Since no precise date had been decided on, their waiting was habitual, but more vague in its manner. This Ephrata community was also communist and had been organized according to rules conceived for Utopian living. It, too, was organized for celibacy in the framework of a monasticism that included both men and women, but this time accompanied by a sort of third order which, incidentally, was the only part of the community to survive after they joined forces with the German Seventh Day Adventists. The fact of their decline should not make one overlook the influence of this community, whose mother house gave birth to chapter houses in other parts of the colony, notably at Snowhill[35] and probably at Oley.[36] Like the Kelpius settlement, the people of Ephrata seem to have had considerable influence throughout the region either by virtue of their numerous visitors, their writings, or their reputation.[37]

The community founded by Jemima Wilkinson was another millenarian enterprise, this one contemporary to the Shakers and quite possibly in imitation of them. A. J. MacDonald, the nineteenth-century Owenite, in his unfinished study of American communities, ends a discussion of the subject by saying that he was at a loss to see any difference between Jemima Wilkinson and the Shakers.[38] Did some defectors from Jemima Wilkinson's "Jerusalem" come to join the Shakers, or did Jemima Wilkinson simply try to copy Ann Lee?[39] Dates of the relevant events favor the second hypothesis. At any rate, similarities between the two sects abound.

Jemima had been born into a family with many children. She became a Quaker, but also attended meetings conducted by the evangelizing Methodist, George Whitefield. She is supposed to have simulated a resurrection in order to substantiate his message—another acting out of Revelation 11:11. Like Ann Lee she first established churches, inviting men and women to leave their families and join her group. Like Ann Lee, she found a patron, and then, with the help of this rich and influential judge, in 1788 the "Universal Friend"—that was the name she chose for herself—began to found communities. "Jerusalem," located in "the wilderness" near Lake Seneca, New York, was the prototype. Jemima's ambition was to bring forth on earth a holy church of the chosen which would join her in celebrating the first resurrection and be ready, like her, to bear witness on the day when Christ would come down from heaven.[40] Jemima's millenarian credo was accompanied by the usual characteristics, and the communist part of her doctrine probably caused some difficulties with the rich benefactor who withdrew his support after spending thousands of dollars on the project. According to the consecrated formula, their ideal of perfection demanded that members be "neither marrying nor giving in marriage" and that "those who had wives should be as though they had none." There were no successors. In 1819 Jerusalem was abandoned.

With the turn of the century and the successful conclusion of the Revolutionary War, one would expect to find a waning of millenarianism in America. Nothing of the sort occurred. The first decades of the nineteenth century furnish many examples of its vitality. The most sizeable of the millenarian movements was, of course, the Millerite phenomenon. The twenty-first of March 1843 was the date William Miller set for the end of the world. This American farmer and veteran of the Revolution had calculated the date after meditating on the Book of Daniel and the Revelation of Saint John the Divine.[41] For eight years he was a missionary preacher whose message was based on dramatic descriptions of the impending Last Judgment. Then, in 1839, the collaboration of a Baptist minister gave the movement a wider field of influence. In 1840 Miller disseminated his message in a special publication called "Signs of the Times," and soon believers were gathering around him. His followers are thought to have been numbered in the tens of thousands. Miller aspired to ecumenism, and on 14 October 1840 he addressed an invitation to Christians of all denominations to assemble and explain their beliefs to each other. A similar encounter would later bring the Millerites and the Shakers into dialogue, although after an exchange of "explanations," neither side altered any of its beliefs.[42]

The Millerite boom was tremendous. So was the disappointment it engendered on 22 March 1843, despite

Miller's proposal that the date be set ahead one year. Such stirrings of revival spirit were not lost on others, particularly the Shakers. They interpreted this new sign of the times as another chapter in their own Old Testament. After this disappointment of 1843, a number of Millerites were welcomed into their ranks, and these new members found in Shakerism what they needed in order to remain faithful to their millenarian convictions. This was not the first time that the Shakers acted as parasites on a religious revival. Both the Kentucky and New Lebanon revivals had already contributed mightily to Shaker recruitment—and for similar reasons.

Moreover, Millerite notions of the millennium reverberated throughout the country, reinforcing, expressing, or sparking off other religious phenomena that were a setting for the growth of the Shaker societies and testified to the spiritual atmosphere in which they thrived. A few examples of these phenomena should suffice.

Eric Jansson, the founder of a Swedish community at Bishop Hill, cast himself in a leading role for the Second Advent of Christ. His anticlerical millenarianism had led him to found a theocratic community which lasted from 1846 to 1862. F. T. Howland, a Quaker, was inspired by the Millerite revival to found a community with the characteristic name of Adonai Shomo or "the Lord is at hand." Howland claimed to have received instructions from the Holy Spirit, which had given him the gift of tongues and prophecy. According to its charter, goods in this community were to be held in common as in the days of the apostles. It lasted from 1861 to 1897. Even more explicitly millenarian was Peter Armstrong, who founded the community of Celesta in order to gather together in a distant Pennsylvania valley the 144,000 believers chosen to herald the Coming of the Lord. The first group to arrive at Celesta consisted of little more than the founder, his wife, and their seven children. In 1863 they were joined by four other believers. The slowness in recruiting did not discourage Peter Armstrong, and in his letters to friends "on the outside" he pleaded with them to leave the world in order to escape Judgment Day and not to be discouraged by the supposed impossibility of feeding and housing 144,000 believers in this wild country. Armstrong reasoned that if one is doing the work of God, there should be nothing to fear.

Hinds, who has described these experiments, adds that there were many similar millenarian communities in America during the first half of the nineteenth century.[43] Indeed, in 1844 William Miller himself declared that he had the names and addresses of some 3,000 preachers, all of whom were actively proclaiming the imminent end of the world.[44]

It was the questions raised in the public's mind by these American millenarian movements that gave the Shakers the opportunity to evolve progressively their own questions and their own answers.

III. Shaker Millenarianism

In Shaker millenarianism one can discern with something approaching certainty two distinct layers of thought: on the one hand, there are the fundamental themes contributed by Ann Lee and the early disciples; on the other, there are the calculated reckonings of later generations of ministers and theologians who had joined the movement. The early Shakers, who were crude and unlettered, showed little concern with the Bible and had small competence for the niceties of scriptural discussion. In distinguishing between the two layers of Shaker thought we would do well to start with the contribution of the later generations, since the abundance of written records they left are the most easily understood. Finally, we shall have to consider a third factor that was progressively grafted onto the body of Shaker thought: the political factor, wrapped in prophecies about the fate of the American nation.

In our cursory review of the various stages in the development of both American and European millenarianism, we have already seen several examples of the role played by dates and the calculations by which these dates have been determined: 1260 for Joachim of Floris, 1527 for Hans Hut, 1657 for the Fifth Monarchy Men, 1689 for Jurieu, 1844 for William Miller, and so on.[45]

Millenarian calculations were generally made a priori, that is, before the event occurred. Thus they are semi-prophetic in character. Calculations made by Shaker theologians differ from the others in that they were made a posteriori, that is, after the essential events had already taken place. This accounts for the justificatory note which characterizes their presentation.

The basic facts of the Shaker appraisal are actually quite inconsistent and vary according to the period of the society's history under consideration. But without going into details that are tiresome and really of secondary importance, it is possible to discern the following broad outlines of prophetic data as presented in the *Testimony:*[46]

1. 2300 : The number of years that must pass before the sanctuary can be purified
2. − 533 : The date B.C. when this prophecy was made
3. =1747 : Date when the Wardleys began their ministry
4. −1290 : Years of desolation
5. = 457 : The "abomination that maketh desolate" under Pope Leo I
6. +1335 : Years of waiting for promises to be fulfilled
7. =1792 : Year in which the Church was organized in "Gospel Order"

And the following are the sources of the figures:

1. 2300: "And he said unto me, Unto two thousand and three hundred days; then shall the sanctuary be cleansed" (Daniel 8:14).

2. −533: The date that the Shaker writer attributed to

the writing of the Book of Daniel. He adopts traditional opinion which placed it in the sixth century B.C.[47]

3. =1747: Date obtained by subtracting no. 2 from no. 1, when the *days* prophesied by Daniel are counted as normal *years*.

4. −1290: "And from the time that the daily sacrifice shall be taken away, and the abomination that maketh desolate set up, there shall be a thousand and two hundred and ninety days" (Daniel 12:11).

5. =457: Date obtained by subtracting no. 4 from no. 3. This is justified by a chapter of ecclesiastic history borrowed from Mosheim. In the year 457 Pope Leo I proclaimed the doctrine that united in the person of Christ there were two distinct natures, the human and the divine. "Here we find," explains the Shaker text, "the origin of this anti-christian doctrine of *two distinct natures in Christ* so generally maintained by the reputed orthodox professors of Christianity, not from Christ, but from Leo, the first sovereign prince of Antichrist."[48] The Shakers, like other dissident sects of the same type, supported "adoptionism."[49] By denying the validity of doctrine of Christ's divinity, they were attacking not only the fact that it excluded all others but also (and perhaps above all) the idea that this deification of Jesus had been effected by a human authority which, in so doing, had deified itself, since it claimed to be the only legitimate interpreter and sole authentic voice of the man-God.

6. +1335: "Blessed is he that waiteth, and cometh to the thousand three hundred and five and thirty days" (Daniel 12:12).

7. =1792: Obtained by adding no. 5 to no. 6. For discussion of the organization of Shaker society and "The Gospel Order," see below, chapter 4, section entitled "The Second Phase."

As one can see, all references used in making this calculation have been taken from the Book of Daniel. Elsewhere one can find supplementary explanations based on passages of "Revelation," particularly chapter 11, in the verses about the "two witnesses" and what happened to them. Two verses in particular are cited: ". . . and the holy city shall they [the Gentiles] tread under foot forty and two months. And I will give power unto my two witnesses, and they shall prophesy a thousand two hundred and three-score days, clothed in sackcloth" (Revelation 11:2–3).

And here is the Shaker commentary on these verses: The forty-two months (Revelation 11:2) or three and a half years make 1,278 days. This is not the same as the 1,260 in Revelation 11:3, since it was formulated in a different manner. The two figures should be counted from A.D. 457, the year of the "abomination" when Pope Leo I proclaimed the doctrine of two distinct natures in Christ. This determines two dates:

1. 457 + 1278 = A.D. 1735
2. 457 + 1260 = A.D. 1717

The first date, 1735, is the one on which the Gentiles were to cease trampling on the Holy City. The second date, 1717, is the one on which the witnesses would cease prophesying in sackcloth.

Shaker apologists point out that during the period indicated by the dates 1717 and 1735, freedom of speech and religion was introduced in civilized lands, notably by William of Orange in England, 1689,[50] and by Peter the Great in Russia, 1721.[51]

Accordingly, during or about the year 1717, the witnesses ceased prophesying in sackcloth. "Those who under the reign of persecution, were branded with the odious name of *heretics, wild fanatics* and *enthusiasts,* were now distinguished by the milder appellation of *dissenters, puritans* and *new lights.*"[52]

Similarly, around the year 1735, "there remained no power in the civil government to persecute unto death any people for their religious principles. Nor had the priesthood of the established churches any legal authority to hinder these Witnesses from the free exercise of their religious faith, or to prevent the declaration of their testimony to the people."[53] Taking advantage of the possibilities afforded by this providential dispensation of religious freedom, the

Witnesses of Truth began to rediscover more and more of the beautiful simplicity of the Gospels, and this revelation came to them at the end of the 1290 days predicted by Daniel.

Later, Elder Frederick Evans was to establish 1792 as the date which simultaneously marked the end of the 1,260 days of the two witnesses in sackcloth and the end of the 1,260 days that the Woman spent in the Wilderness (another number from Revelation). According to Evans, religious freedom did not come to the Shakers until after the American Revolution. Using the language of Revelation 12:16, he said that freedom of belief in victorious America was the earth opening her mouth and swallowing up the flood of religious persecution which the dragon had cast out of his mouth.[54] Thanks to this great upheaval, the Woman in the Wilderness (Ann Lee) had escaped from the Dragon (which was the English Church and state).[55] This was, of course, a further Americanization of prophetic chronology. But although one is not bound to pay any more attention to these variations than did the Shakers themselves, they are nonetheless interesting for what they can tell us about the Shaker state of mind and philosophy of history.

THE BASIC THEMES

Quite obviously, it makes no sense to evoke any superiority in their often unfounded and always tiresome calculations to explain the appeal of the Shaker universe to religious natures caught in the millenarian eddies of Europe and America. Strange as it may seem, the basic reasons for its appeal lie in Shaker realism, which was linked to an unusual interpretation of the Scriptures that the millenarians themselves recognized as contrary to their own traditional principles.

The sundry themes of this prevailing non-Shaker millenarianism can be summarized in four propositions:

1. The advent is *ahead* of us.
2. It will *come down* from the *heavens*.
3. It will be *instantaneous* and *overwhelming*.

4. It *requires perfection* (loyalty to community over family).

The themes of Shaker millenarianism can be reduced to a similar series of four propositions that would contradict the validity of the ones cited above if Shaker theorists had not made them look like their inner "truths" rather than their contradictions:

1. The Advent is *behind* us. It was begun by Ann Lee.
2. It *comes out* of the *earth.*
3. It will be *slow* and *evolutionary.*
4. If it requires perfection that is because *it is perfection* (community over family) *which opens the way.*

These four themes—feminism, immanence, evolution, and perfectionism—form the basis of the Shakers' millenarian doctrine.

Feminism. We have already pointed out that the central idea in Ann Lee's "revelation" was the conflict between two incompatible modes of living (generation versus regeneration), and that she was determined to view this incompatibility as a worldwide, present, and historical fact.

Now for the Shakers there was no need to wait for the Advent in order to know a mode of living in which the conflict would be resolved. It had already been achieved at the time of the Second Coming as embodied by Ann Lee. Through her and the society she founded, the Kingdom of God had been inaugurated on earth. One entire chapter of the *Millennial Church* is devoted to demonstrating what it calls "The Manifestation of Christ in the Female."[56] Everything contributed to supporting the claims of Ann Lee: "The Church was the body of Christ: and as Adam had a body containing the substance of male and female, before Eve was taken from it; so had Christ. Therefore, as Christ had then been manifested in the male only, and not in the female . . .," the text implies that just as the feminine principle of Eve had been immanent in Adam, so the feminine principle, or what the apostles called the Church, had been immanent in Christ. It then continues by saying that the apostles were under the necessity of using this figure of speech "till the female was taken from his spiritual body, and placed in her proper order, as a distinct character. But the time is now arrived, and the female is made manifest; therefore it is no longer necessary to use figurative language in speaking of these things: for we can now plainly declare the Spirit and the Bride."[57]

Thus it was that the new mode which was to reconcile the contradiction between the modes of generation and regeneration already existed, and that the fact of its being brought into existence by a woman, far from being a liability, lent it an extra credibility. On the social level this idea attracted the interest of men like Frederick Evans, for whom feminism was the keystone of social reform. What about the religious level? A conversation between Joseph Meacham and Mother Ann, as reported in the *Testimonies*, reveals what the first generation of Shakers thought about this aspect of their millenarian doctrine. Joseph Meacham, the stern Baptist preacher, was objecting to the Apostle Paul's command that women should not be allowed to speak in church. Mother Ann replied, "As the order of nature requires a man and a woman to produce offspring, so where they both stand in their proper order, the man is the first, and the woman the second, in the government of the family. . . but when the man is gone, the right of government belongs to the woman; so is the family of Christ."[58] It is quite probable that through this little parable Ann Lee meant to question the male monoply of religious functions. She did so by insinuating that this monopoly had already revealed men to be powerless either to replace Christ or to prevent his absence, be it literal or figurative, be it the person or his work. In a sense Ann was blaming the male monopoly for the waning of Christ's mission on earth. Did the Baptist minister feel that he was being personally attacked? The *Testimonies* tell us that

this answer opened a vast field of contemplation to Joseph, and filled his mind with great light and understanding concerning the spiritual work of God. He clearly saw that the New Creation could not be perfect in its order, without a father, and a mother. . . . He saw Jesus Christ to be the Father of the Spiritual Creation, who was now absent; and he saw Ann Lee to be the Mother of all who were now begotten in the regeneration; and she, being present in the body, the power and authority of Christ on earth was committed to her; and to her appurtained the right of leading and governing all her spiritual children[59]

For the Shakers, everything in the course of history seems to have happened according to a series of *as if's:*

1. *As if* the process of creating a proletariat had culminated in the religious proletarianizing of women
2. *As if* this dispossession of women had, in turn, produced its own opposite
3. *As if* this opposite, pushed to the extreme, was giving birth to the Woman Messiah.

The theme is not absolutely unheard of. One finds it, in one form or another, in the historical byways leading to modern socialism. One has only to consider the followers of Saint-Simon.[60]

Immanence. The Scriptures affirm in several places that when Christ returns to earth men will see him "coming in the clouds of heaven" (Matthew 24:30 and 26:64; Revelation 1:7). This explains why at given moments in Christian history groups of men have withdrawn from the mainstream of human activities in order to be unencumbered when they face the great Event. Some have retired to the mountains, like the Taborites; some have searched the heavens, like the Kelpian community in Philadelphia; others have wandered about aimlessly, like the followers of Hans Hut or the Canadian Doukhobors.

The Shaker texts argue that for such millenarians the difficulty came from giving to the prophecy a "natural" interpretation, which is to say an interpretation leading them to expect physical movement through those celebrated clouds.[61] What is needed, concluded the Shakers, is a spiritual interpretation of the prophecy. Those "clouds are not the common clouds of the atmosphere, but *the clouds of Heaven;* therefore they must be heavenly clouds—clouds of faithful witnesses of God who are ready and willing to embrace the testimony of Christ, whenever and wherever it shall appear; and to declare it to the world without restraint and without disguise."[62] The Scriptures use the word several times in this sense: "Who are these that fly as a cloud and as doves to their windows?" (Isaiah 60:8); "Wherefore, seeing we also are compassed about with so great a cloud of witnesses . . ." (Hebrews 12:1).[63]

Now these "clouds of witnesses," according to an analysis by Elder Calvin Green in the *Millennial Church,* are none other than the various tiny religious groups which emigrated to America, both before and during the Shaker experiment, and which were composed of people who, like the Shakers, wanted to live a life more or less modeled on the one preached by Christ's apostles. Indefinite in number and vague in density, they were indeed like clouds, even to the eternal renewal of their presence on the scene. Thus it was not necessary for the Kingdom of God to pass through space and come down from above in some magical operation. It came directly out of the inner heavens of men's minds by a movement in time, examples of which could be seen all around the observer.

Evolution. This emergence of the Spirit from the inner heavens had none of the eruptive suddenness of the traditional Parousia. Yet was not the Advent's suddenness a characteristic that had been categorically affirmed in the Scriptures? "For as the lightning cometh out of the east and shineth even unto the west; so shall also the coming of the Son of man be" (Matthew 24:27).

Lightning? Shaker exegetes take issue with this translation of the Greek word *Astrapê.* Is it not, they query, rather a matter of sunlight or, even more simply, daylight or dawning or shining in an east-to-west direction? Parallel texts, they say, seem to confirm this idea.[64] In any event, are we not obliged to take into account the fact that the first translators of the Bible were haunted by the idea of an instantaneous

Advent and therefore likely to distort the original text, especially in places where words in the original lent themselves to an ambiguous reading?[65] Therefore we should conclude that the text is referring to the Day or "Millennial Day" which will enter the history of mankind like sunshine inundating the countryside, leaving nothing untouched. Dusk comes to one place at the same moment that dawn breaks onto another. In this manner the light or the Day of the Lord does not appear everywhere at the same time and with equal brilliance. Being neither universal nor instantaneous, and certainly not universally instantaneous, the light shines in a varied and graduated fashion.[66]

For the Shakers it was dawn *hic et nunc.* The "cloud of witnessess" testified to this. Another piece of evidence was "the shackling of Satan" by the chain of great events which had established religious freedom in the world and which, in doing so, had invalidated all ecclesiastic persecution, that mighty weapon of the Antichrist. Other pieces of evidence: the spirit of religious tolerance itself, the spread of pacifism, progress in the abolition of slavery, and a general improvement in man's lot, to say nothing of the religious revivals that were breaking out all over the country.[67] All were movements or historical realities in respect to which the Shakers were either beneficiaries or contributors. At the very least, to Shaker eyes they looked like stages in the preparation of a New Age in which it would be the Shaker mission to preach "the everlasting gospel . . . to every nation, kindred, tongue and people."[68]

Perfectionism. "And woe unto them that are with child and to them that give suck in those days!" said Jesus in his prophetic discourse (Matthew 24:19). As stated in Matthew, this curse could not frighten or upset the Shakers, since they did not believe in a sudden, surprise appearance of the Spirit. However, in a doubly roundabout way, it did affect them just the same. In the first place, there was the Malthusian subterfuge implicit in the early practices of the society. The fact of this implicit discipline among the early Shakers seems all the more plausible when one considers that it occurs later, this time explicitly, in the socio-religious experiments of similar groups, such as the Rappites.[69] But above all, there was the theological bypass which led the Shakers to their interpretation of the Judgment by Fire. This form of judgment might have been deemed less sudden, but it was certainly no less merciless than others men have predicted.

In a significant passage of the *Millennial Church* we read that educated Christians generally believe the world will be destroyed by fire and that many people expect a flood of fire and brimstone to inundate the earth and destroy in a flash all its evil inhabitants. The text tells us that:

We firmly believe the world will come to an end and that it will be destroyed by fire. And we also believe and confidently testify, that this fire has already commenced; because we have felt its operation upon our own souls, and have found it to be, in very deed, a consuming fire to lust and pride, and every other corruption of man's fallen nature. This fire, we have no doubt will burn with increasing power, and many will yet feel its purifying effects; and all who come fairly into it may depend on having their lust and pride, their selfishness and avarice, their deceit and hypocrisy, their envy, malice and hatred together with all their evil deeds and evil imaginations, effectively consumed by its power; and when this burning is completed, they will find themselves among that happy number "upon whom the ends of the world are come" (First Corinthians 10:11). But those who shall be found unwilling to come into this fire, by the way of the cross, and to consign their lusts and corruptions to its purifying flames, will at length be compelled to fell the fire of those very lusts burning in them, with inextinguishable fury, and they will not be able to help themselves.[70]

"Their lust is their torment," as Ann Lee had already proclaimed.[71]

Here and there in Ann Lee's preaching, as in the theological commentaries of the *Millennial Church*, the millenarian aspect of their message squeezed the Shakers into a tight corner of perfectionism. But, to be complete, we should immediately add that *this* perfectionism they preached is the very kind which, when lived, produces a millenarian vision.

E. T. Clark presents this aspect of Shaker doctrine by

citing a letter he received from a religious leader in a contemporary American evangelist sect:

By sending and carrying the gospel to every part of the globe, we hasten the return of Christ and thereby cut off hatred, selfishness, divorce, murder, theft, all manner of disease, prevent the birth of untold generations who would be born, reared, be hellbound, die, and be in torment. Look at all the damnable things I could prevent and the souls I could keep out of hell by their not being born, not because I have done anything to carnally prevent conception, but by fulfilling Christ's mission, he returns and then no more souls are born for hell and all the wretchedness that is becoming more rampant.[72]

This is exactly the Shaker point of view. When someone raised an objection by saying, "if this be perfection, then are you not, by desiring all men to be perfect, seeking the end of mankind and, by putting an end to human survival, are you not bringing about the end of the world?" the reply was: "Precisely." And the Shaker apologists explained that they deemed it right and just that man's natural family be dissolved and disappear in the presence of Christ's family, which in the eternal Kingdom of God is the basis of all social order.[73]

It remains to say that, according to Shaker theology, the resurrection of the body is another "natural" idea and, as such, should be filed away in the same folder of errors as the notion that Christ will descend through the clouds and that the world will end in a flood of fire and brimstone. For the Shakers the only real resurrection is an earthly experience of angelic life.[74] Imagine the exaltation of those first generations of believers when they saw that the Kingdom of God was beginning really to exist, and observed that the Day of the Lord as well as the end of the world was near at hand. Imagine how this exaltation must have intensified as, more and more, they watched the revival preachers escape less and less from the trap of their own predictions, while the Shakers were "taking up their cross against the flesh" and joining their bodies and their worldly goods together in communities that were growing in number and in prosperity. The world was truly about to reach its end or, in other words, attain its point of perfection, the moment at which it would disappear. The more perfect its life, the nearer would be its death in time, and vice versa.

A millenarianism often needs to invoke the menace of some punitive force such as the king, the people, an archangel, the barbarian horde, or the Saracens. The Shakers found this force in the young American nation. They had hardly set foot in the country when the War of Independence broke out. They were newcomers, English, and conscientious objectors. This gave the Americans three good reasons to be uneasy. They threw Ann Lee and a few others into jail and even threatened to send them back through the British lines. However, the loyalty of the little group to the American cause was soon established. Consider the story of Zadock Wright, a Tory loyal to the king who, because he had refused to espouse the cause of the Revolution, was thrown into the Albany prison and had joined the Shakers at Niskeyuna, while he was on parole in the king's district, that is Albany. Mother Ann had been locked up because of her suspicious pacifism. Zadock Wright was a tormented soul whose heart had been touched by the fervors of a religious revival, and he told Ann Lee about his own pacifist scruples. Then Mother Ann taught him to see the Revolution in a different perspective, and she convinced him that this war was an act of Providence which would open the way for the Gospel in America. According to the narrative in the *Testimonies*, Zadock Wright then saw clearly that it would be impossible for England to win, since the hand of God was in the Revolution, and because, for the sake of the Gospel, America was obliged to separate from Great Britain.[75] This conversation is undoubtedly part of the origin of the traditional portrait of Mother Ann as a prophet of the American victory. And it is in this tradition, pushed to the extreme, that a Shaker writer would later celebrate the defeat of the English, calling it the defeat of the "European God."

On the part of the believers this rallying to the cause of the colonists implied a secret hope that the religious policies of the American state would gravitate toward Shaker principles. In itself this was not an Utopian hope. Historically, had not Buddhism, Manichaeism, and Bogomilism found favor with the Emperor Asoka, the Uigur Khan, and the King of Bosnia, respectively, and had not each one of these religions grown under a despot's powerful protection to become a quasi-official faith? The Shakers probably had no knowledge of these antecedents, but despite their principle of nonconformism, a kind of inner Shaker logic led them time and again to seek out the support of the rich and mighty. Frederick Evans would frankly propose to Leo Tolstoi that he accept the title of Elder in the Shaker Societies to be founded in Russia and promised to obtain for him the consent and protection of the Czar.[76] During the 1837–1847 revival the Shakers sent a book of their "revelations" to all the ruling sovereigns of the world (although only the King of Sweden deigned to reply with an acknowledgment). In America the society sent its publication to all the dignitaries of the new republic. One answer must have seemed exceptionally important, judging by the fervor with which it has repeatedly been recorded in Shaker literature. A copy of the *Testimony of Christ's Second Appearing* was sent to Thomas Jefferson. He is quoted by the Shakers as having said: "I have read it through three times, and I pronounce it the best Church History that ever was written, and if its exegesis of Christian principles is maintained and sustained by a practical life, it is destined eventually to overthrow all other religions."[77] From this point of view, Shaker beliefs were — or were imagined to be — in a fair way to becoming the American religion; accordingly, America herself became one of the great Shaker themes. This attitude was not without its ups and downs, and Shaker hesitations about the millennial significance of the country were determined by varying interpretations of the government's silence on the subject. But there were, especially during the early years, moments of great enthusiasm during which the American people were seen as the champions of the new gospel of the Second Coming. Such moments afforded the Shakers their greatest sense of fulfillment.

Something of this spirit would remain in the last Shaker formulas. After the lessons learned as a consequence of fifty years of crises, conflicts, and failures, they would come back to the old formula of limitless peaceful coexistence between the New Heaven and the New Land. This New Heaven would, of course, be Shakerism transformed into a general religion—hopefully. The New Land would be America's republican and secular ideals brought to all the people—also, hopefully. In a later chapter we shall see how this transformation was structured.

Any thorough analysis of Shaker millenarianism should be preceded by a chapter on sociological theory, establishing a set of sociological categories for millenarianism in general. Yet solely on the basis of the Shaker example, we can point out the relativity of the two categories most frequently evoked: *postmillenarianism,* a belief that the Advent involves long labor and progressive betterment effected by man *in time* (for some this progressive betterment is the necessary condition of the Advent, for others it is the cause of its occurrence); and *premillenarianism,* a belief implying that the Advent will occur as a sudden intervention effected by God, a physical act *in space.* God, a physical act *in space.*

These two categories of millenarian thought are clearly exemplified on the extremities of the millenarian spectrum. Thus the first category is neatly represented by millenarian socialism inspired by the doctrines of Robert Owen or, even beyond that, by certain brands of Christian socialism. The second category is illustrated by the frantic waiting of the Kelpian community, the Millerite groups, and the followers of Hans Hut.

Yet on closer examination Shaker hopes for heaven on earth fall into neither of the two categories. For the True Believers the postmillenarian formula was too physical in its methods to achieve their desired end, and the premillenarian formula was based on too "natural" a conception of what that end would be. The first was, so to speak, too immanent for them; the second, too transcendent. More precisely, the Shakers were seeking transcendence in immanence itself, and they sought to achieve this by creating a world which would no longer be "of this world," yet nevertheless would be here, now, and real. Their Utopia was concrete—as concrete as a refusal. But for them this refusal was an organizational thing to which they had given ontological status. They wanted both faith and action: faith in the future reign of a transcendental reality which had somehow been interiorized here and now in the substance of human relations; and action through the development of communities which, instead of being workshops where a man labors to prolong his natural life, would be primarily laboratories of self-denial where he could demonstrate the death of what was "natural" in the life we live.

That is why it was necessary for them to prophesy the "end of the world." Perhaps, since they were convinced that this end was at hand, they thought it logical to announce: "The end is here, therefore live like angels." But also, and perhaps above all, in order to bring about the end of the world, they felt the need to add another message: "Live like angels and, insofar as you do so, you shall see that the end of the world is already here." Lastly, behind this concept of a reciprocal relation between faith and action, there was the prodigious Shaker project of creating a universal refusal of existence. In a final victorious conflagration this refusal "to be" would constitute their reply to the never-ending defeat of a world which from generation to generation had, in every sense of the word, been the embodiment of evil.

CHAPTER FOUR

The Sociological Phases
of Shaker History

I. Chronology of the Historical Stages

Chronologically, what we call the history of the Shakers begins at one of several dates: either in 1770, the date when
Ann Lee had her "revelation" in a Manchester prison; or in
1774, the date when the first group of Shakers set sail for
America; or in September 1776, the date when they gathered
together in the Niskeyuna "wilderness"; or finally, in the
years 1779–1780, the period of their first series of "conversions" (the Shaker Pentecost).

Today this history has nearly reached its end. In 1953 E. D.
Andrews counted fifty members and foretold the complete
disappearance of the sect in the near future. In the issue of
21 March 1949 *Life* magazine recorded the semiextinction
of the group in a picture story entitled "Death of a Sect."[1]

In the previous chapters we have sorted out the chain of
events up to the year 1774. Obviously, there is no question
here of going into a detailed account of Shaker history from
that date to our times. The story has already been recorded
in many different ways.[2] Here we shall simply indicate a few
of the main events which have served as its landmarks.

1774–1776. When the first group arrived in New York
City on 6 August 1774, they seem to have dispersed voluntarily. John Hocknell and William Lee left to explore the

Hudson Valley and, perhaps following the advice of a sympathetic Quaker, fixed their choice on a tract of land at Niskeyuna.[3] Then John Hocknell left for England, apparently to collect the capital needed to buy the land they had decided on. During Hocknell's absence most of the group moved to Albany, where each of the various members worked at his special trade. Ann Lee, after going as far as Albany, returned to New York City, where she and her husband found work, he as a blacksmith, and she as a housemaid. This is the period during which Abraham Stanley fell sick and finally broke off all relations with Ann Lee.[4] Hocknell came back from England by way of Philadelphia in December 1775 and stayed in New York City until February 1776. Sometime after this date the whole group, minus Stanley but augmented by several new arrivals from England, gathered together in Albany.[5] They bought their land and prepared for a new community by clearing the ground and erecting suitable buildings, so that by September 1776, in the woods of Watervliet, near Niskeyuna, about seven miles northwest of Albany, "in the wilderness," they had established a permanent settlement. This was to be a place where, according to a Shaker text, "they could enjoy their faith in peace, amid the tumults of war in which the country was then involved."[6] This last remark from the *Millennial Church* throws a singular light on the nature of this Shaker flight to the wilderness. The monastic retreat at Niskeyuna served at the same time, and perhaps above all, as a forest refuge for dissidents. The war with England, which began in Boston in April 1775, had, by the month of June, spread throughout the colonies, and within a year it was known as the War of Independence. The outbreak of hostilities was perhaps not unconnected with the fact that when John Hocknell returned from England in December 1775, he debarked in Philadelphia rather than in New York City,[7] nor with the fact that it was in September 1776 that that the group as a whole withdrew into the wilderness. Later Shakers were firm in their denial that this non-participation in the American Revolution indicated a latent sympathy with the British, but at the time Shaker adversaries did not fail to take advantage of this opportunity to accuse them of it publicly.[8]

1776–1779. These were years of solitude, while they improved their new settlement and, so the texts tell us, fortified themselves spiritually. Years of impatience, too, even among the disciples. Then, in 1779, Ann Lee informed her companions that "the time was just at hand when many would come and embrace the gospel, and directed them to make provisions for it, which they did according to their abilities."[9] It was was about this time that the American victory at Saratoga (October 1777), followed by the American alliance with France (January–February 1778), forced the British to carry their campaign further south, into Virginia and the Carolinas.

1780–1781. This was the year of the great Baptist revival at New Lebanon. According to *Millennial Church*, in May 1780 some of the revivalists "providentially" visited Mother Ann and her little family.[10] Another Shaker text throws light on the "providential" reasons for this visit. In *Shakerism, Its Meaning and Its Message* White and Taylor describe the Baptist preacher who played a large role in organizing it. This was Joseph Meacham, of whom they said:

Laboring for an increase of light and for redemption from the power of evil, he entered the dark days of the Revolution, that time of war, when passion and frenzy seemed to turn men to demons and let loose hordes of evil spirits to bear sway over mind and matter. At such times, men and women of religious nature turn in disgust from the emptiness and rottenness of society in church and state and exercise themselves toward God. Joseph Meacham became a leader among such spirits.[11]

It is then quite probable that when Joseph Meacham and his revivalists came into the Watervliet forest, they were seeking the same thing that the Shakers had found there: a place of refuge where they could remain on the sidelines of the war. Ann Lee's group was English; Meacham's was American; yet difference of nationality did not prevent them from getting along together. The stock of provisions collected as a result of Mother Ann's foresight surely had had something to do with this;[12] the magical effect of Shaker religious exercises did the rest. A first network of converts was woven: "Many from various parts of the country, and of almost every denomination, embraced the faith of the society."[13] One of the first converts was Joseph Meacham himself; he later became the first American leader of the movement.

But outside Niskeyuna the war was still going on. And since these zealous converters were systematically calling on people to become conscientious objectors, since they were almost all English, fresh off the boat, and since they were proselytizing behind the American lines, the inevitable happened: the Shakers were accused of weakening colonists' resistance to the enemy.[14] During the spring of 1780 Mother Ann and the principal Shakers were thrown into prison, and she was threatened with banishment to territory held by the British Army: a reprisal that the prisoners interpreted as a counteroffensive by the "old Heaven" and the "old land."[15] Then, finally, they were set free, possibly because they were judged inoffensive, possibly because they had identified themselves with the right side by prophesying an American victory,[16] possibly because freedom of speech and religion had become firmly enough entrenched in America to permit the presence of some conscientious objectors.[17]

May 1781–September 1783. The first Shaker missionary expedition, the only one led by the founding Mother herself. Her companions were three men (William Lee, James Whittaker and Samuel Fitch) and two women (Mary Partington and Margaret Leeland). The missionary expedition had been prepared by conversations with interested people who had visited the Shakers at Niskeyuna. Homes of converts living in other areas were to serve as bases of operation. For two and a half years the three couples of itinerant preachers (another old dissident tradition)[18] wandered up and down the states of Massachusetts and New York and into Connecticut. The ground had been well prepared by a religious revival and by the war. Preachings, conversions, meetings, and hostile mobs were scattered all along the trail until 4

September 1783, when the pilgrims of the Second Advent returned to Niskeyuna.[19]

1784–1787. This is a period of mourning. The English generation of Shakers was rendered leaderless by the deaths of the three greats: William Lee (21 July 1784), Ann Lee (8 September 1784), and James Whittaker (20 July 1787).

James Whittaker had assumed the role of leader on the death of Ann Lee. We have already pointed out how his coming to power marked the departure of what remained of the old guard from England.[20] For three years under his leadership the movement continued on course, although it has been pointed out that after 1785 there was a fourteen-year lull in recruitment.[21]

1787–1803. During this period Joseph Meacham, the former Baptist preacher, assumed power as the first American leader. He was invested with responsibility for the flock on the very day of Whittaker's funeral. This ascension to leadership was not achieved without friction. But Meacham knew what he wanted to do, and two months after his investiture the Shakers started their first "gathering," a word they used for the process or organizing believers into a community.

About the reasons for this first "gathering" the Shakers generally say little except that Mother Ann had prophesied the operation and appointed Joseph Meacham to carry it through to completion.[22] That is quite possibly true. Nevertheless, behind this explanation, which may well be tinged with hindsight, one can see the signs of a process grounded in more prosaic realities.

First of all, the series of conversions, at Niskeyuna as well as on the missionary trail, had not occurred without giving rise to a wave of eccentricities and excesses. Since this same phenomenon would later mark the first years of a movement as coldly rational as Marxism,[23] what is more natural than to see it in the beginnings of a movement like the Shakers', whose specialty was the unleashing of "enthusiasms"? In 1823 the Shakers themselves implicitly admitted the problem.[24] At least they recognized that it was time to discriminate between use and abuse in their religious practices.

On the other hand, if this turning point in Shaker history became crucial, it was because of a very special requirement in Shaker life, a need that was related to the inner logic determining the society's development.

Up to this point the "True Believers" were still living as they had always lived, generally on their own farms, united together simply by the spiritual solidarity of those who share the same faith (in this case, faith in the Second Advent) and the same religious practices: notably, the observance of the cross, which is to say renunciation of marriage or at least of its consummation. Periodic pilgrimages to the mother-house for a retreat assured the group that individual fervors would be maintained.

Now, according to records of later court trials, we know that it was rare for a husband and wife to be converted by the Shakers at the same time. And in cases where only one of the partners joined the sect, the famous problem of cohabitation was immediately raised, just as it had been raised in the family of the founder herself.[25] The spreading of the gospel had multiplied such cases, and it is very likely that Joseph Meacham's decisions were based on observations of this state of affairs. A new kind of human relationship could not survive in the framework of the old social structure. The sense of brotherhood that had been so frustrated under the old structure could be realized by all only in a new context — one in which, since everything belonged to everyone, nobody would be materially bound to anybody else, and in which the sexes would be joined together in religious exercises of a type replacing the old physical intimacies, now become untenable. This new framework was the Family. "True Believers" who had decided to erase from their lives all notions of a past or future marriage of the flesh were brought together and incorporated into Families; this is the precise meaning of a "gathering." The first "gathering" was at Mount Lebanon in September 1787. This place would soon become known as the "Holy Mount" and replace Niskeyuna as the center of

Shakerism, although the community (Watervliet) later established at Niskeyuna was given the mystic name of "Valley of Wisdom." Others followed: Hancock, Harvard, Shirley, Enfield, Canterbury, Alfred, New Gloucester, and so on. The chronology and topographic details of these communities will be given later in this study. It is understandable that a movement so occupied with internal reorganization was not very interested in making new conquests.

Indeed, the desired formula does not seem to have been found all at once. In 1795 the first oral Covenant was replaced by a written one, and this written one went through a series of modifications.[26] The Family structure, as planned by Joseph Meacham, was revised during the period 1811–1814 by his successor Lucy Wright, the Eldress who had already shared the authority with Meacham before his death. In 1796 there was an important disagreement on an issue raised by the elder in charge of the "Order of Children."[27] And lastly, the property brought to the society by newly "gathered" converts often gave rise to delicate legal questions, two of which reappear quite regularly in the records: (1) Is the contribution of property to the community irreversible in the case of a "True Believer" who decides to leave the church? (2) When a newly "gathered" member is already married, does his property stay "in the world" with the "ungathered" spouse? Shaker elders of the nineteenth century were to pay minute attention to these questions of property and money.

This period of growth and organization was also, thanks to the inspiration of Joseph Meacham, a time of intense religious fervor and austere observances.[28]

1804–1821. The year 1804 inaugurated a new stage in the growth of the Shaker Society, this time through the famous religious revival in Kentucky.[29] In the cold of January 1805, having received encouraging news of a religious ferment in that section, three Shaker preachers, this time three men, set off on a two-month journey of forced marches and fell into the extraordinary religious fervor of the Kentucky revival. The procedures that had worked so well in New York, Massachusetts, Connecticut, and Maine were repeated again in the Midwest. A Presbyterian minister, playing the role filled fifteen years earlier by Joseph Meacham, acted as link between the Shaker preachers and the local population. He was destined to have a strong influence on the course of Shaker literature. This was Richard McNemar, a leader among the New Lights who withdrew from the Synod of Kentucky.[30] Through him, preachings were arranged; later in the wake of the sermons came conversions and, finally, a "gathering." These encounters produced the Kentucky and Ohio societies,[31] the liveliest, most verbal,[32] most active in recruiting, and also the first to disappear.[33]

This is also the period of faultfinding pamphlets[34] and, in reply, Shaker apologetics[35]—a time of theological self-justification[36] and of brushes with the law when the War of 1812 reopened the old question of the legal status of conscientious objectors. In addition, there were the Shaker campaign against the family; the society's predisposition for acquiring a maximum amount of the goods and properties along with its new converts; the Shaker penchant for storing produce and extending their domains; the severity of Shaker schools for children and the harsh manner of correcting the misbehavior of novices. These were all used as justifications for attacking the Shakers at their most vulnerable point: the undeniable and ever-growing prosperity of the Shaker communities.

1821–1847. This was likewise a period of great activity (see Chart no. 3), and it is likely that the Shaker movement reached its apogee around 1850 (see Chart no. 8). The entire period is dominated, on the one hand, by competition from the nonreligious socialisms, especially the Owenites and the Fourierists, and on the other hand, by a general religious transformation manifesting America's reaction to these European philosophies. Notably, there was an evolution either toward a Utopian postmillenarianism, as the gradual mutation of G. Ripley[37] from a transcendentalist to a Fourieristic position remarkably attests, or toward a premillenarianism, of which the turmoil caused by William Miller[38] and perhaps the growing influence of Swedenborg[39] were different facets. During this period the whole millenarian show was ultimately played out against a backdrop of panic caused by the economic crisis of 1837.

Shakerism was still vigorous enough to take advantage of these various historical changes. The preface of the second edition of *Millennial Church*, written in 1848, at the end of this period, mentions the failure of the Owenites and the Fourierists and subtly uses it as an example to attract to the Shaker fold those whose hopes have been frustrated. More and more Shaker writers tended to present their case rationally or at least as a sort of gnosis, and certain converts, like Frederick Evans, would later be drawn to Shakerism precisely because of this mystical rationalism.

Finally, 1837–1847 was another period of religious revival, but this time it occurred within the sanctum, behind the closed doors of the society itself. There was communication with the spirit of those long dead;[40] there were disparate and long-winded revelations,[41] new songs and new dances, laboriously written letters to the great of the world,[42] the spread of vegetarianism and the prohibition of tobacco,[43] and last but not least, the tiresome, insipid, soulful inebriation that was midway between a Sunday School performance and a spiritualist seance.[44] It was around this time that Joseph Smith founded his community at Nauvoo for the greater glory of the Book of Mormon, and that William Miller gathered his flock of Adventists to witness the Second Coming. Neither of the events was lost on the Shakers. There is a reminiscence of Mormonism in their choice of literary genre and even in the content of their writings.[45] As for the Millerites, after those lectures on doctrine and those ecumenical confrontations, followed by the great disappointment, many of them had joined the ranks of the True Believers.[46]

1847–1861. White and Taylor, who were at once judges and actors in the Shaker drama, noted that the years 1821–1861 were "forty years of growth." Actually, as we have already indicated, the growth probably stopped around 1850, during the years when the societies in the West had not yet weakened significantly and those in the East had not yet reached the point of their greatest expansion, so that, adding the minus to the plus, one gets a sort of maximum for the society as a whole. Following the great 1847 revival within the society, there was a fallow period of twenty years during which the machine started to get rusty. They were living on their capital in every sense of the word: properties, manpower, and cultural achievements. Their leaders watered down the Shaker message, vulgarized both principles and details of the societal structure,[47] and composed catechisms as well as catalogues of rules for good behavior.[48] There was no renewal of the great tradition in writing. The Shaker reputation took on an importance that was inversely proportional to the vitality of the sect. This was also the period of "beautiful souls" whose obituaries encumbered the society's publications.[49] The Shakers still shed light all around them, but the star that was the source of this brilliance was ready to die out.

1861–1892. This thirty-year period inaugurated by the shock of the Civil War was dominated by the great figure of Elder Frederick W. Evans. It is through him that reporters like Charles Nordhoff and Elie Reclus came to know and write about the Shakers. A onetime disciple of Owen, after his conversion of Shakerism he carved himself a prominent niche in the history of the United Society. Along with Joseph Meacham and Richard McNemar, but less than Ann Lee, he remains one of the foremost personalities of the movement. Unlike so many of the society's uncultured or narrow-minded members, Evans had read, traveled, and absorbed vast blocks of modern culture from the eighteenth and nineteenth centuries. He liked to announce his loyalty to Voltaire and Paine. Realizing the element of myth and nonsense in the notion of a sudden worldwide conversion to Shakerism, he tried to resolve their problem by a reflective conversion of Shakerism to the world. He was the Shaker humanist. He talked firmly and loudly, and his voice carried far. Twice he went to England to plead the Shaker cause in the mother country. By reason of magnanimity and megalomania, he conducted a correspondence with people the world over, and in his writings he delivered the time-worn revivalist warnings with the accents of a great social reformer or even a revolutionary. Socialism, pacifism, philanthropy: under Evans the young Shaker generation was instructed to become involved with these causes dear to the contemporary world. Evan's personal writings were numerous and varied.[50] None of this prevented him from holding firmly to his Shaker principles: he appealed directly to Lincoln on the question of conscientious objectors and their rights; yet he was equally firm, and not without a certain wiliness, when it came to settling problems involving the financial aspects of military service.[51]

The early generation of Shakers had ambitious dreams of a millenarian church coextensive with a world in which paradise as well as hell had an earthly existence, a world that would one day undergo a "judgment by fire."[52] Joseph Meacham, the realist, had begun to organize, on a smaller scale, yet consistent with Shaker principles, a series of communities that would constitute an antiworld, thus leaving the outside world free to evolve in its own way according to its own logic of perdition. Frederick Evans, who was still more of a realist than Meacham, tended to admit the validity of life in that outside world and thus merely claimed for the Shakers the role of an elite corps in the avant-garde of world progress.[53]

His adversaries did not miss the opportunity to accuse Evans and his policies of being the cause of Shaker decline. The truth is that these policies were not the cause: they were an effect; they represented the only possible way of prolonging the life of this moribund organism condemned by its own inadaptibility. The Shakers had experienced religious revivals. But in an age when men were learning to determine the course of history for themselves, revivals were becoming increasingly rare and suspect. Despite the often dubious illuminism evoked to prolong their survival, despite efforts by Evans and other elders to save the substance of their enterprise by Malthusian, Tolstoian, and Georgic arguments, the day of Shakerism had passed.[54]

1892–1950 (?). The various communities carried on, barely alive, until they finally disappeared one by one. The religious ceremonies became less frequent or were not performed at all. Certain of the rites were secularized.[55] Confession was suppressed.[56] Dancing became wooden.[57] Singing became increasingly dependent on instrumental accompaniment.[58] The revelations of other years were locked up in the archives.[59] At times they even called on the local Presbyterian minister to officiate at a burial.[60] Willingly or unwillingly, they opened their doors for social and commercial exchanges with their neighbors.[61] Engravings which had long been forbidden began to appear on their walls. Books and magazines "of the world" could be found on the library shelves.[62] Moreover, the pyramidic distribution of ages and generations was unbalanced and tilted on the side of old men and women.[63] Casuistry was proliferating.[64] Craft techniques, no matter how ingenious, produced goods costing more than what was manufactured in "the world" by a vital, growing industry.[65] Even farm income was declining. The principle of self-sufficiency was forsaken, to the despair of the older generation.[66] The number of hired workers increased.[67] Young people no longer brought new energies to revitalize the society and break the rhythm of decay.[68] And more and more of the older generation of Shakers were beginning to reconsider the decision that had once led them to assure their salvation by subordinating self to the society now that they began to feel a spiritual torpor and a dreaded sense of futility in the enterprise.

In 1904 White and Taylor, the two Shaker historians who were writing the story of the society's past at a time when everything was falling to pieces around them, asked the question: "Is Shakerism dying?" "Nay," they replied, "not unless God and Christ and eternal verities are failing."[69] Their optimistic answer could have had one of several meanings: either something such as "We shall win in the end because we are the strongest," or "It is only a matter of an eclipse," or "This wasting away will, in time, bring about an unforeseeable and unforeseen change of fortune." In 1904 the Shakers still held to the bravura passage of the first hypothesis. In 1909, according to a letter cited by Daryl Chase, Shaker optimism was still being fed by the hope that God would intervene like a thunderbolt on behalf of his people.[70] In 1936 Shakers were explaining that the society had already achieved its mission and that from the time of its inception, God had planned for them to disappear when their work had been completed.[71] In 1949 the few survivors in a New Hampshire community were still clinging philosophically to this unpretentious theory.[72]

II. The Sociological Phases in Shaker History

Historically, such were the principal landmarks in the nearly two hundred years of the Shaker adventure. Looked at from a distance, the adventure may appear quite banal. But on closer examination one can see in it the changing fortunes of a many-sided movement in which the millenarian strivings of a *church* live on in the organization of an *order*, before being lost in the decline of a *sect* which was no longer concerned with anything but petty sectarian problems.

The titles of Shaker publications through the years testify to this change of fortune. First, the masterful *Millennial Church*, followed by the growth of the *United Society of Believers*. And then, last on the scene, something called *Shakerism*. In their first works members of the society had been content to identify themselves as a people "called Shakers," but finally, Shaker writers came to accept, without any explanations, the abstract term *Shakerism*.

It is possible to set approximate dates for these three sociological stages. The first goes from the founding of Niskeyuna in 1776 to the death of James Whittaker in 1787. The second stage starts with the first "gathering" in 1787 and continues through the final efforts of Frederick Evans at the end of the nineteenth century. The third stage covers the years of the twentieth century during which sectarian interests became more and more the central concern.

But these dates are deceptive, for, sociologically, the problem is not so much a matter of a discernable, neat chronology as of parallel or interlocking phases or elements, each of which is always present as a potential, even when it is not an active factor in determining action and decisions. This means that the phases indicated in subsequent paragraphs will be not so much classifications drawn from some preestablished system for understanding as descriptions of certain modes of being. We are less concerned with ecclesiology than with phenomenology.

FIRST PHASE: THE MILLENNIAL CHURCH AS A MISSIONARY ENTERPRISE

One would be tempted to call their enterprise a missionary "revival" if, unlike John Wesley, the Shakers had not very early articulated their determination to break with all existing churches and even to replace them. Indeed, for the "secularized" millenarianisms they denounced in the various churches, the Shakers intended to substitute not so much another church as the whole world, which had itself been "millenarianized."

This phase is centrifugal, without identifiable limits in space, the rapidity of diffusion in space implying no more than the brevity or even the telescoping of time. It is a phase characterized by spontaneous expression in song and in dance.[73] It is a phase of irrationality and charisma manifested in unintelligible behavior and paradoxical metaphysics. In the last analysis it is an antinomian phase: inspiration alone made the law, and the person who felt himself inspired considered that he was not to be judged by any traditional set of values.[74]

This phase extends back in time to the English prehistory of the Shaker movement,[75] and reached its apogee during the American religious revivals. The first revival attended by the Shakers was at New Lebanon. It started as a reaction in Baptist circles to the Great Awakening that had been set in motion and was being sustained by the missionary followers of George Whitefield. Back in England the Shaker Society had been born on the fringe of Methodism; in America it was on the fringes of this same Methodism that it would have their first chance to grow in numbers.

Opinion in the Baptist Church was divided on the subject of the revival. Those who looked on it with favor were called the "New Lights." As we have already noted, Joseph Meacham and his group were New Light Baptists. Although Shaker "enthusiasm" had nothing to contribute to the "enthusiasm" of this revival, it did find there a source of renewal.[76] But to the millenarian hopes raised by the Baptist preachers, the Shakers brought an immediate, precise, practical, and imperative answer.[77] Thus they were able to harvest conversions whose seeds had been planted by others.

Daryl Chase adds two other examples of conversion to the one of Joseph Meacham's Baptist group at New Lebanon. The first of these is the story of Benjamin Thompson, who had been converted by Benjamin Randall during the New Light revival in New Hampshire. Later, when passing through Albany, Thompson met and preached his fervor to the Shakers, and the Shakers had replied in kind. The result of this confrontation was Mother Ann's decision to send two of her best missionaries into New Hampshire, where they would carry the gospel to the New Light congregations. The missionaries succeeded in persuading some two hundred Baptists to join the Millennial Church, and these converts were among the most important members of the congregation. Baptist annals record bitter complaints of the difficulties caused in their ranks by the Shakers.[78]

Chase's other example is the story of one Shadrack Ireland, a George Whitefield convert in Massachusetts. The feminist and family aspects of Ireland's message seem to have been quite similar to Shaker doctrines. His followers had built him a house similar to the "Square House" of the

Kelpians in Philadelphia. He had predicted his own resurrection on the third or the ninth day. When Mother Ann arrived on the scene several weeks after his death and found his disappointed followers still waiting, she succeeded in regrouping just about all of the flock, except those leaders who were still hoping to inherit the master's authority. One of these leaders (a "Judas," as the Shaker writer called him) found a way to take advantage of his legal position and obliged Mother Ann and her converts to buy the "Square House" back from him.[79]

Daryl Chase notes that some of these new converts were able and sensible people, but that most of their number were lunatics and revival fanatics, ever ready to abandon a prophet for a Messiah. This was the sensitive chord that Shaker preaching had to touch.

In the second revival, the one of 1800 that started in Kentucky, there was the same denominational base of Presbyterians, Methodists, and Baptists. This revival was characterized by the same phenomenon of "enthusiasm," examples of which have come down to us through detailed descriptions written by the participants.[80]

The Shaker missionaries reached Kentucky, then America's western frontier, in 1805, rather late for a revival that had been going on for five years, and which, if it accomplished nothing else, had prepared the spiritual explosion of which the Shakers would be the beneficiaries.

As early as June 1800 one notes an assembly of the "awakened congregations," followed by a series of camp meetings.[81] It was not long before the ministry and the churches themselves reacted to the renewal of religious feelings unleashed by revival sermons. Even some of the Presbyterian ministers forgot the language of their previous indoctrination and spoke like the gospel of salvation.[82] Julia Neal cites a passage in the unpublished autobiography of an elder who had been a Presbyterian minister before joining the Shakers. Analyzing this crisis in which he had himself played a role, Elder John Rankin noted that at the time of the Kentucky revival the leaders of the church hoped for nothing more than an increase in membership and a deepening of religious feelings. They had not foreseen that the revival spirit would imply a reexamination of all the doctrines of the church. Many of the ministers taking part in the revival soon found themselves in disagreement with their own denominations and concluded that at the root of these mysterious manifestations there was an honest desire for justice which the established churches had found no way of satisfying.[83] This reconsideration of church doctrine implied, among other things, the right to follow one's individual revelation[84] and the duty to uphold the idea of an equalitarian brotherhood, in the spirit of which the name of brother and sister was to be used for all members, rich or poor, black or white. It was on these questions that the gap widened between the revivalists and their churches. In 1805, when the Shakers arrived, a split had already been established. The Shakers exploited it effectively, as is evidenced by the fact that between 1805 and 1825 the western societies gathered in 1,800 new members.[85]

The third revival was the one which the Shakers often called the Great Revival. It flourished, approximately, from 1837 to 1847. In the previous chapters we have already noted a few of its social and religious coordinates.

In his study of the Millerite movement Harkness endeavored to lay bare the relation between the rise of Millerism and the economic depression that led to the panic of 1837.[86] From other sources we know the effect of bankruptcies on the growth of the Mormons.[87] It is quite possible that the Shaker economic structure, based on separate, self-sufficient, agriculture-oriented communities had proved itself to be particularly resistant to financial disasters. Yet one should note a possible relation between the date of the crash and the one on which the revival started. On 10 May 1837 New York banks had to suspend all payments in cash, a measure soon put into effect by all banks in the country.[88] According to Daryl Chase the Shaker revival started on 16 August 1837.[89] Children went into trances. A fourteen-year-old girl, Ann Maria Goff, began to have visions: in a

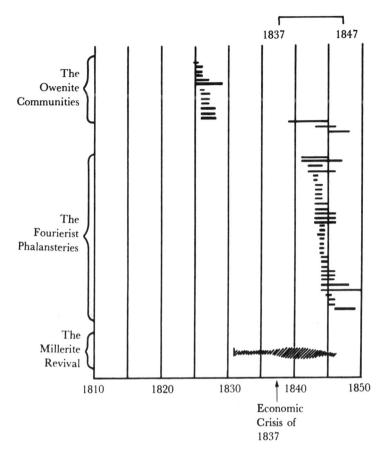

CHART 3. *The Great Shaker Revival: 1837–1847*

dazzling white house she saw a large number of girls in golden dresses and decorated with stars on their shoulders and feet; on their heads there were crowns, and around their hands, halos of bright light; Jesus, who was placing his right hand on their heads and calling them his little children, seemed to feel a great tenderness for them. Visions such as this continued to appear in Watervliet until January 1838. The ministry at New Lebanon quickly forwarded news of these visions to the other Shaker societies. The result was a chain reaction of similar spirit manifestations that rapidly produced a full-fledged revival.

In Shaker History * 105

One can evaluate the Great Revival by the abundance of revelations, although only a portion of these were published, and even they have come down to us only by chance in publications written sometimes as much as fifty or sixty years after the events,[90] for such books were taken out of circulation by the ministry,[91] and the material was debated and even refused by certain societies.[92] Later in our study the analysis of the internal political structure of Shaker societies will reveal the all-powerful role of the New Lebanon ministry in orienting and supervising this spiritual ferment. The first revival had produced Joseph Meacham, who subsequently became leader of the movement. The second revival had produced Richard McNemar, who, although converted to the Millennial Church, steadfastly refused to join the Church Order (this refusal would later be the pretext for his disgrace).[93] The third revival was, if not initiated, at least strictly controlled by the established authorities, who knew, from the experience in Kentucky, all the possible effects of a revival on an existing socio-religious structure. The ministry had the final word when it validated a revelation from Mother Ann in which the founder declared that she would have no "gift" for any of her children except those who lived in perfect union with the ministry and the elders.[94] The clever trick was, of course, to draw out of prophecy itself a means of neutralizing its own effect on the believers.

Thus, without any sudden changes or surprises, the Great Revival dragged out and fed on the flame of its own inspiration. No new societies were founded, but it was then that the old ones received new mystical names.[95] New ties were effected with the spiritualists, of whom the Shakers claimed to have been predecessors.[96] It was the period that produced Philemon Stewart's *The Holy Sacred and Divine Roll and Book*, of which five-hundred copies were sent into the world to the "rulers of all nations." The King of Sweden was the only recipient who acknowledged the gift.[97]

Most of the spirit messages are identified as such. Some come close to apocryphal literature,[98] but they are exceptions to the rule. A brochure like *Calvin's Confession* gives all the necessary precisions as to its literary genre in the title.[99] Although this text of 1842 was not edited and titled until 1904, at a time when the Shakers themselves seemed to have considered this type of writing with the eyes of historian or an archivist, the substance of *Calvin's Confession* can be considered typical of the euphoric effusions during the Great Revival. It deals mostly with Calvin's repentance for having judged himself to be the only man who understood the gospel of Christ and for having thus taken sides with "the bishops." In so doing, he had joined the ranks of the persecutors; for in a world where Papists burned reformers and reformers burned Papists, both Papists and reformers burned like heretics, and all of them were real Christians, if ever people were worthy of that name.[100] His execution of Michel Servetus was the subject of a particularly contrite avowal. In this posthumous confession Calvin spoke of it in the presence of Michel Servetus himself, and the whole manner can be described as a heavenly transposition of the Shaker ritual.[101] Numerous great historical figures came in this way to bolster the Shaker cause after having appeared before their celestial tribunal.[102]

The earthly repercussions of these heavenly interventions were for the most part seen in an intensification of the ascetic and disciplinarian rule of life. One vision called for the standardizing of blue and grey as the colors for all garments worn by the believers—an innovation that did not fail to call forth recriminations from those societies which had stocked cloth of other colors.[103] But above all, this period saw a renewal of the temperance movement.

Dietary laws were not part of early Shaker practices. It was only in 1828 that the United Society was affected by the temperance wave that rolled over the entire country. As recently as 1823 a Shaker had set up a distillery and during the following year started to sell his whiskey on the market. It was not until 1828 that this sale was forbidden and that the church ruled against the use of alcohol except when advised by a doctor. A similar prohibition was ruled against tobacco;[104] but apparently this was not very effective, since White and Taylor note that "many an old Shaker saint rested and consoled herself with her pipe."[105]

After prohibitionist influence, starting in 1837, came the influence of Sylvester Graham's vegetarianism,[106] which was also the cause of much discussion among the various societies. Both of these influences had been revealed in visions during the years 1837–1847. The returning spirits of those who had founded the faith expressed themselves very clearly. The forbidding of tobacco came in 1840, and in 1843 the *Holy Sacred and Divine Roll and Book* played a large role in reviving the discussion of dietary laws. But the battle was not yet won. It was not until 1873 that the death of the tobacco habit is announced in the *Shaker Manifesto*.[107] And for a long time kitchens of the various societies continued the practice of serving two menus, each representing a different diet.[108] The effort to impose a temperance regime and special dietary laws was not exclusively the result of pseudo-revelations. The visions were more of a secondary step, reflecting the tenacious interest of certain rationalistic elders on this subject, notably Frederick Evans and Daniel Frazer.[109] It is even possible that sexual considerations played a role in their reasoning.[110] Such rationalizing is just one more indication of permanent transitions between the mode of revival and the mode of organization.

SECOND PHASE: THE ORGANIZATION OF THE ORDER:
THE "GOSPEL ORDER" IN THE "UNITED SOCIETY"

The second phase, which is the organizing of the order, dates from 1787, the time of the first "gathering" at Mount Lebanon. This means that it fits into the first phase at an early date and that, in turn, this first phase is in step with the organizational phase until the middle of the nineteenth century (second revival, the years following 1804; third revival, 1837–1847). But from then on the mechanisms of the order tend to determine the course of revival inspiration.

From the moment that unlimited expansion in space

fails to bring man any nearer to the Advent, from the moment that waiting begins to hang heavy and time persists in every sense of that word, three courses of action are open to a believer:

1. *He can disappear immediately,* individually or collectively, and salute this disappearance as a favor unwillingly granted by an Antichrist who dominates this world in which his reign is ever growing and eternal. One sees an example of this in the Raskol, where millenarianism was sometimes expressed in a wave of suicides.[111] Likewise, one finds traces of this type of violence in the martyrdom courted by popular revolts among the Jews and in the uprising of the Circoncellions. The "endura" of the Cathari—insofar as any of them really fasted themselves to death—might be considered a more discreet indication of this option.

2. *He can adapt to the historical situation* by making it optional for a small group in the church to live by a discipline which had originally been declared mandatory for all its members. Thus the Manichaeans tolerated a lower order who performed productive labor for the congregation. Thus, if we believe Shaker exegeses, did Saint Paul tolerate marriage among the Corinthians, and, in a more general way, did the Christian Church progressively cease struggling with "the world" and come to tolerate not only marriage but also private property and military service for those whom it called "its people."

At least twice in Shaker history there was explicit evidence of this temptation to adjust spiritual discipline to practical needs. This would have transformed the society into a system of spiritual bonds, enabling the members of the church to remain religiously united, although they would no longer hold all their goods in common[112] and no longer refuse to marry.[113] The Shakers never yielded to the temptation. In fact, they dated the beginning of the decadence of early Christianity from the time that the apostles, in order to reach a larger Gentile audience, yielded to similar temptations.

3. *Lastly, he can resist the course of history.* Anabaptist his-

torians remind us that in similar circumstances this was the Anabaptist solution. After refusing to transform their church into a worldly institution in order to win the world to their cause, the Anabaptists established an increasing number of places where they could live without making the usual distinction between the church and the world, places that would be both extrachurch and antiworld.[114] This was also the Shaker option. We have already pointed out how, when put into practice, their doctrine of spiritual renewal led them, logically, to undertake the socio-economic experiment of pacifist communities in which all property was held in common.

It is probable that this centripetal movement of withdrawal to a place of security where they could consolidate what they had already achieved was envisaged as a temporary expedient. Since they had never provided their church structure with the classic distinction between two states, a state of perfection and a state of imperfection (the three part division of the three orders reflects, as we shall see, quite a different set of criteria), the Shakers could appeal to only two categories: the world of the saved — that is, of their church — and the world of the lost — that is, of everything else. Thus the societies were conceived either as citadels from which they could send forth new missionary expeditions or as havens of refuge for those who would escape the contradictions of life in the world. The goal of the revivals never ceased to be felt in the organization of the "Gospel Order." It was for tactical reasons that the church had "gathered" its members into a religious order, and for many years that order would be motivated by a nostalgia for its first project, which was to become one with the world.

The experiment lasted for a hundred years before the structure of the order was modified at the instigation of Elder Frederick Evans. In the book of Evans's selected writings published after his death[115] there are allusions to a dispute between the new and the old generations on this question of modifying the structure: on the one hand, there were the old believers, set in their ways and, according to

Evans, backward; on the other hand, there were the new believers who would like to start all over again, even if this seemed illogical. Evans sided with the young.

After the Shakers' first one-hundred-year cycle, Evans envisaged another cycle which would begin by modifying some of the basic principles of the first one, even if this meant changing the canon laws of the society. He expressed himself clearly on this subject in a letter to Alexander Webb dated 23 March 1891:

I have just received a long letter from a preacher who states that he has been studying the *Old* and *New Testment* for 25 years; and he wonders that such a man as I am cannot see the absurdity of celibacy, seeing that it would inevitably exterminate the race. This idea was held by the Shakers themselves, until I came foreward as a theologian. I soon saw that there were to be *two orders*—the natural and the spiritual: that clears away obstructions—"New Heavens and a New Earth, wherein shall dwell righteousness." All reforms among the nations have reference to one or the other of these two orders. Hitherto, when men like Leo Tolstoi began to see what genuine Christianity called for, they applied it to mankind en masse. It "made confusion worse confounded." The infidel cried, "Superstition"; the priesthood, "Heresy," and all saw that it was "impracticable." Ann Lee *began* the process of unravelling "the mystery of godliness and of iniquity"; but she saw only in the light of one cycle. Now we see—begin to see, in the light of the second cycle, and two orders are recognized, where, heretofore, only one was admissible, and instead of being accused of designing to "run the world out," the literati, who will go to the encyclopedias in the libraries for information, will learn that they have been misled by *authentic* Shaker works, and that all cyclopedias need to be revised on this point.[116]

In a letter of the preceding year Evans had already pointed out a discussion of this subject published in a brochure entitled *Two Orders*. "*Two Orders*," he explained, "will solve many problems that have hitherto confounded the wise and prudent, and will redeem humanity from many forms of evil."[117] It is evident that during the second half of the nineteenth century a decisive change in Shaker thought was taking place. The new orientation is perfectly clear in Evans's letter. He does not go so far as to make a distinction within the church between the Perfect or the elect and the Auditors or ordinary believers, as the Manichaeans did. Nor does he distinguish between advice and commandments as had been the custom in Christianity.[118] His letter does reaffirm the distinction between the church and the world, the nonsecular church and the nonecclesiastic world, but the second element, the world, is henceforth recognized as, in its own right, a valid order and positive factor in millenarianism.

In place of the old vision according to which heaven and hell were to become progressively more immanent to the world and more and more distinct from each other,[119] Evans substituted a vision in which this progressive immanence and ever increasing differentiation applied to the New Heaven (Shakerism) and to the New World (American republicanism). In the letter of the *Two Orders* he wrote: "Truth will triumph. Shakerism and Republicanism will exist amongst all peoples, as the waters cover the sea."[120]

THIRD PHASE: THE DECLINE AND WANING OF A "SECT"

Symptoms of decline broke out in the last decade of the nineteenth century. In reality they had already been on the scene for a long time. For forty years the membership had been thinning out, although in the year 1874 it was still sufficiently large for an optimistic celebration of the Shaker centennial. Julia Neal cites a marginal note in the official chronicle of this occasion at South Union. The first sentence is an exclamatory recognition of the fact that the sixth of August 1874 marks a hundred years since Mother Ann Lee and her little band had set sail for America, carrying with them news of the eternal gospel for all those who hungered and thirsted for justice. The chronicler then adds that he hopes the next hundred years will see the gospel finally spread to the ends of the earth.[121] Nevertheless, despite an appearance of economic expansion (which was, however, marked by more business failures than successes),[122] the general decline that had begun during the Civil War grew more and more acute.

It is not difficult to determine the mechanics of this disintegration, whose multiple symptoms have already been noted.[123] Industrial production of consumer goods had driven the products of Shaker artisans out of the market, with the result that community workshops were closed and the believers became customers at the neighborhood store, despite the reluctance of older members to go outside the society for supplies. Now the production of these artisans represented, as was so often the case, the off-season work assuring year-round employment for the manpower needed to operate the Shaker farms. Thus the recruitment of new members, which had already dwindled because of the scarcity of a psychologically conditioned public, was diminished even more by the shrinking of the economic demand within the society. As a result, during their busy seasons the society was obliged to hire more workers from the outside, a policy that tended to contaminate the Shaker atmosphere by bringing the winds of the world into the sanctum. This brought about more defections, which were sadly recorded by the Shaker chroniclers. The following, for example, are entries from the record of Pleasant Hill Society in Kentucky:[124]

Lydia and Mary Secrest went to the world from the center family. Silly lambs, you will wish you were in the fold when the wolves get you!

February, 1861: Tabitha Shuter, silly lamb, left the East House for the wide, cold and heartless world!

April 24, 1864: Illinois Green absconded from the West family. What a spectacle! Nearly forty years old and starting out in the wide world, hunting flesh!

Soon this diminished rhythm of recruitment and the dwindling number of believers forced the Shakers to discontinue many of their social services because there was no longer a sufficient number of people to make these economically feasible.

"The Shaker products that derived most directly from agriculture were the last to be given up," notes Marguerite Melcher. Naturally. But the time came when the disproportion between the number of landowners and the acreage to be cultivated was flagrant. Salaries were too high. Taxes were too burdensome.[125] Then came the period of expedients. Julia Neal lists a whole series undertaken by South Union, one of the Western societies. They tried raising sheep, a classic solution by which tilled fields are converted into pasture. In 1908 the trustees rented their lands for five years to a company prospecting for oil. In 1911 there were fifteen hired hands and only seventeen members. In 1912 they sold one of their unoccupied buildings. Despite all their efforts, the situation was obviously becoming untenable. In September 1922 the elders at New Lebanon decided to sell everything at auction. Only nine Shakers remained in the family, and they were given a choice between retirement in a Shaker home or $10,000. Eight out of nine decided to take the money. Two of these married each other and received, as a wedding gift, the automobile that the society had acquired in 1915. Only Elder Logan Johns refused the money and chose to end his days in Shaker company.[126]

The events at this moment of dissolution constitute the result of an experiment and, as such, should be remembered. They were certainly largely determined by the fact that a technical society was liquidating an agricultural and artisan society, and that the Shakers, who had been born *in* and raised *for* the simpler life could only perish in the new society that was replacing it. But also these events throw light on the psychological choices that, together with economic and technical pressures, were shaking the foundation of the United Society. A desire for freedom of action which would enable them to participate in the busy world of events, the call of adventure, or simply the nostalgia to be humans among other human beings—all these urges had become stronger than the imperatives of a discipline which had lost its reason for being. Their refuge was turning into a trap, and the security they had sought there could no longer be hoped for. Moreover had not Elder Evans proclaimed that the history of men in the world was a healthy thing? For those eight Shakers who chose to start a new life, the world of men would not have seemed so healthy and alive if their Shaker "heaven" had not irrevocably dissolved.

III. Sociological Phases as they Appear in Shaker Activities

The development of certain characteristic activities correspond to the sociological phases of Shaker history and are both the effects and signs of them. As such, they can be observed in many examples.

PHASES IN SHAKER CRAFTS AND FURNITURE MAKING

In his detailed studies of Shaker furniture and handicrafts Edward Andrews reaches conclusions that corroborate the preceding analysis. He explains that the culture and corresponding craftsmanship of the Shakers passed through three fairly distinct periods:

i. Organization into communities was a gradual process, five years elapsing from the time when Ann Lee's small colony at Niskeyuna first attracted attention (1780) to the time when the meeting-house at New Lebanon was raised, signifying the advent of a new cult. From 1787 to about 1794 converts were numerous, and all the New England and New York societies (with the exception of the colony at Sodus Bay) were founded. In the latter year the "testimony was considered closed," and attention was concentrated on consolidating the religious order and giving it meaning and form. Until the turn of the century the United Society remained detached, obscure and numerically static. During the formative stage, economic policies were formulated, characteristic industries started, dwellings and shops erected; but the production of furniture was limited. Craftsmanship was breaking away from countryside traditions, experimenting with new forms, and in the process exhibiting a somewhat unstable character.

ii. By 1800 the Shaker system had become firmly established; its essential principles had become sufficiently operative to affect the secular activities of the sect; and distinct conventions in workmanship had been adopted. Until about the time of the Civil War, the culture of the Believers retained a pure and unselfconscious intensity. The members of the sect were dominated by very precise doctrines and a strict though not autocratic leadership. Reading and social intercourse were confined largely to religious channels. The Church pursued its unworldly but industrious way, independent in its beliefs and practices. Conditions were favorable to the development of a true folk art; and it was to this period, when the rapid growth of the society (from 1,000 members in 1800 to a maximum of 6,000 in 1850–1860) involved a steady demand for domestic appurtenances, that the production of furniture was largely confined. So great, in fact, was the productivity of the joiners and wood turners that we can hope only to sample, pictorially and textually, the distinctive types and their main modifications.

iii. By the close of the Civil War the numerical decline of Shakerism, due to various economic-religious causes, had become definitely manifest. In 1875, the recorded population was only 2,500, and by 1900 it had dwindled to a scant 1,000 again. But more important than the decrease in numbers (which removed the need for additional supplies of furniture) was the partial disintegration of the earlier pure and isolated culture. The characteristic Shaker dance rituals were slowly modified and eventually abandoned; instrumental music and more conservative songs displaced the early chants and folk spirituals; the forces of religious ardor, holding compact the life of the sect, were wearing themselves out. The relaxation of the primary religious controls, with their attendant repressions and restraints, and the infusion of "liberal" or "broadening" ideas helped to undermine the solidarity of the order. With the influx of visitors, the employment of hired labor and the removal of restrictions on reading, contacts with the "world" became more frequent. The interiors of Shaker homes began to lose something of their severe restraint and economy: pictures appeared on the walls, secular books and newspapers on the shelves; and flowers were cultivated for their beauty and fragrance alone. The presence of all sorts of worldly gear indicated that the barriers against a sinful society had been lowered. Taste began to shift from a natural acceptance of the simple furnishings of the traditional household to a mild dissatisfaction with such simplicity and a longing for decoration and small luxuries. The furniture made in this period bears frequent evidence of the influence of Victorian style and taste, and suffers in contrast with the early forms.[127]

PHASES IN THE SHAKER DANCE

One of the oldest descriptions of Shaker dancing is found in a 1781 pamphlet by Valentine Rathbun and is quoted by Andrews in his book on Shaker music. Writing about the first meetings at Niskeyuna, Rathbun said:

> In the best part of their worship everyone acts for himself, and almost every one different from the other; one will stand with his arms extended, acting over odd postures, which they call signs; another will be dancing, and sometimes hopping on one leg about the floor; another will fall to turning around, so swift, that if it be a woman, her clothes will be so filled with the wind, as though they were kept out by a hoop; another will be prostrate on the floor; another will be talking with somebody; and some sitting by, smoking their pipes; some groaning most dismally; some trembling extremely; others acting as though all their nerves were convulsed; others swinging their arms, with all vigor, as though they were turning a wheel, etc. Then all break off, and have a spell of smoking, and sometimes great fits of laughter. . . . They have several such exercises in a day, especially on the Sabbath.[128]

Rathbun was a Baptist preacher and this description is a report from the period of the first revival. From what he says it is evident that Shaker behavior is not much different from frenzied movements of the revival itself. William Plumer[129] and Barbé-Marbois[130] have left us similar descriptions of Shaker dancing during this same period.

With the consolidation of the order this early spontaneity disappeared. Andrews notes that it became known as the "promiscuous" manner and was forbidden after Meacham's death in 1796. Later, the frenzies of Kentucky Revival would create new problems to which the formalized, ritualized dance, probably the work of Joseph Meacham, was a necessary and unavoidable solution. On the relation in dance between the voluntary and the involuntary, the ordered and the frenzied, a later Shaker writer has left us an interesting analysis:

. . . In the height of their ecstacy, they were constrained to worship God in the dance.

This was not voluntary. They were irresistibly compelled to go forth in the dances by some invisible hand! Many attempted to resist the impulse until they were forced to comply, by other involuntary acts still more mortifying. The only way that they could avoid the latter, was by yielding to the former. They soon considered it their privilege to rejoice before the Lord, and go "forth in the dances of them that make merry." When I describe to you these mortifying exercises, you will not think strange, that to avoid them, they cheerfully went forth in the dance before the Lord. The spirit of the revival led them to express their joy and gladness in this way. This, you may perceive, was a prelude to the Gospel Order that was soon to succeed. My object is to show, that this was a work of preparation, as the event has absolutely proved to a demonstration.

I wish now to show you the exercises of an involuntary kind, to which these people were subjected, that appear to have been substituted in room [sic] of the *"falling exercise,"* as it was called, at which I have just hinted. The principal of these were the *rolling exercise, the jerks,* and *the barks.*

The rolling exercise consisted in being cast down in a violent manner, doubled with the head and feet together, and rolled over and over, like a wheel, or stretched, in a prostrate manner, turned swiftly over and over like a log. This was considered very debasing and mortifying, especially if the person was taken in this manner, through the mud, and sullied from head to foot.

Still more mortifying were the *jerks.* Nothing in nature could better represent this strange and unaccountable operation, than for one to goad another, alternately on everyside, with a spear of red hot iron. The exercise commonly began in the head, which would fly backward and forward, and from side to side, with a quick jolt, which the person would naturally labor to suppress, but in vain; and the more any one labored to stay himself, and be sober, the more he staggered, and the more rapidly his twitches increased. He must, necessarily go as he was stimulated, whether with a violent dash on the ground, or bounce from place to place, like a foot ball; or hop round with head, limbs and trunk, twitching and jolting in every direction, as if they must inevitably fly asunder. And how such could escape without injury, was no small wonder to spectators. By this strange operation, the human frame was commonly so transformed and disfigured, as to lose every trace of its natural appearance.

Sometimes the head would be twisted to the right and left, to a half round, with such velocity that not a feature could be discovered, but the face appear as much behind, as before. And in the quick, progressive jerk, it would seem as if the person was transmuted into some other species of creature. Head dresses were of little account among the female jerkers. Even kandkerchiefs, bound tight round the head, would be flirted off almost with the first twitch, and the hair put into the utmost confusion. This was a great inconvenience, to redress which, the generality were shorn, though directly contrary to their confession of faith. Such as were seized with the jerks, were wrested at once, not only from under their own government, but that of every one else, so that it was dangerous to attempt confining them, or touching them in any manner, to whatever danger they were exposed; yet few were hurt except it were such as rebelled against the operation, through wilful and deliberate enmity, and refused to comply with the injunctions, which it came to enforce.

The last possible grade of mortification seemed couched in the *barks!* These frequently accompanied the jerks; nor were they the most mean and contemptible characters, who were the common victims of this disgracing operation; but persons who considered themselves in the foremost rank, possessed of the highest improvements of human nature; and yet in spite of all the efforts of nature, both men and women would be forced to personate that animal, whose name, appropriated to a human creature, is counted the most vulgar stigma—forced, I say; for no argument but force, could induce any one of polite breeding, in a public company, to take the position of a canine animal, move about on all fours, growl, snap the teeth, and bark, in so personating a manner, as to set the eyes and ears of the spectator, at variance.

It was commonly acknowledged by the subjects of these exercises, that they were laid upon them as a chastisement for disobedience, or a stimulus to incite them to some duty or exercise to which they felt opposed. Hence it was perceivable, that the quickest method to find releasement from the jerks and barks, was to engage in the voluntary dance. And such as refused, when this duty and privilege were made known, had to bear these afflicting operations, from month to month, and from year to year, until they wholly lost their original design, and were converted into a badge of honor.[131]

Thus out of the involuntary convulsions of the revivals the "voluntary" dance was born and was given a ritual form by the Shakers. It was probably more rhythmical than measured. Its development approximately parallels the development of singing during the second phase of Shaker history. Andrews has given us a detailed analysis of the various figures from the "Square Order Shuffle" (the simplest one) to the many complex patterns elaborated during the revival of 1837–1847.

At the same time a theological justification was worked out with references to the Scriptures. Had not David exorcised the frenzies of King Saul just as the Shaker dance exorcised the "barks" and the "jerks"? And had not David himself danced in front of the Ark?[132] Perhaps in the nude? But such exegeses are really rationalizations that came after the event. They are no more than justifications of preexisting attitudes and, as such, they constitute no basis for an explanation of the genesis of Shaker dances.

Finally, for this activity as for so many others, the end of the Civil War marked the beginning of its decline.

PHASES IN SHAKER SINGING

Andrews has an affection for Shaker music and, in his overall evaluation of their songs, he says that, although the words may be distinctly Shaker, this sacred music belongs to the great tradition of all popular religious singing. In their joyous mood, their rhythms, often in their structure (for example, in the kinds of repetition), these lively Shaker songs suggest the jingling tunes of children's games, the merry folksongs of primitive America, the exuberant and spontaneous excesses of the young of heart all over the world. But the phases of the society's development have also clearly been marked by the way these songs evolved.

Following the wordless tunes of the early period, the first Shaker songs with words belonged to the musical tradition of Baptist and Methodist hymns, to which the Shakers added certain elements drawn from popular ballads and love songs of the times.

To this body of musical literature the Great Revival added many collections of musical messages from the spirit world: "During the period of the so-called 'manifestations' many 'native' songs were received from Indian spirits or from the shades of Eskimos, Negroes, Abyssinians, Hottentots, Chinese and other races. . . . When Indian spirits came into the Shaker Church, the instruments (mediums) would become so 'possessed' that they sang Indian songs, whooped, danced and behaved generally in the manner of savages."[133] The Shakers needed no interpreter to understand these messages or feel their contagious enthusiasm, since they had had daily contact with both Negroes and Indians. Their hymns probably evolved in a manner similar to the Negro spirituals, although, without the blood transfusion that so sensationally vitalized the spirituals, Shaker improvizing never really produced much more than pale imitations of music already known.[134] These songs were not written down until the society was well into the organizational phase of its history. Until 1806 hymns were still learned by heart. A system of musical notation was introduced in 1807. It underwent many revisions until a system of notation by letters was adapted for exclusive use. Conventional musical notation does not appear among the Shakers until the last quarter of the nineteenth century. In *The Gift to Be Simple* Andrews gives examples from all the different periods. After the Civil War the Shakers started to use an accordian accompaniment for their songs—a plaster corset to lend form to a body gone flabby.

EVOLUTION OF SHAKER LITERARY GENRES THROUGH
THE THREE HISTORICAL PHASES

By setting up a chart representing the chronology and distribution by genre of the principal writings by and about the Shakers, and by superimposing on these patterns the

CHART 4
Chronological and Categorical Breakdown of Writings and Publications

	1781–1790	1791–1800	1801–1810	1811–1820	1821–1830	1831–1840	1841–1850	1851–1860
BY SHAKERS								
Catechisms	—	—	—	—	—	—	2	—
Catalogues	—	—	—	—	—	—	2	1
Practices	—	—	—	—	2	1	2	—
Biographies	—	—	—	—	—	—	—	1
Sermons	—	—	—	—	1	—	1	—
Moral Instruction	—	—	—	—	—	—	13	—
Brochures	—	—	—	—	—	1	—	3
General Notices	1	—	—	—	1	1	—	—
Legends	—	—	—	1	1	—	—	—
Liturgy	—	—	—	1	—	1	5	1
Theology	—	—	1	1	1	1	—	—
History	—	—	1	—	—	—	—	—
Constitutions	—	1	—	—	—	1	—	—
Legal Cases	—	—	—	3	—	1	5	—
Apologia	—	—	1	4	3	1	1	—
Total	1	1	3	10	9	8	31	6
ABOUT SHAKERS								
Pamphlets	4	1	1	4	5	—	2	1
Travel Literature	3	2	1	1	2	4	2	—
Journalism	—	—	—	—	1	—	—	—
Notes	—	—	—	1	—	2	—	—
General Inventories	—	—	—	—	—	—	2	1
General History	—	—	—	—	—	—	—	—
Monographs	—	—	—	—	—	—	—	—
Sociology	—	—	—	—	—	—	—	—
Bibliographies	—	—	—	—	—	—	—	—
Total	7	3	2	6	8	6	6	2

corresponding phases in Shaker development, one is led to make the following observations (see Chart no. 4).

1. Noting the course of these writings from 1774, when Ann Lee began her public life by recruiting her own group out of the Wardley circle, to 1792, when the "gathering" of the Gospel Order really became stabilized, one is led to make the following observation: during this period, when the movement experienced a maximum of existence, it at the same time allowed itself a minimum of verbal expression. Until 1780 it led a quiet life. And even then, when the re-

1861– 1870	1871– 1880	1881– 1890	1891– 1900	1901– 1910	1911– 1920	1921– 1930	1931– 1940	1941– 1950	1951– 1955	Total
—	—	—	3	1	—	—	—	—	—	6
1	1	—	—	—	—	—	—	—	—	5
2	1	—	—	—	—	—	—	—	—	9
2	—	—	2	—	—	—	—	—	—	5
—	—	—	—	—	—	—	—	—	—	2
1	1	—	—	—	—	—	—	—	—	15
6	14	14	14	3	—	—	—	—	—	55
—	—	1	—	1	—	—	—	—	—	5
—	1	1	—	—	—	—	—	—	—	4
—	4	1	2	1	—	—	—	—	—	16
—	—	—	—	—	—	—	—	—	—	4
—	—	—	—	—	—	—	—	—	—	1
—	1	—	—	—	—	—	—	—	—	3
2	—	—	—	—	—	—	—	—	—	11
—	1	—	—	—	—	—	—	—	—	11
14	24	17	22	6	—	—	—	—	—	152
—	—	—	—	—	—	—	—	—	—	18
—	—	—	—	—	—	—	—	—	—	15
—	3	3	—	—	—	—	—	—	—	7
—	—	—	—	—	1	—	—	—	—	4
2	5	2	11	6	1	4	3	3	—	40
—	1	—	2	—	2	2	1	2	1	11
—	—	—	1	7	—	—	2	2	—	12
—	—	—	—	—	—	1	3	—	—	4
—	—	—	—	3	—	—	1	—	—	4
2	9	5	14	16	3	8	10	7	1	115

vivalists invited Shaker leaders to speak, none of them turned to writing. The only document dating from this period is a 1790 tract, and it seems to have been written to carry the Shaker message to someone who was deaf and thus unable to hear the sermons.

The history of these years was not written down in detail until 1816, when the ministry began collecting material for the *Testimonies*. This work is at once the *Golden Legend*, the *Fioretti*, the *Vitae Fratrum*, and even the Shaker Gospel. It is made up of accounts told by those who witnessed the early events of Shaker history. However, in reading the text one should remember that twenty to forty years had elapsed between the event and the reporting of it in writing.

The only contemporary records of those first events date from 1781, or about seventeen years after the early dissidence. These can be found in contemporary accounts of the first group's Atlantic crossing and in the first anti-Shaker pamphlets.

2. After the silent phase came a period of articulation during which all Shaker literature falls into one of four categories: a series of apologetics, each one of which is coupled with the pamphlet to which it constitutes an answer; a series of theological writings, from which stemmed the two great works: the *Testimonies* and *Millennial Church;* a series of juridical reports in which one finds the arguments used by the Shakers in American courts of law, largely for cases involving the three great legal problems of the sect: family, private property, and conscientious objection; finally, a mystical series which includes abundant records of the spirit-messages received and published during the Great Revival. This last series, as well as the catechistic writings that followed it, already belongs to the literature of the Shaker decline.

The period from 1806 to 1830 produced the best of Shaker writing, just as it represents the apogee of Shaker recruitment.

3. Shaker writing following the Civil War falls neatly into two periods. First there was a period of literary renewal which continued until the end of the century. On the one hand, this was evidenced by an extraordinary abundance of small brochures daubing the old Shaker theses with modernism. On the other hand, following the writings of J. H. Noyes and C. Nordhoff, the society enjoyed a notoriety which brought it a cascade of honorable mentions in non-Shaker books treating the "American communities."

This was followed by a second and last period of Shaker literature: the period of its extinction. White and Taylor's book, published in 1905, is the swan song. Men had never written as much or better about the Shakers. But the literature on them changed to a reflective genre, and "Shakerism" was once more without a voice. It was replaced by what one might call a sympathetic "Shakerology."

IV. Chronology, Topology, and Statistics

After this documentation, one ought to be able to pinpoint and codify these phases of Shaker history. The fluidity of the first phase offers hardly more than an impression of displacements in space (the missionary trips which have already been mentioned), yet they outline the network of societies to come.

Locations, longevity, and size: these are the units of measurement for defining the outlines of Shaker evolution in the second and third phases. But these measurements cannot be ascertained with an equal degree of precision.

INVENTORY OF THE SOCIETIES

A certain number of lists have been tabulated by Nordhoff,[135] Sears,[136] Dow,[137] Melcher,[138] Bestor, and Andrews (the most scholarly).[139] To these one can add lists extracted either from Shaker chronicles such as White and Taylor[140] or from the lists of addresses that appear on the last pages of such books as Evans's *Compendium*.[141]

In general, inventories agree neither on number, nor on name or dates. Indeed, dates that are given sometimes indicate the founding of the church, sometimes the first moment of the "gathering," sometimes the day when the meetinghouse was completed. This lack of standardized methods for recording events affects any estimate of the number of believers at any given time. Since there was a distinction between the "convert" who had joined the church and the "believer" who had been "gathered" into one of the societies, when one sees a figure on total membership, the question arises: Are these all the members of the church or are they only those members who have been gathered into "Gospel Order"? Apparently this distinction was very real, since in *Millennial Church* it is stipulated that "there are also numbers in various parts of the United States who have embraced the faith of the Society, but whose circumstances have not, as yet, admitted of their being gathered into a regular body."[142] It is then likely that the figures generally given on total membership apply only to those actually living in a Shaker community and tell us nothing of those church members living away from any order. We shall see later how these figures include both the junior and senior orders (sometimes referred to as the junior and senior class) but say nothing about the novitiate order (or class).[143]

A study of the internal evidence offered by these different inventories has given the results schematized by Chart no. 6, which lists the various societies in order of their appearance, and indicates location, longevity, and size (see p. 134).

STATISTICS ON MEMBERSHIP

The two sources of statistics on membership are, of course, records of Shaker computations and the U.S. Census. The figures obtained from these two sources do not agree, and moreover, there is a sizeable coefficient of relativity for each set of figures.

The Shaker sources. The Shaker sources are admittedly not very substantial. The figures furnished by *Millennial Church* for the first half of the nineteenth century are not accurately dated, and the author admits that he is giving approximations: "between fifty and a hundred persons," "about 300," "about 200," "more than 200," and so on.[144] Apparently the Shakers clung to this habit of approximations. In 1914, when J. Prudhommeaux asked the Shakers at Mount Lebanon how many members were left in the movement, he got a vague reply which led him to note that "the Shakers do not seem to be well informed on the statistics that concern them."[145]

Was this vagueness due to a religious horror of the very principle of taking a census, a protest of the sort that has led some dissenting groups to refuse any civil status whatsoever? This seems unlikely. A more probable reason for this reluctance to be counted is found in a suggestive footnote in *Millennial Church* which says:

We are, as yet, but a small people and few in number, compared with the vast multitudes enrolled in the catalogue of other denominations; but when we consider the testimony of Jesus Christ that: "Strait is the gate, and narrow is the way, which leadeth unto life, and few there be that find it," we cannot but feel a sense of thankfulness for that mercy of God which has called us to be numbered with the chosen few; and to us it is a matter of more importance to increase in the principles of peace and righteousness, than to increase in numbers. Yet we feel a firm reliance upon the promise of God, by the mouth of his prophets: "I will multiply them and they shall not be few; I will also glorify them and they shall not be small. A little one shall become a thousand, and a small one a strong nation: I the Lord will hasten it in his time." See Isa. 60:22 and Jer. 30:19.[146]

This note from *Millennial Church* makes the inferiority complex of the Shakers as clear as their manner of sublimating it. Any church which aspires to universality and claims to be destined to attain it according to a progressively accelerating rhythm of acceptance by the world will reveal a natural tendency to close its eyes to the facts when its base of operations is narrow or, more especially, shrinking. Thus the only figures furnished by the Shakers apply to the phase of their expansion: ten or twelve people in 1780, more than 4,000 in 1823, as noted on pages 75 and 84 of *Millennial Church*. There will hardly be any others. Evans's *Compendium*, first published in 1858, pretty much repeats the same figures, lowering them slightly for the West and compensating for this by a slight increase for the East.

Apparently, Evans's approximations enabled him to reassure himself tacitly about the status quo without ever letting any special questions on the subject bother him. Besides, as we have seen in the discussion of Evans's distinction between the two orders (in section II of this chapter), he had a new ideological principle to help him understand why the Shakers were no longer increasing in numbers.[147]

The United States census. The first census was made in 1790, and since then, at ten year intervals, the Americans have continued to count their numbers. Can the census reports be relied on for an accurate account of Shaker numbers through the years? No. For this, there are several reasons. First, not all of the census reports furnish statistics on the Shakers in particular. Next, even when they are given, the data are incomplete. Lastly, even if the data were complete, the Census Bureau itself admits that the items on which the U.S. Census is based do not permit one to interpret the figures for total Shaker membership as a valid statistic for the number of members living in the Shaker societies.

It was not until the Seventh Census, in 1850, that Americans began to record statistics on religious affiliation. Relevant statistics of the Tenth Census were not published, and it was not until 1906 that these results were analyzed separately and published under the title: *Religious Bodies.*

Limiting ourselves to the nineteenth century and the Seventh (1850), Eighth (1860), and Ninth (1870) Census counts, we do have statistics with a certain homogeneity and regular periodicity. But the figures given apply to the number of churches, and considering the ambiguity of the term *church,* which can mean either an ecclesiastic organization or a building in which religious services are held, their statistics are not reliable for religions in general. Not until the Ninth Census was a distinction made between the two senses of the word *church.* However, after the distinction was made, there was no modification in census statistics on the Shakers.

The census figures tabulated the number of members in a church only indirectly and approximately. In the preface to the Seventh Census the editors explained that they were not listing the number of members in each religious denomination or even the number of people attending church. The census recorded only the capacity of the church buildings to accommodate those who would worship there.[148]

In the report of the Ninth Census there was a résumé of these figures for the years 1850, 1860, and 1870, as they applied to the Shakers.[149] These are reproduced in Table 4.1. When Hepworth Dixon used this table to set the total Shaker membership at 6,000 for the year 1860,[150] his figure was both more and less than the reality: more, because of the criterion used in making the count; less, because some of the societies then in existence were not included in the census.

The Eleventh Census of 1890, made on the same basis, sets the total membership at 4,049, an equally ambiguous figure.[151]

Finally, based on the most recent set of homogenous figures, here are the statistics for the years 1906, 1916, 1926, and 1936, as published in *Religious Bodies* (1936). The decline of the Shakers is pitilessly evident.[152]

	1906	1916	1926	1936
Members	516	367	192	92
Churches	15	12	6	3

Estimates of Shaker population made by observers. Very often one will come across a monograph with valid statistics for one of the societies or for a part of a society's history. Some, like the one by Dow,[153] can be discounted since the figures are obviously just approximations. The analyses which remain the most valid are those by Charles Nordhoff and Daryl Chase.

A résumé of Nordhoff's analysis in his 1875 book on America's communist societies is here reproduced in Chart no. 5. It is evident that if one were to make a more complete statistical analysis of the Shaker adventure, a chart like this would be needed, decade by decade, for the century and a half of the society's existence. Although this tabulation is unfortunately the only one of its kind, at least it permits us to verify some of the information garnered from other sources previously indicated.

Even within its limits, this tabulation of Nordhoff points up several traits of the people called Shakers. It is im-

TABLE 4.1
Population of the Shaker Societies
(According to U.S. Census)

SOCIETIES	1850		1860		1870	
	Churches	Accommo-dations	Churches	Accommo-dations	Edifices	Sittings
Conn.	—	—	—	—	1	300
Ky.	2	1,500	—	—	2	1,600
Maine	—	—	2	550	2	700
Mass.	4	1,050	2	850	2	700
N.H.	—	—	2	600	2	300
N.Y.	3	1,300	3	1,600	3	2,300
Ohio	2	1,300	3	1,600	4	2,100

CHART 5*
Population of the Shaker Societies

Society.	No. of Families or Separate Communities.	Adults.		Youth under 21.		Total, 1874.	Population, 1823.	Greatest Population.	Acres of Land.	Hired Laborers.
		Male.	Female.	Male.	Female.					
Alfred, Me.	2	20	30	8	12	70	200	200	1100	15–20
New Gloucester, Me.	2	20	36	4	10	70	150	150	2000	15–20
Canterbury, N.H.	3	35	70	14	26	145	200	300	3000	6
Enfield, N.H.	3	29	76	8	27	140	200	330	3000	20–35
Enfield, Conn.	4	24	48	18	25	115	200	200	3300	15
Harvard, Mass.	4	17	57	4	12	90	200	200	1800	16
Shirley, Mass.	2	6	30	4	8	48	150	150	2000	10
Hancock, Mass.	3	23	42	13	20	98	–	300	3500	25
Tyringham, Mass.	1	6	11	0	0	17	–	–	1000	6
Mount Lebanon, N.Y.	7	115	221	21	26	383	500–600	600	3000	–
Watervliet, N.Y.	4	75	100	20	40	235	200	350	4500	75
Groveland, N.Y.	2	18	30	3	6	57	150 in 1836.	200	2280	8
North Union, O.	3	41	44	6	11	102	–	200	1355	9
Union Village, O.	4	75	92	20	28	215	600	600	4500	70
Watervliet, O.	2	16	32	3	4	55	100	100	1300	10
White Water, O.	3	34	51	6	9	100	150	150	1500	10
Pleasant Hill, Ky.	5	56	114	25	50	245	450	490	4200	20
South Union, Ky.	4	85	105	15	25	230	349	349	6000	15
Eighteen Societies	58	695	1189	192	339	2415	–	–	49,335	–

The returns of land include, for the most part, only the home farms; and several of the societies own considerable quantities of real estate in distant states, of which I could get no precise returns.

*from Charles Nordhoff, *The Communistic Societies of the United States* (New York, 1875), p. 256.

possible to see any age pyramid, since the only age categories cited are "over" and "under" twenty years old. However, given the Shaker mode of recruitment, even if an age pyramid were available, it would not have its usual meaning. Yet from this table we can note:

The proportion of men to women: 58 men to every 100 women over twenty years of age; 56 boys for every 100 girls under twenty-one years of age.

The proportion of those under and over twenty-one: over twenty-one, 78 percent; under twenty-one, 22 percent.

The proportion of hired workers to believers: about 18 hired hands for every 100 believers. However, here it is possible that the hired hands represent the seasonal help brought in by the Shakers as needed.

The other statistical analysis is from the appendix to Daryl Chase's thesis on the early Shakers.[154] His figures have been gleaned from documents in the archives. Although they come at irregular intervals, they do form good points of reference for an historical study (see Chart no. 7). Their conversion into a graph (see Chart no. 8) is of doubtful value because of the irregular intervals between the points of reference. Nevertheless, one can use Chase's data to obtain with some degree of precision a population curve for Mount Lebanon (see Chart no. 9), and it is possible to compare this Mount Lebanon curve with the one produced by its sole church Family (see Chart no. 10).

In summary, from the preceding body of material one can make the following general observations:

1. The phase of Shaker growth coincides with the first two revivals or at least with their immediate effects. The effects of the revival in the West were both greater and more unstable.

2. The apogee of Shaker fortunes occurred about 1830. It was due to a sustained increase of membership in the Eastern societies, which tended to offset the loss of blood in the West (see Chart no. 7).

3. The decline turns into collapse after the Civil War. At

this date religious life, even in the citadel of Mount Lebanon, starts slowing down (see Chart no. 8).

4. It is possible to discern the areas in which there was the greatest resistance to disintegration. The East resisted it longer than the West. And in the East the church Family, which was the highest of the church orders, resisted better than the church body as a whole, as one can see by studying the data on Mount Lebanon. Moreover, the distinction between the orders (class, Family) tended to disappear. From the very beginning of the society the junior orders had been conceived as formulas for a period of transition, and many lukewarm converts used this structural latitude as a way of taking temporary advantage of Shaker membership without any real commitment. They were called "winter Shakers," an allusion to their temporary retreat into a "Family," which they used as a place of refuge during the stormy winter season, but which they left with the coming of spring. The closer one comes to the end of the century, the less distinction there is between the orders. The individual Shaker tended to identify himself purely and simply with the membership as a whole: the Church Order (see Chart no. 10).

5. The curves obtained from the data in Chase can not be projected beyond the year 1900. The general movement of the society after 1900 is pitilessly revealed in the graph of the eight figures given in the Census Bureau's *Religious Bodies* (see Chart no. 11).

These various analyses cover the social history of the Shaker Society in respect to those elements that have astounded observers: its longevity, its some 17,000 members, its 20 communities, its missionary effectiveness, its extraordinary rites for worship, its prosperity, its ambition, its tenacity. The prehistory of the society sets it in relation to the old world of Europe. The history proper sets its relation to the new world of America. The next step in our study is to examine the structure that held the society together (chapters 5 and 6), before asking ourselves what it was in the Shaker consciousness that exalted them.

CHART 6. *Chart of the Shaker Societies*

Lasted from — to — (1780 1800 10 20 30 40 50 60 70 80 90 1900 10 20 30 40 50)

NAMES	STATE AND COUNTY	No. of Families	The Millennial Church for 20th Cent.	Melcher for Max. Pop.	Nordhoff for Pop. 1875	Chase for Total Membership
MT. LEBANON	COLUMBIA, NEW YORK	8	550	600	383	3019
NISKEYUNA (Watervliet)	ALBANY, NEW YORK	4	200	350	235	2668
HANCOCK	BERKSHIRE, MASSACHUSETTS	3	300	300	98	548
ENFIELD	HARTFORD, CONNECTICUT	5	200	350	140	739
HARVARD	WORCESTER, MASSACHUSETTS	4	200	200	90	—
TYRINGHAM	BERKSHIRE, MASSACHUSETTS	3	100	100	17	241
CANTERBURY	MERRIMACK, NEW HAMPSHIRE	3	200	280	145	746
ENFIELD	GRAFTON, NEW HAMPSHIRE	3	200	350	140	183
SHIRLEY	MIDDLESEX, MASSACHUSETTS	3	150	150	48	869
ALFRED	YORK, MAINE	3	200	200	70	241
SABBATHDAY LAKE (New Gloucester)	CUMBERLAND, MAINE	3	150	150	70	165
GORHAM	CUMBERLAND, MAINE	?	—	—	—	—
UNION VILLAGE	WARREN, OHIO	6	600	600	215	3873
WATERVLIET	MONTGOMERY, OHIO	2	100	100	55	127
SOUTH UNION	LOGAN, KENTUCKY	4	350	350	230	676
PLEASANT HILL	MERCER, KENTUCKY	8	450	490	245	494
WEST UNION	SULLIVAN, INDIANA	3	—	200	—	—
SAVOY	BERKSHIRE, MASSACHUSETTS	?	—	—	—	—
NORTH UNION	CUYAHOGA, OHIO	3	—	200	102	407
WHITEWATER	HAMILTON, OHIO	3	—	150	100	491
GROVELAND	LIVINGSTON, NEW YORK	3	—	200	57	793
NARCOOSSEE	FLORIDA	2	—	200	—	—
WHITE OAK	GEORGIA	?	—	—	—	—

CHART 7
Membership of Shaker Communities at Different Dates (according to the count made by Daryl Chase)

	1803	1817	1819	1821	1823	1829	1830	1833	1838	1840	1842	1847	1848	1852	1856	1862	1869	1877	1898	1911	1915
Mt. Lebanon	351		469						428		431		416								150
Watervliet	61		189		240	227												200			
Groveland														111							
Shirley	92					100															
Hancock	142		222			240															
Harvard	101					160					116[1]							70			
Tyringham	52																				
Enfield (NH)	132					198		214													
Canterbury	159					213		219													
Enfield (Conn.)	146					310															
Sabbathday Lake	168																				
Alfred	125								234	110							60				
North Union										200		160							70		
Union Village		600					452	502						380	200	100				22	
Whitewater														144							
Watervliet												60		52							
Pleasant Hill								500						345		250					5
South Union								300				300		238		250					
Busro Creek				152																	

1 Sears.

CHART 8. *Changes of Membership in the Principal Shaker Communities*

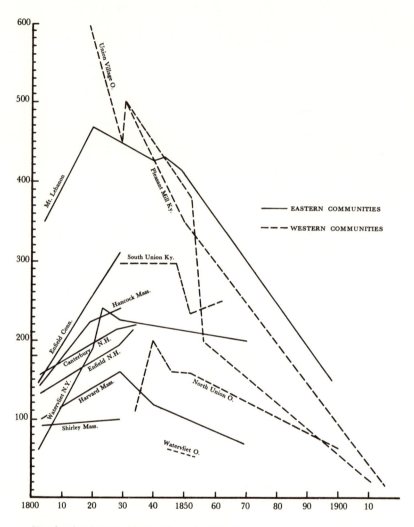

*Based on data from Daryl Chase, "The Early Shakers"
(Ph.D. diss., University of Chicago, 1938).

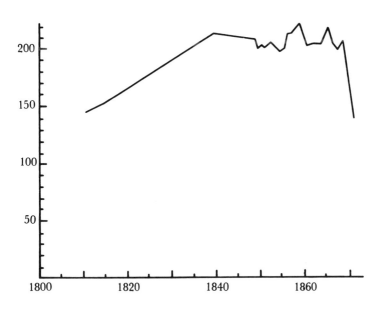

CHART 9. *Number of Members in the Church Family at Mount Lebanon*

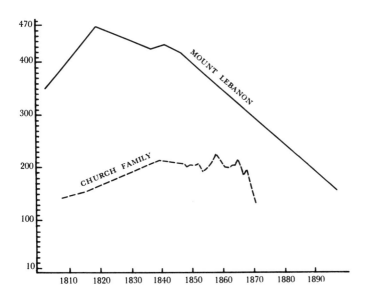

CHART 10. *Comparison of Mount Lebanon and its Church Family: Number of Members*

MOUNT LEBANON

CHURCH FAMILY

Chronology, Topology & Statistics * 137

CHART 11. *Shaker Decline in the Twentieth Century*

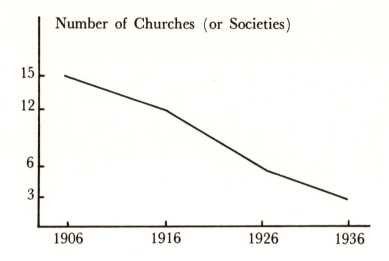

Number of Churches (or Societies)

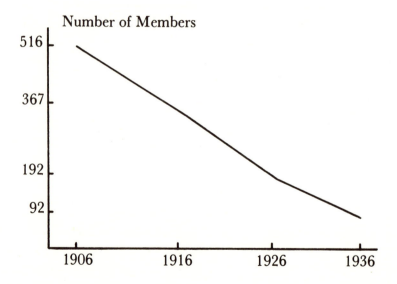

Number of Members

CHAPTER FIVE

Distinguishing Between the Church & the World; Ascetic Feminism

THE BASIC principle on which the Shakers established their church as an institution apart from and opposite to "the world" can be stated in a twofold proposition: on the one hand, affirmatively, salvation comes through the Family; on the other hand, negatively, "marriage of the flesh is a covenant with death and an agreement with Hell."[1]

This two-edged premise can be found in one form or another in the program of many other religious and social nonconformities. By making a rapid survey of these myriad dissidences, one can set up a grid providing coordinates for a preliminary examination of the Shaker problem.

Whether we examine the doctrines of the pre-Christian dissidents (such as Buddhists and Essenes) or the early Christians (such as Montanists) or choose to study the dualistic dissidences (Manichaean or para-Manichaean), medieval nonconformities or post-Reformation peripheral developments, the sectarian proliferation of the Raskol, the mushrooming of "religious communism" in America, or even certain anarchic strains visible just before and after the events of 1848, we see the ubiquitous, simultaneous, correlative dual presence of a demand and a refusal.

The demand is always that there be a religious role for women. This may take one of several forms: either that women be accorded membership in a religious order open to both sexes (Messalians, Apostolics, Shakers), in a segregated all-female order (Buddhists), or in some intermediate type of organization (the Therapeutae, the Kelpians, the Ephratists, the Shakers in "Gospel Order"); or that women be accepted on an equal footing with men as missionary preachers (Montanists, Cevenoles, and so forth); or that woman be raised to a preeminent position in the hierarchy of authority or veneration, be it as prophetess, priestess, or goddess-mother.

The refusal is always a refusal of those roles assigned to women by and in established society. This may take one of several forms:

Either refusal to bear children: This is not necessarily a condemnation of sexuality. The Manichaeans refused to have sexual relations in order not to bear children; the Shakers reversed the Manichaean reasoning and refused to bear children because they did not want to have sexual relations.

Or refusal to marry: This is a refusal of marriage as sanctioned by the church or society and does not necessarily mean disapproval of sexual union. Examples of this may be seen in the Raskol and, to some extent, among the Cevenoles.

Or refusal to have sexual relations: This refusal is not always considered as a refusal to bear children, as in the case of the "Koreshan Unity," whose members fervently believed in the possibility of virgin births. This refusal of sexual relations demanded a special explanation from the Shakers,[2] who generally maintained a position rejecting not only reproduction but also all types of sexual union, be it legal, civil, or ecclesiastic.

In every option cited above, it is as if a woman was expected to renounce some aspect of her femininity in order to affirm some aspect of religious life. Yet the admission of women to religious functions opens the way for recognition of feminine values and even feminism.

It is a delicate task to define the kind of femininity renounced and the quality of religious life gained, and then to determine the reciprocal relation between the two. There are at least two complicating factors:

1. The psycho-sociological motives determining this double attitude, particularly in the following four categories:

    (a) *Ethicol-religious motives*. The tendency to identify the works of the flesh with guilt feelings must be seen in relation to a contrasting religious attitude which glorifies fecundity and interprets sterility as a curse. The relation between these two attitudes, both ethico-religious, is especially significant when the religious glorification of childbirth is a reigning idea; for, in that case, feelings of sexual guilt imply a need for moral reform.

    (b) *Socio-demographic motives*. This is "the refusal of the oppressed to satisfy the demands of their oppressors by supplying them tiny creatures to be exploited, creatures whose birth brings to their needy families only an increase of poverty."[3] We have already discussed this attitude of the Bogomils, and we shall take it up again later.[4]

    (c) *Poetic-mystical motives*. These are present when conjugal relations are dominated by the attitude of platonic or courtly love, or even a feeling of fellowship, be it religious, semireligious, or other.

    (d) *Antiecclesiastic motives*. These are particularly apparent in the behavior of the Raskol. In refusing the church, the dissidents were led to renounce the sacraments; this in turn led them to renounce marriage, either by marrying without the church's sacraments, by inventing some other sacrament, or by inventing some kind of free union. An unequivocal renunciation of marriage leads either to rituals for inducing exaltation (Khlysti, Shakers) or rituals of inhibition (going so far as castratation among the Skoptsy).[5] The Cevenoles as well as the Raskol were caught in this type of renunciation.

2. The second complicating factor comes from the ambivalence of the motives listed above, since they usually, and sometimes simultaneously, induce one of two contradictory attitudes: Either a rigorous sexual asceticism of which the most extreme form is the religious castration that is to ordinary asceticism what a suicidal hunger strike is to fasting.[6] Or "free love"; this expression, in turn, has several different layers of meaning:

   (a) A societal sense: freedom to love without restrictions as to class. This, perhaps, is what a vestige of Manichaeanism was leading the Mazdakites to demand.[7]

   (b) A biological sense: the separation of the sexual and reproductive functions, as at Oneida.

   (c) A juridical sense: "free love" versus the legal or religious indissolubility of marriage. In this sense "free love" is a refusal to recognize any need for social or religious sanctions in a personal relation.

   (d) A libertarian sense: In this context "free love" may lead to polygamy (the Munster community, the Mormons) or to institutionalized promiscuity (American bundling, the "Club de la Chopinette"). It may also lead to moral, scientific, or even religious experimentation, as in the permissiveness of certain anarchist circles, the "complex marriage" of the Oneida community, and the sexual practices during at least one phase of the Palestinian cooperatives.[8]

A preliminary grid such as we have set up here serves only to delimit the problem for discussion, and does not exhaust its possibilities. It should, at the very least, enable us to situate the special case of the Shakers.

Any examination of this special case is complicated by the problem of evolution within the society. "Why did you become a Shaker?" Lacking any questionnaires for the different phases of the society's evolution, we can only study Shaker writings and, through them, deduce the writers' motives for giving the reasons they did. Why, then, did some twenty thousand men and women, during the years between 1770 and 1900, decide to become Shakers, and what made them stand by that decision? In trying to answer this question, we shall examine successively the psychological basis of the decision, its ideological arguments, and the social behavior that it produced.

I. The Psychological Basis for the Shaker Decision

We know that among the Manichaeans, with whom Augustine was once connected, the rule forbidding reproduction was considered more basic than the ban on sexual relations. Man's desire to procreate was considered more sinful than his desire for carnal pleasure. If a Manichaean ("believer") took a wife, he was instructed not to have sexual relations during her periods of fertility. Thus it was that the sexual act was considered even more impure when it led to childbirth. The same line of reasoning is found in the neo-Manichaean aspects of Albigensian doctrine.[9]

Among the Shakers, at least at first sight, the attitude seems to have been the opposite. If, for them, procreation became and remained a sin, that is because it could not be achieved without first indulging in sexual relations.

According to this line of thought, if an act of procreation were possible without indulging in sexual gratification, it would no longer be forbidden by the Shaker code of morality.

This position is clearly stated in the *Millennial Church.*

Therefore, those who still plead the law of nature, or the law of God which is: "Be fruitful and multiply" to justify sexual coition . . . ought first to examine their secret motives in it; and if they are able to lay the propensities of lust entirely aside, and enter upon that work without the influence of any other motive than solely that of obeying the will of God, in the propagation of a legitimate offspring, to be the heirs of the kingdom of Heaven, then they are able to fulfil the law of nature.[10]

Writing about the character of Baudelaire, Jean-Paul Sartre said that "in general, the poet considered sin to be a form of eroticism." This judgment can also be applied to the Shakers. The psychological experiences forming the background of the *Millennial Church* seem to presuppose a tacit adoption of the principle as stated by Baudelaire himself, when he affimed "that the sole and supreme pleasure in the act of love lies in the certain knowledge that one is doing something evil, and that, from the time of their birth, both men and women are aware that evil is the source of all physical delight." This sounds like what Mother Ann experienced or like what she labored, through her confessional techniques, to bring to the light of consciousness in her disciples, for without this personal experience of evil as "the source of all physical delight," how can a reflective person accept the principle that in physical pleasure all evil is to be found? But from this point on, Baudelaire's position and the Shaker attitude lead to very different patterns of behavior. Baudelaire, as Sartre tells us, "chose the path of evil, and this meant that he had chosen to feel guilty."[11] One can imagine Sartre saying of the Shakers that "since they chose the path of goodness, this meant that they had chosen to feel justified and perfect." And, in fact, the Shaker elders admitted that they were no longer able to sin. In the *Testimonies* we read that when inquirers asked them, "Are you perfect? Do you live without sin?" the elders answered, "The power of God, revealed in this day, does enable souls to cease from sin; and we have received that power; we have actually left off committing sin, and we live in daily obedience to the will of God."[12]

This inculpation of human love, which is a priori bound to erotic pleasure, is the dominant subject in Shaker preaching. In *Millennial Church* we read the following condemnation: "Ask of those who, from their infancy, have kept themselves pure and uncontaminated with any of these filthy gratifications, even till the nuptial ceremony had sanctioned the deed, what were the sensations which succeeded the loss of their purity? The candid and honest answer will, invariably, be found to be, *disappointment, shame and disgust.*"[13] This indignation against the life of the flesh is what the early Shaker sermons and, later, their tracts would strive to provoke and sustain in their listeners and their readers.

In the early years of Shakerism ideological considerations played a very minor role. Shaker preachers preferred the emotional shock brought about by the unveiling of personal secrets. Mother Ann and the elders conducted their testimony of the spirit by accusing themselves and those they loved. Thus, in recounting one of her visions, Ann Lee described the destruction of all humanity, not only of those now alive but also of past generations, and said that in her revelation she had seen them as they were, shrouded in darkness and obscurity; and among them, she said, were many familiar faces, including her own mother. According to the *Testimonies*, Ann added that when she recognized her mother in this vision, she cried out to God, for she had always thought her mother to be a good woman, if such ever existed on earth.[14]

These testimonies, helped along perhaps by a talent for reading character, were sometimes followed by a foreboding summons commanding dissemblers and recalcitrants to answer questions: "Kneel down, you haughty creature and confess your sins."[15] On one occasion when a farmer, trying not to be influenced by the gospel message, was etching the ground with his whip, Ann peremptorily summoned him, "Put down that whip and hear the word of God, you idle old man."[16] Sometimes she would astound her listeners by telling them the secret sins of their lives.[17] Several anecdotes lead one to conclude that a predilection for shock techniques led the early Shakers to use corporal punishment when this was deemed necessary to firm up the wavering intentions of a postulant. This is not surprising. Similar behavior has been attributed to Père Lacordaire and others who were directing the souls of novices in nineteenth-century France. William Lee was the man for this corporal persuasion.[18] Certain candidates who failed to be convinced by William's strong arm later complained of the treatment, saying they could not understand the reason for the beating he had given them. On the whole, however, the insistent theme of Shaker sermonizing was "darkness." Sometimes this made a terrifying tableau, as in Ann Lee's description of the regions of darkness and the lost souls she had "seen" there who were in such distress and agony that tears had worn lines like gutters in their cheeks.[19] Sometimes this preaching was deceitful and deliberately upsetting, as in the following commentary on the chapter of Genesis treating the consequences of man's first sin:

God always dispenses his judgments according to the nature of the offense. But in this case there does not appear to be any punishment inflicted upon the hand or the mouth; but the parts to which pertain the power of generation, are now, for the first time, condemned to feel shame. . . . This guilty passion of shame seems to be peculiarly connected with that libidinous act which first produced it; so that it naturally shuns the light, and seeks to cover itself in the shades of darkness, secluded even from the eyes of the most intimate friends. Is not this fact, of itself, a most striking evidence that there is something, either in the act itself, or which is inseparably connected with it, which never came from God?[20]

Guilt complexes that had ripened in the end-of-the-world revival atmosphere, of which the Shaker meetings were both cause and effect, were heightened by these persistent warnings, and prospective converts were tormented by testimonies and summons to repent. After being exaggerated to the point of obsession in the contagious atmosphere of collective avowals, chants, and trances, such guilt feelings were discharged through "confessions." These Shaker confessions, thoroughly organized and strictly required of everyone, were made orally to the elders, men or women.[21] The confession was always of *all* one's sins and was made in a fever of repentence. For those who underwent the ritual it constituted both a baptism in the Spirit and a vow to enter the church, and thus it implied not only a renouncing of the past but a commitment to the future. Mother Ann in the *Testimonies* tells us that the first offering that God looks for from a sinner is that he make a full confession of all his sins and that he then abandon them forever.[22]

The way to abandon one's sins was clear; it was the way indicated in the gospel of the Second Coming, which said in effect that one must give up marriage in the flesh if one is to be married to the Lamb and take part in Christ's Resurrection; for those worthy of taking part in Christ's Resurrection are neither married nor given in marriage, but are like the angels.[23] This, according to the *Testimonies*, was Mother Ann's message to married people during those first meetings in America.

From the moment a church member made his "decision," a wall of fire separated him from those who dwelled in the world. The convert had turned his back on the order of generation, which was the kingdon of darkness, and had entered into the kingdom of light to live in the order of regeneration.[24] Once the "decision" had been made, there could be no compromise between the two modes of living. Before it, he had been in the world. After it, he lived in the church. At no time in its history did the society set up any intermediary order.

Previous to this "decision" the believer had known love of self, and this was a flaw in his love of God. "For it has already been established that the love men bear for their natural relations . . . is a love rivaling men's love for Christ."[25] After this "decision" has been made, the love of God specifically requires a renouncement of self, that and nothing else.[26]

With the passing of the years the Shakers came to admit a certain validity to life in the order of the world. However, for the first generation of the society, there was a veritable ban on all contact with everything in the "order of generation." Daryl Chase quotes a letter written by a young man to his brother "in the flesh":

I now tell you that I don't want you to come here, *to see me:* for I don't wish to see you, nor your wife; except you come as seekers after righteousness; or to bear your cross. When you come for this purpose, I will be a friend to you both. . . . What, therefore, can the pleasure amount to in meeting with me . . . ? And on the other hand, what pleasure could I or your friend believers have with you, and your wife present . . . ? Hoping that we may meet in the destinies of a higher life, I am respectfully & affectionately . . .[27]

One can only agree with Chase's conclusion that "the Shaker conscience never really admitted that there were two ways of life, each of which was, in its own right, acceptable. In the privacy of the Shaker conscience there was only one life that mattered; and that was his life as a spiritual athlete of celibacy. The other was the common way for ordinary mankind."[28]

II. The Ideological Arguments

As it developed through the years, Shakerism borrowed from the theological and ideological arsenal of the various congregations to which its message was addressed. This enabled the Shakers to use premises already agreed on, and from them to draw conclusions of Shaker design. The very nature of these recurring themes and their constant repetition produced a progressively clearer conception of the original Shaker intuition. Thus it was that, at the core of the Shaker imperative, there appeared an awareness of how the guilt they abhorred was somehow determined by the society in which they lived. Historically, this awareness of the relation between man's sense of sin and the society in which he lives occurred just when the Shakers were drawing up the outlines of their metaphysical charter.

We have already explained how the original Shaker choice was not determined by any specific internal or external, psychological or sociological forces, but that some choice had to be made and that this became the Shaker choice by virtue of adopting one system of motivations rather than another.[29] On the other hand, the Shaker choice cannot be reduced to the sum of its post facto justifications any more than this set of justifications can be understood as the product of the original choice which, individually and in toto, they imply.[30] It is like Pascal's classic dialectic: "M. de Roannez said: 'I know the reasons afterward, but before that happens I am simply pleased or displeased by an event without knowing the reasons why. I will not discover them until later. I am of the opinion that when one is displeased it is not because of the reasons one will discover later; one only finds those reasons because the displeasure has already occurred.'"[31] This is probably the way to evaluate the ideological arguments used to explain the Shaker "decision."

These can be reduced to two types: on the one hand, there are the theological arguments and exegeses based on biblical texts; on the other hand, there are the philosophical arguments based on notions as diverse as Hindu thought, communist practices, and Malthusian theory.

THEOLOGICAL AND EXEGETIC ARGUMENTS

On their own initiative the Shakers never invoked biblical texts to prove their doctrine. Moreover, their notion of never-ending revelation discouraged them from giving any holy book unlimited veneration.[32]

But the milieu in which the Shakers preached their message was one in which the Bible was venerated as the Holy Book. Moreover, the first educated converts of the Millennial Church were for the most part pastors of other sects. As preachers, quite naturally, they reflected on this new "message" in the same terms and according to the same methods they already knew, be it only to reconsider the familiar material from the new point of view. This is how the

Shaker "faith" gave birth to a biblical, historical, and even doctrinal theology. It is the biblical theology that is of special interest to us in this section.

A whole study could be made of it alone. It would be possible — and necessary — to catalogue all the biblical texts cited by the various Shaker theologians, determine the frequency of their use, uncover implicit distinctions, and compile and compare their content.[33] Indeed, it is surprising that a task like this was never undertaken by some scholar among the later generations of True Believers.

However, even without a scholarly study, it is evident that quotations from two series of texts appear with the highest frequency in Shaker writings. These are the verses in Genesis dealing with original sin and the passages in the New Testament on marriage. The commentaries of these passages explain the nature of sin, sex, and marriage: original sin was the sexual act, and this resulted in the institution of marriage; marriage, insofar as it implies sexual union, is both the result of man's original Fall and the cause of an even greater sin.

OLD TESTAMENT TEXTS

On the subject of the chapter in Genesis in which Adam and Eve, encouraged by the serpent, eat the forbidden fruit and thus lose their right to live in paradise, the Shaker commentaries are explicit: "Their eating the fruit was the very act by which Adam knew Eve his wife."[34] It remains to distinguish between authorized commentary and more recent invention in the Shaker thesis.

THE DEFINITION OF ORIGINAL SIN

For the Shakers the original sin of Adam and Eve was to have sexual intercourse *unseasonably*. What does that mean?

In the *Testimony* we read:

Would it not be just and right in a wise and prudent parent who should plant an apple tree among the trees of his garden, more excellent than the rest, for the express use of his children, to lay them under an entire prohibition from eating or touching that tree, until the fruit was ready for use? . . . And should the children, through some disorderly influence upon their youthful appetites, be so deceived by the appearance of the blossoms or green fruit, as to pluck and eat them, would not this be an express violation of the law of nature in that case, as well as of the express command of their parent? . . . Thus in the creation of man, by the very law of his existence his seed was in himself; and, had his conduct been regulated according to God's appointment, he would have propagated his own species agreeable to the will of the Creator, and also according to the law of nature, in the times and seasons which He appointed . . . But as they [Adam and Eve] did not like to retain God in their knowledge, and were influenced by the serpent to counteract his laws, they were unseasonably led by the devil into the knowledge of generation instead of being led or directed by the law of God.[35]

This comparison and the many commentaries in the same vein enable us to define several points of the Shaker doctrine on original sin:

1. Physically, this sin was an act of obedience to the commands of lust; formally, it was an act of disobedience to the laws of God.

2. The first sin was not so much the act of coition according to the laws of nature as it was an unseasonable sexual union, in which the rhythms of individual lust were imposed in such a way that they violated the natural rhythms of procreation. If the act was essentially evil, this is because it led to an *irrational* reproduction of the species, and thus was against both the wishes of nature and the divine laws of God.

3. The first sin was original in the sense that it marked the origin of mankind. The malevolence of the act was soon revealed in the child it engendered. This was Cain, who grew up to become the assassin of his own brother. Posterity, which inherited the original weakness, has been reliving it ever since; and every time there is a sexual union prolonging and renewing the original choice, the sin grows

heavier under the weight of the additional darkness. The more men that will be born, the more fruit there will be to pick on the tree of sin.

By this last twist of reason Shaker theologians thought they were opposing a coherent and organic doctrine to the juridical dogma of the "professors of Christianity," who believed that suffering was "a punishment inflicted on mankind for an act of disobedience committed by their first parents."[36] In contrast to most Christian thought, the Shakers (basing their doctrine on Ezekiel 18:20)[37] insisted on two things: (a) that the sons of Adam might afterward become guilty of the same sin by their own acts, and in that case would justly deserve punishment; and (b) that Adam's sons will fall into sin all the more easily since an inclination for this particular sin was an integral part of the act to which they owe their births.[38]

JUSTIFICATIONS FOR THIS DEFINITION

The commentaries and exegeses of the text in Genesis are sufficiently numerous to make one suspect that this reading of the text is not self-evident. This leads one to conclude that the Shakers multiplied the number of commentaries in order to make it appear that their interpretation was the predominating one.

Taking umbrage in the following verses of Milton, cited in the *Testimony*:

> But that false fruit
> Carnal desire inflaming; he on Eve
> Began to cast lascivious eyes; she him
> As wantonly repaid; in lust they burn . . .

Shaker theologians packed their arguments with explanations of how Adam and Eve had been "unseasonably" led to sexual coition by the wiles of the serpent, and that, no matter what image the chroniclers may have used, "this lust was in reality the forbidden fruit of which they partook."[39] In explaining the importance and the meaning of the word "unseasonably" they evoked reasons rooted in the more or less conscious background of the Shaker decision. No less than six of these are listed in *Millennial Church.*

1. "The sentence denounced upon the woman." What was the sense of this multiplication of sorrows in childbirth and this desire which henceforth made women dependent on man (Genesis 3:16)?

Why this rigorous sentence? Is not God just and righteous? Most certainly; and therefore he dispenses punishments according to the nature of the offense. . . . From the very nature of the curse denounced upon the woman, the discerning mind will readily perceive what the nature of the offense was. . . . This slavish subjection is often carried to such a shocking extent, that many females have suffered an unnatural and premature death, in consequence of the unseasonable and excessive indulgence of this passion in the man.[40]

It is difficult not to suppose that this is a reference to Ann Lee's childhood and, particularly, to the death of her mother when Ann was still a young girl.[41]

2. "The evident violation of the order of nature, in a total disregard to times and seasons, in the work of generation." Here again the Shaker reasoning moves from the known effect back to the supposed cause. Man "is eagerly bent upon the acts of generation, but seeks none of its fruits; the desire of offspring is not his motive; his rule of action is dictated only by his inordinate passions. The insatiable nature of his lust knows no bounds, submits to no order and cares for no times nor seasons; except it be the time and season of darkness which is so congenial to his lawless and shameful works."[42]

3. "The shame which is generally found to be inseparable from the act of sexual coition." Adam and Eve made themselves aprons of fig leaves. Men and women have sexual intercourse under the cover of night. We have already seen how this idea was used by Shaker preachers.[43]

4. "The vile use and shameful abuse of this lawless propensity." This line of reasoning is intended for those who

would make a distinction between the use of marriage and the abuse of sexuality, Adam-like use and Satanic abuse.[44] There is no way of contradicting this categorical view that marriage is to sexuality as war is to murder. Just as war is murder that has been legalized socially and psychologically by a civilization, marriage is lust that has been socially and psychologically legalized by an institution.[45]

5. "This alluring passion holds out promises of pleasure which can never be realized." We have already cited one text on this subject. There are many others.[46]

6. "It is the natural source and foundation of all other evil propensities in human nature." This is followed by a commentary on James 1:15, supported by an extract from a speech to the Grand Jury at the Court of General Sessions in Albany, June 1821, to the effect that criminality in character is related to youthful visits to the city's houses of prostitution.[47]

It is obvious that these justifications for a belief in original sin are not drawn from any close critical reading of Genesis; they have been extrapolated out of the private lives of the commentators. Those Shaker commentators had all experienced an evil which they believed to be universal, and they had interpreted it as the effect of another, no less universal, evil somehow involved in the first chapter of man's history on earth. Certain passages in Genesis lend themselves to this interpretation. It was these passages which were remembered and referred to.

LATER AMENDMENTS TO THE FABLE

In their early doctrine Shaker pessimism did not usually go any further than the commentaries discussed in the preceding paragraphs. It was not until the second and third generation that their theories acquired a body of Satanic legend. As examples of this, we cite a poem and a theological digression.

The poem is one that was partially quoted by Charles Gide, who had read it in Nordhoff. The American scholar had found it in a Shaker collection edited by the society in Watervliet, Ohio, in 1833. Here are the last stanzas in which the First Adam is telling his descendants how Satan disguised himself as Eve's husband and became the father of mankind.

When I with guile was overcome,
    And fell a victim to the beast,
My station first he did assume,
    Then on the spoil did richly feast.
Soon as the life had left my soul,
He took possession of the whole.

He plunder'd all my mental pow'rs,
    My visage, stature, speech and gait;
And, in a word, in a few hours,
    He was first Adam placed in state:
He took my wife, he took my name;
All but his nature was the same.

Now see him hide, and skulk about,
    Just like a beast, and even worse,
Till God in anger drove him out,
    And doom'd him to an endless curse.
O hear the whole creation groan!
The Man of Sin has took the throne!

Now in my name this beast can plead,
    How God commanded him at first
To multiply his wretched seed,
    Through the base medium of his lust.
O horrid cheat! O subtle plan!
A hellish beast assumes the man!

This is your father in my name:
    Your pedigree ye now may know:
He early from perdition came,
    And to perdition he must go.
And all his race with him shall share
Eternal darkness and despair.

(from *A Selection of Hymns and Poems; For the Use of Believers*, ed. Philos Harmoniae, pseud. of Richard McNemar [Watervliet, Ohio, 1833]

The Shakers' reason for amending the biblical legend is quite clear. Doctrinally, nothing bothered them more than the command God gave to Adam and Eve (Genesis 1:28) to be fruitful and multiply. This verse was a stumbling block for the believers, and they were forever asking their elders to supply them with explanations. Generally the elders did nothing more than cite appropriate passages from *Millennial Church* in which it was explained that this command was given before the Fall and has since been invalidated by the Gospel of Christ. But it was only normal that on a lyrical level the Shakers would stubbornly continue to exercise their talents on this difficult point. Adam and God, his creator, are the main characters in the drama, and when they come into conflict, the first question to ask is about the authenticity of that man who sinned with Eve. The poem does this by reviving the old legend that Satan was the illegitimate father of the human race. There is, however, a second question that can be asked, this one about the authenticity of that God. Although the Shakers did not generally seem familiar with this question (at least in their published works), there is an explicit exposition of it in one of the Shaker theological treatises. In a fumbling manner the author evokes the ancient theme of a wrathful God responsible for Old Testament justice. This is George Albert Lomas's *Plain Talks upon Practical Religion* . . . (Albany, 1873), especially in the chapter entitled: "Are you Not Failing to Keep the Command: 'Go forth and Multiply'?"

"Certainly," was Lomas's answer. "This command given to Adam and his followers, is not binding on Christ and his disciples. He who gave this command to Adam and Eve either changed the order of his government when he declared: 'Behold I make all things new!' or else it was not the same God!" Lomas inclined to the latter opinion:

The God of the Old Testament was an encourager of reproduction, war, etc., and his chosen people, the Jews, were the most prominent actors in most properly keeping this "great commandment," and to subdue their enemies by fighting. Adam was "the old man," "of the earth, earthy." Christ was not a breeder of human beings; can his *followers* be? Reproduction did not belong to his kingdom of Resurrection. . . . *There never has been, nor ever can be, a child born under Christian auspices,* any more than *war* can be called a Christian institution. Children of the world, Jews and many professional but not practical Christians marry, fight, lust after the gods of the world; and if these are ever proper, these are the proper parties to do them. But Christ is the "new man," "the Lord from heaven," and in heaven these things are not known. The God of Adam and of the Jews commands his subjects to marry, learn the arts of war, vote and fight to-day as in the past; and his subjects obey, no matter by what name they are denominated. In Christ there is neither husband nor wife, no fleshly lusts nor reproductions. The God of the Christians is not worshipped by the married; nor by the warriors; nor by selfish property holders; nor by him nor her, who, not being married, nor soldiers, nor rich, nor poor, but who engage in fleshly lusts of the body or mind! "Who then, can be saved?" "Those who follow the Lamb whithersoever he goeth!" And those who plead for the "great command," and who believe in war, in private property and other lusts, are just as much Christians as Jesus was *when he practiced these things!* The God of Adam is not the God nor Father of the Christian. Jesus was not born under a Christian dispensation, and cared as little about "the world running out," and the fulfillment of the command to Adam, as do his true followers.[48]

In basing his argument on Christ's message, Lomas obviously presupposes the Shaker exegesis of the New Testament.

PASSAGES IN THE NEW TESTAMENT

There have been numerous and complicated skirmishes around many of the texts in the New Testament. The following will serve as examples:

Certain members of the early Christian community were married and lived conjugally with their wives (1 Corinthians 7). Were not these people Christians too? *Answer:*

If they were Christians, the same apostle calls them carnal, and severely reproves them for their carnality (1 Corinthians, 3:1–4). But as the time had not then arrived for a full revelation of the man of sin to be made, and as that revelation was necessarily connected with the second coming of Christ: therefore these Corinthian Christians, who were with so much difficulty persuaded to renounce their former licentious practices, were tolerated in living, in some measure, according to the course of the world. The same toleration was also extended to other gentile churches; but the church of Jerusalem seems to have preserved a greater measure of purity than any other. For it is evident that without abstaining from all fleshly connections, they could not have lived together in one united interest as they did.[49]

Another objection: Did not Christ honor with his presence a marriage feast in Cana? If so, he could not have considered this marriage evil. *Answer*:

Christ's enemies adopted this line of reasoning to prove him a "gluttonous man, a wine-bibber, a friend of publicans and sinners." . . . In making these visits, the Savior of the world had a noble object in view, which was to preach the gospel to poor fallen creatures, who were thus lost in sin and wickedness, and to teach them, by precept and example, a better manner of life. . . . The miracle of turning water into wine, on that particular occasion . . . was for a far more important purpose than to sanction matrimony or promote intemperance. . . . It was designed and eminently calculated to be a figurative representation of his own spiritual marriage at the period of his second coming.[50]

But the two texts which were the most resistant to Shaker exegesis were the fifth chapter of Paul's Epistle to the Ephesians and the nineteenth chapter of the Gospel according to Saint Matthew. The most interesting Shaker exegesis of these texts can be found in *Millennial Church* and in a curious little tract called *Shakers. A Correspondence between Mary F. C[arr], of Mount Holly City, and a Shaker Sister Sarah L[ucas] of Union Village, Ohio* (Union Village, 1868). This is the edited correspondence of a Shaker sister and a prospective postulant. The letters of the postulant constitute a veritable little questionnaire, and the answers from Sister Sarah take the form of a guide to correct thinking.

The Shaker interpretation of chapter five of the Epistle to the Ephesians can be understood through their commentary on another text (1 Timothy 4:1–3) which was resistant to the society's doctrine: "Now the Spirit speaketh expressly, that in the latter times some shall depart from the faith, giving heed to seducing spirits and the doctrines of devils; speaking lies in hypocrisy; having their conscience seared with a hot iron; forbidding to marry, *and commanding* to abstain from meats, which God hath created to be received with thanksgiving of them which believe and know the truth."

When this text was used to make matters theologically difficult for the Shakers, they replied by denying that it applied to them, saying that in this passage Paul is condemning those who *forbid* marriage and that forbidding implies coercion, whereas the Shakers left one free to make the decision for oneself; and this, as they took pains to point out, has not always been the case in the history of Christian churches. They read Paul's epistles in a light that was different from the usual way of understanding his testimony. Paul, they said, was undoubtedly alluding to spiritual marriage, and this is corroborated by his language on other occasions: 1 Corinthians 6:17, 2 Corinthians 11:2, Romans 7:4, and Ephesians 5:32. Verse 32 in Ephesians 5 was their key to understanding Paul's thought: "This is a great mystery: but I speak concerning Christ and the church." This, said the Shakers, if the marriage that Paul was constantly referring to and the one which was forbidden by the apostates he spoke of in his first epistle to Timothy. In all the Christian denominations those who burn for pleasure oppose this interpretation precisely because it condemns their carnal corruption. When one reads Paul in this light, the accusation that the Shakers forbid marriage is turned back onto the accusors, who, as the Shakers pointed out, were not only giving themselves unlimited freedom to pursue their pleasures, but were also clamoring against the virgin purity of the life which the apostle was recommending *as the only true marriage.* It is interesting to note, in passing, that this exegesis of Ephesians 5:32 is the same as the one proposed by Saint Jerome.[51]

The Shakers also had a special reading of Matthew 19:3–6, which is the passage containing Jesus' celebrated command to the Pharisees: "For this cause shall a man leave father and mother, and shall cleave to his wife; and they twain shall be one flesh. . . . What therefore God hath joined together, let not man put asunder." Are not Shaker practices contrary to this injuction? This is what worried the postulant, Mary Carr, and what led Sister Sarah to reply that Jesus certainly did encourage men to forsake their wives and that to do this he evoked all the awards of earth, heaven, and eternity. She cites the Bible again: "And every one that hath forsaken houses, or brethren, or sisters, or father, or mother, or wife, or children, or lands, for my name's sake, shall receive a hundredfold, and shall inherit everlasting life" (Matthew 19:29). Sister Sarah points out that, in Mark's account of the same conversation, Jesus went on to say that such a man "shall receive a hundredfold *now in this time . . .* and in the world to come eternal life" (Mark 10:30). Would Jesus have made promises like this and encouraged men to leave their wives if he were later going to forbid such actions? Sister Sarah says she would not dare accuse Jesus of being so inconsistent. She therefore invites her correspondent to examine with her the passages which are supposed to contradict these commands and these promises, and if possible, to see how the supposed inconsistency in the various words of Christ was illusory. Then she cites Mark 10:2: "And the Pharisees came to him and asked him, is it lawful for a man to put away his wife? tempting him." The first thing to note in this passage is that the Pharisees asked Jesus about the law, not about the gospel. They wanted to know not his own teachings on the subject but what Moses had taught. They were asking: Is it legal?—which to them meant: Is it according to the laws of Moses? That is why Jesus first answered them with a question of his own: "What did Moses command you?" and they replied in turn that Moses had permitted divorce. At this point, in Mark's account of the conversation, Jesus took exception to the teachings of Moses and invoked a more ancient law: "*From the beginning of the creation* God made them male and female. For this cause shall a man leave his father and mother, and cleave to his wife, etc." But that, wrote Sarah, was the old Adamic law, the law God gave to the first Adam. It certainly cannot be considered the same as the Gospel, for those who testify for Christ have crucified the flesh; and this means "the one flesh" of the couple as well as the rest. It was lawful for the first Adam to "leave his father and mother, and cleave to his wife." It is lawful for the "Second Man" to abandon father, mother *and also his wife* in order to follow Christ.[52]

And on another occasion, continued Sister Sarah, Jesus assured his disciples that "there is no man that hath left house, or parents, or brethren or wife, or children, for the kingdom of God's sake, who shall not receive manifold more in this present time, and in the world to come life everlasting" (Luke 18:29–30). In Mark 10:30 the apostle enumerates those things that are to be enjoyed in the present life replacing those which one has abandoned: "houses, and brethren, and sisters, and mothers, and children, and lands." Since the names of what was to be received a hundredfold were the names of spiritual relationships, the name *wife* which had figured among the things to be abandoned is not found among the names of what was to be enjoyed in Christ, for the name *wife* denotes a carnal relation.[53]

With one last remark, Sister Sarah reminds her correspondent that forsaking one's wife for Christ does not necessarily mean a separation, as does divorce. It only means that one is giving up the "married relation," and not the relation with the person or persons. As Paul said, a man can treat his wife as if she were his sister, with no other relation existing between them except that of brother and sister in Christ.[54]

Sister Sarah summarizes her statement of the Shaker position by saying that there are two orders, generation and regeneration, the order of the *old* man, which is of the earth and on the earth, and the order of the *new* man, which is with Christ in heaven. If we cannot belong to both orders that is because in Adam we die and in Christ we are resurrected. Therefore it behooves us to turn from the old man and his lusts, and assume the life of the new man who is born for justice and true holiness. If we chose a life of "generation," we fall under the law of Moses as promulgated in the twelfth chapter of Leviticus. If we chose to follow Christ into a life of "regeneration," we are raised above the Mosaic law, which is a system of commandments and penalties adapted to the order of "generation." The Gospel is a system of grace and a gracious invitation to the holy life.[55]

It is quite clear that Shaker writers quickly fall back into their clichés. At any rate, as far as the Gospel and Jesus were concerned, they spoke with great conviction. Frederick Evans summarized this Shaker certainty with his phrase: "Jesus was a Shaker."[56] Evans later assimilated Jesus and his first disciples to the Essenes, and announced with similar conviction: "Jesus was an Essene."[57]

III. The Philosophical Arguments

The Shakers, especially during the third phase of their existence, were always looking for references which might confirm their position.

A short treatise entitled *The Motherhood of God*, published in 1903, assembles a whole battery of them to support the fundamental thesis of Shaker theology on the duality or bisexuality of God, a thesis which was buttressed by their ideological notions of equality between the sexes. In principle, they drew this thesis from the Book of Genesis. Had not God said: "Let us make man in our image, after our likeness"? And, in doing so, had He not created both man and woman? This means that both male and female share the essence of God.[58]

One does not have to be told that behind this call for a

new archetype was the Father-Mother God. Man's exploitation of women for thousands of years had been, according to the Shakers, one of the principal causes of failure in human history. The tide would turn with the liberation of women. Fourier had advanced a similar view, but the Shakers did not seem to have known it. However, they did seize on Darwin's hypothesis of an androgenous ancestor, and they took careful note of the fact that, according to physiologists, each sex includes, in undeveloped form, the organs of its opposite. Finally and above all, since the exploitation of woman by man had been rationalized in the ideology of a male God, they welcomed the support of every reference which, by corroborating their view of the Motherhood of God, also served to undermine the authority of that suspect ideology.

G. Van der Leeuw notes that in the history of religion there are two main groups: religions of the Father-God, who lives in heaven, where he creates and does things that influence life on earth; and religions of the Mother-God, who lives on earth, where she reproduces her kind and embraces the beginning and the end of everything.[59] This immanentism characteristic of Mother-God religions is found in Shaker theology. A number of believers once attended a meeting of theosophists and came away impressed by several of the analyses they had heard. A specialist in the cabala had explained to them that the Jewish scholars who transcribed the Bible had systematically masculinized the idea of God. A Hinduist, after explaining that the Vedanta teaches the Motherhood of God, had added the following gloss, which is quite similar to Van der Leeuw's and was therefore joyously underscored by the Shakers: "As long as the conception of God remains as extra-cosmic, separate from nature which is passive, so long will He appear as Father alone. The more we see God as resident in nature, the more we understand that God is our Mother as well as our Father." Then he had gone on to say that "in the Rig Veda, the oldest of Hindu scriptures, the divine Mother is described as all in all. *She produced the Father.* . . . It is for this reason that women are so highly honored, and revered by the Hindus. There is no country in the world except India, where God, the supreme being, is worshipped from time immemorial as the divine mother of the universe." The Shaker report of the theosophy meeting concludes by saying that when we think of nature not as something passive and inert but as divine energy, then we can understand that God is a prodigious whole in whom the male and the female principles exist at one and the same time. Then we no longer see nature as separated from God, but see her as an aspect of divine energy that has become manifest. The universe is not a chaos; it is a harmonious whole. Each stage of evolution suggests a hidden design. This is why we speak of this energy as "the intelligent eternal, cosmic Mother of the universe."[60]

Eldress Anna White, who had been present at this meeting, immediately wrote to all the speakers, telling them that these verities had been revealed to Ann Lee and had been taught by the Shakers for more than a hundred years: "For us too, the universe is a harmonious whole and the eternal cosmic energy is the mother of the universe." This spontaneous rediscovery of themes from antiquity gave the Shakers new arguments for their mode of life, just as this Shaker mode of life had enabled them to develop these themes as principles of their own. They knew that "truth came with the light of renunciation, the renunciation of a lower for a higher life." They reasoned that if God was really a man-woman, then should not men and women live together as gods and goddesses or, at the very least, as angels? These accounts of the theosophy meeting were gathered together and distributed in the form of a brochure so that the True Believers might learn of the new theoretical confirmations of their Shaker doctrine.

Another philosophical argument was drawn from their experience with communism and can be summed up in a single sentence: "In virgin life alone is community possible." If one hungers for "communism," one should join a Family. Outside the Family there can be no community.

Aristotle had tried to prove that only private property could assure a peaceful life. The Shakers, on the other hand, affirmed that private property gives birth to conflicts, and that property conflicts are always tied to the idea of marriage. This principle was abridged by D. Fraser in the following apothegm: "The law of marriage order is 'me and thine.' Touch me and mine and I will fight." Conclusion: to end wars, do away with private property; to do away with private property, end marriage.

It so happened that, from 1820 on, the socialist movement in America was in full agreement with the first proposition of the Shaker argument and (at least for the Fourierist and Owenite groups) in partial agreement with the second. The Shakers tried hard to make these propositions serve their own conclusions. The attempt to do this is clearly seen in the clever *captatio benevolentiae*, which constitutes the "Introductory Remarks" added to the 1848 edition of *Millennial Church*. The following are the principal sections of these prefatory remarks:

During the present century, many attempts have been made to form associations upon the plan of a community of interest, in various parts of Europe and the United States of America. Many societies have been formed in part or wholly upon this plan. But it is well known that with all their wisdom, skill, benevolent designs, unity of intention, convenience of location, confidence of success, they have soon failed in their expectations, and been scattered as before. . . .

Now let any candid person examine the causes by which associations (formed for good purposes no doubt) so often fail, and he will find that it arises from the partial and selfish relations, of husbands, wives and children, and other kindred relations, together with the jealousies and evil surmises naturally rising therefrom. Therefore, all who attempt to establish and support such a system by any power of nature, or by any human wisdom, or indeed by any means short of self-denial, integrity of principle, and real chastity of person, will most certainly fail in the end. . . .

For that nature is partial and selfish, and inclines to seek its own indulgence and self-gratification, and is therefore incompatible with that principle of universal love and disinterested benevolence, which is indispensable to the maintenance of a united interest in all things, in any society or community whatever."[61]

These remarks lead to the Shaker conclusion that in only two cases have such communities succeeded and lasted for any considerable length of time. The first was in Jerusalem, in the days of the apostles; the second was in America, where the Shakers established the communities of the Second Coming. In both Jerusalem and America the communities were based on the replacement of "natural" families of husbands and wives by "spiritual" families of brothers and sisters. The Shakers believed that history had proved their point.[62]

The last of the philosophical arguments was Malthusian. Malthus's essays appeared in 1798 and 1803. Their influence on Shaker theorizing came fairly late, and one meets hardly any Malthusian ideas before the period of the great rationalist elders during the second half of the nineteenth century.

Frederick Evans lectured on the Malthusian problem to his London audience:

Remember Herschel's problem: he says take the diameter of this earth as the base of a pyramid, and if Adam and Eve had propagated without any checks to population from war, famine and disease, the inhabitants, standing upon one another's heads, would extend to the sun and twenty-seven times beyond. . . . Malthus provided you with a remedy; you have your remedies to-day; you have your wars, you have your famines, your pestilences. Where are you? Are these normal—are these according to God and to nature? They are certainly not according to the millennial order of things, for the time was to come when war should cease to the ends of the earth, and the nations should learn war no more. As a Shaker, then, I ask you what is your remedy for this increase in population? You have none, and the remedy, my friends, that I propose to you is the institution of the Christ order, the remedy that Jesus of Nazareth provided, that there should be so many Christians on this earth living a pure celibate life, so as to keep in check the populative principle, leaving the natural order far better off than it is now.[63]

One finds similar allusions in such other Shaker writings as the brochure *Aletheian Believers* from the pen of A. G. Hollister, the editor of Shaker catechisms.[64] But the most consistent presentation is undoubtedly found in Richard Pelham's *A Shaker's Answer to the Oft-Repeated Question: "What Would Become of the World If All Should Become Shakers?"* It was published in 1868 and often reprinted.

This long treatise is organized around the following themes:

1. There would be no great loss if everyone imitated the Shakers, since the world was heading toward its end anyway.

2. The task has been divided among those who imitate Christ and those who do not imitate him. Many are called, few are chosen. This division of labor has been forseen.

3. To reproduce one's kind is not a law of nature. It is indubitably natural, under normal conditions, to use one's reproductive powers and produce children; but it is also perfectly obvious that no law of nature requires man to do so. On the contrary, it is the smallest quantity of seed that is generally used for replanting; the greatest part is destined to be consumed.

4. Next comes the theme that is more properly Malthusian:

The time is approaching when the unrestrained generation of the human species will over-populate the earth. A modern writer informs us that our earth contains thirty-two billions of acres; that the present population is one billion and one hundred thousand; and that this population doubles every sixty years, despite wars and all other calamities. At this rate, in less than 300 years there will be only one acre each for every human being, and in 500 years there would be about nine human beings for every acre! *Malthus, the great political economist,* in his work on population says: "Population, when unchecked, would be doubled in every generation, or rather, that it increases in a geometrical ratio; while food can be made to increase, at furthest, only in arithmetical ratio." At this rate of increase, in 500 years population would be more than a million times its present numbers; but, in the most favorable circumstances, the produce of a country could hardly be, uniformly and permanently, increased to twenty times its amount every five hundred years; which, however, would be only arithmetical progression, as compared with the geometrical increase of inhabitants. From these two different rates of increase, it results, that powerful checks on population must be constantly in action.

He continues by "Shakerizing" the Malthusian view:

Thus we see there must somewhere exist a conservative principle in Nature to meet this exigency. And what should that be but the *disuse* of the reproductive organs, and the assumption of a higher sphere, or spiritual life, — the life of Christ? Malthus admits that "abstinence from marriage" must constitute one of those "powerful checks"; but what is mere abstinence from marriage without the religious element? There is no principle in human nature but this powerful enough to cope with man's lust, and restrain him from something worse than mere marriage.

Pelham concludes his presentation by picturing the superiority of continent mankind over reproductive mankind:

That there is an element of continence in the human soul which will yet be more fully developed, is most evident. It has manifested itself more or less from the beginning of the race. It cropped out in the community of Essenes among the Jews, and indeed the Nazarites before them, the Theraputae of Egypt, and the monastics of all Europe and America during the whole Christian era. It may be traced among the Brahmins and ascetics of the East, and has flourished for unknown ages among the followers of the Grand Lama in Thibet. The support of the *vestal virgins* in the Roman temples as priestesses, shows the innate veneration of the human soul for the continent and virgin character, as connected with religion. This order of virgin priestesses was kept up for at least a thousand years in succession. We believe that the time for the more perfect development and organization of this great conservative principle is come, and that it will operate and be gradually extended in order that it may be fully and practically investigated, clearly understood and firmly established for future and more general adoption as it becomes more necessary. Hear what A. J. David says: "When mankind shall have become *spiritually larger* and *finer in body* they will have fewer and fewer children. Down in the lower stratum of society, behold how populous! Take the early races; they propagate rapidly? Earth's mothers have been broken down by their exceedingly numerous progeny. Rise higher in the scale, and the married have fewer children and less frequently. Rise still higher in the *mental* scale, and you can easily believe the time will come that *reproduction will cease!*" . . . It requires but little reflection to discover that as mankind reforms and complies with the sanitary laws of life and health, as well as those of procreation, the population of the earth will increase with an increasing ratio. A large majority may then be reserved from the work of reproduction, in accordance with the general laws of Nature in every other department of mundane life, and may pass into the higher, or inner life, at the expense and sacrifice of the generative principle.[65]

This supreme argument, which was an echo of Mother Ann's primitive intuitions, as seen in her reprimand to Beulah Rude,[66] can also be found in certain contemporary theological treatises.[67] At any rate, it was the main line of defense for Shaker asceticism. After a hundred years of maturation, the economic and demographic forces operative at the time of the society's conception could once more be clearly seen.

Taken as a whole, these arguments illuminate the relation between the way the Shakers were affected by their psychosociological environment and the way they reacted to their discovery of the forces determining that environment. Faced with a world which, in practice destined them for the role of victims, the Shakers reacted with a theory explaining how the world was predestined to be guilty. Their ideological arguments generalized this reciprocal relation by putting it in the context of a universal catastrophe and universal guilt. Their solution was to eliminate the problem by withdrawing from the world and creating for themselves a new environment of universal salvation and justification. This was the Millennial Church, whose first bridgeheads for recruitment in the world were appeals to man's guilty conscience and a call for him to revolt against his existence as a victim. Later the appeal became a promise of integration in a community of those who had been "justified." Theoretical justification came from the new ideology; practical justification was found in a new kind of behavior. Ideology and behavior validated each other, and taken together they validated the initial Shaker "revelation."

IV. Shaker Behavior

Ad intra, this behavior implied that marriage was forbidden and that loyalty was to the Family. *Ad extra*, this behavior amounted to what one might call a renunciation of the sacrament.

INTERDICTION OF MARRIAGE

It is not possible to deduce a consistent attitude from the Shaker statements about marriage unless one considers them in terms of the sociological phases that marked the development of the movement. How else can one reconcile Ann Lee's testimony that marriage in the flesh is a pact with death and an alliance with hell, with the reverent remarks of Sister Sarah, who wrote to a future postulant, Mary Carr, that the marriage relation, providing the laws of God and nature are strictly observed and that carnal exchange occurs only for the purpose of reproduction, is undeniably God's method for peopling the earth.[68]

It is possible to trace the evolution of this attitude. In the first phase of Shaker thought, marriage was indeed considered to be hell on earth because it is impossible to consummate this relationship without reactivating the sin which lies dormant in the blood of every human being. The duty of the married couple was to de-marry each other, since it is not possible to partake both of generation and regeneration. No distinction was made between the use of marriage and the abuse of lust. For the early Shakers an authentic use of marriage would be to achieve reproduction without pleasuring the flesh, and this is something that they were sure could never occur. Mother Ann was careful not to force anyone, but she was firm in her opinion that he who enters marriage is entering the gates of hell. According to Mother Ann, those who chose to live by the flesh were certainly free to do so, although her visions had assured her that those who satisfied their lust would suffer punishments proportionate to their violation of the laws of God and nature.[69]

However, after this first phase, the natural resistance of human dough to the millennarian leaven opened the way for another point of view on the subject. The theory of marriage as a pact with hell was soon paralleled by the theory of marriage as offering "the lesser sin." In the *Testimonies* Mother Ann denies that she forbids marriage to those who are incapable of taking up their cross and sacrificing all carnal pleasure in order to enter the Kingdom of God. To such men she advised that they acquire a wife to whom they would remain attentive and faithful and with whom they would engender legal children. "For, of all lustful gratifications, that is the least sin."[70]

This theory of marriage as a concession to human weakness obviously claimed the support of the celebrated verse number 9 of Paul's First Epistle to the Corinthians. But according to the Shakers, there was one fundamental difference between their attitude and Paul's. The apostle had made this concession for believers who were already members of the church. In doing so, he had invented a new ecclesiastical type of what D. Fraser called the "Christian-Pagan Church," made up of "mad Galatians and pleasure-loving Corinthians." In the primitive type "Pentecostal Church" full participation had been denied to Christian Gentiles who married or owned slaves; such halfway members were tolerated by the early sect, but only as a sort of outer appendage, and they remained essentially outsiders.[71]

The Shakers, on the other hand, had always refused to make any concession other than the one for "halfway" members found in the early Pentecostal Church. But those "lesser sinners," no matter how strong their faith, never gained entrance to the Shaker sanctum. We have already seen how even the prestige of a new revelation from Ann Lee could not influence the Shakers to relax this intransigent attitude.[72] On this principle at least, the Shakers tolerated no addenda to their revelation.

Yet, given the process of the society's inner and outer evolution, it is quite probable that during the modernist phase of the last decades this sector of the "lesser sin" was growing, taking on substance, and being recognized in more positive terms. Sister Sarah's description of marriage as God's way of peopling the earth was certainly not current among the Shakers, and even in the case of the good sister the text is contradicted by the context. Yet it is a fact that the "Adamic" law of marriage was assuming, more and more, a position of peaceful coexistence with the "Evangelical" law of nonmarriage or de-marrying.

Already in the 1848 edition of *Millennial Church* one finds a footnote muting the text's stern demonstration that there is fundamentally no difference between legal marriage and promiscuous lust: "We would not be understood to condemn matrimony, in itself considered, among natural people; for in its primitive institution, in the order of nature, it was good; but our object is to point out the abuses cloaked under it, as now practiced, not only by the world at large, but even by those who call themselves Christians."[73] This qualification comes as an afterthought and is, for all that, a very small one, since the Shakers assumed that this "natural" or "Adamic" state of marriage had never really existed and remained unrealizable.

Yet this is the breach through which Frederick Evans would pass his views on the Second Cycle, repudiating the universal interdiction of marriage.[74] Evans would say that henceforth there would be two orders, the order of generation, which is of the New Land, and the order of regeneration, which is of the New Heaven; and that these two orders were equally responsible for making a contribution to the course of universal evolution.[75]

In his London lecture Evans had insisted on justifying the

Shakers for clinging to their old concept, and in doing so he made the problem just about disappear:

If God made man male and female and said to them, "Multiply and replenish the earth," as He said to all the animals in creation, I take it that it was simply a law of nature that all animal creation, as all the vegetable, should reproduce after their kind, and there is no objection to it. We take no ground against it; we grant you the order fully, freely. That which is spiritual is not first, but that which is natural, and afterwards that which is spiritual. How then is Shakerism opposed to the marriage relation? Not at all. "If it is right for you to be celibates, is it not right for everybody?" I say nay; I say, in the words of Jesus when he was answering the question put to him by the Pharisees about the marriage relation and condemning divorce, that Moses allowed it, not because it was right, but because of the hardness of their hearts, because of their low conditions, just as Brigham Young states that one man and one woman is the order, but that he permits polygamy because of the conditions of the people.[76]

Unless this frankness is feigned, one is led to interpret statements like this as an indication that Evans, from time to time, wished he could have rewritten some of the basic texts of the True Believers.[77]

In the treatise by Richard Pelham, already cited, the writer, despite or perhaps because of his Malthusian ideas, went one step further. Unlike Evans, he was reluctant to exclude human reproduction not only from the natural order but from the supernatural order. "The great Architect," he explained, "has diverse grades of workmen, all necessary in their places . . . to complete the building." The married and the unmarried have their functions in this building, as do the hodcarriers and bricklayers or the painters and decorators. As for the eternal salvation attributed to different functions, Pelham was willing to leave that for the Master Builder to decide, since he knew that the fate of all lies in the hands of a single power who alone determines such things.[78]

In Pelham's treatise we see how, once again, the Shaker

principle of celibacy was saved by becoming, with the passing of time, a formula for all humanity. In Anna White's essay on the Motherhood of God, the confrontation of Shaker celibacy and the world did not exceed existing proportions, and the elders calmly gave her message of peaceful coexistence in straightforward language: "Side by side with the millions whose work is on the plane of nature, who in lawful wedlock should be producing children, healthy, well-developed in body, brain and soul, well trained and well cared for, are the thousands of others, who, by nature, spiritual development, the gifts and call of God, are adapted for life on the spiritual plane, the life which turns from the marriage of earth to the spiritual union of the heavenly state."[79] It is already 1903.

Thus the original vision of a confrontation between heaven and hell which, when immanent, would bring about the Last Judgment and the end of this world, was slowly replaced by a vision of complementary earthly tasks to be performed, side by side, in such a way as to permit life in the world to continue. Millenarianism did not go up in smoke, but henceforth its fate was linked to a consciously spiritualized Malthusian strain which, quite possibly, had from the very beginning been the secret spring of its Christianity.

THE EMPHASIS ON THE FAMILY

The forbidding of marriage was a corollary to the Shaker refusal of reproduction; and, as such, it was the negative aspect of their ascetic femininism. But this interdiction cannot be fully understood unless also seen in the positive light of their message: the development of the Family.

The prestige of the Shaker Family was great. The potential postulant of Sister Sarah's correspondence began her first letter with a nostalgic reminiscence of her visit the previous summer to Union Village. Despite her clear memory of the neatly ordered houses in the quiet repose of the countryside far from the noise and fevers of the world, she was at a loss to express in words the initial effect of the place, which she compared to a green oasis in the desert of life.

The prestige of the Shaker Family was bolstered by the society's writers, who did not hesitate to favor it by denigrating family life in the outside world. A. G. Hollister, the catechist, was particularly adept at this.[80]

In the face of this denigration so slyly sustained by the Shaker writers, the Family offered a cause with some pretensions to greatness: its emphasis on woman as the motive force in a large human enterprise. This emphasis was, above all, religious, based on a belief in the Motherhood of God. It would be more accurate to say that, for the Shaker Family, God's bisexuality was the archtype for all parental relations.

At the summit of life and at the beginning of time were our eternal parents: Almighty God and Holy Mother Wisdom. The conception of the God-Mother as wisdom was, obviously, of biblical inspiration. Shaker exegesis identified this wisdom with the Spirit.[81] As for the three male Gods of the Trinity, they were considered to be an invention of the churches.[82] We have already seen how, quite late in the story, the God-Mother tended to merge with the eternal, intelligent, and creative energy, immanent to life on earth, the material matrix of the world.[83]

Next came "our heavenly parents," which is to say Jesus, the carpenter's son, and Ann Lee, the blacksmith's daughter. The former was described in adoptionist terms.[84] He had carried the latter within him, just as Adam had carried Eve as part of his own body.[85] When her time came, Ann had consummated her spiritual marriage with Christ. The *Testimonies* give a full account of those visions and her declarations about them. Christ was the second Adam; Ann was the second Eve.[86] She was married to Christ.[87] She walked with him, hand in hand, through the gardens of Heaven.[88] She felt his blood running through her soul and washing her, and so on.[89]

Then finally came "our spiritual parents," which is to say our father in the faith. These were the first church elders, particularly Father Joseph Meacham and Mother Lucy Wright, who had brought the church into Gospel Order.

This archetypal relation presided over all relations within

the society. The communities, the meetings, the religious authorities, everything was *dual.* This duality rapidly produced a new type of person, the eldress. In Egypt of the third millennium, demands for social reform had been preceded by the people's demands to partake in those religious rites which opened the way to immortality. In the evolution of Shaker society it was as if the feminist movement, which had been so active during the prehistory of socialism, particularly in nineteenth-century America, was being preceded by a religious feminism that would bestow on the eldress all the rights and privileges of the elder. "The Shaker Eldress is a bishop. . . . She is a pastor. . . . She is the family mother." [90] More generally, the Shakers claimed to have left the rites of Aaron and the Levites (the priests who married and had children and passed the privileges of priesthood to their firstborn), and to have gone back to the universal ministry of Melchizedek, King and priest of Salem, who was without father, mother, or children born of the flesh. [91] The first extension of this opening up of ecclesiastic privileges was to enlarge the religious role of women.

The eldress was a pastor: "To her come the members of her flock, soul by soul, with the burden of sin, the frailty of nature, the weakness of character. To God, before her as witness, is confession made. . . . She must focalize the rays of divine love, connect the soul to God, impart the germ of heavenly life, etc. . . . ."[92] The eldress was even a bishop: "She must know the trend of spiritual, intellectual and humanitarian movements in the outer world and the inner and outer status of the numerous branches of the Shaker Order." She was also a *teacher:* "No pastor of an outside church has more the function of public teacher than the Eldress in the simple Shaker meeting, where all are free to give forth whatever gift of the spirit they may feel, in song, exercise, exhortation or experience. In association and harmony with the Elder, she must know the needs of the hour and the minute, must direct, control, inspire."[93] And finally, she is Family mother. In this role her religious importance is matched by a social preeminence which, among other attributes, won over the Owenite, Frederick Evans.[94]

It was under Evans's influence that feminism within Shaker society began to make common cause with the movement in the outside world for the right of women to vote and hold office. During his London lecture, which was a mine of Shaker ideas, Evans spoke in a pure Shaker style, saying that when he surveyed the Christian nations and saw what had happened to their social systems, as in London, he was struck by a great lack — that the people were not satisfied, that they were ill-fed, ill-dressed, and ill-lodged. Why? Was it the fault of their form of government? This led him to remark that London was governed by men, that women were not represented. True, England did have a Queen (Victoria), but she reigned as a man, not as a woman. The British Parliament, the House of Lords, and the House of Commons did not include any women to represent the people. Why was this so? At least half the population was made up of women, and they had the same faculties of reason and feeling as the men. Why were they subject to laws, penalties, and taxes, yet had no voice in determining what these should be? We Shakers, he said, believe in the fundamental truth that the Divinity is both male and female. The heavenly Mother and Father reign together over the world, and consequently, every normal human government ought to follow this form, recognizing the two eternal elements in mankind, the male and the female. And so, observed Evans, the British government seemed to him to be abnormal and unnatural.[95]

Evans's remarks are a good indication of the prestige of the Family. This prestige was all the more real in that, given the jungle of competition, it was the Family which gave both men and women alike an enviable standard of living. Sister Sarah's postulant had sighed in admiration of those neatly arranged houses. Shaker property was indeed legendary, and there were many technical improvements invented by the Shakers to simplify household chores and economize the labor of women assigned to do housework in the various communities. Materially as well as spiritually, the Shaker

Family promoted the importance of women as members of the society.

As for the men, some were drawn to a community like this simply because it represented an attempt to reverse thousands of years of history, but for women it was normal to be attracted to an enterprise which so enhanced their status. In the 1708 inventory of the French Prophets, men predominated: there were about two for every woman. But in 1875, according to Nordhoff's statistics, there were 58 men for every 100 women above the age of twenty-one, and 56 boys for every 100 girls. In 1891 Evans complained that the recruitment of men was falling.[96] And, finally, we note that the last surviving Shakers are elderly ladies. It is quite likely that on the political level the general campaign for women's rights undercut both the feminism and the religious theories of the Shakers. As for the economic advantages of women's participation in the production and industrialized distribution of consumer items, this double phenomenon would invade the modern world on a scale which the artisan workshops of the Shaker communities could not match, and which rapidly made them obsolete.

RENUNCIATION OF THE MARRIAGE SACRAMENT

Through their many shifts in doctrine the Shakers were able to admit that there was a certain natural validity, even a certain spiritual rightness, in the conjugal union of man and woman. But as we have already pointed out, on one point they remained firm, and this is something they held in common with many religious dissidences: they refused to consider marriage a sacrament. In their eyes the union of man and woman could be tolerated as "the lesser sin" and even merit a certain respect, but they never imagined that it could be officially sanctioned by a church. The conjugal union may have been accepted as a "lesser sin," but to make this sin into a sacrament was the greatest sin of all.

The authors of *Millennial Church* comment on the reasons for this radical attitude. For them the marriage sacrament legalizes lust, just as the so-called holy wars legalized murder: "Doubtless the sanction of a legal ceremony gives a license which, assisted by the shades of darkness, removes all restraint from the feelings of those who do not look beyond it, especially where the mind has been previously polluted by lascivious gratifications; so that they can now indulge their concupiscience in the dark, without shame or remorse."[97]

For the Shakers, decadence in the Christian Church began with the establishing of marriage as a religious institution. And by the same token, this suggests another of their attitudes that was similar to certain medieval dissidences: the refusal of any representation of the crucifix. In fact, for the Shakers, and for the Gospel as they interpreted it, "to take up one's cross" had a very precise meaning: it was a personal commitment to renunciation as a way of life and to the realization of this through chastity and the communal ownership of worldly goods. The Christian adventure went adrift the moment churches began to help their members carry this "cross," relieving them of the responsibility of carrying it themselves (since it approved of their marriage), and nevertheless offering them, through subterfuges of doctrine, all the advantages of Christ. The false prophets of the Antichrist, according to the *Millennial Church*, teach that the unjust can inherit the realm of God through the goodness of Christ. This doctrine, according to the Shaker authors, has been taught ever since Christianity became a popular religion and has infiltrated all branches of the orthodox church.[98] Now the popularity of this doctrine lay in its veneration of symbols representing the Crucifixion. As an object of worship, the crucifix replaced the Crucifixion, making it possible for the real event to live on in its symbolic substitution. "This was done by substituting the form of a wooden cross in the place of practical self denial and *making the show of religion* supply the place of reality. Hence when the Emperor Constantine assumed a Christian name, he formed such a cross for his standard, under which he prosecuted his bloody wars, and fought his way to the throne."[99]

Thus Shakerism was implicitly iconoclastic. Images were

considered a sign of religious decadence. The rooms reserved for religious meetings remained for a long time, if not always, bare of "representative" art. The people who assembled there were the True Believers, "who had taken up their cross of the flesh." All the others were to wait outside, in the church courtyard.

Unfortunately, there is no way to arrive at a figure giving the proportion of those who, in taking up their cross, had to de-marry. Judging by the polemic literature, they were more numerous during the early period of the church than during the later years. This ritual of de-marriage was perhaps the most significant characteristic of Shaker behavior. Through it we get the Shaker references to the Pauline privilege.

In her correspondence Sister Sarah alludes to this rite of de-marriage and explains that it is different from a divorce.[100] It was especially difficult when husband and wife were not "converted" at the same time. Practically, the difficulties caused by the arrangement were similar to those which the founding mother had encountered when she tried to live "innocently" with her husband. For it was rare that husband and wife were "converted" at the same time. Quite apart from the lawsuits over property, the psychological frustrations engendered by this conjugal arrangement would have sufficed to create unbearable tensions in the de-married couple.

What happened if the new convert remained at home, in his own house? In such cases the other spouse was obliged to obey the rules for cohabitation stipulated by Shaker morality. Mother Ann was sometimes successful in obtaining this. In the *Testimonies* we read that "after Nathan Cole embraced the gospel, his wife, Molly who still remained in unbelief went to see Mother Ann, and asked liberty to continue her usual custom of attending the Baptist meeting, which was contrary to Nathan's feelings. Mother replied, 'You must confess your sins and be obedient to your husband. I cannot counsel you otherwise; if I do your children will be lost; for, through the believing husband, the children will be sanctified.' "[101]

Most of the time this cohabitation proved difficult, and in such cases the recalcitrant member of the couple was often besieged until he, too, made the "decision" of belief. Daniel Rathbun, in his violent pamphlet addressed to James Whittaker, described how he had seen a certain Samuel Fitch summon his wife, his son, and his daughter to the meeting and how Fitch had made them kneel down in front of the people assembled. Then, in a most solemn manner, Fitch had renounced them, saying that they were no longer his wife and children, and that he was no longer husband and father. After describing this scene Rathbun accused the Shakers of using all sorts of pressures and "other methods" for sowing discord between husbands and wives. He closed this passage of his pamphlet by asking Elder James Whittaker if such behavior could not be called "preventing marriage."[102]

Later lawsuits confirm the accusation that pressures were applied. The testimony given by Mary Cummings before a commission of the New Hampshire legislature is particularly suggestive on this score:

My maiden name was Mary McGrath. I was born in Dorchester, New Hampshire, and married Edward Cummings, in 1827; I am the mother of eight children, five of whom are now living; my husband and children are all living with the Shakers; my husband is here to-night; I now live at Sanbornton Bridge; and since my husband has been at the Shakers I have worked out in different places to get a livelihood. My husband joined the Society four years ago last March, and moved his family there at the same time. At that time we owned a farm in Hebron, which was sold in October following, for $1,475.00; we had, also, a horse, carts, wagons, two cows a heifer, &c., &c. Mr. Cummings took all his property to the Shakers. My oldest son was fifteen years old; another ten or eleven; a third, eight or nine. My youngest child was seven months old when I moved there. When I married, my husband was a member of the Congregational Church in Groton; afterwards he renounced the churches, joined the Osgoodites, and preached about, which business he followed about three years. He then joined the Shakers. After he told me he was going to join the Shakers, two of the brethren came to visit me and tried to induce me to join them: afterwards the same two brethren and two sisters came to visit me.

They told me I had better join; that if I did not I should be left alone; that if I would go I might have my children; otherwise they would be taken from me. My husband told me that if I would go, I should have a house by myself and the youngest children. That if I did not go with him, he would take the children away from me, sell the farm and the rest of the property, leave me alone and advertise me in the public print. I could do no other way; so I consented to go. After I got there they kept no one of their promises. I was put into a little building, called the centre building; my children were all taken from me, except my babe which was seven months old; and in three months from that time my little babe, only ten months old, was taken from me. At first I was permitted to sleep with it, for a few nights; but soon that was refused me, and I was forbid to go at all into the house where my children were. Since I left the Shakers, I have been to see my children three or four times. They were brought into a room — the boys with one of the brethren, and the girls with one of the sisters. I was once refused permission to see where my children slept, and was once permitted to see. When I urged and besought them to let me see my children, I was told that the gospel required me to labor out of my natural affections.

I never signed the deed conveying away our farm till after I went to the Shakers. John Lyon, a leading Elder, urged me to sign the deed; told me that it would be for my interest to sign it. My husband brought me the deed and requested me to sign; then Lyon and the sisters persuaded me; and by means of persuasion and threats I signed it.

My husband gave me five dollars, when I was there, about three weeks ago, which is all the money I have received from him since he joined the Shakers four years ago. I have supported myself by my own labor, since I left.[103]

The Shaker conscience never seemed to have been bothered by complaints like those of Mrs. Cummings. Their replies invariably invoked the principle of religious freedom, so dear to American hearts, and the Bible, which was no less cherished by American society.

In 1828 the Shakers affirmed before a commission of the New Hampshire legislature that if a man or woman who joined their community had other previous obligations through a contract of marriage, then it was the duty of the society to take care of both parties with kindness and Christian charity. If the husband and wife were unable to live together in peace, they should be separated by mutual agreement and their properties should be divided between them with justice and equity. And so the society permitted a separation of husband and wife only when the partner who did not have the faith conducted himself in such a manner that the believer, after conscientiously fulfilling all his moral obligations, felt justified by the laws of God and man in asking for a final separation.[104]

Any remaining ambiguities in this Shaker statement of position and practice disappear when one compares it to a passage in Joseph Dyer's refutation of the scurrilous anti-Shaker pamphlet written by his wife Mary. Dyer explained that in respect to marriage the Shaker position was exactly that of Saint Paul in his letter to the Corinthians: "If any brother hath a wife that believeth not, and she be pleased to dwell with him, let him not put her away. And the woman which hath a husband that believeth not, and if he be pleased to dwell with her, let her not leave him" (1 Corinthians 7:12–13). Such was the faith and principle governing the Shaker attitude toward the marriage contract. Dyer continued his explanation by stating that when a person who was married under the law joined the society, they considered him bound to do all that the law required in the marriage contract. And, he concluded, since there is nothing in the law that requires sexual cohabitation when this is against one's conscience, there is nothing in the marriage contract, as understood by law, that is contrary to the belief of the Shakers. Likewise, there is nothing in the Shaker faith that is contrary to the laws governing marriage.[105]

We can take our conclusion for this analysis from Daniel Fraser's *The Music of the Spheres*. After enumerating seven steps in the reasoning that led the Shakers to rediscover the cornerstone of "true Christianity," Fraser concludes that if one examines the marriage system closely and takes into consideration all the facts, one will see that all the evidence points to a single principle: "marriage is not a Christian institution."[106]

CHAPTER SIX

Distinctions Within the United Society: Communism & Theocracy

AN 1834 document, written in the style of a guided tour, describes the four stages in the personal evolution of every True Believer as he pursues his spiritual adventure.[1]

The first stage is his separation from the world. In chapter 5 we discussed the difficulties and dramas involved in taking this step. Each of the succeeding stages corresponds to one of the behavioral distinctions whereby a Shaker's spiritual progress is manifested in the world of "real" events. Such documents as are available make it possible to affirm that this process of individual spiritual perfection resulted in the development of three distinct codes of behavior: one governing the members of the Family, one governing the actions of the Family considered as a unit, and one governing the whole Shaker Society in its relations with the American people.

It was the functioning of this threefold constitution that enabled the Millennial Church to organize itself into the United Society of Believers.

I. The Families in the Society

It was not until 1786, or the beginning of the second phase of Shaker history, that the Millennial Church was gathered in Gospel Order. In the process, the church was transformed into the "Church Order," and this Church Order was the beginning of what would be known as the United Society, that is to say, the association of all those believers, gathered and ungathered, who had "taken up their cross" and thus made a break with the ways of the world.

In general the membership of the United Society tended to coincide with the membership of the Church Order. This tendency is evident in the membership statistics of Mount Lebanon[2] and is confirmed by Charles Nordhoff's study.[3] But during the early years there was a very real distinction between the Church Order and the United Society. McNemar, the great Shaker writer, induced many believers to sign the Church Covenant, but he never signed it himself, arguing in his paper that the two life styles were quite different and that, personallly, he was fit only for the lower order.[4]

Although one could become a member of the United Society by simply adopting its moral code, membership in the Church Order required an economic commitment— the surrender of one's worldly goods to the community. Membership in the society was always considered to be merely a first step or transitional stage between life in the world and life in the Church Order. "Since the work of God is an increasing work, neither families nor individuals, if they remain faithful, can long be satisfied with anything less than Gospel perfection. As one gains in faith and understanding, one soon feels the want of a nearer relation to the Society and a greater separation from the world. Those who do not gain this will, of course, fall back to the world."[5] Despite all his services to the society, McNemar ultimately fell victim to this line of thought.[6]

This intransigent attitude did not go uncontested. During the years 1815–1820 the leaders of the society were strongly tempted to dissociate spiritual life from the problem of economic organization. A letter sent to Richard McNemar and published by him predicted the ruination of the Shaker communities unless there was an immediate reorganization according to new principles. The writer proposed to McNemar that the church be divided into two distinct and separate orders, one spiritual, the other material, and that each of these orders be responsible for choosing its own leaders.[7] By dissociating the ecclesiastical structure from the cooperative structure, the writer hoped to make responsibility more commensurate with competence and, at the same time, enable the society to classify its new members according to their abilities and interests. Enterprises like the Shakers' have always been bothered by the problem of economic management. The economy as such has special needs, and those chosen to manage it often have a tendency to oppose directives issued in the interest of spiritual uniformity. The early monasteries were not immune to such worries, as one can see by reading between the lines of the complaints made by John Cassian.[8] At any rate, this problem caused considerable disturbance during the first years of the Shaker enterprise.[9]

In its development the Shaker Family structure was caught between two conflicting tendencies: on the one hand, in the name of millenarian perfectionism, there was a centripetal tendency toward communal life and collective ownership of goods; on the other hand, in the interest of maintaining a peripheral spirituality for those still less than perfect, there was a centrifugal tendency toward admission of private possessions and individual management. This tendency to admit the existence of a marginal state of perfection not only made it possible for the Shakers to accomodate a certain degree of freedom, but also served to make the spiritually desirable life look a little less impossible to achieve.

This refusal to make an absolute dissociation between their demand for ecclesiastic uniformity and the needs of economic collectivism led the Shakers to seek a maximum of coincidence of the two; their solution was to institute a graduated typology for the Families, making the extent to which a member participates in the collective economy a criterion for determining his degree of spiritual integration with the church.

THE THREE TYPES OF FAMILIES

In New England and the Midwest there were, in all, about twenty "societies," for which Chart no. 6 gives the names, locations, and dates.[10] Each society was subdivided into from two to six "Families." Each Family contained from 30 to 150 members and was usually designated by its geographical position in respect to the society headquarters (North Family, South Family, and so on). Thus the Family was the geographical unit of the United Society. According to available lists, there were about 60 of them, corresponding approximately to the 6,000 members attributed to the Shakers during their period of greatest prosperity.

On this geographical classification the Shakers superimposed an organizational classification whereby members were divided into "classes" or "orders," sometimes also called "Families." The particular "class" ("order" or "Family") that dominated in a community varied from geographical location ("Family") to geographical location. There were three groups in this organizational classification.

First or *Novitiate Class* (or *Order*, or *Family*)
Second or *Junior Class* (or *Order*, or *Family*)
Third or *Senior Class* (or *Order*, or *Family*)

The distinction between these groups was essentially economic. Using the Shaker's own vocabulary, one can say that members of the first class were "in separation," in the second class were "in cooperation," and in the third class were "in community." Detailed and precise descriptions of these organizational groups can be found in Shaker texts, particularly in didactic writings such as Seth Y. Well's *Brief Expostion* (1834) and Evan's *Compendium* (1859).[11]

CHART 12. *Chart of Shaker Distinctions*

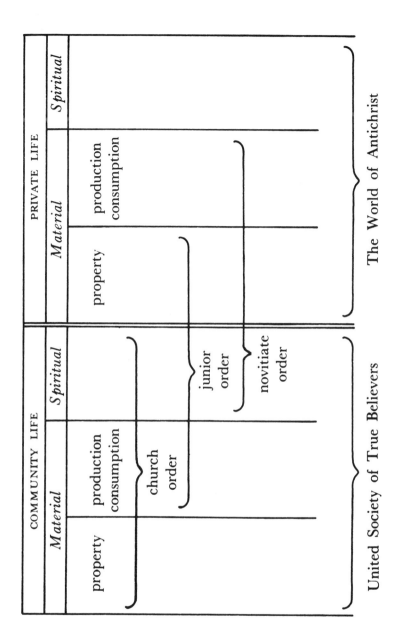

COMMUNITY LIFE

Material | *Spiritual*

property | production consumption

church order

junior order

novitiate order

United Society of True Believers

PRIVATE LIFE

Material | *Spiritual*

property | production consumption

The World of Antichrist

First or novitiate class (or order, or family). "First" in this case does not mean preeminent. Quite the contrary. This is the first stage, therefore the lowest level of the Shaker hierarchy. In the words of the Shaker formula, members of the novitiate class have received the gift of faith, but have chosen to live with their natural families and direct their own temporal affairs. All who wish to do so may live according to this arrangement and are counted among the brothers and sisters in Christ just so long as they respect his law.[12]

The two main features of this order are clear: (1) Religious dependence: as members of a religious community they are necessarily under the supervision of their religious leaders. (2) Economic independence: members of this class are not governed by the society as far as their property, children, or natural families are concerned. In respect to those things they are as free as the members of any other sect, yet they enjoy the spiritual privilege of being Shakers and keep their membership in the society so long as they do not violate the faith or moral principles of the Millennial Church.[13] This economic independence made members of the novitiate class vulnerable to a discreet reminder that they were always free to make a donation to the religious or charitable activities of the society.[14]

Second or junior class (or order, or Family). Shaker converts of this class still owned their property but had ceased using all or part of it in order to join the production-consumption cooperative which constituted the economic infrastructure of a Family.

Laws governing their behavior as members of a Family were very carefully worked out. They were required to sign a contract stipulating the gratuitous nature of the exchange. To the Family they made a gratuitous offering of goods and services; from the Family they gratuitously received food, lodging, and clothing, according to their needs, along with medical care and assurance that they would be cared for in their old age. Thus no junior member of a Family could receive a salary.[15]

In cases when the junior member agreed that the Family

could use all or part of his property (cattle, farm machinery, and so forth), an inventory was usually taken and signed.[16] The contract permitting its use stipulated that no interest or rental would be charged, although some agreements did make provisions for eventual reimbursement.[17] Should the junior member leave the Family, only those goods inscribed on the inventory would be returned to him.

The junior class Shaker could also, if he so wished, sign away certain parts of his property to the Family. Shaker writers insist that, far from encouraging this arrangement, the custom of the society had always been to discourage believers from making premature decisions, not only because such decisions were considered irrevocable, but also because experience had proved them to be a frequent source of quibbling over petty problems. The Shakers did not abstain from such objurgations, but they gave them a spiritual or religious twist, reminding the members of the junior class that they would remain in a state of imperfection until they had taken the decisive step.[18]

Third or senior class (or order, or Family) or church order or church Family. Members of this group categorically renounced not only the use of their property but also the property itself. Made as a solemn gift, their worldly goods became part of the common, jointly-held, inalienable property of the society, and the new first class member signed a covenant to this effect. This Shaker Covenant will be discussed in detail in the next sections.

Entrance to this class of Shakers was strictly controlled. It was forbidden to minors. Adults were required to get the approval of their heirs and their creditors. They were expected to have analyzed the Covenant thoroughly and to have recognized that, once signed, it would be irrevocable. Should the first-class Shaker later leave the Family, he would lose everything except what the generous nature of the society was in the habit of granting him. In this way members of the senior order were economically absorbed into the community. Having given their all, they were assured that all would be given to them. Moreover, their decision made them members of the class from which the elders were selected to govern the various Families. Qualitatively, this class was, of course, superior to the others; with the withering away of the membership in the lower classes, this superiority became quantitative as well.[19]

THE HISTORICAL DEVELOPMENT OF
THE THREE TYPES OF FAMILIES

Theological treatises written during the second and third phases of Shaker history advance the idea that if one is a socialist, one is automatically a Shaker. This line of reasoning, as we have already pointed out, can be found in the "Introductory Remarks" which preface the 1848 edition of *Millennial Church*.[20] It is also found in Frederick Evans's account of his personal intellectual Odyssey.[21] Historically, this line of reasoning reverses the process as it really occurred. Contrary to the latter-day theologians, the Millennial Church did not create Shakerism because its members wanted to be socialists. The Millennial Church was made up of Shakers; that is why it produced a kind of socialism.

In moving toward a communistic society, the church was really doing no more than duplicating a process which had become almost ritual among the religious immigrant groups moving into the New World.[22] We have already pointed out that the Pilgrim Fathers of the *Mayflower* inaugurated their adventure in the New World by experimenting for several months with a kind of socialism.[23] But without going back that far in history, one can say that for most of the nineteenth-century American community experiments (at least for those founded by immigrants from Europe) the struggle for existence under difficult conditions produced a certain egalitarian attitude which, when coupled with a millenarian nostalgia, determined the socialist form of their communities.

Consider the case of the Rappites. They did not arrive in New Harmony with the express intention of practicing common owership of goods and property; but when they gathered around their leaders in this unknown land, where everything seemed so hostile, they observed that a few of them had resources and that most of them were in dire need. Their religious orientation led them to compare themselves to the first Christians in Jerusalem surrounded by Gentiles, and it was the analogy between the two predicaments that gave birth to an analogous solution. In Judea, acting on the advice of the apostles, the rich had shared their wordly goods with the poor. The rich among the Rappites decided to do likewise, and this was not so difficult for them, since their belief in Christ's imminent return to earth had rendered them almost indifferent to personal property.[24]

It was the same with the founders of Zoar. In his *American Communities* W. A. Hinds tells how the first Separatists at Zoar were so poor that they had to hire themselves out to the surrounding farms as laborers. During the Atlantic crossing from Germany the rich had shared their fortunes with the needy, but all expected that once the voyage ended they would return to a regime of private property. However, some of the exiles had no money to pay for their share of the land, and others were too ill, old, or feeble to earn a living. Their leaders and his advisors were made to understand that the only way of avoiding a catastrophe was to form a communistic society. The decision to do this was made in 1819.[25]

The same thing happened at Amana at about the same period (1842–1846). In the beginning no one spoke about a community. Each one bought a piece of land commensurate with his financial resources, intending to live simply as a Christian congregation. It was the practical necessity of looking to the temporal welfare of all the members that led to communism.[26]

Likewise at Bishop Hill, the Swedish community started its existence as a religious dissidence and was led to socialism by a combination of millenarianism and poverty. Olaf Janson, the founder, had intended to separate the "children of God" from the rest of the wicked world and take them to America, which would be their base for conquering the globe. When this had been achieved, the millennium would begin.[27] Poverty brought them to their senses. Without money, food, or medicines, the Jansonites faced the hard winter of 1847–1848, shivering in holes in the ground and huddled together in sheds built against the hillsides. The result was another experiment in communal living.

In each of these cases it was the sense of brotherhood in the framework of a religious ideal brought from Europe that fomented on American soil some form of economic communism as a way around obstacles which threatened to undermine the religious ideal. This was also to be the case with the Shakers.

One of the elders wrote a letter to Alex Kent[28] explaining that, properly speaking, the Shakers were not a community. The elder considered the society to be a church, a gathering of people united by a spiritual vision. He thought that it was only secondarily and incidentally that the Shakers could be called communists, since their communism was accessory to the main goal, which was spiritual. This, said the elder, was what distinguished the Families of the United Society from other efforts to establish communist communities on the American continent, and he mentioned the Owenites, the Fourierists, and so on.

An example of this is the establishment of the mother chapter at Niskeyuna.[29] Frederick Evans described the spontaneous creation of that first communist community in a letter to Robert D. Owen:

The inspiration that made them Shakers led them to be good to each other, to clothe the naked, to feed the hungry, even when they were their own persecutors. They loved each other so genuinely, so practically, that each one felt it a privilege and a duty to let every other brother and sister possess all that he possessed and enjoy all that he himself enjoyed. They had all things in common. They learned by experience that the direct tendency of their new religion was to include all those who would embrace it in the form of a new communal relation, and that this was the legitimate and inevitable consequence.[30]

Thus, before Shaker communism became the subject of theological arguments, it was, first of all, purely and simply an accomplished social fact. This tendency to collective ownership of worldly goods was, of course, unconsciously present in Ann Lee's "Revelation." When nothing really belonged to anyone in particular, then everything belonged to everyone generally. This transformation into a collectivist society led the Shakers to resurrect the theoretical justifications used by the early Christians, and from this developed their theological demonstration of communism:

Does Christianity admit of private property? We answer this emphatically *in the negative*. Affections for private property are the sequences of self-love, and this is un–Christian; they are opposed to the equality of the good things of this life or of any other; they lead to the formation of earthly families and generative attachments, and not to Christian life. Christian life and love draw souls into a communion of interests in all things, after the pattern of Pentecost; and heavenly families, whether formed on earth or in the spirit land, are virginal in character, with communion of interests in all things fully prevailing.[31]

Quite incidentally, the Shakers related another argument, this one practical, to the theological and experiential justifications for holding property in common. The believers had been told that, if only it were possible for members to leave the society at will, repossess the goods they had contributed, and receive just remuneration for the work they had done, the society would grow and have more influence among the people. Seth Y. Wells, in his "Exposition Continued. . . ,"[32] gave a Shaker reply to this type of suggestion. His first reaction to it was practical: Who would keep the books, calculate interest, and estimate the changing values of the properties that had passed into Shaker control? Where was the man with sufficient mathematical skill first to calculate the real value of the workdays contributed by all those people and then to make fair deductions for their room, board, laundry, clothing, medical care, and other expenses of daily living? All these calculations, Wells explained, would have to be made if each member of the society was to keep his own private interest under an equitable system of just remuneration. Without such detailed accounts, regularly kept, how could any court rightfully judge the amount to be paid for a year's work or the amount to be deducted for necessary and incidental expenses? The Shaker writer left the answer to this problem of bookkeeping to those already involved in it or to those who wanted to establish a society organized for this sort of record-keeping. Let them make their calculations! They would soon discover that a community founded on this basis could not prosper. The practical difficulties and resulting confusion would inevitably bring about its dissolution.

Actually, as far as the bookkeeping for individual properties was concerned, the Shakers never went any further than the inventory of goods brought into the society by new members of the junior order, although sometimes they calculated a property's value when reimbursement was later called for. Their communal life made them ill-equipped to calculate the value of goods produced by any one person. Moreover, any attempts they might have made to systematize such calculations, as in the Joseph Warren communities, could hardly have been considered encouraging.[33] The Shaker reluctance or inability to make these calculations is especially significant in that it underscores another aspect of their enterprise. Egalitarian communities like these, in which each received goods and services according to his needs, had nothing in common with enterprises whose prosperity comes from increasing the rate of production and where any such acceleration implies a system for evaluating the work contributed by each member. In communities like the Shakers', when abundance did occur, it was the result of an accumulation of capital in the form of gifts, free labor, and land speculation. But before such abundance could be realized, the believers lived under a regime of penury, implying egalitarian consumption of goods produced and a system of distribution which refused not only to calculate interest on capital loaned but also to remunerate members for work that had been done. The fact that no interest was paid for the use of capital contributed by members destroyed the motivation for capitalism within the community, and the absence of a graduated payscale prevented the "managers" from developing into an economic class distinct from the rest of the community.

On the other hand, when considered as economic units the various communities looked like bastions of capitalism. The Shaker drive for profit was legendary: the best of everything went into the treasury, and individual members were given only what they needed to continue working. Members were not burdened with the expense of reproducing their kind, and certain texts lead one to think that for some of them this was a joyous relief rather than a sacrifice.[34]

Asceticism sometimes led to stinginess.[35] And it should be pointed out that most of the Shaker lawsuits were over questions of money.[36] Evans admitted that the societies had acted like agrarian capitalists.[37] This question of gain or profit is related to another problem: the worker whose only remuneration came in the form of egalitarian consumption tended to become indifferent to his work. Absence of distinctions in the kinds of work to be done and a general leveling of individual possibilities for improvement contributed to the indifference. When times were bad, Shaker communism made it possible for them to stand together; when times were good, especially when prosperity meant an improved life within the community, it favored this tendency toward inertia.

When one considers two types of recurring difficulties, the outlines of the "classes" or "Families" come into sharper focus. The first type occurred when only one partner in a married couple was converted. We have already seen how the Shakers handled such cases and how they based their behavior on the directives given by the Apostle Paul in his first Epistle to the Corinthians.[38]

In some cases the application of Paul's principles led to peaceful cohabitation. When this occurred, the "converted" partner stayed with his or her own natural family and was obviously placed in the Shaker's novitiate order. This was the solution for those who accepted imperfection as a "lesser evil," as suggests George Lomas in *Plain Talks*.[39]

Sometimes the religious differences ended in the separation of husband and wife. In such cases the Shakers persuaded the couple to divide up their property. In several cases unbelieving wives sued the society to recover property which their husbands, in the fervor of conversion, had signed over to the collectivity. In general, American law was quite severe with such "converts." A Kentucky law of 1812 provided that in cases of conversion like this, all property should pass into the hands of the partner remaining in the world; an Ohio law of 1811 gives the court the right to decide how much of the property a "convert" may take with him into the society. These legal barriers explain why the Shakers tried so hard to persuade even unbelieving wives to follow their husbands into the society. We cited an odious example of this in the deposition made by Mrs. Mary Cummings before the New Hampshire legislature—odious, that is, if one believes the story as recounted by the victim.[40]

In cases when both husband and wife had been converted and both wanted to join a Shaker community, there still remained the problem of the children who were too young to make that kind of decision for themselves. In such cases, in order to avoid legal complications, the Shakers proposed that compromises be reached by mutual consent. One such compromise was an "equitable" repartition of all property in the following proportions: eight parts to the father, four to the mother, two to each son, one to each daughter. These proportions of 8:4 and 2:1 indicate that there were limits to Shaker feminism, since their doctrine of religious equality of the sexes did not prevent them from judging a man to be, economically at least, worth twice as much as a woman. Once their property was divided, husband and wife were free to turn it over to the society if they so wished. Heirs who had already attained legal age were given their due share. The shares of any minor heirs were to be put in the hands of trustees who would manage the property until the heirs came of age.[41] This rule of repartition was not imposed on novitiates, but it was proposed to them as a custom of the society. Usually, considerable time would elapse between a person's "conversion" and such a settling of his worldly accounts. This corresponded to the time spent by the postulant in the novitiate and junior orders.

This first type of difficulty occurred at the moment when a postulant entered the society, and it was generally caused by women. A second type of difficulty occurred at the moment of leaving the society (this did happen), and it was generally caused by men. These were men who, after giving all their worldly goods to the society and working without payment for several years, found themselves once more faced with the problem of making a living, and who therefore wanted to reconstitute some instrument of production, usually a farm. Such men would turn to the society and ask that they be given back their lands. Demands like this were the cause of many lawsuits.

A certain J. Witcher, testifying before the New Hampshire Legislature in 1848, said:

I have lived with the Shakers sixteen years; was fifteen when I went there. My grandfather once owned the farm where the Shakers now live; he became a Shaker; my father lived at the Shakers. My sisters lived at the Shakers for about twenty-two years each. All I received for my services for sixteen years was $100. My sisters never received anything. My father became poor and was going upon the town, and as I had just left the Shakers and had nothing, I spoke to them to give him some help to keep him off the town. They refused on the ground that the property was all in common at the Shakers and they consequently had nothing to give.[42]

Such depositions did not find the Shakers unprotected. The text of the Covenant — which will be discussed later — previously signed by the defecting Shaker, protected the interests of the United Society. J. Witcher was bitter on this subject: "I signed the Covenant when I was about twenty-one years old. This is an instrument protecting the Society against claims for services."

Despite all their precautions, the battle was a hot one on

this point. In Kentucky a certain John Whitbey, who figured on a list of such signatures, asked the court for the right to sue the Shaker societies even though they had no juridical status. This was a subtle way of reorienting the debate and creating doubts about the legal significance of the Covenant he had signed.[43] Likewise in Kentucky, when two ex-Shakers named Gass and Banta sued the Pleasant Hill Society to recover their property, they invoked both the egalitarian principle and their right to repossess what they had contributed to the society.[44] However, the court upheld the Shaker argument, declaring that the plaintiffs were owners of Shaker property only so long as they were members of the "societies." Once they left a society, they ceased to have any claims to its property. Their suit was rejected. The fact that the Shakers themselves insisted on publishing reports of these trials is ample indication the decisions reached were not always unfavorable to their interests.[45]

This sort of legal squabbling led the Shakers to be doubly cautious about the wording on contracts which regulated entrance to the various classes. It also led them to clarify the distinctions between the junior and senior orders, to arrange for an inventory of a member's possessions when he entered the junior order, and to establish, whenever circumstances would permit, a more liberal policy toward those who left the society. Julia Neal notes that it was always Shaker policy to give each member leaving the church Family a sum proportionate to the value of the property he had brought to the society, and to supply him with the tools necessary for beginning his life anew.[46] Indeed, certain Shaker texts state that the trustees were under a moral obligation to reimburse those defectors whose entrance into a Family had contributed to its subsequent prosperity. But they insisted that they were not legally bound to make such generous gestures.

Thus, through a series of crises, the Shakers developed a code governing a believer's rights and obligations as he moved in and out of the various stages leading to full membership in the Church Order. As they evolved, these regulations were codified in the Covenants.

In 1788 the Covenant was an oral agreement among the members of the church; then in 1795 it was put into writing and signed. It underwent modifications in 1801, 1805, 1822, 1829, and 1832. Moreover, the various local societies adapted it to their special needs and purposes. Without making any judgment or even claiming to make a comparative analysis of these texts, we can take a sampling of what was produced. Our sampling will include three examples: (1) the 1795 transcription of the 1788 oral covenant; (2) a covenant signed by members entering the lower orders; (3) a few extracts from the edition of the Shaker constitution, or Church Covenant, revised in the early 1830s.

1. The 1795 Transcription of the 1788 Oral Covenant[47]

In the year of our Lord one thousand seven hundred and eighty-eight, the year in which most of the members of the Church were gathered, the following order and Covenant was then, and from time to time after, made known and understood, received, and entered into by us, members of the Church, agreeably to our understanding of the order and Covenant of the Church in gospel order.

It then was, and still is our faith, being confirmed by our experience, that there can be no Church in complete order according to the law of Christ, without a joint-interest and union, in which all the members have an equal right and privilege according to their calling and needs, in things spiritual and temporal.

And in this, we have a greater privilege and opportunity of doing good to each other, as well as to the rest of mankind, and of receiving according to our needs, jointly and equally, one with another, agreeably to the following articles of Covenant.

First. All, or as many of us as were of age to act for ourselves, who offered ourselves as members of the Church, were to do it freely and voluntarily as a religious duty, and according to our own faith and desire.

Second. Youth and children, being under age, were not to be received as members or as being under the immediate care and government of the Church, except by the request of free consent, of both their parents, if living; but if they were left by one of their parents to the care of the other, then by the request of free consent of that parent, but if the child had no parents, then by the request or free consent of such person or persons as had just and lawful right in the care of the child, together with the child's own desire.

Third. All who were received as members, being of age, who had any substance or property and were free from debt or any just demand from those that were without, such as creditors or heirs, were allowed to bring in their substance as their natural and lawful right; and to give it as a part of the joint-interest of the Church, according to their own faith and desire; to be under the order and government of the Deacons or overseers of the temporal interest of the Church, for the use and support of the Church, or for any other use that the gospel might require, according to the understanding and discretion of those members with whom it was intrusted, and who were appointed to that office and care.

Fourth. All the members 'who were received into the Church were to possess one joint-interest as a religious right; that is, all were to have just and equal rights and privileges according to their needs in the use of all things in the church — without any difference being made, on account of what any of us brought in, so long as we remained in obedience to the order and government of the Church, and were holden in relation as members. All the members were, likewise, equally holden, according to their abilities, to maintain and support one joint-interest in union and conformity to the order and government of the Church.

Fifth. As it was not the duty nor purpose of the Church in uniting into Church-order to gather and lay up an interest of this world's goods, but what we became possessed of by honest industry, more than for our own support, was to be devoted to charitable uses, for the relief of the poor and such other uses as the gospel might require. Therefore, it was and still is our faith never to bring debt or blame against the Church or each other for any interest or services which we have bestowed to the joint-interest of the Church, but freely to give our time and talents, as Brethren and Sisters, for the mutual good one of another and other charitable uses, according to the order of the Church.

Marguerite Melcher says that in 1801, when the growing prosperity of the northern Shaker communities demanded new provisions for the business management of the Shaker property, the two following paragraphs were added:

And we do, by these presents, solemnly covenant with each other for ourselves and assigns, never hereafter to bring debt or demand against the said Deacons, nor their successors, nor against any member of the Church or community, jointly or severally, on account of any of our services or property thus devoted and consecrated to the aforesaid sacred and charitable uses.

And we also covenant with each other to subject ourselves in union, as Brethren and Sisters, who are called to follow Christ in Regeneration, in obedience to the order, rules and government of the Church. And this covenant shall be a sufficient witness for us before all men and in all cases relating to the possession, order, and use of the joint-interest of the Church. In testimony whereof, we have, both Brethren and Sisters, hereunto subscribed our names, in the presence of each other, this twenty-fourth day of June, in the year of our Lord, one thousand eight hundred and one.

2. *A Covenant Signed by Members Entering a Lower Order*

The following text was found by Daryl Chase in the archives of the New York Historical Society.[48] It was to be signed by postulants seeking admission into the novitiate order of the church:

Whereas, I, the undersigned, have this day attached myself as probationary member to the United Society of Believers at _____ and being my desire to live with said Society according to the known faith and customs thereof, that I may receive the benefits arising from the observance of the rules, regulations, moral and religious instructions of the same.

Therefore, agreeable to the custom of said Society, I hereby covenant, promise and agree, that I will never prefer any account, claim, nor demand against the said Society, or any member or members thereof, for the use of any money or property brought into said Society, nor for any labor or service which I may perform or render while residing in the same, over and above what I may receive in food, clothing, washing, and other necessary support: And, whereas, it is further mutually understood and agreed that I shall be free to withdraw from said Society whenever I am dissatisfied therewith, and that after sufficient and timely notice shall have been given by me I shall receive all the money and other property which I brought into said Society, or their value at the time it was brought in.

Therefore I further agree and promise that so long as I am permitted to enjoy the benefits and privileges of said Society I will faithfully conform to the rules thereof, and will not find fault with the said rules, requirements, regulations, worship or teachings, by acting or speaking against the same so as to create dissatisfaction disunion, or inharmony in the Family; provided this shall not be so construed as to prevent a free and respectful inquiry of the leading authority into the reasons of said rules and regulations; and if I shall fail to comply with this agreement such failure shall be deemed sufficient cause for loss of membership with said Society, and upon being desired so to do by the leading suthority of the Family in which I reside will peaceably withdraw from the same.

Witness my hand the _____ day of _____ A.D. 18 ____

3. Extracts from Revised Shaker Covenant

In 1873 Roxalana L. Grosvenor edited a complete text of the Shaker Covenant claiming that this was the first time it had been published. This Boston edition of the Shaker Covenant fills eight large pages. The last paragraphs offer a profusion of formulas, all suggesting the same obsessive need to protect the society from members who, after leaving the church, might ask a civil court to invalidate the economic decision made when they first entered the Church Order.

Article 6, Section 5: As we esteem the mutual possession and enjoyment of the consecrated interest and privileges of the Church a valuable consideration, fully adequate to any amount of personal interest, labor or service, devoted or consecrated by any individual; we, therefore, covenant and agree, in conformity with an established and well-known principle of the Church, that no person whatever under its care and protection, can be employed for wages of any kind, on his or her individual account, and that no ground is or can be afforded for the recovery of any property or service devoted or consecrated as aforesaid; and it is also agreed that in case of the removal of any member or members from one family, society or branch of the Church to another, his, her or their previous signature or signatures to the Church or Family Covenant from whence such member or members shall have removed, shall forever bar all claims which are incompatible with the true intent and meaning of the Covenant, in the same manner as if such removal had not taken place. . . .

Article 7, Section 1: According to the faith of the Gospel which we have received and agreeable to the uniform practice of the Church of Christ from its first establishment in this Society, we convenant and agree to dedicate, devote, consecrate and give up, and by this Covenant we do solemnly and conscientiously dedicate, devote, consecrate and give up ourselves and services together with all our temporal interest to the service of God and the support and benefit of the Church of this community, and to such other pious and charitable purposes as the Gospel may require, to be under the care and direction of such elders, deacons, and trustees as are or may be appointed and established in the Church by the authority aforesaid.

Article 7, Section 2: Whereas, in pursuance of the requirement of the Gospel, and in the full exercise of our faith, reason and understanding, we have freely and voluntarily sacrificed all self-interest, and consecrated and devoted our persons, services and property, as aforesaid, to the pious and benevolent purposes of the Gospel; Therefore, we do hereby solemnly and conscientiously, for ourselves and our heirs, release and quitclaim to the deacons, or acting trustees of the church for the time being, for the uses and purposes aforesaid, all our private personal right, title, interest, claim and demand of, in and to the estate, interest, property, and appurtenances so consecrated, devoted and given up; and we hereby jointly and severally promise and declare in the presence of God, and before these witnesses that we will never hereafter, neither directly nor indirectly, under any circumstances whatever, contrary to the stipulations of this covenant, make nor require any account of any interest, property, labor, or service, nor any division thereof which is, has been, or may be devoted by us, or any of us, to the uses and purposes aforesaid, nor bring any charge of debt or damage, nor hold any claim, nor demand whatever against the church or society, nor against any member thereof, on account of any property or service given, rendered, devoted or consecrated to the aforesaid sacred and charitable purposes.

In confirmation of all the aforesaid statements, covenants, promises, and articles of agreement, we have hereunto subscribed our names and affixed our seals, commencing on this _____ day of _____ in the year of our Lord one thousand eight hundred and _____.[49]

The communal structure implied by these texts is quite clear. It is summed up in Chart no. 12. For the Shakers in general and, above all, for the Church Order, there was no question of organizing a system of worker participation or even a cooperative. All their property was held in common and nothing was transferable to an individual. This was not collective ownership in the usual sense, according to which the property as a whole would belong to the people as a whole, nor was it really property jointly held. For above and beyond all questions of individual ownership rises the right to eminent domain asserted by the Millennial Church. According to the Shakers' own principles, this right of eminent domain could be justified only as a stewardship of properties held "for charitable uses, for the relief of the poor and such other uses as the Gospel might require."[50] To make a comparison, this is halfway between the ecclesiastic conception of church property as the patrimony of the poor[51] and the Marxist principle that property is the eminent domain of humanity as a whole.[52]

The Family was too much concerned with work and production to be a charitable organization,[53] but it was also too monastic to be compared to a Russian collective. However, it did resemble a refuge and it did create an atmosphere of productivity. Like both the Hôtel Dieu and the collective farm, the Shaker Family was conscious of serving a larger goal and therefore holding its properties in the name of something other than itself. That is why, like those other institutions, the Family was haunted by a curious religion of work.

THE RELIGION OF SHAKER COMMUNISM

Shaker acts of charity were addressed not only to the poor, the disinherited, the homeless, and the orphans of the world, but also to their fellow believers. There was a veritable decentralization of economic activity in the cooperative interplay of the various families and communities, and this help, all gratuitous, seems to have been taken for granted. Between the years 1805 and 1813 more than $18,000 was sent from the East to the West so that the new communities in Kentucky and Ohio might acquire more land, and in 1814 the Eastern communities sent $1,515 to Union Village to finance the return of those whom the war and the Indians had driven from Busro Creek.[54] They called this last sum a "free gift and charitable donation." There were many other gifts like it, all part of the Shakers' intercommunity cooperation.

But the style of Shaker communism can be seen most clearly in the religious justifications given for their group behavior. We have already pointed out the role played by the comparison which the True Believers made between themselves and the Pentecostal communities of early Christianity. This was not the only biblical justification for Shaker communism. They also claimed to be inspired by the Mosaic laws or, to use the phrase of Frederick Evans, by "Mosaic communism."

This reference to the Mosaic texts is not unusual in the history of cooperative communities.[55] Elder Evans was particularly fervent on the subject; and these texts were probably responsible for the manner in which the Shakers celebrated Sunday. The relation between cyclical periods of repose and economic activity fascinated Evans. In the essay appended to his *Autobiography* he reflected on the fact that the ancient Jews had four Sabbaths: the Sabbath of days, the Sabbath of months, the Sabbath of years, and the Sabbath of Sabbaths. On the Sabbath of days no one worked for anyone else, but everyone consumed alike, as all had done when God gave them manna in the desert. The Sabbath of months was the harvest season, when the poor man could glean in the fields of his rich neighbor and so make up for some of the inadequacies of his own production. The Sabbath of years was the time one settled one's debts. The Sabbath of Sabbaths was the day when the land itself would be redistributed.

Evans remarked that the Jews cultivated their lands scientifically and explained that when they came into the land of Canaan each family received a lot which was to be his homestead. He cited as another principle of Mosaic law that all men have a right to the land on which they live. This, said Evans, is the law of nature and the law of God, and quite contrary to the laws found in Christianity.[56] Evans based his defense of Shaker agrarian policies on this theory of the community's eminent domain, a theory which the Families had already put into practice and justified by citations from both Old and New Testaments. The elder argued that individual ownership of land was at the origin of all the social upheavals in the modern world.[57]

To these theoretical justifications of religious communism the Shakers added a practical consideration: their theory and special practice of Holy Communion. We know that, directly or indirectly, it was their theories about food which influenced the Manichaeans to abandon the Eucharist. They replaced the Lord's Supper with a refinement in their own eating habits whereby "light" would be distilled from the body of the Elect who had consumed foods containing varying amounts of "darkness."[58] There is some similarity between this Manichaean "refinement" and Shaker practices, but above all there are differences. The similarity: both Shakers and Manichaeans rejected the Eucharist as it was practiced in other Christian churches. The main difference: dietary laws played only a secondary (and later) role in the Shaker repast.[59]

The Shakers gave many reasons for dropping the sacrament of Holy Communion; among these were the following: the early Christian church did not practice it;[60] a large part of the Lord's Supper ceremony follows the Old Testament law and should be considered as nothing more than a prefiguration of the law Christ was to announce;[61] although the Eucharist is a symbol of union, it has been the cause of bitter disputes and disunion among Christians;[62] the fact that the Lord said, "Do this in remembrance of me," does not establish the sacrament of the Eucharist any more than his command, "Do as I have done to you," made a sacrament of washing each other's feet.[63]

Last and above all, the Shakers felt that the sacrament as it existed in other churches was a travesty of Christian reality; for, they said, reality was to be found only in a community living and breathing according to the principles of Christ. Although dietary laws played practically no part in Shaker life, they believed that eating was the fundamental act of living. For them the basic rule of the table was to eliminate all social distinctions during this fundamental act of human life, and they believed that this was achieved in the Shaker community and nowhere else, since the members of this community had died to themselves and to the world. Everytime they sat down at table together, they were witness to the death of the Lord (1 Cor. 11:26) and the life which emanated from his sacrifice (John 6:48–56).

In the *Millennial Church* the reader is reminded that confessions of religious fervor and rituals of bread and wine are no equivalent to what is felt by true disciples of Christ. On the other hand, says the Shaker text, the greatest practical demonstration of authentic love and disinterested goodness that can be given on earth is found in places where all are blessed with a heart and a soul, where the rich and the poor can eat and drink together at the same table, serenely sharing a common good and mutually participating, both spiritually and temporally, in each other's joys and sorrows. The authors of the *Millennial Church* then explain that in communities patterned after those established by the early Christians, where believers ate and drank together in harmony and Christian love, members can participate in the Lord's Supper every day. In such places of belief, harmony, and love they can truly announce the death of the Lord by their own example, showing all that they have died to selfish and particularist nature, and that by so dying they have been raised to a level of spiritual life never attained by the religions of the world.[64]

In the last analysis, it looks as if the Shakers, like the Manichaeans, wanted to dispense with the Eucharist as a sacrament and substitute for it the *immanent reality* of a transubstantiation. The Manichaeans had called for a transubstantiation of physical nature in the body of the individual Perfect. The Shakers called for a transubstantiation of human society and its "generations" in the community of regenerated believers. For both Shakers and Manichaeans the traditional idea of a sacrament was no more than a ritual curtain covering a reality that was not there. For the Shakers, just as the only baptism was the Baptism of the Spirit by an act of confession and a decision to "take up one's cross," the only Eucharist was a collective consumption of what had been collectively produced; and for them it was these economic practices which day by day fashioned and refashioned the Family body in which the blood of the Spirit circulated. Thus it was that the Shaker meal transformed communism into a religion. It was their custom to eat in silence and to kneel in silent prayer before and after every meal. They never forgot the lesson of the Quakers that silence is the supreme form of praying.[65]

II. Members in the Families

One might expect to find that the socio-economic egalitarianism among the Shakers would have made their Families resemble certain anarchist communities in which, historically, an exaggerated fear of authority quickly induced a disintegration of the whole social body. There were a dozen of these anarchist groups in France at the beginning of the twentieth century,[66] and they abounded in nineteenth-century America,[67] but between them and the Shakers there was no resemblance at all. The Shaker Families should be classed under the genus of authority and the species of religious authority. They were early dominated by a rigidly organized hierarchy which seems to have rapidly gained control of the movement at the very time when, paradoxically, the movement was claiming that everyone had an equal right to prophesy.

After describing how the Shakers' religious communism dictated an individual's relation to goods and property, it remains for us to examine how their "political theocracy" regulated his relations with other people.

THE HIERARCHICAL STRUCTURE

From top to bottom the structure of a Shaker society was affected by the fact that it was a joint enterprise of men and women, and that, consequently, all responsibilities were shared by couples, sometimes even by two couples. Thus a Family had two men ministers and two women ministers, two elders and two eldresses, two deacons and two deaconesses.[68] This hierarchy of double offices was theocratic. In it the old aphorism about all things coming from the Lord appeared to be literally true, and later we shall examine how the Shakers managed to make the prerogatives of power originate in a manifestation of the Spirit. Most Christian reform movements, especially since the Reformation, have tried for some degree of democracy in religion and have returned to the folk custom of popular elections. This was not true of the Shakers, who considered any system of elections within the church as a contrivance of the Antichrist. For them the election of bishops by popular vote during the first centuries of the Christian era was an undeniable sign that church decadence had already set in.[69]

The Ministry

The ministry was usually a team of four leaders, both men and women, who held almost absolute power over their particular society, sometimes over two or three societies that had been federated into a bishopric. There was one ministry for each society or bishopric. The ministry at Mount Lebanon dominated all the others and, consequently, all the other societies. This domination was never seriously challenged, despite the autonomous tendencies of the societies in the West.

Since the ministry had the largest voice in designating all responsibilities within its particular society or bishopric, since the ministry of Mount Lebanon dominated all the others, and since the leading elder at Mount Lebanon dominated the other three members of the four-person team, this last-named elder was the man (or woman) who wielded supreme power over the entire society. Thus an examination of how he was chosen should disclose the source of authority in the Shaker hierarchy. Investiture of the ministries in the other societies followed similar rules.[70]

In principle, God chose Ann Lee, who chose James Whittaker, who chose Joseph Meacham, and so on. The lines of authority appeared to follow a principle of "parental" succession.[71] Yet, as indicated by disputes over the second and third investitures, this principle does not seem to have been constitutionally established any more than its mode of application. After those first three investitures, the selection of a new leader was facilitated by the fact that the surviving members of the four-man ministry were all in favor of the same person to fill the vacant post, and that the former leading elder, when still alive, would most likely have told them his choice of successor. This is summed up in the *Millennial Church* by a statement to the effect that all ministers are chosen from the Church Order by their predecessors, and that their authority is confirmed and established by a spontaneous unanimity of the whole church body.[72]

This notion of spontaneous unanimity was not entirely a figure of speech; and, at least during the early years of the society, when a candidate for the ministry faced the assembled members of the Church Order, the confrontation seemed to be a veritable trial of force. At least that is the impression one gets from the Shaker accounts of the investiture of James Whittaker and James Meacham, the second and third successors to Ann Lee.

White and Taylor describe how after Mother Ann's funeral James Whittaker spoke to the audience and begged his brothers and sisters to pray for him and to help him follow the path of God, saying that they had to be more vigilant and faithful than ever, since those most capable of protecting the flock were no longer present. According to this account, Whittaker's address was so solemnly impressive, so effectively mixed with tears, that everyone was profoundly moved, and it became evident that the mantle of Mother Ann had fallen onto him. At this point Elders Joseph Meacham, Calvin Harlow, and John Hocknell stepped forward and recognized him as their elder.[73] However, the choice had not always been so evident. In another passage of the same text we read that "after Mother Ann's death, the faith of all had been tried, few knowing on whom the gift of leadership would fall." In the end it was the American faction, probably supported by the Shakers' English patron, John Hocknell, which had carried the day and accepted Whittaker despite the opposition of James Shepherd and John Partington. These two men, who had been members of the original group of English immigrants, preferred to secede from the society rather than submit to the leadership of James Whittaker. White and Taylor explain that their opposition was concealed from the rest of the membership "as a matter of prudence."[74] and that Whittaker did not reveal until later that he had had a disagreement with them.

When Joseph Meacham succeeded James Whittaker, his investiture was carried out in the same two stages: first, a showdown with the leaders; second, ratification by an assembly, with a unanimity which was implicit rather than expressed by vote. Once again the confrontation began with the funeral oration honoring the dead elder. Joseph Meacham, his younger brother David, and Calvin Harlow were candidates for the position of leading elder left vacant by Whittaker. These men addressed the audience, which was particularly numerous for the occasion, and "for a time Elder Joseph felt the silent opposition of the people of the place who were in attendance. The oppression was so great that at the grave he shook and trembled from head to foot, and then spoke under the influence of the Spirit with such power that even Believers marveled. He declared that the work of God would increase and the power of God would overcome all things."[75] The sight of the Pentecostal powers descending on Elder Joseph was supposed to be the sign of his election, but on this particular occasion the choice did not seem to have won the unanimous consent of the assembly, and for two months he shared the leadership with his partners, David Meacham and Calvin Harlow. Then, after two months had passed, the copartners left on a mission to the societies in the East, leaving Joseph Meacham at the Mount Lebanon headquarters to begin his great task of "gathering." Only then did his investiture seem permanent. White and Taylor tell us that Meacham's work was so mighty and that God's will was so manifest in the progress made by the people, that when the other two elders returned from their mission, they clearly saw that God had annointed him as leader of the flock. On their own initiative, they recognized him as their elder (first stage). And the unanimous agreement with which the believers accepted this designation was "cordial and spontaneous"[76] (second stage).

After the ministry of Joseph Meacham, the church was in Gospel Order. Its system of four elders selected by cooptation minimized the uncertainties of parental succession. Codification and simplification of this process for selecting the leading elder is found in the Covenant:

The said primary administration of parental authority has been and is perpetuated as follows: Namely, that the first in that office and calling possesses the right given by the sanction of divine authority, through the first founders of this Society, to prescribe or direct any regulation or appointment which they may judge most proper and necessary respecting the Ministry or any other important matter which may concern the welfare of Church, subsequent to their decease. But in case no such regulation or appointment be so prescribed or directed, then the right to direct and authorize such regulation and appointment devolves upon the surviving members of the Ministry. . . . Such appointments being officially communicated to all concerned, and receiving the general approbation of the Church, are confirmed and supported in the Society.[77]

This same process applied to the choice of ministries in the individual societies, with the extra provision that all appointments were to be approved by the Mount Lebanon ministry, which was recognized as the center of directives for the United Society.[78]

As for the ministry itself, it was absolute. All decisions, both spiritual and practical, and all nominations of elders, trustees, and deacons were in its hands.

The Trustees

On the level of the "society" or "bishopric" the absolute power of the ministry was matched by an economic power granted to a number of superdeacons or bursars, called "trustees." They were responsible for the economic and financial management of the community. As custodians of the goods and property of the local societies, they were in charge of all transactions (buying and selling to the world), all accounting, and the records for the archives.[79] All commercial and juridical operations were done in their name and over their signature. The local assembly had no power to ask for an audit or a report of stewardship. Since the trustees had complete control of all buying, selling, stocking, and loaning, their economic powers set them above the deacons, who were responsible for managing all work within the Family.[80]

The trustees' freedom of action and the powers related to the performance of their duties were, however, severely controlled by the ministers. In their presence the trustee had to sign a formal declaration attesting that in the name of, in the place of, and in the interests of the society, he assumed responsibility for the goods and properties listed on a detailed inventory that had been made at the time when he had taken office. His accounts were examined once a year by the ministry in the presence of witnesses. In sum, there was a continuous, careful, and sometimes bothersome check brought to bear on the lives of these businessmen–believers, exposed as they were to all the dangers attending contact with the outside world. Trustees traveled by twos and threes. They were not permitted to go on trips lasting more than four weeks. They were forbidden to participate in unnecessary conversations with people of the world. And when conversations did become necessary, the trustees were expected to give an accurate account of them to the ministry.

In the last analysis, being a trustee was a delicate job. If a trustee committed the serious sin of incurring debts for the community or if he committed the no less serious sin of becoming too important in his job, he was recalled and replaced.[81] Among the Shakers a job like this was not an envious one, and the Covenant made provisions for cases when the post was "wholly vacant"—the only position for which this clause was deemed necessary. It was also the only post in the Shaker hierarchy which women did not hold along with the men.

Elders and Deacons

On the Family level the eldership and the deaconry repeated the functions performed on the society level by the ministry and the trustees (see Chart no. 13). On this level also the elders were four in number, half men and half women. They were responsible for the spiritual guidance of the Family: for instructions, advice, conduct of the daily meetings, encouragements, reprimands, and so on. They were named to the post by the ministry, and after assuming office, they participated, in an unspecified way (probably as consultants), in the decisions of the ministry and the election of the trustees. Deacons and deaconesses were likewise named to their jobs by the ministry after consultation with the Family elders. They were responsible for the organization and management of all work in the Family except commercial operations, which were left to the trustees. They acted as both personnel and production managers;

CHART 13. *Power Structure in the United Society*

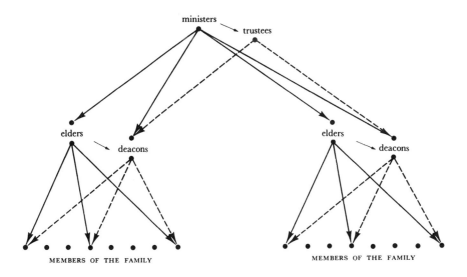

all caretakers and foremen were under their orders. They supervised, checked, and, when necessary, guided the members of the Family in their different tasks.[82] They were responsible for maintaining the greatest possible balance between production and consumption in the Family (auto-consumption), even if this meant calling on the trustees for help when this balance was threatened in one way or another.

Thus the deacons were dependent on the general supply office, managed by the trusteeship of the society, and on the collective priorate, composed of the four Family elders. The Shakers valued the deaconry. In its functions of stewardship they thought they had restored an apostolic institution of the old Pentecostal community.

This distribution of responsibility and the decentralization of economic practices called for a rigid centralization of political authority. As can be seen in Chart no. 13, which represents the interplay of powers, the lines of authority avoid dictatorship only on one point: the at least tacit assent of the assembly of believers, who must recognize the presence of the Spirit in the leading elder. Thus it would have been theoretically possible for a wave of rebelling prophecies to break through the lines of authority even though, because of an esoteric cooptation, they formed a closed circuit. In fact, this type of competing voice did appear at the time of the first successions, but did not seem to have had any consequences. After 1830 the administration brought prophesying under control. Indeed, it was at about that time that the prophets or "instruments," as they were called, began transmitting messages from Ann Lee to the effect that the founding Mother would not recognize as her children any of those who resisted the authority of the established ministry. Daryl Chase quotes a cynical observation by a Western minister, one of McNemar's adversaries. At first, he had been served by "revelations" supporting his antagonism to McNemar, but later he was disserved by other "revelations" opposing his campaign against the vegetarian dietary laws which were making life miserable for all good Shakers who enjoyed meat, pork, tea, coffee, and tobacco. He said: "Every time I have consulted an instrument he has told me that I am right." The cynical minister went on to say that he doubted very much if there was a single example in the East or in the West of a minister who had clearly stated his convictions on what was good and what was bad, and to whom the visionary had not invariably answered all questions in a way favorable to the minister's point of view. He added that this was undoubtedly the case when the messages came through forbidding the use of meat in the Harvard society, in Massachusetts, and then spread to all the other societies in the country. The minister finished his remarks on convenient "revelations" by suggesting that if the Harvard ministry had been convinced that butter and potatoes should not be eaten, then there would certainly have been an abundance of messages from the spirit world to confirm this opinion, and the potato blight would have been offered as incontestable proof of the vision's authenticity.[83]

To complete the picture of the Shaker power structure

one should add that those to whom the Covenant had given plenary powers were not required to give any account of their activities to their Families or to their societies;[84] all appeals to a superior authority were transmitted only through the channels of the hierarchy;[85] and expulsion was the penalty for anyone who questioned the good faith of those wielding authority.[86] With this in mind, one can understand the disillusioned remark of Hervey Elkins, who defected from the Shakers after fifteen years in the senior order: "The Shaker Government in many points resembles that of the military."[87] What Elkin's attitude does not take into consideration is that it was this rigid structure which had made possible the Shaker success during the first half of the century; nor does it recognize that, at the time of Elkin's writing, this severe discipline appeared doubly rigid, since the evils it was invented to combat were already beginning to lose their significance.

LIVING CONDITIONS OF THE MEMBERS

To get a more complete picture of daily life in the Shaker communities, we must examine their living conditions, their working conditions, and their socio-economic code of behavior.

Living Conditions

These were described in detail by Charles Nordhoff. From his monograph and the memoirs of Hervey Elkins, which Nordhoff had consulted, one can glean a wealth of details, to which should be added all those so meticulously compiled by Edward D. Andrews.[88]

The daily schedule. Shaker life followed a regular rhythm for the day and for the week. The daily schedule went something like this:

4:30 A.M. (or 5:30 in winter): Rise to the sound of the bell. Kneel for a short silent prayer. Personal ablutions. Clean the room.

6:00 A.M. (*or 6:30*): Breakfast, preceded and followed, as were all the meals, by kneeling for a silent prayer. Food was eaten in silence.

Morning Work Period: Work in the house, in the fields, or in the workshops.

11:50 A.M.: The bell indicates end of the work period.

12:00 A.M.: Noon meal, in the same manner as breakfast. Men, women, and children at separate tables. Sometimes there are separate tables for vegetarians and nonvegetarians.

Afternoon Work Period:

5:50 P.M.: End of afternoon period.

6:00 P.M.: Evening meal.

7:30–8:00 P.M.: During this half hour, a deep silence. Each member retires to his room, where the occupants of the room stand together in one or two lines, bending forward, supporting themselves by placing their hands on their knees, and holding this position without falling backward and without falling asleep. (This was the position for silent prayer.)

8:00 P.M. (*or 8:30*): Daily meeting.

9:00 P.M. (*or 9:30*): Curfew.

The weekly rhythm was marked by the different types of daily meetings and by the solemn regulations for behavior on Sunday.

Monday: Information meeting in which members listen to letters from other societies, articles clipped from newspapers (carefully avoiding all mention of accidents and crimes), extracts from magazines (especially opinions on events of historical importance).

Tuesday: Meeting for singing and dancing.

Wednesday: Meeting organized for exchange of ideas and various kinds of conversation, "including ones in which nothing is said," according to Hervey Elkins.

Thursday: "Laboring meeting." This is a religious gathering, probably similar to the "Radenije" of the Khlysti. It is likely to include an exhausting dance to rhythms which arouse a collective exultation.

Friday: More songs and dances.

Saturday: Weekly religious service of the society. All Families meet together in the meetinghouse for this occasion. Talks by the ministers and the elders. Songs and dances.

Sunday: Absolute rest. No profane reading, no work, no cooking, no washing, no hair-cutting, no nail-paring, no shoe-shining, and so forth. The evening meal was pushed ahead to 4:00 P.M. During the evening period groups of four to ten brothers and groups of a like number of sisters would visit each other for conversation on the news of the week and the affairs of the society as well as those of the world outside. Sunday meetings may be held in the "meetinghouse" (church Family) or in the assembly hall found in each Family house. These meetings and the dancing and singing have been described by visitors from the "world" in many printed accounts. (This is the only occasion when the Shakers would get together in groups smaller than the Family. Careful attention was paid to any personal ties which might develop during these conversation periods, and to avoid them the composition of the visiting groups was carefully controlled, varied, and often modified.)[89]

Relations between men and women except during the official colloquies, were reduced to a silent copresence at table. The rules of the order had assembled them under the same roof, but a draconian custom separated them from each other once they were there. Men and women did not shake hands; they worked in separate workshops, ate in the same dining hall but at separate tables, and assembled in the same meetinghouse, but were in separate groups for services, dances, and singing. Even the elders and the ministers were subject to this reserve. The Shaker sisters cleaned the brothers' rooms and took care of their clothes, but this was not the occasion for any personal contacts. Every morning after rising and performing his ablutions, the brother would fold his bedclothes over two chairs, open the windows to air out the room, and then leave. The house-keeping sisters did not come into the men's rooms until after they had left. During the workday a sister was not permitted to enter one of the brothers' workshops unless she was accompanied by another woman. No brother and sister were allowed to engage in conversation except in the presence of a third person. And if the brothers or sisters needed any technical help from each other, they were required to make a formal request for this through the deacon or the deaconess. Thus there was a continual dividing line between the sexes in this mixed monasticism.[90]

The Shaker community was like a cloister. No one could leave his Family without the permission of the elders. Conversation between members of different Families was forbidden unless such interchange was necessary. In that case the talk was succinct and discreet. A brother who shook hands with a woman unbeliever, or a sister who touched a man unbeliever, was expected to tell the elders about it before appearing at the next Shaker meeting. Such gestures were tolerated only when it was the outsider who had been the first to extend his hand. All visits to the outside world, even to one's own natural family, were forbidden, except in cases where such visits were likely to result in a conversion. All visits from one Shaker society to another were controlled by the ministry, who prescribed the number and names of the visitors and told the group exactly what path to follow in going there and in coming back.

Thus the Shakers, in their daily lives, were concerned only with themselves and were physically bound together. The Family life had as its center the Family house, and for them this building played a role similar to the one played by the "longhouses" in the ethnologists' descriptions of joint-families in primitive societies. All members of the Family lived in the same big house. Only the ministers had private apartments and workshops. The upper floors of the Family house was divided into rooms which could lodge from four to eight people. Each room contained a bed for each occupant, the necessary toilet equipment, a mirror, a stove for heat in the winter, a writing table, and an abundance of chairs which, when they were not in use, were hung on the wall. A wide hallway separated the men's dormitory from the women. On the floor, but not nailed down, there were soft-colored mats made by the Shakers themselves.

On the ground floor were the kitchens, pantries, store-rooms, and the large common dining hall. The novitiate Family house had an extra, separate dining hall which served as an inn for visitors to the community.

Surrounding the Family house were the different out-buildings necessary for work: the sisters' workshop, where they made clothes, baskets, and so on; the brothers' work-shop, where they did woodwork and made brooms and brushes; the laundry, the stables, the fruit-sorting shed, the mill, the furniture shop, the metal working shop, and so on. Everyone who visited these communities noticed the striking cleanliness of both buildings and grounds. On the walls, as visitors never failed to remark, were the wooden pegs from which the Shakers hung unused objects such as hats, baskets, and empty chairs.[91]

Building construction was simple and excluded any archi-tectural effects meant to beautify the appearance. When Nordhoff asked Elder Frederick Evans whether, if they were to build anew, they would aim at more beautiful struc-tures, Evans replied: "No, the beautiful, as you call it is absurd and abnormal. It has no business with us. The divine man has no right to waste money upon what you would call beauty, in his house or in his daily life, while there are people living in misery." He went on to explain to Nordhoff that "in building anew, he would take care to have more light, a more equal distribution of heat, and a more general care for protection and comfort, because these things tend to health and long life. But no beauty."[92]

There are many available drawings, engravings, and photographs of the Shaker buildings, rooms, costumes, and interior furnishings to supplement those details gleaned from writings by and about the believers. In fact, enough information is given to make certain analogies between these living conditions and those in an abbey or a convent, although the Shakers themselves insistantly refused to admit that there was any similarity. When the societies began to disband, the buildings were secularized. Bestor reports that some of them were converted into schools and at least two of them were used as prison farms.[93]

All reports agree that working conditions among the Shakers were humane and pleasant. The collective rhythm gave their workday an attractive liveliness. As a rule the men worked outside, the women, inside. Thus the taboo which separated the sexes also prevented women from practicing certain trades. "Suppose a woman wanted, in your Family, to be a blacksmith, would you consent?" Nordhoff asked Elder Evans. "No," was the reply, "because this would bring men and women into relations which we do not think wise."[94] Yet the women did have their own workshop, where certain collective trades were allowed. Moreover, a system of alternating jobs, carefully regulated by the deacons, made it possible to vary the different tasks. The young women were assigned to washing and ironing. As for the kitchen and related services, those tasks were apparently not enjoyed and were done by the month in rotation.[95]

There was a similar system of alternation in the men's jobs. One visitor thought he saw in this a vestige of Fourierism. But work on the land was always the basic activity for Shaker men. "Every commune, to prosper, must be founded, so far as its industry goes, on agriculture," said Elder Evans. "Only the simple labors and manners of a farming people can hold a community together. Wherever we have departed from this rule to go into manufacturing, we have blundered."[96] Evans also expected these rural labors to result in a maximum of economic self-rule, which, he thought, was the only sound way to set up the moral and material welfare of a community. "Moreover, a community, he said, should as far as possible, make or produce all it uses."[97]

No exceptions were made in the obligation to perform manual labor. Even the ministers and the elders were expected to do their share. True, the ministers did lodge apart, but they had a workshop of their own, and when Nordhoff visited Mount Lebanon, he watched the four ministers make baskets during the time left over from their trips and the administrative tasks.[98]

Their refusal to set up industry and their demand for

self-rule made it impossible for the Shakers to organize a collective activity that would complement agriculture. This led them, en masse, to become extraordinarily skillful artisans. Indeed, Shaker-made chairs were widely sold in the Eastern United States. In MacLean's bibliography numbers 160–85 are devoted to Shaker publications concerning their own manufactured products. Herbs and medicinal powders predominated, but this was not the only field in which they showed their ingenuity. In their list of Shaker inventions are many things which, after all, were no more than lucky finds or even possibly some pirated ideas. However, it is quite possible that these believers did rediscover for themselves things that others had already found or invented elsewhere. Nevertheless, their list is very impressive and suggests a wide range of interests.

We can skip over the horse collar and the metal pen point, which they claim to have invented,[99] and divide Shaker contributions into three categories: inventions for improving men's productivity, inventions for economizing women's labor, and inventions contributing to the increased comfort of the community.

To the first category belong the following techniques and machines, claimed as Shaker invention: the screw propeller, a rotary harrow, a turbine water wheel, a threshing machine, a way of joining wood with tenon and mortise, a planing machine, a circular saw, a washing machine, a nail-cutting machine, a machine for twisting whip handles and lashes, a technique for making chairs, a foundry for ironware, a way of making brooms, brushes, and mats, a technique for drying corn, and so forth. To the second category belong pot handles, butter workers, clothespins, machines to cut fruit and shell peas, a silk reeling machine, a four-compartment rotary oven, and so on.

These Shaker ascetics must have had some taste for certain material comforts, since they included in their list the invention of cast-iron stoves to replace fireplaces, a hot-air heater for winter, and a ventilator for cooling the kitchen in summer.[100]

There is no doubt that both the working conditions and

the products produced were determined by the fact that the Shakers lived in a community of craftsmen. They were never able and never wanted to transform it into a technical society.[101] Thus, with the passing of time, they were unable to meet industrial competition, and as soon as they began to make purchases in a market furnished by big industry, the Shaker artisans had to shut down their shops. Evans complained about this bitterly: "We used to have more looms than now, but cloth is sold so cheaply that we gradually began to buy. It is a mistake; we buy more cheaply than we can make, but our home-made cloth is much better that what we can buy; and we have now to make three pairs of trousers, for instance, where before we made one. Thus our little looms would even now be more profitable—to say nothing of the independence we secure in working them."[102] One would almost think this was Ghandi speaking. This was not the only similarity between the Shakers and the principles of the Indian leader.[103]

The Socio-Economic Code of Behavior

Religious movements tending toward dualism have always looked down on production, particularly agricultural production. Buddha judged that a monk who cultivated the land should do penance, and the Manichaeans were barely tolerant of those who worked the land, since they considered this a sign of and a cause of imperfection.[104] But in the case of the Shakers, who transferred these doubts to industrial production, all suspicion disappeared as soon as they considered agriculture or, more generally, the human labor invested in it. "Hands to work and heart to God." The Shakers remained faithful to Mother Ann's slogan. The Shaker code of morality was based on the value of work, thrift, and asceticism, and it made the hope of salvation synonymous with the practice of economic virtues. In this they are not unlike the Methodists,[105] but in the case of the Shakers they applied this work-morality to the structure of their paramonastic community.

Work: "At Enfield, New Hampshire, some of the Believers in that place, having more zeal than wisdom and understanding, imbibed a notion that they were not to continue in this world but a few years, and concluded that they need not make any further provisions for a living, in consequence of which they made a very undue use of their property, by squandering it away in a profuse manner.... On hearing of it, Mother ... bade them go home and set out apple trees, and raise calves, and make provisions as though they were to live a thousand years, and gather something to do good with."[106]

Speaking to the reapers, Mother Ann said: "Cut your grain clean; God has caused it to grow, and you ought to be careful to save it."[107] To Lucy Bishop, who was scrubbing a room, she said: "Clean your room well; for good spirits will not live where there is dirt. There is no dirt in heaven."[108] On another occasion, speaking to some other sisters who had been washing the floor, she said: "You ought to be neat, and clean; for there are no slovens nor sluts in heaven."[109] On another occasion she said: "The devil tempts others, but, an idle person tempts the devil. When you are at work, doing your duty in the gift of God, the devil can have no power over you, because then there is no room for temptations." And again: "I am prudent and saving of every temporal blessing which I receive, as though I had labored for it with my own hands; and you ought to be so too."[110]

Thrift: "Cornelius Goodale, being at the Church at Watervliet, in January, 1784, and being, at that time, under some embarrassments in his temporal circumstances, asked Mother Ann if it would not be better for him to sell his farm, and buy a less one, and so pay his debts. Mother Ann answered, 'You better not. The people of God do not sell their farms to pay their debts; but they put their hands to work, and gather something by their industry, to pay their debts with, and keep their farms.'"[111]

Here is another example: "In the last year of Mother's ministry, a number of Brethen and Sisters being assembled together at Watervliet, Mother spoke very largely concerning the great loss of the American people in many things, and particularly, concerning their involving themselves in debt. She directed her discourse on this subject mostly to one who was very deeply involved and not able to clear himself. She said, 'You will go and run into debt, and not only bring yourself into bondage, but your family also, and bring distress on your creditors; such evil management will forever be a loss to the soul till the creditors are paid, and the soul finds repentance.'"[112]

Asceticism: Shaker daily life did not seem to include any particular system for doing penance. Repentance was part of the prayer during the weekly "laboring meeting" or during the half-hour of silent meditation at the end of the workday. Repentance was also related to their way of life and work. Their cleanliness seems to have been obsessive. The expression "neat and clean" recurs in almost every one of Mother Ann's admonitions.[113] She favored the life of hardship. She condemned the Shaker sisters for huddling around the fire.[114] She forbade idle conversation as time lost from work. In matter of dress, furniture, and table settings she required her people to be simple, practical, and modest. No silver tableware, no jewels, no tablecloths were permitted. The Shakers lived standing up. Laziness, play, and self-indulgence were rigorously proscribed.[115] Shaker furniture will long testify to this inspiration.[116]

From the tone of these moral warnings of Mother Ann, one concludes that Shaker economic efficiency was closely tied to their idea of salvation: There are no idlers in heaven. Laziness tempts the devil. There is another passage in the *Testimonies* which sums up this question with a description of the difficulties Mother Ann and the elders had in instructing the believers how to manage their temporal affairs. They repeatedly told their flock to be industrious, to put their hands to work and their hearts to God, to be neat and clean, to be careful managers, to use the things of the world as if they were not really using them at all, to be prudent and economical, to waste nothing and to let nothing spoil out of carelessness, to avoid both avarice and prodigality, to be good and charitable to the poor, and to incur no debts. The passage continues by explaining that these things were prescribed for the believers in order to assure them spiritual blessings, and that experience had abundantly proved that those who showed small faith in temporal things failed to find blessings in their spiritual life. Thus, concludes this passage of the *Testimonies*, a faithful and wise use of one's time and one's talents in temporal matters was essential if one wished to fall heir to true riches.[117]

After statements such as these it is not surprising that the theme of justification *by faith* found little support among these people so concerned with works, including economic works. In Dunlavy's *Manifesto* we read that, considering all the Apostle James wrote about faith and justification by faith, it is remarkable that he never said "by faith alone."[118] The Epistle of James was one of the Shaker's favorite texts, and Mother Ann loved to have people read the first chapter aloud to her, starting with verse twenty-two:[119] "Be ye doers of the word and not hearers only." She must have relished this text.

III. The United Society in its Relations with the American People

To complete this outline of the socio-economic structure of the United Society we must consider how the Shakers reacted to the big problems of the outside world. This includes the society's attitude to the economic problems of hired and slave labor and its reaction to the socio-political problems raised by the fact of war.

The question of hired labor has already appeared several times in chapter 4 of this study.[120] It was the Shakers' own greediness for land that gave rise to this question. During the first decades of the nineteenth century land was an excellent investment and the Shakers invested all they could muster—

"immoderately," as Frederick Evans explained to Nordhoff. The disproportion between the amount of land owned by a society and the number of productive members in the society led the Shakers to the sordid solution of using adolescents to cultivate the extra fields. They would first "adopt" the youngster and then expect him to work for his subsistence. This abuse grew to such an extent that, in 1850, the State of New York passed a law limiting the amount of land the Shakers could own and the number of apprentices they could acquire. Many of the believers balked at this system. Evans believed that they had everything to lose by maintaining such extended domains, and said that the problems of expansion required all the working hours of their most talented members for projects involving non-Shaker workers on lands outside the Family enclave. He told Nordhoff that any economic advantages were far outweighed by the moral dangers involved.[121]

The end of this period of property expansion coincided with a drop in Shaker recruitment. Previously, there had been too much land for too few men. Henceforth, there would be fewer and fewer men, for the same amount of land, and the practice of engaging hired labor was intensified. The more enlightened elders felt very guilty about this. The letter to Alex Kent cited in chapter 4[122] is a late indication of this malaise, which had started about the middle of the century. Hepworth Dixon reported that for many years the Shakers had bought every piece of land that was for sale, with the result that by midcentury they owned more land than they could cultivate and had to call on the men in neighboring villages for help. These men, reported Dixon, worked easily with the Shakers and under their orders. But, remarked the author of *New America*, it was quite possible that a situation like this, mixing the work of laymen with the work of saints and, of course, submitting the lay worker to a landowner, would develop into a kind of rural feudalism, giving the Shaker owners all the profits and assigning to the others a subordinate rank and the small remuneration of serfs bound to the soil. Dixon said that the Shaker leaders were already aware of this, and since the spiritual purpose for which they had made so many sacrifices in no way resembled the business goals that they were about to achieve, these leaders were beginning to ask themselves whether they had been unfaithful to their principles and whether they should get rid of all land in excess of their needs.[123] The fact is that recruiting declined at a faster rate than the liquidation of excess lands. Not only did the Shaker domains shrink in size, but, one after another, the societies themselves were going to disappear.

The question of slavery was far from simple for the Shakers. Ann Lee's message was certainly antislavery, and the *Testimonies* record a vision in which she saw the poor Negroes, whom white society scorned, saved from their low estate, riding high in the sky with crowns on their heads.[124] But this glorious redemption of the spirit had nothing to do with the problem of liberating black slaves, and the problem of slavery appeared very early in Shaker history in two forms: the owning of slaves and the hiring of slaves owned by others.

The problem of slave ownership was rapidly resolved. Julia Neal in her monograph on South Union has described how this came about. At first there was a black Family, composed of Negroes who belonged either to believers or to the society. This experiment would have been similar to the well-known experiment of Francis Wright at Nashoba, Tennessee,[125] if the Shakers' "black Family" had integrated blacks and whites and if emancipation had been envisaged either as a *fait accompli* or something to come in the future. It is clear that nothing of the sort occurred, since in 1816 the Shaker slave owners were still disputing the question with their ministers. It was only after 1819 that emancipation of slaves became general in the society. In 1830 the last Shaker slave was freed — about fifty years after Ann Lee's message.[126]

The question of the hiring of slaves belonging to non-Shakers was much more difficult. Slaves offered a convenient and cheap solution to the problem of cultivating their over-extended lands, and the Shakers did not hesitate to take advantage of the opportunity to use them. Although in 1836 South Union decided that in principle they would no longer rent black slaves,[127] Daryl Chase points out that in 1862, 140 acres of wheat belonging to this society were still being cultivated by slaves rented from their owners.[128] Justifications were not hard to find. The believers maintained that work was less brutal and more human on their farms and that the slaves preferred to come there. Then there was always the possibility of a conversion, such as the case of Brother Jonah, who, after laboring twenty years on the Shaker farm for a rent of $120 a year paid to his master, was finally bought by the Shakers for $800. He died a year later. In any case, in this geographical location, it was dangerous to be thought an abolitionist.

The New England societies rebelled against these justifications of slavery presented by the societies in Kentucky and Ohio. They accused the Western communities of wanting to get the maximum amount of labor for the least amount of money. Slave labor cost only seven or ten dollars a month per man. No white laborer or free Negro could afford to work for such wages. They challenged the Western societies to pay the Negroes a decent wage, saying that with the difference between this wage and what was paid to his owner, the Negro would soon be able to buy his freedom.[129]

But the Western societies managed to avoid the fundamental questions, as can be seen in the following questionnaire, which in 1860 Elder John Rankin of South Union sent to some of his Northern brethren:

First: Shall *money* or property which has been obtained by the sale of Negro slaves be refused or accepted by the Church of Christ?

Second: If refused how far removed from the sweat and blood of the slave must money or property be, in order to render such money or property acceptable to the Church? Our sugar and coffee come directly from the toiling slave through his master and is acceptable. Should money be equally so?

Third: There is a sister of twenty-five years standing in the society and fifteen years in the Church whose father, in Tennessee, being the owner of some slaves, died intestate. By the laws of that state, 'made and provided' the court has to sell the property, slaves included. The proceeds of this sale brings to the heirs, $2,000 each. We have received for the heir who is with us, $1,600 and soon will have the balance. When Question Number One is answered, we will know what to do.[130]

The tone of the letter reveals how its writer would have the questions answered. We do not know how the Northern brethren replied. At any rate, the Emancipation Act at the end of the Civil War would soon cut the Gordian knot of such specious reasoning.

The attitude of the Shakers during and after the Civil War is a key to understanding their relationship with the rest of the country. Despite the numerous lawsuits, they had lived under a tolerant regime which had permitted them to grow and had spared them from persecutions. It looked as if Ann Lee's prophecy had come true. The New World had proved to be a land favorable to the Gospel, and the Shakers periodically repeated their gratitude:

The effect of the American Revolution was the institution of a Republican form of Government, which entitled all to an equal right in political and religious belief. Thus America became the land of free thought and free speech. . . . This prepared the way for the organization of the *Shaker Church* [in America] where the unadulterated principles of Christianity were recognized and wrought out in the daily lives of its members. Hence the product of this Republican Government was the establishment of a *spiritual* government, moving in a corresponding line with the regulations of the civil polity, yet exceeding it in purity and holiness, although the interior order will be dependent for its increase of members upon the outward order.[131]

But their loyalty was particularly put to the test during the War of Independence and the Civil War. During the first of these wars the founding Mother was thrown into prison and the believers were pestered by mobs and plagued with a flood of pamphlets partly because of their supposed sympathy with the British. Nevertheless, they managed to come through the Revolution without renouncing their pacifism. James

Whittaker told Labdiel Adams, minister of Luneburg, Massachusetts: "We will fight your enemy and the enemy of all mankind, that is, the devil."[132] A goodly number of veterans from this war and from the War of 1812 swelled the Shaker ranks. Their army pensions accumulated in the National Treasury because the Shaker Society refused to collect this pay for military service. Hundreds of thousands of dollars were involved in these uncollected pensions. The money was never collected, but it was not going to be lost to the Shaker cause.

In the decades immediately following the Revolution, state legislation varied on military service. Some states exempted the Shakers from military conscription, some demanded that they pay for replacements, others demanded that they serve in the armed forces. The Shakers learned to take advantage of this diversity. Thus, since the laws in Massachusetts were more lenient, the ministry of Mount Lebanon sent the New York brethren to live in one of the Massachusetts societies long enough to be considered residents of that state and reap the benefit of the exemptions which the Bay State provided for religious groups such as the Shakers and the Quakers.[133] Apparently they would also sometimes put an end to the state's harassing by agreeing to pay for a replacement.

During the Civil War the question was raised again. The government of the North claimed the right to conscript young Shaker men in states under its control, and the Shakers replied by refusing not only to be conscripted but also to pay a fine or hire a substitute. This is the way they had acted in 1815.[134] Their refusal to serve in the army did not, however, prevent them from furnishing help in the form of lodging, food, and forage when these were requisitioned by one side or the other.

The Northern government used force to impose its law. Young Shakers were forcibly enrolled in the Army and then, because of their passive resistance, they were thrown into irons. At one point Elder Evans presented a petition personally to President Lincoln. The President must have appreciated the elder's willfulness, because he told him: "You ought to be made to fight. We need regiments of just such men as you." But Evans had something to offer in exchange: the $600,000 in undrawn pensions that legally belonged to the society through those Shaker brethren who were veterans of preceding wars. In consideration of this sum, the government sent the Shaker recruits back to their Families on indefinite furlough. Shaker cooperation in past wars had been good enough to pay for their noncooperation in the present one. Under the sign of the dollar the Shaker argument seemed most urgent. A similar demand made by the Western societies in 1863[135] also resulted in the recognition of the Shakers' right to be considered conscientious objectors.

Were they living in an ivory tower? Not completely. Ann Lee said that her children should refuse to wage war against other men in order to wage war against Satan. Evans used a similar argument, but for him Satan had the face of agrarian capitalism. He maintained that there would have been no slavery if there had not been a capitalist monopoly of the land.[136] For him land was the primary element of human existence, and wars were settled by "material guarantees" in the form of *more* land accruing to the victors. "And this land," he said, "is held by Government and landholders, in unlimited quantities; it is held from the possession of thousands, who are dependent upon its products, to sustain life from day to day. Those products are yielded only by labor; which labor the landholder extorts from the rightful owner—the dispossessed, landless person, whether male or female. Slavery is the inevitable result; all persons possessing no land are slaves of those who have the land in possession and have robbed them *legally* of their inalienable rights of an inheritance in the earth."[137] Evans had no intentions of taking part in the war, but since he felt that this war had been caused by the agrarian monopolies, he intended to play a role in the revolution against those monopolies. The same theme appears in the writings of another elder, Daniel Fraser. The War of Independence had brought the country political equality, but political equality without economic equality is meaningless. And, argued Fraser, this economic equality would remain nonexistent so long as there was capitalism of the land. This agrarian capitalism was therefore antirepublican.[138]

Not only antirepublican, but also antinatural and anti-Christian, said Evans. This line or reasoning was reported by the French geographer Elie Reclus, who, during his exile after the defeat of the Commune, traveled widely, studying the foreign scene, and spent some time among the Shakers. The words attributed to Evans have certainly been recast by the French writer, but the themes are those of the elder's published works, and it is remarkable to see them reappear in notes taken by an attentive listener at one of the Family sermons. According to Reclus, one night when Elder Evans was speaking in the meetinghouse he turned from the believers to address the audience of those who had come from miles around to watch the picturesque ceremonies and dances of the Shakers:

So now you have looked over these funny, half-crazy people called the Shakers! Good! You think we are apostates and that only you are in possession of Christian truths. . . .

Then let us consider your Christian Republic of the United States. I do not hesitate to affirm that this nation is the most free and most advanced of all. Certainly it is better to live here than under the tyranny of kings and emperors. However, how was this Republic of the United States established? You took possession of an immense territory, you cheated the Indians from whom you bought 100,000 acres of land for a pair of spectacles. Your government has put this land up for sale, this land which belongs to all men, this land to which every worker has a right, and it is being sold in gigantic tracts. When your capitalists gain possession of these tracts, they resell them at prices so excessive that the working farmer could never buy an acre unless the money were lent to him by the seller himself—at enormous rates of interest. Thus the nation is being split into two camps which everyday move further and further apart: the Christians who exploit and the Christians who are exploited! Only yesterday I read that in New York a man who had been unable to pay his debt of money was thrown into prison with common thieves! Your capitalists build factories in which the poor workmen could well envy the fate reserved for slaves under the laws of Moses. Your journalists and your legislators, your judges and your professors, your civil servants, all tell us that it is the usurers who control the public fortune and even that they created it. Why do you look so skeptically at this meeting hall where our miracles occur? Haven't you, yourselves, performed a miracle that we would never have believed if we had not seen it before our eyes. You have managed to create poverty in the land of milk and honey, in a land whose ore beds abound with marble, coal, and iron, where veins of gold and silver are so abundant that it is prudent to exploit them only partially; you have managed to create poverty in a land where crops of corn and wheat are so plentiful that one doesn't know what to do with all one grows! And while your merchants and your industrialists, grown pale with worry and yellow with gastritis, are forever between two thefts and two cases of indigestion, one meets their wives only between two adulteries. Those upper-class Christian ladies with the help of your doctors who specialize in abortions and your druggists who specialize in selling poison, commit foeticide and infanticide more often than their husbands cause bankruptcy. If it were not for the immigrants and the workers, whom your example has not yet corrupted, you would have already depopulated this land so full of promises . . . . And do you think that this will last much longer? No, I say to you! You already have strikes by workers who cannot feed their families on the wages you pay. Abroad, you already have had the Commune in Paris, a revolt of work against usury, a revolt which was crushed with a fury that caused the pavements to run with the blood of the people as it flowed into the sewers. And it is this blood that you have been drinking in the United States, you, like all the rest. Your literature, your newspapers, your businesses, your banks, your religions all drank of it, and your churches also had their thirst satisfied! Do you think that God, the great judge, who has seen all this will forget such things? No, I say. Open your Bibles and read what happened to Babylon. What is this Babylon? It is the society in which you are living at this moment. Who is Babylon's whore? She is your Church, mother of all the abominations that prevail: luxury and poverty, war and slavery, money, capital, speculation, usury, poor houses, insane asylums, prisons, murders, suicides, houses of prostitution, military camps, legal advisors to the medical profession and priests! You drink the brew of fornication. The kings have passed the cup of pleasure to your merchants. . . . And now your sins have risen to the heavens where the Eternal finally takes notice of your iniquities. . . . Leave this place and know that it will not always be possible to laugh at Eternal justice.[139]

Evans was speaking in English. Reclus was writing in French. In reconstructing the speech, the European intellectual was undoubtedly making a very free transcription of what Evans said to the spectators at that Shaker meeting.

It was at about this time (in the 1880s) that, encouraged by such social prophecies, the Shakers began to consider themselves charged with a special mission in American society. This mission was to spread the gospel of an agrarian socialism something like the Georgists' and thus launch a revolutionary movement in which they would play the role of avant-garde. Their good intentions seemed to have led them, momentarily, to forget the facts of reality:

There must be an Order above and in advance of the world, to govern and regulate, or set in order those who forsake it. The spiritual is for that purpose. The present condition of society is no cause of discouragement. The future cannot be determined by the present. Like life, society grows from a principle divinely implanted; it is progressing, bringing the world and its attraction to an ultimate. It is true there is not much increase of members to our Church at present. That is because of the lack of the religious element without; yet many (by degrees) are ripening up to the Gospel work, which is the harvest; and, ere long, a revival of religious and practical truth will occur.[140]

Thus Shaker fortunes began to falter at a time when they were making an effort to define a progressive social program in terms of prophetic religion. It is quite possible that this effort involved a mixture of styles that was not unrelated to the process of decline.

CHAPTER SEVEN

Shaker Ecclesiology &
Shaker Socialism

THE PRECEDING chapters have treated the evolving presence of Shakerism on the historical scene. It is time to show how the existence of Shakerism as a historical fact depended on the Shakers themselves acting out their own idea of world history.

In other words, when a grouping like the Shakers appears at a given time and place, its presence is to be explained by the kind of socio-economic life it has created for itself under the influence of socio-economic forces acting on it from the outside. But insofar as this particular way of organizing life implies aspirations of imposing it as a way of life for everybody else, it also implies that all history is to be understood according to its Shaker categories. Any social movement which claims to represent a radical, new beginning must sooner or later demonstrate that what it began has become absolute. When a movement claims to have inherited a maximum of the past, it is at the same time claiming to represent a maximum of the future. This is why interpretations of the past tend to degenerate into mere geneological charts, while information about the present more or less follows the principles of Procrustes' bed. At any rate, this was the logic behind the Shaker theologians' attitude toward man's history, when they tried to fit the world into the categories of their own archives.

However, before proceeding any further in this analysis,

we should acknowledge that in Shaker thought there is a double relativity. The historical generalizations which their writers brushed over with such absolute authority are really theological concepts; and despite the desire of the individual Shaker to erase all distinctions between science and religion, those theological concepts, no matter how scientific they seemed to be, remained relative to a religious intuition. "I thanked God that I had found a people who were not stereotyped in their religious belief; but who in the progress of spirituality, could change their theological views. — Then a distinction is made between theology and religion? — Certainly. Theology is but the science of religion, while religion is the germ of eternal life, which may be found in every human heart. . . . The cultivation of this germ has produced the increase of the past and the present."[1]

So theology is relative to religion, and any particular religion is, in turn, relative to its own history, since, according to the Shakers, the religions of mankind are as much subject to the evolutionary process as man himself. "We may consider all religions as merely progressive steps by which the human understanding has developed itself in every time and place, and will continue to develop itself in the future."[2] According to this view, the historical generalizations of Shaker theology are hardly more than useful ways of thinking or operational concepts.

This dual relativism in theology did not prevent the Shakers from producing a work of "universal history." This was the well-known *Testimony of Christ's Second Appearing*, which they claimed had evoked such an enthusiastic reaction from Thomas Jefferson. The book is really no more than a collection of facts. Today a compilation like this is of small interest as ecclesiastic history, but the manner in which these facts have been compiled is nevertheless a precious source of information for anyone interested in its author's ecclesiology. His historical narrative is based on a system of preferences, all of which were determined by the theory that there has been a chain of "witnesses." It is this system of preferences that reveals the Shaker mind.

According to the Shakers' own interpretation of the past, they were historically related to the religious dissidences of the first eighteen centuries in the Christian era. To this picture of their past should be added their intent to transform the world in the future, since it was their project for changing the world which brought them into contact with the religious and nonreligious socialisms.

The Shaker reaction to the socialists, quite as much as the socialists' reaction to Shakerism, was to become a kind of test, providing a profile of the Shaker mind at a moment when, ecclesiologically, it was torn between the desire to outstrip the various socialisms and the fear of not being able to meet their competition.

I. The Chain of Witnesses

According to Shaker theology, the religious history of mankind is divided into four periods, the figure "4" being justified by a series of biblical references (Ezek. 47, Rev. 5, Zech. 2).

1. From the Creation to the Exodus
2. From the Exodus to John the Baptist
3. From Christ's First Appearance to his Second Appearance in the person of Ann Lee.
4. From the Second Appearance of Christ to the end of the world

During the first period[3] Abraham was given the law of circumcision: "the first outward sign of a practical cross against the fallen nature of the flesh." The Shakers considered this to be one more proof of man's original sin: "Let it be remembered, that this first permanent cross which God required of his people was one which pointed directly to the very nature and foundation of man's loss from God." It was also a sign of things to come: "Abraham being found faithful to obey the commands of God thus far, and to keep the law of circumcision, God according to his promise, blessed him with a son in his old age. And here it is worthy of remark, that this child of promise was not generated according to the will of the flesh, in the days of his youth." Sarah was no longer fecund, and Abraham had ceased to have intercourse with her. And then Abraham agreed to sacrifice this son of God's promise:[4] "The law of circumcision was the first visible sign which pointed to the destruction of the root of sin. And the offering up of Isaac was a prelude to all those ceremonial sacrifices under the law, which had a special reference to the great sacrifice of the Son of God, and to the final sacrifice of his followers of all the ties and beloved objects of nature."[5]

During the second period Moses was held responsible for two kinds of laws: on the one hand, his laws governing production and property, which have already been discussed;[6] on the other hand, his code governing ritual impurities, which the Shaker theologians interpreted as laws to check reproduction and lust.[7] This tribute to Moses does not tally with some of the accusations which the Shakers made against the Jewish God, calling him a "God of generation." The tribute, however, is more basic than the accusation, since it can be found in the oldest and most doctrinal of the Shaker texts, the *Millennial Church*[8] and the *Testimony*.[9]

The fourth period along with the various ways of interpreting it, has already been covered in our discussion of the relations between Shaker millenarianism and American millenarianism.

It is the third period (the years between Christ and Ann Lee) that contained the celebrated Chain of Witnesses, so central to Shaker theory. Actually this theory was not exclusive to the Shakers. It was based on material drawn from two works which are quoted at length in the *Testimony*: Robertson's *Ecclesiastical Researches* (Cambridge edition, 1792) and A. Maclaine's English translation of Mosheim's *Histoire ecclésiatique* (Philadelphia, 1797). To these sources of Shaker theory should be added the eleven volumes of Dr. Lardner's *Collected Works*, published in 1788. As for studies presenting similar historical interpretations, there is a closely related theory in the voluminous work by I. de Beausobre, who antedated the Shakers,[10] and another in Broadbent's more recent work, *The Pilgrim Church.*[11]

According to the Shakers, this third period subdivides into five phases of unequal length:

1. The Jewish Christian Church or apostolic church or Pentecostal community, founded on the sacredness of celibacy, common property, and interdiction of war and slavery.

2. The Gentile Christian Church, which was a concession made by the apostles to their pagan converts. Slavery and war were still forbidden, but marriage and private property were permitted, although regulated by Mosaic law. Evans held that unless one understands the difference between the Jewish and the Gentile Christian Church, the various books of the New Testament are incomprehensible.

3. The Roman Catholic Church came into being when the Gentile Christian Church began to deteriorate. Like the Lollards, the Hussites, and many others, the Shakers saw the Catholic period as beginning with the "Constantinization" of the church. In this phase there appeared holy wars, systematic religious persecution by the Inquisition, monopoly of the land, slavery, oaths, codification of marriage, and codification of monasticism; in sum: "the adulterous mixture of Church and State, right and wrong, peace and war, humility and pride, monastic celibacy and sacramental marriage, hebraism and Mahometanism, Christianity and Heathenism, all commingled together in Christendom."[12] In a word, it was Babylon or the Beast who, according to John's apocalyptic vision, would come to scourge the survivers of the original church.[13]

4. The Protestant Church. For the Shakers this was not much different from the Church of Rome. Evans wrote that both churches permit marriage, private property, union of church and state, ambition, oaths, persecutions, wars, slavery, and monopoly of the land. Both taught that salvation is assured in a far-off, unknown world for those who make proper use of water (baptism), bread, wine, and blood (the Eucha-

rist).[14] Both believe in the murder of the most virtuous man the world has ever produced, and both have faith in the magical qualities of a wooden cross, the instrument of Christ's crucifixion.[15]

5. The Protestant sects, such as the Baptists, the Quakers, and the Methodists. These, too, were treated severely, but, as we shall see, the Shakers had one prejudice in their favor.

Several hundred pages of the *Testimony* are devoted to an analysis of these periods and phases. There can be no question here of even making a résumé. Several of the points have already been touched on, and we shall take a sampling of what seems most significant in the rest.

ON THE PENTECOSTAL COMMUNITY

This is the keystone of Shaker ecclesiology, since the Pentecostal community is supposed to have refused marriage of the flesh and to have carried its cross without making any exceptions. According to John Dunlavy, there are many historical accounts to support this thesis.[16] However, since these historical accounts, despite their abundance, are all either debatable or flawed, the Shaker argument rests largely on an inference made from their own case. It likewise rests on the notion that the Pentecostal community resembled the Essenes. "Jesus was an Essene," affirmed Frederick Evans,[17] and it was his opinion that this was also true of the whole early Christian community.

The following traits were attributed to the Pentecostal community: property held in common, celibacy, nonresistance to force, separation of church and civil government, and power to cure disease.[18] Evans points out that the very same traits were found among the Essenes:

The Essenians were the ripened fruit of the Mosaic dispensation, and the highest order of people that the dispensation could produce. 1. They were communists, holding property in common. 2. They were celibate, neither marrying nor giving in marriage, and had outgrown and risen above the works of generation. The nation furnished them with adults and children to support the Order which was held in high esteem by all parties and sects in Judea. 3. They were children of peace, non-resistants, taking no part even in the religious wars of the Jews. 4. They were vegetarians, observing the command "Thou shalt not kill," without reservation, and considered that he who slew an ox was as he who killed a man. 5. They were hygienic Spiritualists, holding that "it was Egyptian to be sick." They practiced the gift of healing diseases and exorcised evil spirits. 6. As Israel dwelt alone and was not numbered with the nations, so the Essenes dwelt alone, not belonging to any of the parties or sects in Israel. When rebuking the Pharisees and Sadducees as hypocrites, etc., Jesus passed by the Essenes in silence. The Essenians were, many of them, converted on the day of Pentecost, and formed the body of the Jerusalem Church with its extraordinary spiritual origin and the continued gifts of the Spirits in their meetings.[19]

In the passage just quoted (of 1889), Evans gives no sources, but one can guess what they were by comparing his text to a more contemporary work by Charles Edson Robinson, *A Concise History of the United Society of Believers Called Shakers*.[20] Robinson was one of the few non-Shaker writers to publish with a Shaker imprimatur. His book first appeared as a series of articles, starting in January 1891, in *The Manufacturer and Builder*. The first chapter is almost entirely devoted to the Essenes, and the author says that he drew his information from a book by Christian D. Ginsburg, *The Essenes, Their History and Doctrines*, published in London in 1861. It was in this work that Charles Edson Robinson had found the six testimonies which he acknowledged as references. These were texts by Flavius Josephus, Philo, Plinius, Caius Julius Solinus, Porphyrus, and Eusebius of Caesarea. Using this material, Robinson describes at length the Essenes' way of life and explains that it developed from certain principles found in Leviticus 15:16–33 and Exodus 19:15. He denies that the Essenes were ever like the Pythagoreans, a resemblance which, says Robinson, was once taught by Flavius Josephus and, more recently, by Zeller.[21] Instead, he relates their mode of life to what was proposed by Saint Paul and by Christ. He claimed that Saint Paul was teaching Essene doctrine in his First Epistle to the Corinthians (1 Cor. 7:5–9) and that the religion taught by Christ and the apostles has many traits in common with Essene beliefs.[22] Finally, Robinson salutes the Shakers as the legitimate heirs to this early combination of Essene doctrine and Christianity. "There is at the present day a society of Christians found, we are told, only in America, which have many of the characteristics of the Essenes. Indeed, they have so many features in common, one is almost led to think that the United Society of Believers called Shakers are but the lineal descendants of the Essenes. . . . Christ and his Apostles were Essenes in many of the features of the religion which they taught. Equally true is this of the Society of Shakers. And neither do we find any other religious sect so closely following the teaching of the Essenes, and of Christ and his Apostles, as do the Shakers."[23]

Evans inferred that the Pentecostal community had been recruited among the Essenes and had pushed his inference one step further than Robinson, who pointed out that the Essenes wavered on the question of celibacy[24] and that they seemed to have established an intermediate religious category for married people. Earlier, in the light of Shaker experience, Evans inferred that before this capitulation to human nature was manifested in the Gentile Christian Church, it was quite possible that the old Jewish Christian Church had undergone a revival of Essenism.

ON THE "CONSTANTINIZATION" OF THE CHURCH

Improving on or anticipating a well-worn theme, the Shakers interpreted the Christianizing of the Roman Empire as an example of Christian imperialism.[25] There are many Shaker pamphlets on this subject. It might be helpful to examine one aspect of their argument, since it provides a supplementary view of Shakerism as defined by the Shakers themselves. This is their analysis of monasticism. In it they reveal a prejudice against conventional monastic life that is common in paramonastic dissidences of this type.

Monasticism, according to the Shakers, was closely related

to the imperialist policies of the Catholic Church, which, by institutionalizing private property and marriage for the main body of believers, made it necessary to set up special monastic orders for the others. By tolerating marriage for one class of Christians, the church made it necessary to impose celibacy on another class of Christians and thus established a division of labor which was fatal to the church's original doctrine. In order to tolerate marriage they made it into a sacrament; and this made it necessary for them to consider celibacy also as a sacred (rather than a human) obligation.[26] For these reasons the Shakers condemned Christian monasticism, to which, despite their protest, their system was so often compared.[27] Their attitude was complicated by the fact that they both praised and repudiated this link with their own past. In the *Manifesto* John Dunlavy writes that if the monastic orders of the Catholic Church have retained a certain purity characteristic of the apostolic community — as indeed they have — and are just about the only element in the church to do so, this does not diminish the claims of the True Church.[28] For the Shakers the distinctions between the monastic orders and the communities of True Believers were legion:

1. The monasteries were selective. They offered a way of perfection to a small group whose spiritual progress was in contrast to the imperfection of the great mass of members in the church, to which the monks never ceased to belong. For the Shakers there was only one kind of holiness, and that was the kind they were trying to achieve. It created no special place in the church for anyone, because it was a holiness to be achieved by all.[29]

2. The monasteries through their special spiritual disciplines, excused the rest of the church from leading the apostolic life, but at the same time the monasteries lived temporally on the gifts and contributions given them by the church. The Shakers, on the other hand, were made self-sufficient by their own efforts, working with their own hands, producing all that was needed for their own survival, with enough left over to share with those in want.[30]

3. In the monasteries, as soon as they entered the order,

members were free of all concerns for husband, wife, or children. Among the Shakers membership was offered to everyone, married and unmarried, old and young, who wanted to be saved by taking up his cross.

4. In the monasteries the monks were bound by an oath, a solemn vow of celibacy. Among the Shakers faith and love of truth were the only bonds.[31]

5. The monasteries have been supported by public approval and the power of the law. The Shakers have been denounced as the enemies of mankind and a public danger.[32]

The *Manifesto* concludes its presentation of these opposing points of view with a challenge for the monasteries to do as the Shakers had done, to gather together families with varying needs and problems, and to induce parents to work for the children of others as well as their own. Then, says Dunlavy, the world would see their true strength.[33] The *Manifesto* was published in 1818. Fifty years later many of these arguments could have been used against the Shaker position.[34]

With the exception of the monastic orders (and, as we have seen, this exception was not without certain reserves), church history in the period inaugurated by the Emperor Constantine was under the reign of the Antichrist. The *Testimony* calls this empire of the Antichrist "the reign of the most perfect confusion, injustice, deceit and cruelty."[35]

During this period, according to the Shaker view, the True Church took refuge in the various religious dissidences, the historical succession of which constituted what they called the "Chain of Witnesses." In this dramatic series the line of demarcation between the persecuted and the persecutors was that separating the servants of Christ from those who served the Antichrist.[36]

ON THE CHAIN OF WITNESSES

A passage in the *Testimony* sums up Shaker thought on this subject. After citing without any particular order Cerdon, Marcion, Manichaeus, Novatian, Hierax, Priscillian, the Marcionites, the Manichaeans, the Bogomils, the Cathari, the Beghards, the Picards, the Waldenses, the Albigenses, the Anabaptists, and so forth, the text goes on to say that all these dissidences were manifestations of a tendency toward the true Gospel and a protest against the corrupted religion established in the name of man, not God. This does not mean, says the author of the *Testimony*, that the doctrines and practices of these "witnesses" constituted a system passed down from one to another in some chain of authority; it does mean that they were all influenced by the same invisible Spirit, and that even if there were no real links connecting the various witnesses of the chain, the only differences in their faith and practices were ones of degree.[37]

On the following page of the *Testimony* we read that these witnesses had little or no relation to the Christian world of their time, as should be clear to anyone who considers the history of religious persecutions from Nero to Governor John Endicott.[38] From the beginning of the "decline" to the New England persecutions, using iron, fire, and imprisonment, the persecutors had taken their toll by the thousands and the millions.[39]

Looking at the Shaker list of witnesses, one is struck by the fact that the names do not fall into any particular pattern and that the "Chain" includes a very disparate collection of dissidences. This observation did not completely escape the Shaker writers. It will help us understand their view on the subject if we take a few soundings of Shaker thought. We can do this by examining three different groups of dissidences: the dualist dissidences, the medieval dissidences, and the peripheral dissidences at the time of the Reformation.

THE GROUP OF DUALIST DISSIDENCES

The *Testimony* cites the repressive laws against the Manichaeans during the Christian Empire. This time the Shaker concern is for the Empire, since their sympathies go to the tolerance of Emperor Julian, just as their hostility is vented onto the intolerance of Saint Augustine.[40]

For the substantive part of the question they were obliged to glean whatever obiter dicta they could find in the traditional literature, which, much to their dismay, was the only source of information on Manichaeus and his doctrine. Thus the *Testimony* starts its discussion by saying that Manichaeus' adversaries decried the strictness and austerity of the rule he prescribed to his disciples. And then comes the defense. The Shaker writers claim that although Manichaeus' enemies accused him of coercing the people into a life of mortification and abstinence, it was obviously the persecutors themselves who were guilty of dictating to men's consciences, since the only means of persuasion used by the Manichaeans was the innocent example of their leaders.[41]

Despite their discomfort at having to deal with sources which read like hostile pamphlets,[42] the Shakers were wholly sympathetic with Manichaeus. Their sympathies also went to the neo-Manichaeans.

The Messalians are mentioned only briefly in the *Testimony*. They are identified as "Messalians or Euchytes, which is to say "those who pray." The mention is honorable, but the Shaker writers push them ahead a few hundred years into the twelfth century.[43]

As for the Paulicians, the *Testimony* makes them the descendants of Paul of Samosat in the fourth century. The author notes that the violence with which they were persecuted drove them to "the most desperate measures of defense" (the Paulicians were not particularly partisans of nonviolence)[44] and that this finally pushed them into the arms of the Saracens, who protected them against the rage of their Catholic persecutors.[45] In this case the Shaker sympathies were clearly with Islam, and they claimed that the Arabs and other so-called infidels did not practice persecution until the orthodox Christians taught them. The Saracens persecuted no one, says the *Testimony*. Jews and Christians of all countries lived peacefully among them.[46]

The Shaker text relates the Bogomils to Manichaeanism through their supposed founder, Basilius, an aged and venerable man whom the bloody Emperor Alexius tricked into explaining his doctrine and then condemned to be burned as a heretic in Constantinople.[47]

The Cathari are described as doctrinally related to the Waldenses, the Patarines, and the Beghards. They are supposed to have originated in Spain and to have been the descendants of the Priscillians, who, after eight hundred years of peace, were forced to flee persecution and seek refuge in the valleys of the Pyrenees. From there, under various names, they are supposed to have spread out to France, Germany, and other countries of Europe. The Shakers borrowed this hypothesis from their usual sources.

It is obvious that doctrinal differences matter little in this Shaker inventory of dualistic dissidences. They even manage to find a common denominator for these dualisms in an Anabaptist custom.[48] Another passage, more wisely, renounces any attempt to determine the doctrinal content of these dissidences, saying that it would take an interminable time to calculate their supposed errors on such matters as baptism, the Eucharist, use of the altar, funerals, marriage, and so on.[49] All discussion can finally be reduced to one point: whatever the name and whatever the country, all those who renounced papal superstition and looked for religion in the practice of virtue were a uniform object of persecution by "the Mother of Whores."[50]

THE GROUP OF MEDIEVAL DISSIDENCES

Waldenses, Beghards, and Patarines, although brothers and sisters of the free spirit, were put on the same level as Albigenses, Cathari, Bogomils, and Messalians. This confused grouping had been cited before the Shakers and would be referred to by others after them. The Shakers simply made use of the clichés of their time.

They did, however, refuse to treat the Waldenses as precursors of the Reformation; or rather, they refused to treat the Reformation as the work of the Waldenses' descendants. They noted the Waldenses' exodus to Bohemia and Moravia, but for them the Waldenses' real descendants were the Anabaptists, who were bothered and even persecuted by the Reformers. The *Testimony* tells us that among the Anabaptists who were persecuted during the sixteenth century, one can find the same traits as those found in the Waldenses and the Manichaeans.[51] This triple similarity leads to many difficulties of which the Shakers were not aware.

Against this general background the Shaker account portrays just four men: Pierre de Bruys, Henri de Lausanne, Tanchelm, and Arnauld de Brescia. Since they were all tortured to death, they have a right to a place of honor in the Shaker memorial.[52]

Naturally, the pages of the *Testimony* devoted to medieval dissidences denounce the Inquisition, yet there is no recognition given to the Lollards or the Taborites. Can it be that those groups were too closely associated with memories of the English insurrection of 1381? Were John Ball and Jean Ziska too violent to be included in the Chain of Witnesses? If so, why did the Shakers include a violent leader like Thomas Münzer?

THE PERIPHERAL GROUPS OF THE REFORMATION

Shaker indulgence for Thomas Münzer is in sharp contrast with their severity in judging the great leaders of the Reformation. They criticize the Lutherans, the Calvinists, and the Anglicans on several scores. Indeed, first and foremost, they were persecutors. Calvin condemned Michel Servet to death.[53] Likewise, Luther treated the Anabaptists in the same way that the pagans of antiquity had treated the early Christians.[54] As for the English Reformation, "not only did the Episcopalians in *England* persecute the dissenters; but in *Scotland* and during the commonwealth in England, these persecuted the Episcopalians. And what is perhaps more extraordinary, even in *New England*, where the first colonists fled from the iron hand of oppression at home, they persecuted the Quakers and others who differed from their establishment."[55]

Then, says the *Testimony*, these English Reformers put the

Spirit in the fetters of the word. The scriptures which they had adopted as the Word of God and sole criterion of religious truth led them not only to become inflexible in their respective doctrines but also to quarrel and argue in a scandalous manner and condemn each other to radical judgments followed by exile, imprisonment, and even executions.[56]

Finally and probably most importantly, the Reformers are identified with those whom Saint Paul accused of wanting to forbid marriage. By way of a characteristic interpretation, the Shakers were able to turn one of Luther's own Bible texts against him. This Shaker exegesis is the one which makes a distinction between spiritual marriage, which Christ's disciples called a mystery,[57] and the civil contract of marriage as it was usually practiced among the Gentiles.[58] Not only did the Reformers try to solemnize the civil contract by treating it as a religious ceremony, but also, something which for the Shakers was the sin of sins, they denied the sense of "the spiritual marriage." This last was something that even the Catholic hierarchy had never done.[59]

Shaker bitterness toward the men of the Reformation contrasts with their sympathy for Thomas Münzer and his peasants, including even their armed revolt. The *Testimony* goes to great lengths to explain that however contrary to the spirit of the Gospel may have been the conduct of the peasants when they took up arms against the pitiless cruelty of their oppressors, they have been exonerated by reliable historians who guarantee that the peasants groaned under an intolerably heavy burden which they could no longer carry, and that the excessive tyranny of the nobility had driven them to desperate measures.[60] The extenuating circumstances were the same as those evoked in the case of the Paulicians when they were "driven to desperate measures of defense." As for Münzer, it was he who drew up the list of demands which the peasants presented to their feudal lords. It was circulated throughout Germany. And the Shaker writer, pontificating like a Voltaire, comments: "It was so well written that a Lycurgus would have signed it."

The *Testimony* does not seem to recognize any distinction between Münzer's peasants in arms and the Anabaptist pacifists. These pacifist groups were the descendants of the former Waldenses, through the Moravians, and they had some of the same traits: no priests, no private property, no participation in civil offices, no military service, no established and compulsory religion. They lived in fraternal orders, each one of which was composed of numerous families holding all things in common. In the sixteenth century 20,000 of these Anabaptists were supposed to have been expelled from Moravia.[61] Then came the storm. The influence of the Antichrist in the united power of the Protestants and the Papists produced such an effective drive to exterminate the sixteenth-century Anabaptists that no trace of their faith or their name remains.[62] After the Anabaptists, the Chain of Witnesses survived under another name, the Mennonites. Like the Shakers, they refused to take oaths and to serve in the armed forces. Like the Shakers, they made an absolute distinction between civil and ecclesiastic powers, and so forth. Moravians and Mennonites would remain the Shakers' favorite point of reference. "The Mennonites and the Moravians, what a noble people!" wrote Frederick Evans in a letter to Leo Tolstoi.[63]

What about the two denominations in the Shakers' own backyard, the Quakers and the Methodists? In the *Testimony* a long discussion of Methodist doctrine[64] concludes with an expression of regret that Wesley never really broke with the Anglicans and their idea of communion.[65] A no less lengthy discussion of Quakerism renders hommage to George Fox and the Quaker martyrs in America,[66] and then deplores the influence of Barclay and Penn and the prosperity of the Quaker movement in general.[67] Both Quakerism and Methodism allied themselves with the civil power and came to be considered true Christian sects worthy of protection by the secular arm. For the Shakers this marked the end not only of their suffering but of their spiritual powers.[68]

Despite their reserves, it is evident that the Shakers accepted and envisaged grafting onto their young plant certain groups which, although too conformist for their tastes, gave some hope of regaining spiritual life:

The *Mennonites* and *Moravians* of the present day claim their descent from the ancient heretics; however, by mixing with the spirit of anti-Christian reformers, and embracing their human creeds, their religion has degenerated into a formalism without vital content; yet, in many particulars, they retain some shadow of the ancient virtue in regard to holding civil offices, bearing arms, taking oaths, etc. But the purest descendants and present remains of the ancient witnesses are the people called the Dunkers; some among this people, in a great degree, retain the uprightness and simplicity of their predecessors.[69]

Under the names of *Quakers, Methodists*, New-Light *Presbyterians* and others, even under the most permanent forms that have been established during the dominion of Antichrist, it is undoubtedly certain that there are many souls sincerely looking for redemption from sin; and who, according to their light, are laboring to do the best they can.[70]

Elio Vittorini has sketched the outlines of a summary and contestable phenomenology for Christianity according to which Catholicism is the form Christianity took during the phase of agrarian feudalism, and Protestantism the form it took during the phase of bourgeois commerce and industry; history will have to wait to find out what form it will take during the phase dominated by the international proletariat. However debatable such a phenomenological schema may be, it would have delighted a Shaker writer, who would doubtless have offered the content of Shakerism *en bloc* for Vittorini's third phase.

The principal conclusion of the *Testimony's* system of historical judgments seems to be a radical refusal of the two dominant strains in Christianity (i.e. the Catholics and the Protestants) and a cautious preference for peripheral sects of the Reformation, such as the Moravians, the Mennonites, the Quakers, and the Methodists, all of which were born during crucial phases of the class struggle in Europe.

These phases were also studied by sociologists like Friedrich Engels and Kautsky, who were seeking historical roots for their own ideas. But, and this is another conclusion, the historical judgments made in socialist literature do not coincide with those made by the Shakers in their writings. Socialist literature chooses its heroes from among the militants in the class struggle, sometimes soldiers: men like Jean Ziska and the Taborites, Thomas Münzer and his peasants, and the Levellers. Methodism is suspect precisely because it looks to a conciliation of the classes. Shaker literature, on the other hand, chooses its historical models from among the pacifist Moravians of the Bohemian brotherhood, the Mennonites, and the Quakers; and if the Shakers differ with the Methodists, it is because they have different reasons for the same nonviolent reconciliation.

In a third phase as projected by Elio Vittorini, the phase during which Christianity is confronted by a self-conscious proletariat, Shakerism is something of a leftover. Ecclesiologically, it prolongs the pacifist Christian dissidences which originated during the social upheavals and revolutions of Europe between the fourteenth and the eighteenth centuries. It expects to go beyond the other dissidences by way of a process similar to the one by which early monasticism was, momentarily, set apart from the established church. But in moving beyond the other groups to create what they believed to be a Christian Utopia, the Shakers remained nonetheless short of the socialist ideal; and this ideal, after all, is what their system would be judged by.

In a few of its fundamental ideas Shakerism comes close to socialism: for example, the materialism implicit in its religion of Motherhood,[71] the evolutionism of its religious philosophy,[72] the adoptionism in its Christology, the laicizing of its internal structures, and its admiration of the French eighteenth century. Accordingly, just about the only people whom the Shakers really liked were the founders of the American Republic. For a long time their dream of absorbing society into the church and making monasticism a universal way of life prevented them from reaching an understanding not only with Christian socialists or social reform groups like the Methodists, who seemed content with halfway measures, but also with the nonreligious socialisms such as Owenism and Fourierism, which seemed to lack any spiritual base.

They prudently explored the possibilities opened up by other American religious socialisms. These radical experiments in communal living attracted their interest, but nothing came of these probings. Shakerism remained a hybrid. It was too materialistic, or at least too immanentistic, to be Christian, and too idealistic to understand what was evolving in the socialist organizations. It had a vision of a twofold Utopia: the Utopia of a priestless church within the Utopia of a classless society. It intended to make both these "Utopias" into something real.

It was in order to substantiate the first of these Utopian visions that the Shakers looked to the near and distant past for everything which might corroborate the ecclesiastic structure they had devised. It was in order to substantiate the second aspect of their double Utopia that they turned to the various socialisms both near and far, and from them garnered everything which might justify or amplify their own program of socialization. In this quest for corroboration Shakerism encountered another and illustrious champion of "true Christianity"—Leo Tolstoi.

II. Shaker References to Socialism

Shaker interest in the nineteenth-century socialisms was limited to those aspects which reflected their own concerns. Thus their attention was directed onto socialist solutions for the religious, political, and agrarian problems of their time. There is no example of the Shakers paying any attention to a socialist movement with none of these characteristics. Nonreligious socialisms, especially European industrial socialisms of the Marxist variety, are practically unmentioned in Shaker literature.

In the course of their explorations they examined five areas of socialism with a sympathetic or critical eye, as they probed for possible ways to expand their own experiment and prolong its life in time.

1. The religious "communities" in Germany
2. The religious "communities" in America
3. The Fourierist and Owenite groups
4. American socialisms (Bellamy, Henry George)
5. Tolstoi's Christianity

1. THE GERMAN RELIGIOUS COMMUNITIES

Apart from the Kelpian community, "Das Weib in der Wuste," founded in Germantown and dutifully documented by the Shakers under the heading "cloud of witnesses," and apart from the Bethel and Aurora communes which were founded by a German, Dr. Keil, but peopled largely by Americans,[73] the four great German experiments in communal living were: Ephrata, the Rappites at Harmony-Economy, the Separatists at Zoar, and the Inspirationalists at Amana.[74] The Shakers' acquaintance with these communities was facilitated by the fact that, like the Shaker societies themselves, they seem to have been on a circuit regularly visited by travelers interested in sociological curiosities.[75]

Ephrata. This is the community that caused the authors of the *Testimony* to praise the Dunkers, saying: "The purest descendants, and present remains of the ancient witnesses are the people called the *Dunkers;* some among this people, in a great degree, retain the uprightness and simplicity of their predecessors."[76] It was with elements of these German Baptists who had emigrated to Pennsylvania around 1719 that Conrad Beissel founded the community of Ephrata, referred to above in the section on American millenarianism.[77] The community was well enough known for the Shakers to be aware of its existence, at least by hearsay, but since the rise of Shaker fortunes coincided with the decline of Ephrata, there is no reason to look for any closer relations

CHART 14. *Distribution of Shaker Societies and Other American Communities*

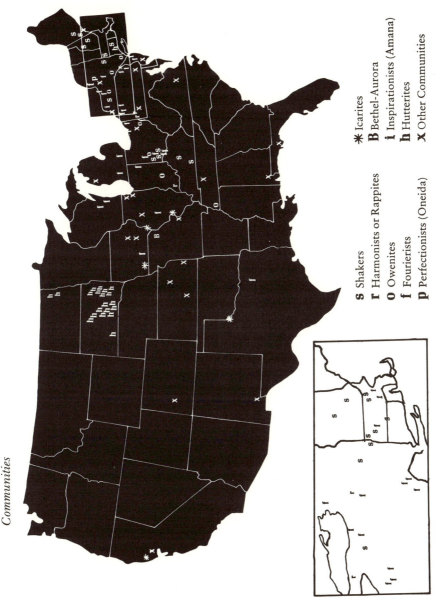

s Shakers
r Harmonists or Rappites
O Owenites
f Fourierists
p Perfectionists (Oneida)

✳ Icarites
B Bethel-Aurora
i Inspirationists (Amana)
h Hutterites
X Other Communities

between them. As far as the Shakers were concerned, it was enough for them to know that here and there, in the past as in the present, the same Spirit had been inspiring men to action.

The Rappites of Harmony-Economy. During their experiment at Busro Creek the Shakers came into close contact with the Rappites. Daryl Chase cites a letter to the Shaker brethren of the East in which they gave an account of this meeting and told how the Harmony Society had moved from near Pittsburg to a place fifty miles from Busro Creek where, two years before, they had established a large and united community.[78] Although communication on religious matters was difficult since the language of Harmony was German, the Shakers were pleased to observe that their neighbors practiced confession of sins and had taken up their cross against the flesh. Two of these people came to live with the Shakers in order to learn their customs and their language. According to this letter to the Eastern brethren, the Shakers judged their neighbors the Rappites to be decidedly strong, rich, charitable, and good people.[79]

The first site of the Harmony community had, in fact, been in Butler County, north of Pittsburg, where they lived from 1805–1814. The Rappites subsequently moved to Posey County in southern Indiana, where they welcomed a new wave of immigrants from Germany. In 1818 there were about a thousand of them in the colony. It was at about that date that their Shaker neighbors wrote the letter cited by Daryl Chase. The Shaker community at Busro had been founded in 1812 and lasted until 1826. Since "Father Rapp" and his people remained at Harmony until 1825, the two neighboring communities had ten years in which to learn about each other's ways.

Rapp had introduced celibacy into his community before they arrived in Indiana. He had notions about the Motherhood of God quite similar to the Shakers', and he had worked out a relationship between perfectionism and millenarianism which was almost identical to Shaker doctrine. Relations between the two communities could therefore be cordial.

Yet they rarely went beyond cordiality. In 1825 Rapp sold the village of Harmony to Robert Owen, who transformed it into New Harmony. The Shakers at Busro Creek welcomed the new leader, but soon they too moved away, dispersing their flock to South Union and other societies in Kentucky and Ohio. During the War of 1812 the Busro community was forced to withdraw to Union Village. After the war the return to Busro had been subsidized by the brethren in the East, who sent substantial sums of money for this purpose.[80] Subsequent to this return the community faced the same difficulties as the ones which were to cause Father Rapp to abandon Indiana, namely, an unhealthy climate, disease, and fevers. "Out of 120 brothers only two were in a state to work."[81]

This separation, however, did not put an end to relations between the Shakers and the Rappites. A Rappite historian points out that in 1850 there was a plan for the group which had been reestablished at Economy to integrate with the Shakers and the Separatists of Zoar.[82]

The Separatists at Zoar. The Zoar community, located on the road between South and North Union, Ohio, was similar to the Rappites in origin, structure, and destiny. The Shakers had ample opportunity to visit these people during trips between their own two Ohio communities. When Issachar Bates, one of the three early Shaker missionaries in the West, broke his arm near the Zoarite village, he was taken in for an extended period of care. According to his report, he could not have been better treated by his own people; and when he left, the Zoarites refused to accept any money for the services they had rendered.

Relations between the two communities were cordial, although the Zoarites, who were communists, preferred their democratic organization to the Shaker theocracy. Moreover, after a short trial period, Zoar had abolished the rule of mandatory celibacy. Thus these two experiments followed different paths.

When Charles Nordhoff visited Zoar, he noted that the oldest man in the community was a ninety-year-old American who had joined the Shakers at the age of fifty and then, at the age of sixty-three, had left them to join the group at Zoar. This example, taken together with the story of Issachar Bates, indicates that the two communities knew each other well. Despite such exchanges, the 1850 project to federate the communities never materialized.[83]

The Inspirationists of Amana. The Shakers were also in dialogue with Amana; and with them, too, they discussed a plan for federation. Documentation of this project is furnished by a letter which B. S. Youngs, author of the *Testimony*, addressed to the members of Amana, proposing that the two societies unite. In his letter, after formally addressing the brothers and sisters in eloquent diplomatic language, Youngs proposed that the two societies unite for more familiar and close relations with each other, and explained that in so doing they would please God, who wishes that all those called by his Holy Spirit, no matter what their nation, their language, or their color, be of one heart and one soul.[84] But, once more, the conversations led to nothing. The Shakers' veneration of Ann Lee and the fact that the Inspirationists practiced marriage made the dialogue difficult and, in the end, useless.

Thus the Shakers did not achieve any meaningful relationship with the German community experiments. No association or federation was established, even though they may have hoped for this, as was indicated by the letter to Amana and the 1850 plan of federation with Zoar and Economy. However, such bonds and similarities as did exist had one positive result. Up to that time the American communal tradition had been German in language and culture. By meshing, even in a limited way, with the lasts gears of that tradition, the Shakers were able to furnish an English language version of it. Through them, the old nostaligia of the Moravians, the Dunkers, and the pietists became naturalized American.[85]

And, reciprocally, the background of these German communities strengthened the Shakers in their own theoretic outlook. Most of them were prosperous. All had a European prehistory quite similar to the Shakers'. All their communities had rules similar to those of the Shakers. It was not difficult to see a kind of preestablished harmony in such parallels. Were they not just so many more demonstrations that "a cloud of witnesses" had announced the Second Coming?[86]

2. THE AMERICAN RELIGIOUS COMMUNITIES

Among the American community experiments based on religion, there were two with a dramatic correlation to the Shakers: The Mormons and the Perfectionists at Oneida.

The Mormons. Although the Mormon establishment cannot be classed as a communal experiment, at one point during their development, there were attempts at instituting a semicommunism. One of these was the Mormons' ill-fated "United Order" or "order of Enoch," modeled after the Shaker community Dunlavy had described in the chapter "United Inheritance" of the *Manifesto*.[87] Moreover, a few Shakers are reported to have passed into the ranks of the Mormons; and the society at North Union, Ohio, was located not far from Joseph Smith's colony. Both were possible avenues for the Mormons' unquestionable literary influence on the believers. Daryl Chase gives a few specific examples of these influences, such as a parchment supposedly written by Saint John the Divine, a new Book of Moses, and a prophetic revelation from some American Indians.

At any rate, a comparison of dates indicates that there was definitely an influence running from the Mormons to the Shakers. In at least one instance examined by Daryl Chase it also quite possibly ran in the opposite direction as well. This was a case of finding a similarity between two hymns — a Mormon hymn and a Shaker hymn. It is also possible that, in composing those hymns, both Mormons and Shakers drew their inspiration from a common source.[88]

Taken altogether, these comparisons indicate a possible influence of Shaker communism on such collectivist ideas as existed among the Mormons. The Rappites may have had a similar effect on the Latter Day Saints.[89] Reciprocally, a Mormon influence on the Shakers was felt, especially during the Great Revival of 1837–1847. It is quite possible that the Shaker leaders were aware of the borrowings from Mormonism in some of the spirit messages, and this may be one of the reasons why so many of them were never published, even by the history-oriented Shakers of the first decade of the twentieth century.[90]

The Shakers reacted to Mormon polygamy by accusing the Mormons of pushing Christianity one step further into "Babylon." Yet they seemed to prefer Mormon polygamy to the practices at Oneida or even to ordinary Christian marriage. After all, were not the Mormons mobilizing lechery into the service of reproduction, making concupiscence less sinful, since, in the process of reproduction, it is distributed among a larger number of wives?[91] Moreover, Mormonism claimed to be a revival of ancient Judaism and taught, as did Moses, that children are a "heritage from the Lord" and "the glory of their parents," and that the law limiting marriage to the sole purpose of reproduction should be considered sacred. According to the Shakers, this reference to Moses is doubly valid because the Mormons did not try to justify polygamy by making it into a sacrament. They *permitted* it, just as Moses permitted divorce. This did not mean that the Shakers thought polygamy just. But in allowing it, just as the Shakers allowed that marriage could be the lesser sin, the Mormons must have felt that it was better to be polygamous than something worse. The reasoning is Evans's. In his *Autobiography* he adds that by permitting polygamy they were avoiding the "social evil of Christendom."[92] In this way the Shakers interpreted their own tolerance of monogamy as the equivalent of the Mormons' tolerance of polygamy; and they believed that both these doctrines of tolerance were preferable to making marriage into a sacrament.

Oneida. The Perfectionists at Oneida and the Shakers of Massachusetts were in frequent contact. The two societies were founded on similar premises, from which they drew opposite conclusions. Their common premise was a belief that the suppression of the family was a step in eliminating private property as in early Christian communism. This led the Shakers to the principle of celibacy for all. It led the Perfectionists to the opposite principle of "complex marriage" or plural marriage. The Shaker principle was based on the impossibility of a conscious, rational, spiritualized procreation. The Oneidist principle was based on the social institution of mutual criticism and the physical technique of male continence,[93] both of which were relied on to assure a voluntary and conscious disjunction of the two aspects of human love: "the amative and the propagative functions." Thus Oneida created for itself an atmosphere of sublimated sexuality and semiscientific eugenics. The community lasted for thirty years. J. Prudhommeaux brought back several photographs of onetime members who had been born of "selected parents." In the end the Oneida community disappeared under the pressure of public opinion. It produced copious documentation.[94]

Like the Shakers, the Perfectionists of Oneida thought they were at the center of the American communitarian movement. Two impressive records of the experiment, the one by Noyes and the one by Hinds, were produced. Naturally, the Shakers denounced the Oneida way as another "Babylonization" of Christianity. Evans called it "disorderly Spiritualism, parent of Free-lovism" and said it led to a diabolic misuse of marriage, in which "they seek how to use it *ad libitum* and still be unfruitful."[95]

But there were two aspects to Oneidism. On the one hand, there was the disjunction of sexuality and reproduction by a special technique of intercourse; on the other hand, based on the individual and collective self-control that this made possible, there was a rationalizing of reproduction itself by what the Perfectionists called "stirpiculture." The Shakers were venomously opposed to the first aspect of this program because it opened the door to sexual activity ad libitum, but they found themselves in sympathy with the second aspect because it proposed that the "propagative functions" be protected by replacing sexual attraction with rational considerations. This second principle of Perfectionism was obviously not valid for the church but was valid for "the World" at a time when Shaker theology began to attribute a certain value of its own to life outside the society. In effect, insofar as the Shakers finally approved the perpetuating of mankind by a decreasing quantity of couples,[96] their principles led them to envisage that this perpetuating would occur according to a system of increasing quality of progeny. That is why from time to time a Shaker elder would become the advocate of the principle of "stirpiculture." Hinds slyly points this out.[97] If this bias of Shaker thought created no agreement, it at least opened up the possibility of discussion with the Perfectionists at Oneida.

At any rate, the people at Oneida, although they deplored the Shakers' ascetic dogmatism,[98] never ceased to treat them with an undeniable respect. Pierrepont Noyes, son of the founder of Oneida, wrote in his memoirs that he once saw his father and Elder Evans having a friendly chat together: "I was struck by the fact that my father treated him as an equal."

In his own *History of American Socialisms*, after transcribing MacDonald's somewhat ironic account of what he had observed among the Shakers, John Humphrey Noyes noted that Shaker influence on American socialists has been so great that they should be given a special place in the story of the old religious communities.[99] According to one of his biographers, Noyes's homage to the Shakers went even further. He was convinced that the success of the Shakers had encouraged the emigrations and communal experiments of the Rappites, the Zoarites, and the Ebenezers.[100] These later experiments in communal living were thought to have been more like echoes of the Shakers than original creations. In England, when Robert Owen set out to convert the world to communism he was, to Noyes's mind, quite consciously following the trail already blazed by the American Shakers. And Noyes, according to his biographer, went so far as to declare that Frenchmen like Saint-Simon and Fourier had been influenced by the Shakers. Retracing the geneology of the community movement, he affirmed: "It is only fair to say that we all owe more to the Shakers than to the socialist planners of the modern world." Shaker success was what supported all the written theories of the French and English groups, and it was what compensated for their failures. He thought it doubtful that Owenism and Fourierism would ever have existed or, at least, ever have had an effect on the practical American people if the Shaker communities had not already been in existence. It was Noyes's opinion that, if one is to do complete justice to Shakerism, it does not suffice to say that the Rappites, the Zoarites, the Ebenezers, the Owenites, and the Fourierists all echo the Shaker enterprise; one must add that the Shakers themselves are the distant echo of the early Christian Church.[101]

Noyes's curious homage seems a bit exaggerated. It is doubly curious because of the fact that Noyes was led to his own social and religious conclusions by a study of early Christianity. The difference between the two exegeses must have given Noyes and Evans much to discuss during their conversations. It would be possible to reconstitute those discussions from the many texts that each of the men has left us, but such a project would lead us away from the problem of Shakerism and take us into the world of Oneida.

In sum, there was an interdependence of similarities and differences among the three main religious community movements in America: The Shakers' movement was based on religious celibacy; the Mormons', at least in part, on patriarchal polygamy; and the Oneida Perfectionists', on plural marriage. All three claimed to be inspired by the Bible. All three opposed marriage as practiced in established Christian churches. This common inspiration and common opposition explain why these groups were relatively so permissive of each other's practices.

The differences in their respective conclusions explain — if not their controversies, since these were practically non-existent — at least the almost complete lack of solidarity among them. The rapid decline of Oneida and the expansion of Mormon activity into an area outside the immediate community only confirmed this indifference.

Shaker relations with the Fourierists were slight. Albert Brisbane, one of the Fourierist pioneers in America, had only scorn for the communal experiments of the Shakers and religious groups such as the Moravians and the Rappites — "those monotonous and monastic efforts." Bestor cites a group of Fourierists from Rochester who repudiated the Shakers, Rappites, and Zoarites, saying that some of their notions are "repugnant," others "hideous." This repudiation did not prevent the Rochester group from appreciating the prosperous condition of the religious communities.[102] The almost total collapse of the ambitious American phalansteries provided the Shakers with an occasion for harsh revenge. Yet the only new members they seem to have picked up from the demise of those communities were from Fruitlands; and this was because of a not very Fourierist dissidence at the Fourierist Brook Farm. One of the founders of Fruitlands, Charles Lane, and his twelve-year-old son spent several years in a Shaker society after the failure of their own collective.[103]

With the Owenites, on the other hand, relations were more complex. They began at an early date and lasted through the failure of the community at New Harmony. The two movements had a certain common background. We know that the French Prophets, like the Methodists, were directly or indirectly influenced by the Moravians. This does not appear very clearly in Shaker history and prehistory except in the homage paid them by the authors of the *Testimony*.[104] On the other hand, in the history of Methodism, this influence is quite evident. Elie Halévy writes:

The Moravians exercised a spiritual authority over several Methodist sympathizers. They had a profound aversion to violence in any form and in this sense were as little revolutionary as the Quakers. This did not prevent them from dreaming of a peaceful transformation of society into a place where people would share the wealth and hold goods in common. The colonies they organized at Herrnhut and at Lamb's Hill in Yorkshire, as well as the Treveca community which Howell Harris later set up on the Moravian model in Wales, were all small closed societies, resembling both the monastery and the *phalanstery*.[105]

This is the period during which Benjamin Ingham and the Moravian communities he founded in Yorkshire were influencing social thought, and it is time for someone to write a detailed account of how an English newspaper accused Ingham of preaching common ownership of property to the English workers.[106] At any rate, after a series of difficulties coming from within and from without, the societies founded by Ingham were dispersed. The fate of the survivors is weighted with significance: "Many of their members transferred their allegiance to the Dalites, a *Scottish sect named after Mr. Dale, a rich Glascow industrialist who later became the father-in-law of Robert Owen.*"[107]

Mr. Dale, the founder, had started life as a journeyman weaver and had become the coowner of New Lanark. At first he had subscribed to the views of the Glassites, a sect found by Robert Glass mainly to combat the power of church and state and to advance the cause of ecclesiastic democracy.[108] Thus, when some of Ingham's disciples joined the Dalites, they were bringing a communitarianism into contact with a congregationalism. Elie Halévy believes we are justified in concluding that "the Moravians and the Methodists linked the mystical communism of the Middle Ages to the lay communism of the nineteenth century."[109]

Without going as far as Elie Halévy in our speculations, it would be interesting to know·if the conversations between Robert Owen and D. Dale, or with Miss Dale, soon to become Mrs. Owen, included a discussion of Ingham and the Moravian societies, and if any of this talk influenced reforms undertaken at New Lanark. Whatever may have been the case, in 1817, when Robert Owen launched his propaganda campaign, one of the English publications (*New Monthly Magazine and Universal Register*) printed long articles about the Moravians, mentioning along with them the Shakers, as well as the Rappites and the Jesuit *Reducciones* in Paraguay.[110] In this way Owenism and Shakerism already had a more or less articulated point in common during their pre-history. This makes it a bit less surprising that the man who was Dale's grandson and Robert Owen's son—Robert Dale Owen—was at one time tempted (although only perfunctorily) to join the Shaker society at Mount Lebanon.[111]

It was not until 1817 that Robert Owen had any factual knowledge of the Shaker organization. Until that time he had been concerned with theories, notably in his *A New View of Society*, which appeared in successive editions between 1813 and 1817. That year a Philadelphia newspaper, the *Aurora*, published two extracts from Owen's book. According to Bestor, this was probably the first time that the message of Owenism reached the American public.[112] Among the readers interested in these extracts was a Philadelphia Quaker named W. S. Warder, who had the idea of sending to the English author, as a practical confirmation of his theories, a short monograph on the Shaker societies of the United States.

At the same time there was another Quaker playing a role in Owen's research. This one was more than a hundred years old. His name was John Bellers, and it was he whom Karl Marx referred to as an "extraordinary mind in political economy." Bellers's treatise, *Proposals for Raising a College of Industry*,[113] was given to Owen by a friend named Francis Place, who had found the brochure in a dusty corner of a library. His comment on presenting his find was supposed to have been: "I've made a great discovery—a book which was supporting your social ideas a century and a half ago." The convergence was a fortunate one. In 1818 Robert Owen added some writings of his own to the essays by Bellers and Warder and published them all under the title *A New View of Society*.

The Warder monograph is honest and in sympathy with its subject. The author expresses a few reserves as to the sectarian dogmatism of the Shakers and the narrowness of their education, and is somewhat skeptical of the Shaker theory of marriage.[114] However, his reserves are presented discreetly, and he places his emphasis on common ownership of property, successful autarky, organization of work, and the general social virtues of the Shakers, whom he describes as "sober, simple, clean, honest, hospitable and generous."[115]

The most interesting page of the book is the foreword, most likely written by Owen himself. It claims that the text to follow will offer the reader simple but convincing proof of the results that can be attained by "the principle of combined labor and expenditure," and may therefore be considered an argument against the present system of mankind. To a liberal and well-informed mind the only objection is a degrading tendency to superstition, which he saw as responsible for the low quality of intelligence manifested in the religious notions and behavior of the Shaking Quakers. But even that, according to the author of the Foreword, does not seem to have prevented these people from making progress, cultivating useful skills, creating a uniformly peaceful atmosphere, and permitting the exercise of truthfulness, decency, and sincerity in their hospitality. That part of the Shaker behavior which arouses enlightened minds to revulsion and pity supplies obvious and abundant proof for the thesis of *A New View of Society*, that "the character is formed *for* and not *by*" the people a man lives with. From this it follows that human beings can be led by the ignorance and folly of society to pervert the most ordinary feelings and necessary inclinations of human nature, and yet, at the same time, like the Quakers, present to those around them a moral character and attitude of inoffensive goodness. These moral qualities are seen in the Shakers to a degree which is unparalleled in the best forms of present-day society. In view of this, is it possible for a reasonable man to doubt that society has the means, even with its limited knowledge, of raising intelligent man as far above his present level of existence as the conduct of those simplehearted Shakers has raised them above the low level of behavior found even in the best ordered town or village under the system reigning in the world today? So wrote Owen in 1818.[116] His homage is not without a note of malice. It reflects almost the same position as the one Friedrich Engels would take a few decades later.

The Shakers were to be in a good position to counter this reasoning after the collapse of the community at New Harmony, but from the very beginning they had Robert Owen on the defensive. When he visited America in 1824, one of his first concerns was to visit the Shaker society at Watervliet. What traces we have of this trip indicate that he found the Shakers placid and intransigent.[117] Owen shook his head in agreement when they explained their social structure, but he turned a deaf ear when the True Believers undertook to dissuade him from his project of founding a community based on a diversity of religious faiths. Later, when he arrived in Indiana, Owen met the Shakers again. They came to visit him in the village that he had acquired from Rapp.[118] There is even a record of two Shakers from Kentucky who came to New Harmony to join Owen's community. That same year Owen's illustrious disciple, Frances Wright, justified her Nashoba project by pointing out, among other things, the precedent of the Shakers.[119] As one can see, Owenite reasoning took the form of citing current examples. To those who remained reluctant or were hostile to the idea of founding a society on a principle other than personal interest and private property, they would oppose, de facto, examples of social milieus based on collective interest and property held in common: the *Reducciones* in Paraguay and the communities of the Moravians, the Rappites, and especially the Shakers.

Thus the Shakers were in a good position to gather in the diehards after the collapse of New Harmony experiment. There were some obscure ones such as D. Latham, his wife, and his daughter, whose arrival was recorded at South Union in 1827. There were others who were more illustrious, such as Frederick Evans, whose spiritual itinerary we have already indicated; Daniel Fraser, who, after meeting Owen in England, joined the Shakers and became one of their great elders; and Sister Jane D. Knight, who entered the Order of Mount Lebanon in 1826 and wrote "Sketch of

Socialistic Experiments," which unfortunately exists only in manuscript form.[120] The Shakers also gathered in whole groups. In May 1827 several survivors from the defunct community of Valley Forge arrived at Mount Lebanon to learn the secret of a communism that works.[121] After some complicated negotiations, about fifty of them were gathered, not counting those who appeared later and among whom, according to White and Taylor, there were many children destined to become solid Shakers.[122] It is quite possible that Owen himself made a visit to Mount Lebanon at this time.[123]

After the wave of Owenites and then the wave of Fourierists had passed, the Shaker texts drew conclusions from the course of events. To the preface in the second edition of the *Millennial Church*, which we have already cited,[124] should be added an essay written in 1853 by William Leonard under the title "Reasons for Which the Attempts to Establish Communities in the World Have Failed." In his essay Leonard pointed out that within the space of a few years more than twenty similar societies had been launched in the United States. Four or five of these were in the State of New York; two were in Ohio, and one or more in New Jersey and Massachusetts; there had been Brook Farm at West Roxbury, Mendon at Hopedale, and a community at Northampton. One group went as far as Wisconsin and tried to start a society on a large scale in that region.

These societies, explained Leonard, had all begun their lives with great zeal. In both Europe and America their founders invariably invoked the success of the Shakers to prove that the thing could be done. But almost all of these enterprises, which had been launched so enthusiastically, became dislocated and saw their members dispersed until hardly a survivor was left to tell the story. If the talents and superior abilities of illustrious men and the generous donations of sympathetic friends could assure the prosperity of foundations like these, they would have done so, for in many cases such men and such gifts were not lacking.[125]

Leonard continues his essay with the usual argument: marriage and private property belong together. The collective community cannot prosper unless marriage is suppressed and abandoned. Families based on marriage and collective ownership of goods are antagonistic elements, and all who try to combine them to make a society whose guiding principles will be procreation and self-interest are trying to dress up something old to look like something new.

There were hazards in this de facto argument: the Shakers did not foresee that in a few decades their society, too, would be dislocated and dispersed, undermining the basis for their sententious discourse.

4. AMERICAN SOCIALISMS

Anyone who thumbs through a history of socialism in the United States or reads the chapter on the collective communities in a book like the one by Morris Hillquit readily perceives that in their development the Shaker societies remained alien to the trade-union movement and the socialist-inspired political parties. Only two associations can be pointed out. One was with Edward Bellamy, the Utopian socialist. The other was with Henry George, an outsider who enjoyed a period of immense popularity in the United States. The Shakers reacted negatively to Bellamy's industrial and centralized socialism. They reacted positively to George's agrarian socialism, with its facile version of a cooperative.

Bellamy's book, *Looking Backward. If Socialism Comes. 2000–1887,* was published in Boston in 1887. B. Ruyer judges it to be inspired by Marx.[126] M. L. Berneri judges it to be inspired by Saint-Simon.[127] Morris Hillquit judges it to be solely the product of the author's observation and personal obsession.[128] Frederick Evans, not without a sour note, judged it to be inspired and determined by the experiments of the Shakers. He wrote in a letter that Bellamy's *Looking Backward* "is a reflection from Shakerism; as the moon reflects the light of the sun, so is Shakerism throwing light upon the sin-darkened earthly order of Church and State."[129]

More explicitly, in another letter dated 23 March 1891,

Evans speaks of having read Bellamy's book when it first came out:

We read Bellamy's Work, when it first came out. He lives in Massachusetts and he has been well acquainted with the Shaker system all his days. He knew of its successful, economic results in settling all disputes about capital and labor; he knew, too, that thousands of human beings had ignored private property for a hundred years; and had taken the ground, that whoso would not work, should not eat; thus making work honorable and aristocratic idleness—made possible by robbery—was shameful, and in a Shaker village, unfashionable. Unfashionable, too, were all the unhealthy, silly modes of disfiguring the well-made, beautiful human form. He saw a people so independently rich, without speculation, that they originated their own modes and manner of living in all respects. Their hygienic habits created healthy bodies, that needed no paints to hide the diseases that lust creates—"the ills that flesh is heir to," a community, where the two sexes live together in sexual purity, while caring for and ministering to one another's daily needs and comforts. Bellamy in his utopian book ignored the Shakers and their achievements, while he appropriated the main facts of their wonderful lives and system to make himself the observed of all observers, for the time being. When Shakerism comes to be read as Bellamy's book is being read—and it will be—it will reveal the source of his plagiarism.[130]

It is difficult to see how Bellamy's great industrial mobilization could be purely and simply a plagiarism of the Shaker system. Obviously, there were a few traits in common: Bellamy's army of women workers, commanded by its own woman-general, might be considered an echo of the teams of Shakeresses directed by their deaconesses and their eldresses. It is also true that the organization of the United Society did evoke the idea of an army for some observers such as Hervey Elkins, with whose writings Bellamy was acquainted.[131] The elimination of salary scales in favor of a common salary for everyone, collective thrift, modes of common consumption, these could all be found in the Shaker societies, and Bellamy may well have taken his ideas from them. Yet Bellamy's socialist Utopia seems both more "statized" and more individualistic than the Shaker system. Moreover—and this is a crucial difference—Bellamy inspired no agrarian community of the Shaker type. All that the movement born of his book really produced was the "Bellamy Club," a political organization whose purpose was to promote the nationalization of industry.

It is quite true that at the time Bellamy's book was published the Shakers considered themselves to be the artisans of a general economic transformation which would someday achieve the political democratization begun under the Declaration of Independence.[132] And when Evans, as in this letter, said that Bellamy's Utopia was a projection of Shakerism, he was referring to the Shakerism he dreamed of and, quite possibly, could not put into words. Except for a few small points,[133] the letter did not criticize the content of Bellamy's book; Evans's only complaint seemed to be that the author had not clearly indicated that Shakerism was his source. *Looking Backward* sold a half million copies in a few years, which was enough to make anyone a little jealous.

The Shakers' bitterness toward Bellamy gave way to frankness and cordiality when they considered the writings of Henry George. The idea of agrarian nationalization was more accessible to the Shakers than the theme of industrial concentration, which Bellamy had treated with such resolute optimism. From remarks that Evans made to Nordhoff, one senses that the Shakers balked at Bellamy's brand of optimism,[134] whereas the Georgist themes infiltrated deep into the political thinking of the great rationalist elders like Evans and Fraser. In the passages already cited from their writings the following motifs of Georgist doctrine were evident: if progress brings nothing but poverty, it is because it has been rendered ineffective by private ownership of the land and the resulting monopolies; the worker rightfully owns only the product of his labors; the land is free, for it was there before the man who cultivates it and cannot be owned; and there should be a system assuring all the citizens of their right to all their country's land.[135]

These propositions were doubly attractive to the Shakers

because of their resemblance to the Mosaic laws, which were so generally appreciated by the Millennial Church and which, perhaps because of what Henry George had written, were increasingly cherished by Frederick Evans.[136] The disagreements between the Georgists and the socialists made an understanding with the socialists even more difficult to reach, but the believers' systematic mistrust of industrial society and politics would have neutralized any entente that might have occurred. Even with the Georgists, their relations were fragile, and when a series of communities were organized according to the tenets of Georgist doctrine, those communities remained formally unrelated to the Shaker societies.[137]

However, during the electoral campaign of 1886, a period of great popular enthusiasm for the Georgists, the Shakers did something they had never done before and would never do again. They actively supported a candidate. Elder Daniel Fraser's "Shaker Support for Henry George" was published in the *New York Tribune* on 26 December 1886. This was in the middle of the electoral campaign. A few days before, in the same newspaper, a short article reported a message sent by Archbishop Corrigan to all the pulpits in the city. In it he had warned his flock to be wary of specious theories claiming to prove that land cannot be owned any more than the air and the sea. This was, of course, a part of Georgist doctrine. According to the pastoral letter, this attack on private property would, if successful, bring stagnation into the spirit of enterprise and rob labor of its essential motivation. The Archbishop agreed that in many cases the rights of workingmen had been trampled on, often in complicity with the law. But does one excess correct another? The workers' just demands should be made, but according to the method that Christ had always taught, etcetera. Naturally, the purpose of reporting this letter in the newspaper was to generalize the Archbishop's criticism of those faithful Catholics and clergy who had compromised themselves by supporting Henry George. Elder Daniel Fraser sent in his reply that very day.[138] It read as follows:

To the Editor of the Tribune: Sir — In your daily of November 23 there is an article headed "The Catholic Pastoral and Mr. George," which says: "Who would burrow in the earth to draw forth its buried treasures, if the very mine he was working were at the mercy of the passer-by? Who would watch with eagerness the season to sow, to reap and to gather the harvest, if he is told that those who stand by the wayside idle are equally entitled to its enjoyment?" If these illustrations support the argument in the preceding sentences, allow me to think that the said argument has no force, because these illustrations never had, nor never can be actualities. Again, Archbishop Corrigan states that "in many instances the rights of the toiler are trampled on, and the fruits of his labor snatched from his grasp; this is done too frequently with the concurrence or at least with the connivance of the law." He adds: "Seek redress of such grievances by the wise methods which the Church is forever teaching." Yes, "forever teaching" and forever leaving the "toilers" in the lurch, as she has done for hundreds of years, and as she has left Daniel O'Connel and Ireland in the lurch to suit her foreign policy. O'Connel died broken-hearted and the Ireland of to-day is the fruit of that policy. Why Henry George should be connected with that Pastoral I fail to see, except to be commended. The whole scope of his teachings is to secure to the "toiler" releasement from "being trampled on" and to prevent the "fruits of his labors being snatched from his grasp."

The wild conduct and talk of some of the "toilers" is mainly due to aggravations and long-continued repression. The press of Christendom today is repressive in the interest of those who trample on the toilers, and are "snatching from his grasp the fruits of his labors." I think the press of your city very English. It has the odor of aristocratic interests. You state: "Any able bodied man can make his way by his labors to the regions in which free land is still open to the settler, and can earn enough on his way to pay all the expenses of his acquisition." With equal extravagance of thought and sentiment the editor of the Tribune might advise the two hundred thousand needlewomen of his city to change their employment. The little busy bee conducts its social affairs with more discretion. It does not send out a single bee and expose it to many hardships on its way to the flowery regions of the West. It deals more kindly with the brother bees. It sends out a colony laden with the sweets of its civilization.

Human social life as manifested to the "toilers" lacks brotherly kindness. However the law has gone forth, "All have an inalienable right to the pursuit of happiness." Give this generality actuality by opening to all access to the elements of human subsistence. And do as the bees do, lading those who are beginning life with the sweets of your civilization.

There are three kinds of political economy or plans of social life. The first is that of Heaven, "Unto this last, even as unto thee, will I give a penny." The second, that of modern Christian civilization, which leaves in the city of New York 200,000 helpless women the victims of destructive competition. And to dispose of its surplus population, its chief factors are war, famine and pestilence. Third, the political economy of justice — opening to all the elements of human subsistence, of which Henry George is an exponent. The attacks of the press upon him impress me unfavorably.

I am an aged man, between eighty and ninety. I advise in the interests of peace, and of security to life and property, that you take a change of base. I have the great happiness of being your friend.

D. Fraser

Mount Lebanon, Columbia County, New York., December 23, 1886

This, then, was the first and the last time that a prominent Shaker would intervene in an electoral campaign. Coincidentally, at about the same time, another prominent man, who was also a stranger to competitive politics and also a communist agrarian, took up the defense of Henry George. "The merit of Henry George is not only to have annihilated the sophisms that religion and science use to justify private property but also to have illuminated the question with such a degree of clarity that one can no longer deny the injustice done in the name of rights to property unless one stops up his ears." This statement was from the pen of Leo Tolstoi. It represents his first point of agreement with the Shakers.

5. LEO TOLSTOI'S CHRISTIANITY

It is interesting to speculate on how the contact was made.[139] All that we know is that Elder Frederick Evans and Leo Tolstoi entered into a relation similar to the one that Tolstoi would later establish with Ghandi. The same inspiration ran through the thought of all three men, but with different results. The America of the 1890s, Tolstoi's immense talent, and the situation of the Hindu masses explain the divergences.

The Shakers published two of the letters from their correspondence in a brochure which can be found in American libraries.[140] It contains a short answer by Tolstoi to a previous letter by Evans, about which nothing is known, and a second long letter by Evans which reads like the swan song of the aging elder. The text of the two letters are so interesting — and rare — that we transcribe them in their entirety.

Toula, Tasnaya Poliana, Russia
February 15, 1891

Elder Frederick W. Evans
Dear Friend and Brother: Thank you for your kind letter.

It gave me great joy to know that you approve of my ideas upon Christianity. I was very much satisfied with your views upon the different expression of religious sentiments, suiting the age of those to whom they are directed. I received the tracts that you sent me, and read them, not only with interest, but with profit; and cannot criticise them, because I agree with everything that is said in them: there is only one question which I should wish to ask you.

You are (as I know), non-resistants. How do you manage to keep communal property — but, nevertheless, property? Do you acknowledge the possibility, for a Christian, to defend property from usurpators? I ask this question because I think that the principle of non-resistance is the chief trait of true Christianity; and that the greatest difficulty, in our time, is to be true to it: how do you manage to do so in your community?

I received your tracts; but you say in your letter that you have sent me books; do you mean that you have sent me books and tracts, or do you call the tracts, books?

I received, more than a year ago, the Oregon paper, *World's Advance Thought.* I have several times seen your articles in it. I am very grateful to the editor for sending this paper; in every number of it I get spiritual nourishment; and, were it not for some spiritualistic tendency which is foreign to me, I should absolutely agree with all its religious views: I like this paper very much.

With sincere respect and love,

Yours truly,
Leo Tolstoi

Tolstoi's question on how to protect communal property reflects his obsession with an idea of which Henry Lasserre has given us several examples in his essay on the Tolstoyan communities. According to the Russian writer, to say that property is held in common rather than individually does not change the fact that ownership of the property is guaranteed by the state, protected by the police, and consequently dependent on force: "The fundamental rule of Christian belief is not only not to use force, but also not to acquire property and not to defend the property one already has." This leitmotif of Tolstoi's thought runs through all his correspondence with the experimental collectives in Russia and in other parts of the world. He comments on this at length in his letters to the Doukhobors of Canada:

The idea of property implies that not only will I refuse to surrender my fortune to whoever wishes to take it from me, but also that I will prevent him from doing so. And it is impossible to defend one's possessions against other people without using violence, which is to say, by fighting or, if necessary, by murder. Without the use of force, without killing, property would never be safe. In cases where we do hold property without using force, this is possible only because our property is guaranteed by professionals whose task it is to use force to protect it. To admit the validity of property is to approve violence and murder, and it makes no sense for a man to refuse military service and police duty if at the same time he is permitted to hold property which can be maintained only by the army and the police. Those who do their military service, perform police duty and own land are acting better than those who refuse all military service and police duty, but also refuse to give up their rights to own property.[141]

It is not surprising that Tolstoi asked the Shakers: "You are (as I know) non-resistants. How do you manage to keep *communal property*—but, *nevertheless, property?*"

It was an embarrassing question. For although they proclaimed that the eminent domain administered by the various societies was in the service of the Gospel and the poor, the Shakers could not overlook the fact that the lands and goods they held in common had been acquired and defended in courts of law.[142] In his reply Evans was uneasy and wavered between two different arguments. In one he pleaded the necessity of passing through a state of imperfection before attaining a greater perfection; in the other he suggested that his greater perfection could be attained under existing American laws, since the country was ruled by a government of the people and that, a priori, such a government could not be conducive to coercion. In his answer Evans sounds like a preacher who has been upset and is short of breath. The text is part timidity, part megalomania, and part passion.

Mount Lebanon, New York, U.S.A.
6 March 1891

Leo Tolstoi

Dear Friend and Brother: — Your welcome letter is received. There is much union of sentiment between us and more union of spirit. Wisdom says, "I love those, who love me; and we love those who are in the same degree of light and truth that we ourselves are in." It is wonderful what clear ideas you have in relation to the definition of the words Christian and Christianity. You are ministered unto by a Christ spirit as Jesus was. It is not for yourself alone, but is for thousands of other souls with whom you are connected who are ripe for the harvest sickle. The end of the world is coming upon them.

Russia is a mighty Empire, it has produced large numbers of spiritual men and women in the past under the first appearing of Christ in the male order. They knew God as a Heavenly Father, but not as a Heavenly Mother. They had a male Priesthood order. They were a John the Baptist people, who looked, waited and prayed for the "coming of our Lord." They were sincere and self-sacrificing, but knew not how to pray *aright*, having been blinded by theological ignorance and consequent error.

The Mennonites and Moravians, what a noble people! And many others bearing different names, but all actuated by the same Christ spirit, down to the Quakers or Friends who came nigh unto the Kingdom of Heaven.

These were the "Two Witnesses" — male and female — who prophesied and prayed and practiced Christian virtues "in part." Religious persecutions have not been "in part," but in whole, and those who brought their opposers to the "Holy Inquisition" or killed them by the thousands under the Duke of Alva or by a "Saint Bartholomew Massacre," thought they were doing God good service.

All the great European nations are *Christian*. War is a permanent institution among them. They are exhausting their national resources, fighting or "in peace preparing to fight." Do they not pray to the same God to help them to kill each other? Could the devil do worse by them?

You ask: "How do you manage to keep communial [sic], but nevertheless, property. Do you think it possible for a Christian to defend property from usurpers?" These are important questions. Jesus said: "Be ye perfect, even as your father in heaven is perfect." That is the *end* of our Christian travel, but is it the *beginning*? Did Jesus come to it while yet in the body? "Jesus was not yet perfected," this was said of him after his death.

If we scrutinize closely the history of Jesus, from birth to death, do we not see a growth from where he was to where he would be? "He saw the travel of his soul and was satisfied." Suppose we had a list of the sins he confessed to John before he was baptized and previous to the time when the Christ Spirit descended upon him, and then suppose we make another list of the various transgressions and violations of the abstract principles of Christianity as you and I *now* see them, what would be the result? Should we not conclude that he was an "elder brother" and "was touched with the feeling of our infirmities"? He had the same nature, and by it "was tempted in all respects like those whom the Christ spirit came to redeem." He was simply "the first born of many brethren," just as Ann Lee was the first born of many sisters.

Of course Antichrist has reversed all this. Those calling themselves Christians have taken the sword and have perished by it. Peter had a sword and a sheath to put it into after he had cut off a man's ear. That was not "non-resistance." What were the Apostles doing with "two swords," and why did Jesus tell his followers to sell their garments and to buy swords?

The Mennonites, Moravians and Quakers were non-resistants. Not until the separation of Church and State by "*the Horns* Infidel powers—that grew out of the Beast" in the American Revolution,[143] could "communial [sic] property" be held by non-resistants. That is the "New Earth," and as it becomes more perfect in its righteousness, the "New Heavens" will be nearer perfect in all the Christian virtues. It will travel from faith to faith through seven cycles, unto the perfect day, the light shining brighter and brighter until the light of "one day shall be as the light of seven days."[144]

We hold and defend our communial [sic] property under the Civil laws of the "New Earth," but in no case, nor under any circumstances should we injure a fellow being. You see that our Civil government is the voice of the people — vox populi vox Dei — and the people who are the rulers are more progressed than are the rulers of Russia, or of any Church-and-State government on the face of the earth.

We, the Shakers, under the American secular government, can carry out the abstract principles, taught by the revelation of the Christ spirit, more perfectly than has hitherto been done by mortal men and women, just as we carry out sexual purity, notwithstanding the sexes are brought face to face in every day of life, being without bolts and bars, in the same household of faith.

You are "pained" at our ideas concerning Ann Lee, and "spirit intercourse" between parties in and out of mortal bodies. I suppose it to be caused by misconceptions of what our views have been and what they are at present. What they were when the "Millennial Church" was written leave to the people of those times. Paul said: "When I was a child, I thought and spake as a child, but when I became a man, I put away childish things and thought and spake as a man."

Should that not be the case with those, who are in the "kingdom of heaven" of whose *increase* and government, to order and establish it in justice and judgment, "there should be no end"? The little stone cut out of the mountain, without hands — by revelation — *grew* and became a great mountain, and filled the earth.

At one time, the God of Israel told Moses that he would not lead the people of Israel hereafter, but that he would appoint an angel in his place, as leader. Israel, instead of increasing with the increase of God, retrograded.

I propose to send you some of my writings and shall be much obliged if you will spare the time to read and criticise them. Why should not theological problems be subject to the same rigid logic that mathematical problems are subject to? And why should not theologians be as cool and self-possessed as are mathematicians? If possible, they should be far more so; they should love one another, and that would be like oil in all parts of a complicated piece of machinery.

Dear friend: Come to Lebanon and see what God hath wrought, then, return and establish the Order in Russia, with consent of the Government, which the Shaker Order can and will obtain for you.

Calvin Green, one of our prophets, many years ago, predicted a glorious spiritual work in Russia, and he was very enthusiastic upon the subject. A Russian minister visited Lebanon and was very friendly. Has not the time arrived? And art not "thou the man?"

In *our* Church, the government is of God. It is not of the people. "Ye have *not* chosen me, but I have chosen you," and Revelation of God is the Rock upon which the Church is founded, and the "gates of Hell" — religious controversy — "will not prevail against it."

We repeat, come and see us, it will do you good. A poor, uneducated factory woman has confounded the wisdom of all *men*, reformers, legislators and scholars who have come to nothing as promoters of human happiness. Their systems have ended, in Christendom, as you now see it, and as Booth and those who inspired him, saw it. The end is coming.

With love to yourself and family I remain your friend,

F. W. Evans

Did anything come out of this correspondence? In view of the great Russian writer's predisposition for this type of communal experiment,[145] it is safe to assume that he was not disconcerted by the somewhat nebulous grandiloquence of the aging elder's style. Most likely, it was Evan's death in 1893 that broke off the exchange.[146]

Tolstoi showed himself in agreement, except on minor points, with the doctrine and practices of the Shakers.[147] Indeed, in its main points Tolstoi's Christianity was essentially identical with the "true Christianity" of the Shakers. Both identified Christianity with nonresistance: "The Christian cannot be a soldier, which is to say an assassin."[148] Both fought the coalition of church and state, of which Tolstoi was himself a victim. Both were practical ecumenists, liberal but not indifferent when confronted with theological and doctrinal variants: "Religious doctrines are numberless, but there is only one religion."[149] Both were radical communists, believing in the eminent domain of God in everything, and forbidding the ownership of property as a violation of God's right: "The essential point on which we should concentrate all our energies is the renunciation of property rights leading to hired labor and tenant farming."[150] Both refused to take oaths: "Brotherly love is incompatible with oaths."[151] Both preached perfectionism through chastity: the Russian, too, was convinced that Christian marriage could not be achieved, but he thought that a couple with children should stay together, living as brother and sister, to assure the education of the young.[152] There are even traces of Shaker millenarianism in Tolstoi's way of answering those who objected that the kind of perfection he preached would bring about the extinction of the race: "If God wants the human race to exist, He will find the way to perpetuate it, if not it will most certainly disappear from the earth."[153] At any rate, adds Tolstoi: "Instead of marrying and producing children it would be far simpler to support and save the millions of little ones who are dying all around us for lack of physical, to say nothing of spiritual, nourishment."[154] That, too, had been a policy of the early Shakers.

Similarities between the two are found even in the secondary characteristics of the Shaker universe and the world of Tolstoi's thought: mistrust of medical aid,[155] vegetarianism,[156] prohibition of tobacco,[157] reluctance to join with urban, industrial civilization,[158] predilection for rural, craft-based autarkies,[159] mistrust of too much schooling, and so on.

There is another important resemblance to be pointed out. Almost all these traits of Tolstoyan typology, as the thesis of M. I. Markovitch has shown, can be found in the attitudes of Mahatma Ghandi, who, a few years later, was to become another of Tolstoi's correspondents.[160] These are the traits which dominated the social architecture discussed in the Ashrams and later inspired the mass movement led by Ghandi. And we know that Ghandi himself likened these traits to those of true Christianity.

On the central point of marriage, Ghandi taught explicitly the Malthusian principles which had been only implied by the Shaker theory. Ann Lee had called marriage the lesser sin. Ghandi called it a lapse from grace, and he has left us the following commentary on this judgment:

Until India becomes a free nation, capable of combatting under-nourishment and remedying its causes, capable of feeding itself during periods of famine, capable of curing malaria, cholera, influenza and other epidemics, we do not have the right to bring children into the world. I cannot conceal from the reader *the discomfort I experience when I hear people discuss the births on our Indian soil. I must admit that for years I have reflected with satisfaction on the possibility of continence putting an end to procreation. . . .*

. . . What I wish to demonstrate is that young or old, blasé or not, it is our duty during the present period to cease giving birth to beings who will inherit our slavery.[161]

This declaration by Ghandi can be compared to the admonitions Mother Ann gave to Beulah Rude. In both cases the remedy was the same. Moreover, it is reminiscent of the old Bogomil legend: "A refusal of the oppressed to satisfy the demands of their oppressors by supplying them tiny creatures to be exploited, creatures whose birth brought to their needy families only an increase of poverty." No doubt about it, lust is a disorder at the very heart of the reproductive act, and for this reason it has been denounced as the original sin.[162]

This encounter of the Shaker doctrines with the Tolstoyan view of life—and, implicitly, with Ghandi's program—is very significant. It suggests that near the end of its cycle Shakerism may have discovered the premises contained in its own latent sources.

From the Shakers to Tolstoi, from Tolstoi to Ghandi, run the threads of a tradition joining the Far East with the Far West that was America at the time of the early Shakers. Ghandi was a Jainist, a member of the ancient religious movement akin to Buddhism, born in the sixth century B.C., and in this religion he found all that he needed to enrich his own conception of the good life. The question to ask is whether this road, which, through Tolstoi, joined Shakerism to Ghandism, is not really a road back, and whether the road forward did not through Jainism and Buddhism, affect the Shaker movement itself.

It must be pointed out, right away, that the stopping-off places on this road twenty-four centuries long are guesswork and indefinite, and that one should not expect them to represent a continuous formal tradition.

It is difficult to know whether or not the homage paid to Manichaeus and the neo-Manichaeans in the *Testimony*[163] is based on a real historical continuity. When one looks farther back than the English Prophets and the French Prophets, connections are hazy and it is not easy to know if and how the Cevenoles were related to the preceding Cathari. And despite the series of dualisms and related doctrines which appeared in the Middle East and in Languedoc from the fourth to the twelfth centuries (Messalians, Paulicians, Bogomiles, Patarines), the Manichaean origins of the Cathari is still problematic.

On the other hand, the line running from Manichaeus to Hindu thought is quite clear: "Wisdom and good works have been brought to us with perfect continuity, from one period to another, by the messengers from God. At one time they came to us through the prophet Buddha in India, at another time through Zoroaster in Persia, and at another time through Jesus in the West. After these came the age of Revelation in which I, Manichaeus, Messenger for the God of Truth, now deliver the Prophecy to Babylon."[164]

We also know that Buddhism exercised a strong, direct influence on Tolstoi. In 1844 the Russian writer registered at the University of Kazan to study Oriental languages and literature. In 1847, in the hospital at Kazan, he was in a bed next to a Buddhist lama with whom he had long talks. All during Tolstoi's life his readings and letter-writing revolved around the religion of the Hindus, the Jainists, and the Buddhists. This has been amply documented by M. I. Markovitch.[165]

The present study makes no attempt to show that there was any ideological influence of the doctrines on each other. The Shakers, Tolstoi, and Ghandi worked out their doctrines independently of one another before the first two exchanged greetings by letter in 1890 and before the second and the third began a longer exchange of ideas in 1908.

A priori or a posteriori, these doctrines all refer to traditions that are similar or are thought to be so; and those lumped together under the names of Buddha, Jesus, and Manichaeus do really advocate the same socio-ecclesiastic types. They even recognize these types in each other, as did Evans and Tolstoi. This recognition of similarities can be a deciding factor in our final evaluation of Shakerism, for they point up what appears to be more of a reinvention than a survival of a doctrinal tradition. If this is so, then the identical behavior at different times and places is not necessarily the result of a single vision that has been passed down orally or in writing from the past. It may simply be a matter of similar situations leading to behavioral solutions which were *later* recognized as common to those of a number of other groups. In such cases we are dealing with a tradition in which it is useless to look for lines of influence. This is the hypothesis proposed by R. Hertz in his interpretation of the material that K. K. Grass made available on the Russian sects. It would also seem to apply to the phenomenon of Shakerism.[166]

Conclusions

The HISTORICAL antecedents claimed by the Shakers thus lead, roughly speaking, to three central sources: the early Christians, who were valued for their similarity to the Essenes and for their Judaic tradition;[1] the Manichaeans and their medieval outcroppings, whose tradition the Shakers evoked only because they wanted to treat the Zend Avesta on the same level as the Bible;[2] and the Buddhists, whom they had got an understanding and feeling of from the writings of Leo Tolstoi and their friendship with the man himself.[3] It is clear that none of these antecedents was a determining factor in the initial development of the Shaker dissidence. It was not until later and a posteriori that the dissidence took on form and substance, when it was looking for corroboration and sanctions in the religious history of mankind. The Shakers found what they were looking for, more or less explicitly stated in the three sources. It was a case of having to establish a heredity before they could talk about any inheritance. What they inherited seems to be a certain typology which itself derived from a certain type of situation.

Correlations as vast as this are likely to be hypothetical, but that has not prevented men from attempting to make them.[4] In 1924, after listening to a memo by M. Meillet on the Gathâ de l'Avesta,[5] Marcel Mauss addressed the Institut Français d'Anthropologie with a series of remarks which may throw some light on our subject. Noting the traits and the popular origin which M. Meillet had attributed to the religious morality and dualism of the Zoroastrians, Mauss thought he could correlate that phenomenon with the phenomena of the Jews (who had prophesied before, during, and after their captivity and had had a psalmodic literature resembling, according to I. Loeb, "une littérature des pauvres") and the Hindu phenomena observed in Jainism and Buddhism. His conclusion was:

It is legitimate to suppose that this immense cultural tremor which was represented throughout the ancient world by equivalent forms of thought and law comes from a single cause which we can only half perceive. This cause is the ascent of the common people to the thought and the freedom to which they have aspired. . . . And we say that, seen in this light, the tremor is everywhere the same. It reveals what the people think and how they work without their masters.[6]

This way of interpreting the triple source which served the Shakers as historical point of reference should be critically examined.

It is impossible to interpret the great religious reforms as social revolutions, and it is doubtful that they were exclusively popular movements. In no case were they proposed by a classless society as a social protest against a class society. But — and this is the point where Marcel Mauss's suggestion should be developed — this religious reform did have social consequences, but of a different nature. For insofar as the established society had a priesthood constituting a class within the existing class structure, the religious reform had social effects. It did not abolish the class society; it simply displaced one of the classes. The one it displaced generally had a hereditary monopoly on revelations, holy books, and rituals, giving it control of the collective conscience on which the existing class system depended for theoretical sanction and moral justification. That is why the kind of groups produced by this religious reform had a corrosive effect on the normal relations between the various social classes, especially when the principle of equality before God came to mean the practice of socio-economic equality among men — as in the

Buddhist assembly, the Essene colony, and the Manichaean or para-Manichaean gatherings.

In this way the Shakers' central struggle against church and state led to the creation of the Family, a social phenomenon in which laymen became clerics without benefit of the form (sacraments, theology) or matter (temples, statues) of a priesthood or ministry which identified with a ruling class or even constituted the ruling class itself. "Church and clergy helped her not," says the Shaker chronicle, telling the story of the poor factory girl, Ann Lee. This chapter in Mother Ann's life has the force of a parable: during the deliberate and quasi administrative absence of the established church there occurred a gratuitous attempt to deproletarianize religion. It is not unlikely that at this point the reforming group was acting out its heritage from the Cévennes, where, without leaders and without pastors, young lay preachers had inspired the assemblies in the wilderness.[7]

This shift from a society with a religious class (the established church) to a religious society with no classes at all has always had both sociological causes and effects. In the case of the Shakers the defection of the established church corresponded to a defection of a whole civilization. Even though they never went so far as to launch a strike of their own, refusing to produce farm products or pay taxes, the Shakers did show some other classic symptoms of social revolt. They refused to reproduce; they refused to work in industry; they refused to take oaths; they refused to do military service; they refused to use money among themselves; they refused to use the courts for personal grievances; they refused to partake in the cultural activities of their day such as schools (usually), instrumental music (before 1870), profane literature, and painting. In sum, they were on strike against society as it was, and had millenarian hopes that by extending their strike over the entire face of the earth they would finally destroy that society.[8] This seems to have been the undisciplined and disappointing social content of the Shakers' class consciousness. It may also be what relates the Shakers to those "communities of the poor" which appeared on the scene in centuries past.

A "community of the poor" is not the same thing as a proletarian organization, which implies behavior and states of mind quite foreign to the Shaker universe. The elder or individual believer could be a Yogi, but he was not a member of the proletariat.

Nevertheless, historically, Shakerism occupied a position at the juncture of these two typologies. Perhaps it even acted as a catalyst, facilitating passage from one to the other. Before rejecting the theses of "utopian socialism" and "religious communism," had not "scientific socialism" drawn ideas from their various experiments and used their example as a springboard for leaping to its own solutions? To answer that question one must first clarify the role of the "new Christianities," including Saint-Simon's, in the formation of nineteenth-century proletarian socialism,[9] and then determine the relation of the German dissidences to the first stirrings of dialectical materialism.[10] Such clarification is the province of another study. Without anticipating its conclusions, but also without referring back to the relations between Owenism and the religious community experiments, there is one notable fact that should be mentioned as having a bearing on the Shaker problem.

In February 1845 Friedrich Engels, one of the first and greatest militants in the Western communist movement, was a speaker at the "agitation" sessions in Germany. We know the various subjects discussed at those meetings and we know which one Engels reserved for himself. He wanted to show that the communist system could be profitable and practical by explaining what had been created by the American communities and, in particular, by the Shakers. Remembering the precision of Engels's communist theory of property (for example, in *Anti-Dühring*),[11] one might well doubt that he would advance such an argument. However, we know his own thought on this subject, since at almost the same date he transcribed a substantial part of his presentation for a publication which was being hunted down by the government as an instrument of communist propaganda in Germany. This study was later included in the Marx-Engels *Gesamt Ausgabe*.[12]

Most of Engels's material comes from John Finch's travel notes as published in the *New Moral World* shortly after Engels had sent that paper his own analysis of continental communism.[13] Aside from an account of the Owenite communities,[14] Engels chose to concentrate his remarks on three of the American experiments that Finch had described:[15] the Rappites at Harmony-Economy, the Separatists at Zoar, and above all, the Shakers. He shrugged off the religious premises as negligible and idealized the socio-economic results, calling them decisive. This text was written in 1845, two years before the communist league rallied around the *Manifesto* to become a proletarian organization. It is strange to learn that one of the last representatives of a religious communism had been invoked to guarantee the practicability of this project, yet that seems to have been Engels's clearly stated intention:

When one talks to people about socialism and communism one quickly learns that they will agree with you in principle and declare that communism is very fine, but quickly add that it is impossible to achieve this in real life. This objection is raised so often that the author deems it useful and necessary to refute it with some facts which are not well known in Germany and which simply invalidate the accusation. Communism, or life and work in a community where all goods are held in common [*Das soziale Leben und Wirken in Gemeinschaft der Güter*], is not only possible but, as we shall see, is already being practiced successfully in many communities of America and in one place in England. . . .

The reader will discover that most of the colonies described here developed out of various religious sects which most of the time fostered paradoxical and completely irrational points of view. On this subject the author is content to say only that such views have nothing to do with communism as such. It is obviously of no importance whether or not the people demonstrating the practical possibility of communal life believe in God, in "20" or have no faith at all. If they do have an irrational religion it constitutes an obstacle to be overcome and if, despite that obstacle, the community is vital and prosperous, how much easier it would have been for others who are free of religious nonsense. Although they are very tolerant, almost all the English socialists have given up religion, and that has not been easy in England where religious bigotry exposes them to denigration and calumny.

In America and, generally speaking, in the world the first to found a society organized according to the principle of common ownership of goods were the people called Shakers. They constitute an unusual sect with special religious ideas; they do not marry, they forbid all intercourse between husband and wife, and have other, similar rules. But those rules are of no importance to us here. As a sect, the Shakers were founded about seventy years ago. The founders were poor folk who gathered together to live in brotherly love under a system of common ownership of property which permitted them to worship God as they saw fit. Although their religious views, particularly the interdiction of marriage, have alienated many people, the Shakers attracted many adherents and now have ten large communities,[16] each of which has from 200 to 800 members. Each one of these communities is a lovely village with well constructed homes, factories, workshops, meeting halls and barns. They have gardens for flowers as well as vegetables, orchards and forests, vineyards, meadows and fields in abundance. They have cattle of the finest quality, horses, cows, sheep, hogs and chickens. In every case there is more than they need. Their barns are full of wheat; their storehouse shelves are stacked with so much cloth that an English traveler who visited them declared that he could not understand why a people who lived in such abundance would still work. According to him, the Shakers labor only to pass the time; otherwise they would have nothing to do. Among them no one is forced to work against his will and no one fusses uselessly in his job. They have no poorhouses no homes for the aged, because they have no poor, no needy, no widows, no abandoned orphans. They know no poverty and have nothing to fear. In their ten villages there is not a single policeman; there are no judges, no lawyers, no soldiers, no prisons, and yet everything functions normally. As far as they are concerned, the laws of the country do not exist, and indeed they could be abolished without anyone in the community knowing the difference, since these peaceful people have never caused anyone to be sent to prison. They live, as we said, owning all their worldly goods in common, and neither business nor money plays any part in their lives. . . .[17]

Thus we see that communal ownership is not absolutely impossible. The success of these people's efforts testifies to the contrary. We also see that people living communally live better and work less, that they have more leisure time in which to develop their minds, and that they become better and more moral men than their neighbors who stayed in the system of private property. This is what Americans, Frenchmen, Englishmen, Belgians and even a large number of Germans have already understood. Everywhere there are people who have made it their task to disseminate this information and who have thrown their lot in with *the party of the community* [*und für die Gemeinschaft partei ergriffen haben*].

This is important news for all men, but it is especially important for the poor workers who possess nothing, who are always spending their wages as soon as they are paid, and who run the inevitable risk of finding themselves without bread to eat. For them this opens the way to an independent life of security and serenity, by giving them equal rights with those who because of their wealth are in a position to bully the worker into becoming a slave. It is for these workers that communism is most important. In other countries the workers form the nucleus of the party calling for common ownership of goods; it is the duty of German workers to take their example to heart.[18]

In the middle of the nineteenth century Christianity was at a turning point, hesitating between a renewal of the church and a reform of society. Is this hesitation not central to Lamennais's thought, and does he not illustrate the blind alley it can lead to? During the same period European communism was hesitating between the semireligious millenarianism of Cabet, Weitling, and even, in some respects, Owen, and a rigorous analysis of self-conscious class struggle. Where does the distant echo of Shakerism fit into this picture? Was it a vestige or rather a revival of early Christianity, which itself carried strains of the great Eurasian religions, as Leo Tolstoi has shown us? Was it a preview of modern socialism, and was it, unwittingly or unwillingly, an integral part of its gestation, as Engels thought?

The significance of the United Society of Believers seems to be that it was caught between two goals, and that it never evolved beyond the stage of this unsurmounted, if not unsurmountable, dilemma. The distant neo-Christianity of the Shakers remained a distant presocialism. Nevertheless, it does claim our attention as a phenomenological phase and might even be called a "missing link," since through it two such different trends or life styles seem to have, momentarily at least, come into rudimentary contact.

Notes

Notes to Introduction

1. I have tried to show this current sociological interest in my bibliographic essay *Dissidence religieuses et socialismes utopiques*, published in *L'Année Sociologique* (1955).

2. E.g. Abbé Grégoire, *Histoire des sectes religieuses* (Paris, 1828–45), 5:220–28; John Hayward, *The Book of Religions* (Boston, 1842), pp. 75–85; I. Daniel Rupp, *He Pasa Ekklesia: An Original History of the Religious Denominations at Present Existing in the United States* (Philadelphia, 1844), pp. 656–62; R. A. Knox, *Enthusiasm, A Chapter in the History of Religion* (Oxford, 1950), pp. 558–66. See also, articles in various dictionaries, particularly the one by Schaff-Herzog.

3. E.g. Mary Hennell, *Outline of the Various Social Systems and Communities Which Have Been Founded on the Principle of Cooperation* (London, 1844); Donald Drew Egbert and Stow Parsons, *Socialism in American Life*, 2 vols. (Princeton, 1952).

4. E.g. W. Plumer, "The Original Shaker Communities in New England," *New England Magazine*, vol. 22 (1900). A correspondence, 1782–83, ed. with a foreword by F. B. Sanborn. A. E. Bestor, *Backwoods Utopias* (no. 2), pp. 44–45.

5. The most flagrant example is the work by H. Semler, *Geschichte des Socialismus und Communismus im Nord Amerika* (Leipzig, 1880).

6. E.g. Mary Marshall Dyer, *A Portraiture of Shakerism, Exhibiting a General View of Their Character and Conduct from the First Appearance of Ann Lee in New-England Down to the Present Time* (Concord [?], 1822).

7. Judgment of J. Prudhommeaux in *Etienne Cabet et l'Icarie* (Paris, 1926), p. 320, n. 2.

8. Rufus Bishop, *Testimonies of the Life, Character, Revelation and Doctrines of Our Blessed Mother Ann Lee and the Elders with Her; through Whom*

the Word of Eternal Life Was Opened in this Day of Christ's Second Appearing, Collected from Living Witnesses in Union with the Church, 1st ed. (Hancock, 1816), 406 pp.; 2nd ed. (Albany, 1888), 302 pp. Rufus Bishop, Testimonies Concerning the Character and Ministry of Mother Ann Lee and the First Witnesses of the Gospel of Christ's Second Appearing, Given by Some of the Aged Brethren and Sisters of the United Society: Including a Few Sketches of Their Own Religious Experiences. Approved by the Church. (Albany, 1827), 178 pp. Precepts of Mother Ann Lee and the Elders (Albany, 1888), 302 pp.

9. Benjamin Seth Youngs, The Testimony of Christ's Second Appearing, Exemplified by the Principles and Practice of the Church of Christ. History of the Progressive Work of God, Extending from the Creation of Man to the "Harvest,"— Comprising The Four Great Dispensations Now Consummating in the Millennial Church. Antichrist's Kingdom, or Churches, Contrasted with the Church of Christ's First and Second Appearing, the Kingdom of the God of Heaven. Published by the United Society Called Shakers. 1st ed. (Lebanon, Ohio, 1808) 600 pp.; 2nd ed. (Albany, 1810) 620 pp.; 3rd ed. (Cincinnati, Ohio, 1823) 574 pp.; 4th ed. (Albany, 1856), 632 pp. John Dunlavy, The Manifesto or a Declaration of the Doctrines and Practice of the Church of Christ (Pleasant Hill, Ky., 1818), 520 pp. Another edition was printed in New York, 1847; 486 pp. Calvin Green, A Summary View of the Millennial Church or United Society of Believers, Commonly Called Shakers, Comprising the Rise, Progress and Practical Order of the Society together with the General Principles of their Faith and Testimony. 1st ed. (1823), 320 pp.; 2nd ed., revised and augmented with approval of the ministry (Albany, 1848), 384 pp.

10. Calvin Green, and Seth Y. Wells, A Declaration of the Society of People Commonly Called Shakers Showing Their Reasons for Refusing to Aid or Abet the Cause of War and Bloodshed by Bearing Arms, Paying Fines, Hiring Substitutes or Rendering any Equivalent for Military Services (Albany, 1815), 200 pp. Observations on the Natural and Constitutional Rights of Conscience in Relation to Military Requisitions on the People Called Shakers (Watervliet, February, 1816), 24 pp. Richard McNemar and Calvin Morell, An Address to the State of Ohio, Protesting against a Certain Clause of the Militia Law Enacted by the Legislature at Their Last Session and Showing the Inconsistency of Military Power Interfering with Persons or Property Consecrated to the Pious and Benevolent Purposes of the Gospel (Lebanon, Ohio, 1818), 24 pp. The Other Side of the Question. In Three Parts: 1. An Explanation of the Proceedings of Eunice Chapman and the Legislature against the United Society Called Shakers in the State of New York. 2. A Refutation of the False Statements of Mary Dyer against the Said Society in the State of New Hampshire. 3. An Account of the Proceedings of Abram Van Vleet, Esq., and His Associates against the Said Society at Union Village, Ohio. Comprising a General Vindication of the Character of Mother and the Elders against the Attacks of Public Slander—the Edicts of a Prejudiced Party—and the Misguided Zeal of Lawless Mobs (Compiled by Eleazer Wright, Calvin Morell, Matthew Houston, and S. Serring.) (Union Village, 1819), 164 pp. Richard McNemar, ed., The Decision of the Court of Appeals (of Ken-

tucky) in a Case of Much Interest to Religious Communities in General and to the Shakers in Particular, to Which Is Prefixed a Brief Illustration of the Ground of Actions (Dayton, Ohio, 1834), 66 pp. A similar text had been published the preceding year: The Shaker Society against Gass and Banta. Brief of a Case in Kentucky (1833), 8 pp. Includes pages 48–58 of No. 57. An Act in Relation to Certain Trusts, 15 April 1839, New York Statutes, 62nd Session, 1839. Also reproduced in New York Assembly Documents, 1849, No. 198, Vol. 3, pp. 10–11. Certification of Administrative Measures of the Shakers before 1830. Account of Some of the Proceedings of the Legislatures of the State of Kentucky and New Hampshire. 1828 . . . in Relation to the People Called Shakers. Republished (New York, 1846). Report of the Examination of the Shakers of Canterbury and Enfield before the New Hampshire Legislature at the November Session, 1848; Including the Testimony at Length; Several Extracts from Shaker Publications; the Bill Which Passed the House of Representatives; the Proceedings in the Pillow Case Together with the Letter of James W. Spinney. (Concord, 1849), 100 pp. Report of the Select Committee on the Subject of the Shakers, 2 April 1849, 13 pp. Included in New York Assembly Documents, 1849, Vol. 3, No. 198. Report of the Trustees of the United Society of Shakers in the Town of New Lebanon, Colombia County, New York, 18 March 1850. Included in New York Senate Documents, 1850, No. 89. John Whitely, Letters and Documents Respecting the Conscription, Arrest and Suffering of Horace Taber, a Member of the United Society. Compiled by John Whitely. (Shirley, Mass., 1863). Durbin Ward, Shaker Income Tax. Application to Commissioner Delano. Brief of Durbin Ward, Counsel for Applicants (Albany, 1869), 21 pp.

11. Millennial Praises, Containing a Collection of Gospel Hymns in Four Parts Adapted to the Day of Christ's Second Appearing Composed for the Use of the People (1812), 288 pp. Philos Harmoniae, A Selection of Hymns and Poems for Use of Believers, Collected from Sundry Authors. (Watervliet, Ohio, 1833), 186 pp. Philos Harmoniae was another pseudonym of Richard McNemar. Book of Hymns and Poems. Isaac Newton Youngs, A Short Abridgement of the Rules of Music with Lessons for Exercise and a Few Observations for New Beginners (New Lebanon, 1843), 40 pp. Haskell Russell, A Musical Expositor; or a Treatise on the Rules and Elements of Music Adapted to the Most Approved Method of Musical Writing (New York, 1847), 83 pp. A Collection of Millennial Hymns Adapted to the Present Order of the Church (Canterbury, New Hampshire, 1847), 200 pp. A Sacred Repository of Anthems and Hymns for Devotional Worship and Praise. Compiled by Maria Hastings and Henry Blinn. (Canterbury, N.H., 1852), 233 pp. Inspirational Hymns and Melodies Illustrative of the Resurrection, Life and Testimony of the Shakers (Albany, 1875), 152 pp. A Selection of Devotional Melodies; Simple in Arrangement, Yet Inspirational (Canterbury, N.H., 1876), 44 pp. A Collection of Harmonies and Melodies Adapted to Sacred Worship (Canterbury, N.H., 1878), 100 pp. Henry Blinn, A Repository of Music, Containing Elementary and Advanced Lessons, Selected from the Works of All Teachers (Canterbury, N.H., 1880), 73 pp. Shaker Anthems and Hymns, Arranged for Divine Worship (Shaker Village,

N.H., 1883). *Original Shaker Music. Published by North Family at Mount Lebanon,* compiled by Daniel Offord, Lucy Bowers and Martha J. Anderson (New York, 1893), 271 pp. *Shaker Hymnal, by the Canterbury Shakers* (Boston, 1908).

12. *A Short Treatise Containing Observations on the Duty of Believers Suitable for the Consideration of Those Who Have Just Arrived at the Age of the Discretion and Understanding to Be Regarded and Put in Practice by All Who Wish to Have Their Lives Agreeable to Themselves and Others. Addressed to Youth.* (New Lebanon, 1823), 36 pp. *A Juvenile Monitor Containing Instructions for Youth and Children, Pointing out Ill Manners and Showing Them How to Behave in the Various Conditions of Childhood and Youth* (New Lebanon, 1823), 20 pp. *Youth's Guide in Zion and Holy Mother's Promise Given by Inspiration at New Lebanon,* 5 January 1842 (Canterbury, 1842), 36 pp. *A Juvenile Guide or Manual of Good Manners, Consisting of Counsels, Instructions, and Rules of Deportment for the Young by Lovers of Youth. In Two Parts.* (Canterbury, 1844), 137 pp. *Circular Concerning the Dress of Believers* (Mount Lebanon, 1866), 12 pp. *Rules for Behavior in Places Consecrated to Worship. Notice to Visitors.* (Shaker Village, N.H., 1876), 2 pp. Henry C. Blinn, *Gentle Manners. A Guide to Good Morals* (East Canterbury, 1899), 79 pp.

13. James Holmes, *A Collection of Useful Hints of Farmers. And Many Valuable Recipes.* (West Gloucester, 1850), 120 pp. There is a previous edition without any title page, 1849. This book was followed by *The Farmer's 2nd Book* and *The Farmer's 3rd Book* (1856). These four items are described in MacLean, Nos. 45, 46, 47, 48. *Improved Shaker Washing Machine, etc., Manufactured and for Sale by the United Society of Shakers, at Shaker Village, New Hampshire* (Concord, 1859), 24 pp. *Catalogue of Herbs, Roots, Barks, Powdered Articles, etc. prepared in the United Society* (New Gloucester, Me., 1864), 15 pp. *Catalogue of Medicinal Plants, Barks, Roots, Seeds, Flowers, and Select Powders, with Their Therapeutic Qualities and Botanical Names; also Pure Vegetable Extracts, Prepared in Vacuo, Ointments, Inpissated Juices, Essential Oils, Double Distilled and Fragrant Waters, etc., Raised, Prepared and Put up in the Most Careful Manner by the United Society of Shakers at Mount Lebanon, N.Y. First Established in 1800, Being the Oldest of the Kind in the Country.* (Albany, 1873), 58 pp.

14. The best known is undoubtedly the Evans–Tolstoi correspondence. See Frederick W. Evans, *Shaker–Russian Correspondence between Count Leo Tolstoi and Elder F. W. Evans* (Mount Lebanon, 1891). There are others.

15. Fayette Mace, *Familiar Dialogues on Shakerism in Which the Principles of the United Society Are Illustrated and Defended* (Portland, 1838), 120 pp. William Leonard, *A Discourse of the Order and Propriety of Divine Inspiration and Revelation Showing the Necessity Thereof in All Ages to Know the Will of God. — Also a Discourse on the Second Appearing of Christ in and through the Order of the Female. — And a Discourse on the Propriety and Necessity of the United Inheritance in All Things in Order to Support a True Christian Community.* (Harvard, Mass., 1853), 88 pp. Frederick W. Evans, *Religious Communism.*

A Lecture by F. W. Evans (Shaker) of Mount Lebanon, Columbia Co., N.Y., U.S.A., Delivered in St. George's Hall, London (6 August 1871) with Introductory Remarks by the Chairman, Mr. Hepworth Dixon, etc. Harvey L. Eads, *Shaker Sermons: Scripto-rational. Containing the Substance of Shaker Theology, together with Replies and Criticisms Logically and Clearly Set Forth* (New York, 1879), 222 pp.

16. The model apologetic brochure is *A Brief Exposition* ed. Seth Y. Wells (Albany, 1834). It was widely circulated. See also Frederick W. Evans, *A Short Treatise on the Second Appearing of Christ in and through the Order of the Female* (Boston, 1853), 24 pp. Frederick W. Evans, *Tests of Divine Inspiration or the Rudimental Principles by Which True and False Revelation in All Eras of the World Can Be Unerringly Discriminated* (New Lebanon, 1853), 128 pp. Frederick W. Evans, *Ann Lee, the Founder of the Shakers. A Biography with Memoirs of John Hocknell, James Meacham, Lucy Wright. Also a Compendium of the Origin, History, Principles, Rules and Regulations, Government and Doctrines of the United Society of Believers in Christ's Second Appearing* (New Lebanon, 1858), 187 pp. Clara Endicott Sears, *Shakers. Duality of the Deity. Or God as Father and Mother.* (Mount Morris, N.Y., 1867), 7 pp. George Albert Lomas, *The Life of Christ is the End of the World* (Watervliet, 1869). Frederick W. Evans, *Shaker Communism or Tests of Divine Inspiration. The Second Christian or Gentile Pentecostal Church as Exemplified by Seventy Communities of Shakers in America* (London, 1871), 120 pp. Frederick W. Evans, *Religious Communism. A Lecture by F. W. Evans (Shaker) of Mount Lebanon, Columbia Co., N.Y., U.S.A., Delivered in St. George's Hall, London (6 August 1871) with Introductory Remarks by the Chairman, Mr. Hepworth Dixon, etc.* Giles B. Avery, *Sketches of "Shakers and Shakerism" Synopsis of Theology of United Society of Believers in Christ's Second Appearing* (Albany, 1883), 35 pp. As for the polemic writings, they occupy a large place in Shaker literature, especially before 1850.

17. Daryl Chase, "The Early Shakers, An Experiment in Religious Communism" (University of Chicago, 1938), pp. 220 *et seq.* Chase refers to collections of Shaker manuscripts in the following libraries: WESTERN RESERVE HISTORICAL SOCIETY (Cleveland). Chase's thesis, written after studying this collection, quotes abundantly from it and describes its scope. The collection includes about 1,800 published titles and 3,000 volumes of manuscripts. PITTSFIELD ATHENEUM (Pittsfield, Mass.) NEW YORK STATE HISTORICAL SOCIETY (Albany, N.Y.) OHIO STATE HISTORICAL SOCIETY (Columbus, Ohio). A. E. Bestor, *Backwoods Utopias. The Sectarian and Owenite Phases of Communitarian Socialism in America* (Philadelphia, 1950). Bibliographical essay, pp. 255–256. A. E. Bestor gives the following bibliographical references. The principle collections of Shaker manuscripts available to the public have been described by Charles Adams in the *New York State Museum Bulletin No. 323* (Albany, March 1941), pp. 123–128. To Mr. Adams' brief note on the collection in the Library of Congress should be added that library's own *Handbook of Manuscripts* (Washington, 1918), pp.

365–366; also the *Librarian of Congress Report,* 1930, pp. 79–80, and the annual report of the *American Historical Association* for 1937, Vol. 1, p. 124; also the unpublished catalogue of the Library. Bestor also cites the manuscript collection at Western Kentucky Teachers College, Bowling Green, Kentucky. This collection was not mentioned by Adams, but has been described by Julia Neal. Bestor's note concludes with a mention of the large private collections, such as the one of Clara Endicott Sears in the Wayside Museum, Harvard, Mass., and the one of Edward Deming Andrews which is described in the bibliographies of his own works.

18. J. P. MacLean, *A Bibliography of Shaker Literature with an Introductory Study* (Columbus, Ohio, 1905), 71 pp.

19. Edward Deming Andrews, *The Community Industries of the Shakers* (Albany: The University of the State of New York, 1932), 322 pp. This book, like the two other Andrews' books was based on the following articles: "Craftsmanship of an American Religious Sect," in *Antiques,* 14 (August 1928), pp. 132–136; "The Furniture of an American Religious Sect," in *Antiques,* 15 (April 1929), pp. 292–296; "The New York Shakers and Their Industries," in *New York State Museum Circular* (2 October 1930); "An Interpretation of Shaker Furniture," in *Antiques,* 23 (January, 1933), pp. 6–9. Edward Deming Andrews, *Shaker Furniture, the Craftsmanship of an American Communal Sect* (New Haven, Yale University Press, 1937). Edward Deming Andrews, *The Gift to Be Simple* (New York, 1940).

20. Marguerite Melcher, *The Shaker Adventure* (Princeton, 1941), 319 pp.

21. Mark Holloway, *Heavens on Earth. Utopian Communities in America, 1680–1880* (London, 1951), 240 pp.

22. This documentation includes: (a) Works in the Bibliothèque Nationale. They are few. The most valuable one is Benjamin Seth Young, *Testimony of Christ's Second Appearing,* 4th ed. (Albany, 1856), hereafter cited as *Testimony.* The copy in the Bibliothèque Nationale turns out to be that which belonged to Abbé Grégoire. (b) The collection of writings and brochures (about 60 of them) gathered together by J. Prudhommeaux. Assigned the task of studying the Fourierist societies in the United States, he brought back (1904) an important collection of documents on all the American communities and, in particular, on the Shakers, whom he had visited at Mount Lebanon. He considered his book on Cabet to be nothing more than a first chapter of a larger work he intended to write. These documents as well as Prudhommeaux's first drafts were made available to me by his son, M. A. Prudhommeaux. (c) Books by Shakers or about Shakers in the catalogue of the British Museum and consulted there. There are many of them. (d) Books made known by other British libraries. (e) Microfilms of documents in American libraries, in particular the thesis by Daryl Chase, "The Early Shakers. An Experiment in Religious Communism" (Ph.D. diss., University of Chicago, 1938), which is valuable for its account of research done in the archives of the Western Reserve

Historical Society, Cleveland, Ohio. It remains to be said that the limits of the material in these works have defined the limits of this analysis.

23. This is the terminology used by E. Troeltsch to characterize what he calls the "Church-Type" and the "Sect-Type." The book by Troeltsch was consulted in the English edition, *The Social Teaching of the Christian Churches*, 2 vols. (London, 1950), 1:331 ff. (trans. from the German: *Die Soziallehren der Christlichen Kirchen und Gruppen* [1912]).

24. "True Believers." This is the name that the Shakers chose for themselves. After 1850 in certain of their books they are even called Aletheians, or the True Aletheians, the True Ones. From other sources we know the important role played by a nostalgia for "True Christianity" in early French socialism (Saint-Simon, Leroux, Considérant, etc.).

25. "The Shakers. A Strict and Utopian Way of Life Has Almost Vanished. Death of a Sect," *Life* (March 21, 1949).

26. G. Gurvitch, *La vocation actuelle de la sociologie* (Paris, 1950), pp. 139, 212.

27. A French sample of the "Great Family" is found in the millenary existence of the Thiernois communities: the Quittard Pnion, the Ferrier, the Dozolme Chevalerias, etc. Cf. A. Bigay, *Le vieux Thiers* (n.p., 1947). The persistence of this "consanguine collectivism" (name given it by P. Lafargue) in these "Families" would later draw the attention of French socialism. Cf. M. Dommanget, "Community Socialism from 1841 to Our Days," in Sylvain Maréchal, *L'égalitaire, l'homme sans Dieu* (Paris, 1950), pp. 424–26. They would also draw the attention of Le Play and his school. See the resumé of Le Play's analysis of the Melouga family community as observed by Cauterets, in E. Demolins, *Les Français d'aujourd'hui. Les types sociaux du Midi et du Centre* (Paris, 1898), pp. 4–29. And see, of course, the recent, as yet unpublished thesis of H. Lefèbre on "Les communautés pyrénéennes."

28. The socio-economic structure of communities like Zoar, on the other hand, is more like that of a village "commune," with its separate households and common ownership of land. The Shaker Family implies not only common ownership of the means of production but also collective modes of consumption, lodging, and feeding.

29. See use of the word in book titles. E.g. W. A. Hinds, *American Communities* (Oneida, N.Y., 1878).

30. A. E. Bestor, "The Evolution of the Socialist Vocabulary," *Journal of the History of Ideas*, vol. 9, no. 3, pp. 259–302. Simply notice that Bestor does not use all the material made available by the commentaries of Engels (i.e. Mega 1, 4, pp. 345, 365 ff.).

31. Cf. below, chap. 6.

32. Troeltsch (see n. 23), 1:336 (in German edition of 1912, p. 370).

33. According to E. Troeltsch, the dominant church is responsible for the pejorative sense of the word *sect:* "Sectarian groups were considered to be atrophies of ecclesiastic Christianity. But this point of view is es-

sentially that of the dominant churches, and is based on the belief that the Church-Type is the only one with a right to exist" (Troeltsch, 1:333–34). Troeltsch does not take into account the point of view of the sect itself, for whom it is rather the established church which is, by the very fact of being established, a subproduct. He tends to see a dialectical relation between the *extensive* Christianity of the churches and the *intensive* Christianity of the sects: intensity and extensiveness being in inverse relation to each other. "What the sects gain in intensity of Christian life they lose in universality" (ibid., p. 337). There is a revaluation of Troeltsch's position in J. Wach, *Types of Religious Experience Christian and Non-Christian* (Chicago, 1951), chap. 9, "Church, Denomination and Sect," pp. 187 ff.

34. On the subject of American "sects" Troeltsch refers to articles by Max Weber: "Kirchen und Sekten in Nord Amerika," in *Christliches Welt* (n.p., 1906), pp. 557–58 ff. These articles were republished in Max Weber, *Gesammelte Aufzätze zur Religionsoziologie* (Tübingen, 1920), 1:207–36, under the title "The Protestantische Sekten und der Geist des Kapitalismus." He does not discuss the Shakers.

35. J. Prudhommeaux, "Un siècle de communisme expérimental aux Etats-Unis," in "Leçons au Collège Libre des Sciences Sociales" (1912), a collection of unpublished lectures.

36. Charles Gide, "Les colonies communistes et coopératives," *Cours au Collège de France, 1927–1928* (Association pour l'enseignement de la coopération, 1928), pp. 24 ff.; trans. Ernest F. Row, *Communist and Cooperative Colonies* (New York: Crowell, 1930).

37. H. Lasserre, *Cooperatisme intégral* (Basel, 1927). Also, W. Thompson, *Pioneer in Community, Henri Lasserre's Contribution to the Fully Cooperative Society* (Toronto, 1949).

38. Martin Buber, *Paths in Utopia* (English trans. London, 1949), pp. 59 ff. "Vollgenossenschaft" has been translated as "full cooperative," which is equivalent to "coopérative intégrale" in French. Buber contrasts it with two other categories: cooperative production and cooperative consumption, of which, according to him, it is a synthesis.

39. H. Infield, *Cooperative Communities at Work* (London, 1947), p. 8. Since 1954 Infield's thought on this subject has evolved. See particularly his "Utopia and Experiment," *Cooperative Living*, vol. 1, no. 3, pp. 1–8 (discussion of Buber), and "Cooperative Community Research and the Sociometric Test," ibid., vol. 3, no. 1, pp. 1–8.

40. We shall see that Shaker societies classified their members into three groups: those who maintain and use property, those who maintain property but do not use it, and those who neither maintain nor use it. It is this third category which constitutes the "Church Order" or the "Senior Order."

41. These figures were established by Julia Williams in "An Analytical Tabulation of the North American Communities: by Type, Longevity, Location" (Master's thesis, University of South Dakota, 1939), and Lee Emerson Deets in "American Idealistic Community Experiments," a re-

port read to the American Sociological Society (1931). They are summarized in a note by Deets in his *The Hutterites: A Study of Social Cohesion* (Gettysburg, 1929), in "American Idealistic Community Experiments," a report read to the American Sociological Society (1931), and "Data from Utopia," *Sociology*, vol. 3, no. 2 (New York, 1940).

42. F. C. Conybeare, *Russian Dissenters* (Cambridge, Mass., 1917).

43. J. W. Eaton and S. M. Katz, *Research Guide on Cooperative Group Farming* (New York, 1942).

44. E. T. Clark, *The Small Sects in America* (New York, 1937; rev. ed. 1949).

45. Pierre Brodin, *Les Quakers en Amérique au XVIIe et au début du XVIIIe siècle* (Paris, 1935).

46. G. W. Bradford, *History of Plymouth Plantation 1620–1647* (Boston, 1912). See also, C. M. Andrews, *The Colonial Period of American History: Vol. 1, The Settlements* (New Haven, 1934), pp. 123–26.

47. From Holland: the colony of Plockhoy and the Labadists. On P. Plockhoy, see his own book, *A Way Propounded to Make the Poor in These and Other Nations Happy by Bringing Together a Fit Suitable and Well Qualified People unto one Household Government or Little Commonwealth* (1659); and John Downie, *Peter Cornelius Plockboy* [sic], *Pioneer of the First Cooperative Commonwealth* (Manchester, Cooperative Union, n.d.). See also, a thesis written by L. D. Harder for Michigan State College, 1950. On the Labadists, see "The Labadist Colony in Maryland," *Johns Hopkins University Studies in Historical and Political Science*, vol. 17, no. 6 (Baltimore, 1899).

48. The numerous German-language community experiments will be analyzed in another work now in preparation. There is a bibliography by Emil Maynen, *Bibliography on German Settlement in Colonial North America* (Leipzig, 1937). Eaton and Katz (see n. 43) list, by experiment, the essential works. A. E. Bestor, in *Backwoods Utopias. The Sectarian and Owenite Phases of Communitarian Socialism in America. 1663–1829* (Philadelphia, 1950), also analyzes the bibliography for several German communities.

49. From Sweden: the Bishop Hill community. The classic work on Bishop Hill is M. A. Mikkelsen, *The Bishop Hill Colony, A Religious Communistic Settlement in Henry County, Illinois* (Baltimore, 1892), p. 80.

50. From Bohemia: through the missionary emigration from Herrnhut led by the famous Count Zinzendorf. See Jacob John Sessler, *Communal Pietism among Early American Moravians* (New York, 1933), p. 265. On the principal community, Bethlehem, a work edited from within the sect, see J. M. Levering, *History of Bethlehem* (Bethlehem, 1903). For a discussion of the adjective *communistic* applied to their system, see ibid., p. 181. Another study is Hellmuth Erbe, *Bethlehem, Pa., Eine Kommunistische Herrnhuter Kolonie des 18 Iahrhunderts* (Stuttgart, 1929). For a recent summary see, W. Senft, "Communisme chrétien," *LeMonde Non-Chrétien* (January-March 1952), pp. 93–100.

51. On this characteristic, see summary and references in Knox,

Enthusiasm, A Chapter in the History of Religion, pp. 168 ff. The same characteristic is noted by E. G. Leonard in his study. Sharing a place of authority with the Bible, he says, is the Protestantism of the Spirit, which goes from the Zwickau prophets and the Anabaptists to today's Pentecostal sects; its history passes through the Quakers, the inspired men of the Cevennes, Swedenborg, the German visionaries, and many others. He adds that historical details on this can be found in monographs devoted to its most visible manifestations and in those contemporary accounts in which communities with this tendency have recorded their past. However, according to him, the history as an ensemble has hardly been touched. See E. G. Leonard, *L'illuminisme dans un protestantisme de constitution récente* (Paris, 1952), p. 5.

52. Harold Bender, *La vision anabaptiste* (Montbéliard, 1950), p. 33. Translation of two articles, one from *Church History* 13 (March 1944): 3–24; the other from the *Mennonite Quarterly Review* (April 1944).

53. On Penn's trips to Europe see Oswald Seidensticker, "William Penn's Travels in Holland and Germany in 1677," *Pennsylvania Magazine of History and Biography*, vol. 2 (1878). On the founding of Pennsylvania following this emigration, see P. Brodin (n. 45), chap. 5, "Une colonie Quaker, la Pennsylvanie," pp. 297–381.

54. See n. 50.

55. Elie Halévy, "Naissance du Méthodisme en Angleterre," *Review de Paris* (August 1906). And see below, chap. 7.

56. W. D. Morris, *The Christian Origins of Social Revolt* (London, 1949), chap. 9, on "The Diggers." The disturbance made by the Diggers coincided with the waning of the English Revolution and Cromwell's eviction of the revolutionary left. The community project of Winstanley (The True Levellers) dates from April 1649. The failure of the Diggers coincided with the rise of the Quakers. This failure is not unrelated to Plockhoy's project of ten years later, in 1659 (see n. 47). According to A. Bestor, this project, which was to end up as one of the first community experiments in America, was precisely the product of crossing the radicalism of the English sects, in which Plockhoy had played a role, with the Dutch Mennonite movement in Holland, in which Anabaptism was still alive. See Bestor (n. 48), p. 27; also H. Bender (n. 52), passim. For the title of Plockhoy's project, see n. 47. The complete title of Winstanley's project was "The True Levellers Standard Advanced or the State of Community Opened and Presented to the Sons of Men" (before 1649).

Notes to Chapter One

1. See above, Introduction, n. 22.
2. Calvin Green and Seth Y. Wells, *A Summary View of the Millennial*

Church, 2d ed. (Albany, 1848). All references are to this edition, hereafter cited as *Millennial Church*.

3. *Testimony*, p. xxiii.

4. *Millennial Church*, p. 8. Italics in original.

5. Ibid., p. 10.

6. Mary Marshall Dyer, *A Portraiture of Shakerism* . . . (Concord [?], 1822 [?]).

7. *Millenial Church*, p. 9.

8. Among her sources Mary Dyer cited E. Calamy, one of the tenacious polemicists against the French Prophets. She also cites Charles Ewen, N. Spinckes, Bishop Hoadly, and others.

9. See below, next section.

10. Jean Cavalier: not to be confused with the Cevenole military leader. This error has been made by certain Shaker historians.

11. Aside from general works on the Camisards and the Cevenole prophets, see A. Dubois, *Les Prophètes cévenols* (Strasbourg, 1861); E. Rauzier, *Les Prophètes cévenols* (Macon, 1893); C. Taylor, *The Camisards* (London, 1893); F. Wattier, *Les Prophètes cévenols* (Paris, 1894). See also the following four studies which are particularly important for the part of history studied here: J. Chavannes, "Les Prophètes cévenols," *Chrétien évangélique* (Lausanne February-May 1869); P. Vesson, "Les Prophètes camisards à Londres, 1706–1714," an extract of the *Mémoires de l'Académie des Sciences, inscriptions et belles-lettres de Toulouse*, ser. 9, vol. 5 (1893); Georges Ascoli, "L'affaire des Prophetès français à Londres," *Revue du XVIIIe Siècle* (1916), pp. 8–28, 85–109; C. Bost, Introduction and notes to *Mémoires inedits d'Abraham Mazel et d'Elie Marion sur la guerre des Cévennes* (London, 1931), vol. 34 of *Publications of the Huguenot Society*.

12. "Récit abrégé des entretiens qu'Elie Marion, Durand Page et Jean Cavalier ont eus avec Mss. les conducteurs d'une des églises françaises de Londres, dite de la Savoye," in *Théâtre sacré des Cévennes* (1707), pp. 143 ff.

13. The study by Ascoli (see n. 11) particularly emphasizes the causes for this anglicization of the French prophesying and the steps in its development.

14. Elie Marion, *Avertissements prophétiques d'Elie Marion, l'un des chefs protestants qui avaient pris les armes dans les Cévennes, ou Discours prononcés par sa bouche sous l'opération de l'Esprit fidèlement reçu dans le le temps qu'il parlait*, published in April 1707, according to Vesson (see n. 11). A copy of the Lacy plagiarism was found by Daryl Chase in the large collection of Shaker literature of the Western Reserve Historical Society. Daryl Chase claims that this copy once belonged to one of the Shaker societies. See Daryl Chase, "The Early Shakers" (Ph.D. diss., University of Chicago, 1938).

15. Ascoli (see n. 11), p. 98.

16. According to Ascoli, p. 101: "On n'en finirait point d'analyser les livres anglais ou français dirigés contre les prophètes" (There were an

endless number of books written in English and in French against the prophets).

17. Cited by Vesson (see n. 11), p. 25.

18. This letter written 4 April 1709 is in the French Protestant Library: *Collection Coqueret, Papiers Rabaut. I.B. Mss 302, pièce 3.* It is followed by a "Répartition des prophètes camisard en tribus" (Dividing the Camisard prophets into tribes), ibid., *pièce 4.* Vesson (pp. 28–29) is probably referring to another list from which the name of John Lacy must have disappeared. Here he is listed in the tribe of Levy. The 150 "prophets" inscribed on this list are divided into groups, 12 to a tribe, except for the tribe of Levy, which numbers 28 members.

19. *Cri d'alarme ou avertissement aux nations qu'ils* [sic] *sortent de Babylone des ténèbres pour entrer dans le repos du Christ* (A cry of alarm or warning to the nations that their peoples should leave the darkness of Babylon to enter a state of peace and rest in Christ), message recorded by Fatio and Pourtalès (1712).

20. Part I, 1712: *Plan de la Justice de Dieu sur terre dans ces derniers jours et de relèvement de la chute de l'homme par son péché;* Part II, 1714: *Quand vous aurez saccagé vous serez saccagés car la lumière est apparue dans ces ténèbres pour les détruire* (Amsterdam, 1714). Quoted by Chavannes (n. 11).

21. Ascoli (see n. 11), p. 100.

22. *Millennial Church,* p. 9.

23. Ibid.

24. Ascoli, p. 100.

25. Ibid., p. 103.

26. Ibid.

27. M. R. Brailsford, *Quaker Women* (London, 1915). See also, Pierre Brodin, *Les Quakers en Amérique* (Paris, 1935), the chapters devoted to Mary Fisher, Ann Austin, Mary Dyer, and others. In this work the Quaker woman Mary Dyer (of the 17th century) is obviously not the same as her namesake discussed above.

28. Ascoli, p. 99.

29. A. Whitrow, *Warnings of the Eternal Spirit* (London, 1709), Preface by Sir Richard Bulkeley.

30. Ascoli, p. 99.

31. See below, this chapter and also chap. 2.

32. John Lacy, *The General Delusion of Christians, Touching the Ways of God's Revealing Himself to and by the Prophets, Evinc'd from Scripture and Primitive Antiquity* (London, 1713). This text was reprinted in 1832 with a preface by Edward Irving. See also, John Lacy, *The Scene of Delusions, by the Reverend Mr. Owen of Warrington, at his Own Earnest Request, Considered and Confuted, by One of the Modern Prophets; and (As It Proves) Partly by Himself* (London, 1723).

33. A Léger, *La jeunesse de Wesley* (Paris, 1910).

34. Quoted by Ascoli, p. 104.

35. See below, chap. 2.

36. A Léger, who emphasizes the large number of people preached to in Bristol and Kingwood, points out a quite opposite tendency in the "Prophets" and underlines a declaration made by Thomas Chubb in 1746 to the effect that "after an initial rapid success the cause of the Prophets had almost completely collapsed" (Léger, pp. 410 ff.).

37. P. de Félice, *Foules en délire. Extases collectives* (Paris, 1947), pp. 219–40. E. G. Leonard, "La part de la jeunesse dans la restauration du protestantisme français au XVIIIe," *Revue de Théologie et d'Action Evangélique* (October 1944), p. 354.

38. See below, chap. 4, "Phases in the Shaker Dance."

39. C. Bost, *Les prédicants protestants* (Paris, 1912), 1:172 ff., 219 ff., 354 ff.

40. *Millennial Church*, p. 9

41. Ibid., pp. 9–10

42. See below, chap. 3

43. Brousson speaks with admiration of Isabeau and Pintarde: going from place to place and from wilderness to wilderness, having meetings in which, with the word of God, they called on the people to be converted, to be sanctified, to rekindle their zeal. Likewise unearthed was the story of some young girls moved by inspiration: Jeanne Durand, Flore Viala, etc. Their stories by M. Pin in *Nicolas Jouanny* (Montpellier, 1930) and commented on by Leonard in "La part de la jeunesse dans la restauration."

44. Ascoli, p. 98.

45. The reference is to *Histoire des amours des Prophètes des Cévennes* by a "protestant captain in the cavalry." Manuscript in the Library of Nîmes: cote no. 197. Despite his evident concern to present a detailed documentation of the facts, the captain's work is obviously a pamphlet. The passage alluded to is on pages 98–100. In the case of the Cevenoles, what appeared to be "preferring love to marriage" may well have, if not its explanation, at least a part of its origin in the legal status of Protestants during the period following 1697–98. The fact that no union was legally valid unless celebrated by a Catholic curate forced them to undertake either a Catholic marriage (thus a semiabjuration) or celibacy or, de facto, some form of free union. The first solution was a subterfuge to avoid abjuration and seems to have been in favor among bourgeois and city people. The second was rare. The third was preferred by the rural population and the working class. This was the union without any official marriage or recognition. Whether or not it had parental blessing, whether or not it had been performed by a minister of the "Desert" or one of some foreign land, whether or not it was recognized in a notarized contract, such a union could easily look like a form of free union and thus be considered an example of an antimatrimonial *bond* simply by virtue of the fact that it remained outside the recognized or imposed forms of matrimony. On this legal situation, see E. G. Leonard, *Le problème du mariage civil et les protestants français au XVIIIe siècle* (Paris, 1942).

46. In his study on the "Khlysti" Séverac remarks that the presence of

both sexes at their meetings gave rise to accusations of promiscuity which he judges to be without foundation. See Séverac, *La secte russe des hommes de Dieu* (Montpellier, 1906). The same situation was often observed in the Middle Ages (one thinks particularly of the Guillemites). See H. E. Lea, *Histoire de l'Inquisition* (Paris, 1902), pp. 100 ff., and *Dictionnaire de théologie catholique,* article on "Guillemites." Whatever truth there may be in these accusations is based on a practice whose traces are found in an often quoted testimony taken from the history of the Inquisition at Limborch: "Item dixit (se audivisse) a quodam quem nominat quod inter quosdam erat opinio aliquorum quod non debebat reputari homo vel mulier virtuosus vel virtuosa nisi se possent ponere nudus cum nuda in uno lecto et tamen non perficerent actum carnalem" (He said that someone he knew told him there are people who had adopted the beliefs that one cannot consider a man or woman virtuous unless they are capable of going to bed together naked without copulating). A passage from a letter written by Daniel Rathbun to James Whittaker, published in an unusually violent pamphlet (Springfield, 1785), suggests that this practice was not unknown to the early Shakers. It may well have played a role in their initiation ritual.

47. According to confidential revelations made by Ann Lee to Daniel Wood in *Testimonies of the Life, Character, Revelations and Doctrines of Mother Ann Lee,* ed. Rufus Bishop, 2d ed. (Albany, 1888), p. 38; hereafter cited as *Testimonies.*

48. See Agnès de la Gorce, *Camisard et Dragons du Roi* (Paris, 1950), p. 190; and E. G. Leonard, *Problèmes et expériences du protestantisme français* (Paris, 1940), pp. 27–29. On the "clear preponderance of the lower or semi-lower classes in the Midi," see ibid., p. 7.

49. See J. Dedieu, *Le rôle politique des protestants français, 1685–1715* (Paris, 1920). His thesis of the politicizing of this uprising is subject to reserve in Leonard, "Le protestantisme français de la Révocation à la Révolution" (see n. 48), p. 137.

50. Frank Puaux, *Les défenseurs de la souveraineté du peuple sous le règne de Louis XIV* (Paris, 1917), pp. 66–74. Rebellious attitudes manifested by their changing loyalties when confronted with the complicated politico-ecclesiastic relations. See Jean Orcibal, *Louis XIV et les protestants* (Paris, 1951).

51. See below, chap. 6, "Communism and Theocracy."

52. For an enumeration of these harassing measures, see O. Douen, *Les premiers pasteurs du désert* (Paris, 1879), 1:72 ff., 80 ff.; also Orcibal, (see n. 50), p. 57, nn. 88–89. On the secularism of the Cevenole meetings and services in the "wilderness," see E. G. Leonard, "Le problème du culte public et de l'Eglise dans le protestantisme français du XVIIIᵉ siècle," *Foi et Vie,* no. 4 (1937), pp. 431–57; also "Les Assemblées du Désert et le problème du culte et de l'Eglise dans le protestantisme français du XVIIIᵉ siècle à nos jours," *Bulletin de la Société Historique du Protestantisme Français* (December 1939). See also, his *Le protestant français* (Paris, 1953).

53. Jurieu, *Lettres pastorales*, "Lettre du 15 Octobre 1686." See Bost, *Les prédicants protestants*, 1:161.

54. Douen, 2:33.

55. C. Brousson, *Lettres et opuscules* (Utrecht, 1701), pp. 36, 125.

56. E. G. Leonard, *Histoire ecclésiastique des Réformés français au XVIIIe siècle* (Paris, 1940), pp. 7–9.

57. Chavannes (see n. 11), pp. 232–33.

58. Procedure described by F. Conybeare in *Russian Dissenters*, Harvard Theological Studies, no. 10 (Cambridge, Mass., 1921), pp. 180 ff. L. Mazoyer, in this same work, makes an allusion suggesting an analogy between distinctions made by the Raskol and those made by the Cevenoles.

59. John Dunlavy, *The Manifesto . . .* (Pleasant Hill, Ky., 1818), p. 316. Also, see below, chap. 5.

60. Jurieu (see n. 53), "Lettre de 12 Janvier 1689."

61. Letter of 7 January 1703, quoted at length by Henry Van Etten, *Chronique de la vie quaker française 1745–1945* (Paris, 1947), p. 29. Although there is no doubt about the opinions of Daniel Raoul, this particular document attributed to him is of doubtful origin.

62. Ibid., p. 36

63. See E. Jaulmes, *Les Quakers français* (Nîmes, 1898), and Van Etten.

Notes to Chapter Two

1. Benjamin Seth Youngs, *Testimony* (Albany, 1856), pp. 24–26.

2. Calvin Green and Seth Youngs Wells, *Millennial Church* (Albany, 1848), p. 10.

3. *Testimony*, p. 10.

4. *Millennial Church*, p. 11.

5. The name "Shakers" was accepted only with the passing of time. It is interesting to compare the use of this word in the titles of the principal publications of the church.

6. *Millennial Church*, p. 5.

7. Ibid., p. 16.

8. Ibid., p. 19.

9. Ibid.

10. Ibid. This expression, which occurs elsewhere, was addressed to those who, given their family situation, had either the means or the courage to accept the new regulations imposed by Ann Lee for emigration.

11. Theo Schroeder, "Shaker Celibacy and Salacity Psychologically Interpreted," *New York Medical Review* (June 1, 1921), pp. 800–05.

12. Schroeder took these facts from a pamphlet by Mary Marshall Dyer, *The Rise and Progress of the Serpent . . .* (Concord, 1847).

13. Schroeder refers in particular to two studies: Ida C., *Heavenly Bride-grooms*, Introduction by Theo Schroeder, reprinted from *Alienist and Neurologist* (1915–17); and "Revivals, Sex and Holy Ghost," *Journal of Abnormal Psychology* vol. 14 (April-June 1919): 34–37.

14. Georges Ascoli, "L'affaire des Prophètes français à Londres," *Revue du dix-huitième siècle*, 3ᵉ année, no. 1 (January-April 1916), p. 88.

15. Pierre Brodin has pointed out the ambiguity of the name "Quaker." He tells us that the surname "Quaker" or "Trembleur" is of a slightly dubious origin. Did the followers of Fox really quake because they were possessed by the Holy Ghost (see Barclay, *Apology*, Prop. II, sect. 8, p. 12, n. 2) or did they call on their listeners to quake at the name of the Lord? See George Fox, *Journal*, rev. ed. (Cambridge, 1952), pp. 1–4. It is possible, says Brodin, that these two interpretations, far from being irreconcilable, are equally true. This ambiguity should also be noticed among the Shakers. The name was first applied to them in derision by the general public and was later claimed in its original form, but with a modification of meaning: "Shakers," those whose vocation is to shake others or be shaken by them. See Frederick Evans, "Religious Communism," in his *Autobiography of a Shaker . . .* (Mount Lebanon, 1888), p. 203.

16. This is the pamphlet: *The Honest Quaker or the Forgeries and Impostures of the Pretended French Prophets and their Abettors Exposed in a Letter from a Quaker to His Friend. Giving an Account of a Sham-Miracle Performed by John L. Esq. in the Body of Elizabeth Grey on the 17th of August Past* (London, 1707).

17. See "Henry Pickworth" in *Dictionary of National Biography*. In his pamphlet against the Quakers, Pickworth would later try to show that the Quakers were Papists and that William Penn was insane when he died. In a reply to these charges, R. Claridge wrote that Pickworth was "mendicassimus et invidiosissimus."

18. On this tradition of "enthusiasm" (i.e. divine inspiration) among the Christian dissidents, see R. A. Knox, *Enthusiasm* (Oxford, 1950).

19. On this topic in general, see Leif Eeg-Olofsson, *The Conception of the Inner Light in Robert Barclay's Theology: A Study in Quakerism* (London, 1954). A masterful study, unfortunately published too late to be more fully used here.

20. See William Penn's preface to George Fox's *Journal*, bicentennial edition, 1:15; also Robert Barclay, *The Anarchy of Ranters* (London, 1676). The latter is cited by Pierre Brodin in *Les Quakers en Amérique au XVIIᵉ et au XVIIIᵉ siècle* (Paris, 1935), p. 13. This "extravagance" was no less real among the Shakers, especially among the first converts. Their "perfectionism" seemed to have created an antinomian strain of which certain nudist practices were perhaps a manifestation. They probably claimed precedent for this particular antinomian privilege by evoking the image of David dancing naked in front of the ark. See Theo Schroeder (n. 11), pp. 804–05.

21. *Millennial Church*, p. 15

22. There were similar scuffles during the first years of the French Prophets. See Ascoli (n. 14).

23. Cited by Daryl Chase. Also in Edward Andrews, *The People Called Shakers* (New York, 1953), p. 4.

24. Andrews, pp. 3 ff.

25. Brodin (see n. 20), p. 37.

26. Ascoli says that in 1718 Mary Keimer was in Pennsylvania to spread the new faith (see n. 14).

27. Thomas Prince, *Chronological History of New England* (Boston, 1736), 1:82. Quoted by Brodin, p. 25.

28. The community of interest appears in a curious work: Royal Ralph Hinman, *The Blue Laws of New Haven Colony Usually Called Blue Laws of Connecticut . . .* (Hartford, 1838). The author's intention was to point out how intolerant were the laws, especially toward the Quakers. This work defending the Quakers includes a short treatise on the Shakers, which is none other than Seth Youngs Wells's *A Brief Exposition of the Established Principles and Regulations of the United Society of Believers called Shakers*, improved edition (Albany, 1834). The author of *Blue Laws* explains that he has added these pages to his own book at the request of a Mr. S. Y. Wells of New Lebanon, N.Y., and that they contain the religious doctrines of the United Society of Believers, commonly called Shakers. He says that he has inserted this material in order to accommodate the Shakers and to offer the public a chance to acquire a deeper knowledge of their religion, which in general has not been understood.

29. Frederick Evans, "Religious Communism," in his *Autobiography of a Shaker and Revelation of the Apocalypse . . .* , new and enl. ed. (New York, 1888), p. 217.

30. *Testimonies* (Albany, 1888), p. 50.

31. On this characteristic of Methodist recruiting, see W. J. Warner, *The Wesleyan Movement in the Industrial Revolution* (London, 1930), pp. 165–66. And on the social structure of this recruiting, see E. Halévy, "Naissance du Méthodisme en Angleterre," *Revue de Paris* (August 1906), p. 853.

32. *Millennial Church*, p. 57.

33. See Warner (n. 31), p. 210 and pass., chap. 5 on "The Wesleyan Avowal of the Economic Ideal," also chap. 6 on "The Practice of the Economic Virtues," and chap. 7 on "The Significance of Wesleyan Philanthropy."

34. *Journal of the Reverend John Wesley*, ed N. Curnock (London, 1938), 2:136.

35. Ibid., p. 226.

36. Ibid., 7:153.

37. *The Letters of John Wesley*, ed. John Taleford (London, 1931), 4:122.

38. This text by James Smith is quoted and exploited by Mary Dyer in *A Portraiture of Shakerism . . .* (Concord, N.H., 1822), pp. 33–35.

39. See J. H. Overton, *The Evangelical Revival in the Eighteenth Century*

(London, 1907), p. 45. The split will gradually widen on the following issues: (1) *The role of the parish:* the Methodists operated vertically on a proletariat that had been uprooted and rendered homogeneous by economic factors, whereas the evangelists saw an advantage in working from a geographic base; (2) *recruitment:* the Methodists recruited from the lower and lower-middle classes, whereas the parish-evangelists made their appeal to the upper and upper-middle classes; (3) *relations between the clergy and the laity:* from the very beginning the Methodists opened the pulpit and gave the responsibility for organizing parish social life to laymen. Eventually, in exceptional cases, they even admitted laymen to the ministry, making Methodism, in the last analysis, a "High Church" of nonconformism. See Elie Halévy, "Naissance du Méthodisme en Angleterre," *Revue de Paris* (August 1906). The evangelists, on the other hand, maintained the laity in strict subordination to the clergy and insisted on observing traditional ecclesiastical order, making them look like a "Low Church" in the established church structure. Thus it was normal for the Shakers to recruit on the fringes of secularized Methodist (and Baptist) societies.

40. A. Dubois, *Les Prophètes Cévenols* (Strasbourg, 1861), pp. 3 ff.

41. The kind of satisfaction that the proletariat could expect in religious matters is indicated by the Shaker accounts of Ann Lee's childhood. See Anna White and Leila Taylor, *Shakerism, Its Meaning and Its Message* (Mount Lebanon, 1905), p. 18. On paternalism in early English religious societies, see Warner, *The Wesleyan Movement in the Industrial Revolution* (London, 1930), pp. 35 ff.

42. At least this is Warner's conclusion (see n. 41), p. 11. He says that religion was frankly used as a soporific for the poor. The paradoxical vulgarization of this view, from an economic perspective, appeared in the well-known *Fable of the Bees* by Mandeville in 1714; there we learn that each hour a child spends reading books represents an hour lost to social good.

43. Thus, in an address approved by a conference of Methodist ministers in Bristol, 1819, we read that the church should persuade its members to have patience and to abandon themselves to the will of God rather than make common cause with the political organizations and the evil of rebellion. John and Barbara Hammond, *The Town Labourer, 1760–1784* (New York, 1917), pp. 283–85, quote this address and add that, in spirit, this preaching was the exact opposite of what was taught by the Trade Union Movement at the time. One preached patience; the other taught impatience.

44. Despite their stinging criticism of the Methodists, the Hammonds (ibid., pp. 286–87) admit that Methodism was, in a very real sense, a training school for better citizens and, in some cases, for better revolutionaries.

45. Paul Mantoux, *La révolution industrielle au XVIIIᵉ siècle: Essai sur les commencements de la grande industrie en Angleterre* (Paris, 1906), p. 365

46. Mantoux (p. 370) cites this description from Gilbert J. French,

Life and Times of Samuel Crompton, Inventor of the Spinning Machine Called the Mule (Manchester, 1860).

47. Mantoux, pp. 418–19.

48. Ibid., pp. 428–29.

49. *Millennial Church,* p. 12.

50. Mantoux, pp. 434.

51. Phrase used by M. Halbwachs in "Réflexions sur un équilibre démographique," *Annales, Sociétés, Civilisations* (October–December 1946).

52. It was during the period 1770–80 that associations of workers began to assert themselves as a mass movement. The law forbidding these coalitions was passed in 1790. See Mantoux, pp. 462, 467–68.

53. According to Shaker tradition, Ann Lee possessed an extraordinary gift for languages. The *Testimonies* (p. 51) claim that she spoke 72 different tongues.

54. *Millennial Church,* p. 12.

55. Toad Lane, later known as Todd Street, is supposed to have been inhabited by blacksmiths and publicans. See Hepworth Dixon, *La nouvelle Amérique,* trans. Chasles (Paris, 1874).

56. See n. 11. This is related in the *Testimonies,* pp. 2–3.

57. Consecrated phrase used by the Shakers when referring to renunciation of sexual relations in marriage.

58. *Testimonies,* p. 246.

59. *Millennial Church,* p. 12.

60. Among the Bogomils social protest first appeared in a myth according to which the duty not to have children expressed a refusal of the oppressed to satisfy the demands of their oppressors for a supply of tiny creatures to be exploited, creatures whose birth brought to their needy families only an increase of poverty. See H. C. Puech and A. Vaillant, *Le traité contre les Bogomiles de Cosmas-le-Prêtre,* trans. and commentary (Paris, 1945), p. 269.

61. *Millennial Church,* p. 13.

62. *Testimonies,* p. 35.

63. W. E. A. Axon, "A Manchester Prophetess," *Transactions of the Historic Society of Lancashire and Cheshire,* 27th Session, 3d ser., vol. 3, Sessions 1874–75 (Liverpool, 1875).

64. *Millennial Church,* pp. 12–13.

65. The one by Colonel Smith, for example, as reported by Mary Dyer in *A Portraiture of Shakerism,* pp. 33–35: "She [Ann Lee] supported the character of a woman of ill-fame in England." Theo Schroeder in his "Shaker Celibacy and Salacity" (see n. 11) uses the Mary Dyer text as his only source for confirming the image of Ann Lee as a shameless fortune-teller, card reader and drunkard, not only in England but also in America. For the Shaker rebuttal, see *A Review of Mary Dyer's Publication Entitled "A Portraiture of Shakerism" Together with Sundry Affidavits Disproving the Truth of Their Assertions* (Concord, 1824).

66. *Millennial Church* p. 19.

67. *Ibid.*

68. *Ibid.,* p. 16.

69. *Testimonies,* p. 37.

70. *Ibid.,* pp. 38–39; *Millennial Church,* pp. 13–14.

71. For the Bogomil relation to monasticism, see Puech's essay (n. 60). For discussion of the Patarines as representing a form of heterosexual monasticism, see Steven Runciman, *Le Manichéisme médiéval* (Paris, 1949), p. 95.

72. For details of this movement toward communal ownership, see below, chap. 6.

73. Detail pointed out by Daryl Chase in "The Early Shakers" (Ph.D. diss., University of Chicago, 1938).

74. White and Taylor (see n. 41), p. 69.

75. *Millennial Church,* p. 45.

76. *Ibid.*

77. *Ibid.,* p. 49.

78. The same expression with the same sense appears in the description of those who left with Ann Lee. See above, n. 10.

79. *Millennial Church,* p. 49.

80. Letter quoted by Chase (see n. 73), p. 52.

81. *Ibid.,* p. 51.

82. *Millennial Church,* p. 50.

83. *Ibid.,* p. 13.

84. All these visions contained references to America and to the establishment of the church in that land. They also reveal an obsessive need never to be separated from Ann Lee. In all of them he claimed to have seen a gold chain that kept the two of them bound together, and he interpreted this as a sign that they would never be separated.

85. *Testimonies,* p. 277.

86. The Niskeyuna colony was, indeed, considered to be the birthplace of the Shaker Families, even after Mount Lebanon had assumed first importance.

87. The equivalent, as expressed by Engels: "When you put men into a situation fit only for animals, those men must decide whether to revolt or to become like beasts" (Friedrich Engels, *Situation de la classe laborieuse en Angleterre,* ed. A. Costes [Paris, 1923], 1:218.

88. Samuel Fitch is supposed to have addressed Ann Lee and said: "Christ is called the Second Adam and thou art the Second Eve." To this Ann is supposed to have replied: "Flesh and blood has not revealed it unto thee, Samuel; but God has" (*Testimonies,* p. 165). All of chapter 13 in the *Testimonies* is devoted to pronouncements made by Ann Lee about the joys of being in heaven.

89. Malthus's first brochure was dated 1798. The second edition, revised and augmented, was published in 1803. P. Froment points out that

the concept of necessary evil is the basis of all Malthus's thinking. See P. Froment, *Démographie économique* (Paris, 1947), p. 114.

90. Karl Marx, *Capital*, ed. Sociales (Paris, 1948), 3:101–02.

91. Engels (see n. 87), 2:13.

92. Ibid., p. 39.

93. *Millennial Church*, p. 12.

94. Engels, 1:218.

95. G. Sencier, "Le Club de la Chopinette et les communistes matérial-istes," in his *Le Babouvisme après Babeuf* (Paris, 1912), pp. 299 ff.

96. Karl Marx, *Propriété privée et communisme*, Mega 1, 3 (Paris), pp. 111–13.

Notes to Chapter Three

1. Distinction made by S. J. Case in *The Millennial Hope* (Chicago, 1918), and repeated by E. T. Clark in *The Small Sects in America* (New York, 1937), p. 25.

2. Revelation 20:6.

3. See G. Bardy, "Millénarisme," in *Dictionnaire de théologie catholique*, and Adolph Harnack, "Millennium," in *Encyclopedia Britannica*.

4. Bardy, "Millénarisme."

5. See below, chap. 7.

6. For a description of the third age in the cycle, see Joachim of Floris, *Concordia Veteris et Novi Testamenti* (Venice, 1519), pp. 21–22; also E. M. Aegerter, *Joachim de Flore, L'Evangile éternel* (Paris, 1928), pass.

7. K. Kautsky, *Vorlaufer des Neueren Sozialismus*, in *Kommunistische Bewe-gungen in Mitte alter* (Stuttgart, 1909), p. 244

8. This is emphasized by Reuben E. E. Harkness in "Social Origins of the Millerite Movement" (Ph.D. diss., University of Chicago, 1927).

9. Clark, *The Small Sects in America*.

10. See Case, *The Millennial Hope*.

11. The relation between Thomas Münzer, leader of the peasants' re-volt, and Joachim of Floris is emphasized in the following works: W. Zimmermann, *Geschichte des Grossen Bauernkriegs*, 1:172–73; Friedrich Engels, *La Guerre des Paysans en Allemagne*, written in London, 1850 (Paris, 1929), p. 65; M. M. Smirin, *Die Volks Reformation des Thomas Münzer und der grosse Bauernkrieg*, trans. from the Russian (Berlin, 1952), pp. 159 ff.

12. Engels (see n. 11), pp. 68–69. See also, K. Mannheim, *Ideology and Utopia*, 5th ed. (London, 1949), pp. 190–204.

13. H. Vedder, *B. Hubmaïer, the Leader of the Anabaptists* (New York, 1905), pp. 159 ff.

14. Clark (see n. 9), p. 32. Paul Hazard, in *La crise de la conscience*

européenne (Paris, 1935), 2:274 ff., has outlined a few similar mystical expectancies during the 18th century: the "Confrérie des Frères angéliques" and the "Culte des Philadelphes."

15. See Vedder.

16. Pierre Jurieu, *L'ésprit de M. Arnaud* (Deventer, 1684).

17. Pierre Jurieu, *Accomplissement des prophéties* (Rotterdam, 1686).

18. Pierre Jurieu, *Apologie pour "l'accomplissement des prophéties"* (Rotterdam, 1686), p. 108.

19. Jurieu (see n. 17).

20. Ibid., chap. 11.

21. Jurieu (see n. 18), p. 8.

22. For the Shaker explanation of Jurieu's timetable for the day of reckoning, see *Millennial Church*, p. 9.

23. The Mechanic Preachers were to the revolutionary left of the 17th century about what the poor priests (who may or may not have stemmed from Wycliff) were to the uprising of 1381. They belong in the quite complicated movement of those who dissented from the Puritan belief that material prosperity comes to men chosen by God, and who countered it with a prophetic faith in predestination of the poor. See David F. Petegorsky, *Left-Wing Democracy in the English War* (London, 1940), pp. 64–65. This text is quoted and commented on in W. D. Morris, *The Christian Origins of Social Revolt* (London, 1949), pp. 97 ff.

24. Harkness (see n. 8), pp. 69 ff.

25. Ibid.

26. G. Winstanley, *The New Law of Righteousness* (London, 1649); commentaries in M. L. Berneri, *Journey through Utopia* (London, 1950), pp. 143 ff.; and Morris (see n. 23), pp. 115 ff.

27. Charles Burrage, "The Fifth Monarchy Insurrections," *English Historical Review* 25 (1910): 722 ff.; also his "Anna Trapnel's Prophecies," ibid., 16 (1911); 566 ff.

28. This traditional identification of the four monarchies (or empires) is now considered to be based on a false premise. See A. Lods, *Histoire de la littérature hébraïque et juive* (Paris, 1950), pp. 842–43.

29. Anna White and Leila Taylor, *Shakerism, Its Meaning and Its Message* (Columbus, Ohio, 1905), p. 160.

30. The date of the Kelpian emigration is approximate in Green's account. He said it occurred "about" a hundred years before his visit (1827). The Kelpians emigrated in 1694.

31. Mark Holloway, *Heavens on Earth: Utopian Communities in America, 1680–1880* (London, 1951), pp. 37 ff.

32. Case (see n. 1).

33. Rousselot de Surgy, *Histoire naturelle et politique de la Pennsylvanie et de l'établissement des Quakers dans cette contreé* (Paris, 1768). This work is composed of two separate accounts: one by a Swedish writer (Halms), the other by a German (Gottlieb Mittelberger). It treats a dozen different church groups in Philadelphia (the English, the Swedish, the German

Lutherans, the Presbyterians, the New Light Presbyterians, the German Reformed, the Calvinists, two Quaker meetings, the Anabaptists, the Roman Catholics, and finally, the "Herrnhutes" or followers of Count Zinzendorf).

34. See below, chap. 7.

35. On Snowhill, see W. A. Hinds, *American Communities* (Chicago, 1908), pp. 25–26.

36. On Oley and the Baumanites, see M. E. Gaddis, "Christian Perfectionism in America" (Ph.D. diss., University of Chicago, 1929).

37. In 1703, for example, the Sabbatarian churches of Rhode Island sent delegates to the "Woman in the Wilderness" community for instruction. See Holloway (n. 31), p. 42, n. 1.

38. This remark was found by J. Prudhommeaux in A. J. MacDonald's notes for his never completed book that was to be called "The Communities of the United States." The remark about Wilkinson and the Shakers was on a page dated 28 May 1853 of the manuscript in the Yale University Library.

39. The first hypothesis is advanced by MacDonald (see n. 38), p. 681; the second is adopted by Holloway (see n. 31), p. 37.

40. Hinds (see n. 35), pp. 27 ff. Hinds lists his sources on p. 31.

41. Harkness (see n. 8), pass.

42. Daryl Chase describes this encounter, as do White and Taylor (see n. 29), pp. 160–70.

43. Hinds (see n. 35), pp. 396 ff.

44. Clark (see n. 9), pp. 32–33.

45. See directly above.

46. P. 530 n.

47. Modern scholarship puts this date in the second century B.C., between 166 and 164 (see Lods, n. 28). This discrepancy alone obviously upsets the entire Shaker computation.

48. *Millennial Church*, pp. 205–06.

49. The Russian Khlysti likewise placed the first holy event in Jordan when Jesus of Nazareth was filled with the Spirit. Their adoptionism is studied by F. C. Conybeare, in *Russian Dissenters* (Cambridge, Mass., 1921), pp. 339 ff.

50. *Testimony*, p. 530.

51. Peter the Great's policies on the church were obviously approved by Shaker writers. See *Millennial Church*, p. 217. For history of this policy, see P. Milioukov, *Histoire de Russie* (Paris, 1935), 1:407 ff.

52. *Millennial Church*, p. 218.

53. Ibid., pp. 217–18.

54. Revelation 12:16: "And the earth helped the woman; and the earth opened her mouth, and swallowed up the flood which the dragon cast out of his mouth."

55. Frederick Evans, *Autobiography of a Shaker* (New York, 1888), pp. 42–43.

56. *Millennial Church*, pp. 258 ff.

57. Ibid., p. 270.

58. *Testimonies*, pp. 16–17.

59. Ibid., pp. 16–17.

60. See M. Thibert, *Le féminisme dans le socialisme français de 1830 à 1850* (Paris, 1926), pass.

61. *Millennial Church*, p. 252.

62. Ibid.

63. Ibid.

64. Ibid., p. 254.

65. Ibid.

66. Ibid., pp. 255–56.

67. Ibid., pp. 256–57.

68. Ibid., p. 258.

69. See Aaron Williams, *The Harmony Society at Economy, Pennsylvania* (Pittsburg, 1886). Their religious ideology resembles that of the Shakers. Population control and family planning can, temporarily, have the same effect. This is what was practiced at Zoar, at Amana, and in certain kibbutzim.

70. *Millennial Church*, p. 160.

71. *Testimonies*, pp. 238–39.

72. Clark (see n. 9), p. 146, n. 34.

73. A. G. Hollister, *Synopsis of the Doctrine Taught by Believers in Christ's Second Appearing* (Mount Lebanon, 1893), pp. 12–13.

74. George Lomas, *Plain Talks upon Practical Religion: Being Candid Answers to Earnest Inquirers* (Albany, 1873), p. 9.

75. *Testimonies*, p. 27.

76. See below, chap. 7, for this Shaker-Russian correspondence.

77. Jefferson's reply is quoted from White and Taylor (see n. 29), p. 321.

Notes to Chapter Four

1. "The Shakers. A Strict and Utopian Way of Life Has Almost Vanished. Death of a Sect," *Life* (March 21, 1949), pp. 143 ff.

2. The three principal works are Anna White and Leila Taylor, *Shakerism and Its Message* (Columbus, Ohio, 1905); Marguerite Melcher, *The Shaker Adventure* (Princeton, 1941); and most recently, Edward D. Andrews, *The People Called Shakers: A Search for the Perfect Society* (New York, 1953).

3. Daryl Chase, "The Early Shakers" (Ph.D. diss., University of Chicago, 1938).

4. See above, chap. 2.

5. *Millennial Church*, p. 23.

6. Ibid.

7. Ibid.

8. See Valentine Rathbun, *A Brief Account of a Religious Scheme . . .* (Boston, 1781); Amos Taylor, *Narrative of the Strange Principles, Conduct and Character of the People Known by the Name of Shakers* (Worcester, Mass. 1782); Daniel Rathbun, *A Letter from Daniel Rathbun of Richmond in the County of Berkshire to James Whittacor [Whittaker] Chief Elder of the Church Called Shakers* (Springfield, Mass., 1785); Abram Van Vleet, *An Account of the Conduct of the Shakers* (Lebanon, Ohio, 1818).

9. *Millennial Church*, p. 23.

10. Ibid., p. 24.

11. White and Taylor (see n. 2), p. 98.

12. *Millennial Church*, p. 23.

13. Ibid., p. 24.

14. Ibid., p. 25. See also, *Testimonies*, pp. 57, 69, 85, 87, and ff.

15. *Millennial Church*, p. 25.

16. See above, chap. 3.

17. *Millennial Church*, p. 26. See also, *Testimonies*, pp. 63–64.

18. One also finds this tradition among the old Messalians. See A. Guillaumont, "Les Messaliens," in *Etudes carmélitaines: Mystique et continence* (Paris, 1952), pp. 133–36. Likewise, one finds this tradition of male and female missionaries traveling together among the itinerant preachers of medieval dissidences, among the Cevenoles, and in certain of the nonconformist sects that sprung from the Raskol.

19. *Millennial Church*, p. 29.

20. See above, chap. 2.

21. White and Taylor (see n. 2).

22. Ibid., p. 71.

23. Using recollections of his youth, Engels did a detailed analysis of this phenomenon in his study "Zur Geschichte des Urchristenums," *Neue Zeit*[1] (1894–95): 4 ff. The article appeared in French under the title "Contribution à l'histoire du Christianisme primitif," *Le Devenir Social*, 1: 27–40, 138–47.

24. "The work was all new to those who embraced it, and the leaders being few in number and the work extensive, *irregularities could not always be foreseen nor prevented*" (*Millennial Church*, pp. 24–25).

25. See above, chap. 2.

26. See below, chap. 6, for text of this Covenant.

27. Both White and Taylor and Andrews mention this first dissidence, which must have been important enough to involve the whole community.

28. White and Taylor (see n. 2), p. 101. See also, W. A. Hinds, who, in *American Communities* (Oneida, 1878), p. 48, quotes Elder George Lomas as admitting that "The severity of our rules can be attributed to Elder Joseph Meacham."

29. See Richard McNemar, *The Kentucky Revival* (Cincinnati, 1807).

30. See Ibid., chap. 3; also, J. P. MacLean, *A Sketch of the Life and Labors of Richard McNemar* (Franklin, Ohio, 1905), chap. 2.

31. For locations and dates, see Chart no. 6.

32. See J. P. MacLean, *A Bibliography of Shaker Literature with an Introductory Study of the Writings and Publications Pertaining to Ohio Believers* (Columbus, Ohio, 1905). In his introduction MacLean emphasises the literary fecundity of these Ohio societies.

33. See Chart no. 8.

34. The New Lebanon Revival had also set off a wave of pamphlets critical of the Shakers. See Thomas Brown, *An Account of the People Called Shakers* . . . (Troy, N.Y. 1812); Eunice Chapman, *Account of the Conduct of the People Called Shakers* . . . (Albany, 1817); Van Vleet, *An Account of the Conduct of the Shakers;* Mary Dyer, *A Brief Statement of the Sufferings of Mary Dyer Occasioned by the Society Called Shakers* (Concord, N.H., 1818).

35. For Shaker apologetics at this period, see Richard McNemar, *Shakerism Detected* . . . (Lebanon, Ohio, and Lexington, Ky., 1811); Calvin Green and Seth Y. Wells, *A Declaration of the Society of People Commonly Called Shakers Showing Their Reasons for Refusing to Aid or Abet the Cause of War* . . . (Albany, 1815); Joseph Dyer, *A Compendious Narrative Elucidating the Character and Conduct of Mary Dyer from the Time of Her Marriage in 1799, till She Left the Society Called Shakers in 1815* . . . (Concord, N.H., 1818), and *The Other Side of the Question* (Cincinnati, 1819), Shaker explanations, refutations, and accounts of what happened in the cases of Eunice Chapman, Mary Dyer, and Abram Van Vleet, compiled by Eleazer Wright, Calvin Morell, Matthew Houston, and S. Serring.

36. For the theological justifications see McNemar, *The Kentucky Revival;* Bejamin S. Youngs and Calvin Green, *Testimony of Christ's Second Appearing* . . . , 1st ed. (Lebanon, Ohio, 1808); John Dunlavy, *The Manifesto or a Declaration of the Doctrines and Practice of the Church of Christ* (Pleasant Hill, Ky., 1818).

37. See B. Frothingham, *G. Ripley* (Boston, 1882), particularly Ripley's last message to his congregation, pp. 63–91.

38. See above, chap. 3.

39. On Swedenborg, Evans wrote that he was the contemporary of Ann and that she once called him her John the Baptist. See Frederick Evans, *Autobiography of a Shaker*, 3d ed. (New York, 1888), p. 40.

40. J. R. Colon, *A Return of Departed Spirits of the Highest Characters of Distinction as Well as the Indiscriminate of All Nations into the Bodies of the Shakers* . . . (Philadelphia, 1843). In this book, dedicated to people of all religions, but most especially to Jews and Roman Catholics, there is an inventory of the personalities with whom they had been in spiritual communication: Washington, Bonaparte, Alexander the Great, etc.

41. For spirit messages, see William Leonard, "Copy of the Record of Divine Instructions . . . ," typed copy of a 1843 spirit message recorded

by "William Leonard Instrument" (Union Village, Ohio, 1904); also William Leonard, "Lives and Sufferings of Christ . . .," typed copy of an 1841 message (Union Village, Ohio, 1904); Calvin Green, "Extract from a Writing Received in the Name of the Prophet Joël," ed. A. G. Hollister under the title *The Law of Life* (Mount Lebanon, 1901); Lucy Wright, *The Gospel Monitor . . .—Copied by Inspiration of Mother Ann's Desire* (Canterbury, N.H.; 1843); J. Lafume, *Calvin's Confession . . .* , ed. A. G. Hollister (Mount Lebanon, 1904); his *Youth's Guide in Zion and Holy Mother's Promise Given by Inspiration at New Lebanon* (Canterbury, N.H., 1842); his *Farewell Address of Ebenezer Bishop of New Lebanon to the Inhabitants of Zion* (Canterbury, N.H., 1850); Philemon Stuart, *A Closing Roll from Holy and Eternal Wisdom, Mother Ann, Father William and Father James to the Children of Zion . . .* (Canterbury, N.H., 1843); his *Circular: Further Directions concerning the Distribution of the Sacred Roll and Book . . .* (New Lebanon, 1843); his *The Holy Word of the Lord God Almighty, the Holy One of Israel to His Chosen People throughout Zion's Habitations . . .* , written by inspiration in 1843, copied in 1904. (n.p., n.d.); Paulina Bates, *The Divine Book of Holy and Eternal Wisdom Revealing the Word of God out of Whose Mouth Goeth Sharp Sword . . .* (Canterbury, N.H., 1849).

42. See Philemon Stewart, *A Holy Sacred and Divine Roll and Book from the Lord of Heaven to the Inhabitants of Earth . . .* (Canterbury, N.H., 1843).

43. See next section on sociological phases.

44. There is no trace here of any direct influence from the *Théâtre sacré des Cévennes*, except through a probable acquaintance with the writings of John Lacy. Nevertheless, here and there in their prophetic moments, the Shakers do reveal certain characteristics of their Cevenole predecessors.

45. See below, chap. 7.

46. White and Taylor note the conversion of a certain Enoch Jacobs, who had been editor of *The Day Star*, a Millerite journal. After Jacobs joined the Shakers in 1846, his paper became a platform for preaching Shaker ideas. White and Taylor (see n. 2) then continue with a more general statement (pp. 170–71) to the effect that the Millerite movement contributed many members to the Shakers, and that Canterbury, Enfield (New Hampshire), and Harvard societies owed most of their growth to this source of converts. E. D. Andrews (see n. 2) notes (p. 292) that in Philadelphia a Shaker mission had "gathered" a Family composed of ex-Millerites—mostly Negro.

47. See H. C. Blinn, *A Little Instructor* (Canterbury, N.H., 1849); H. L. Eads, *The Tailor's Division System, Founded upon and Combined with Actual Measurement; Containing Thirty Diagrams and Designs Reduced to Mathematical Principles* (Union Village, Ohio, 1849), a manual to assure standardization of Shaker costume; H. C. Blinn, *A Concise Catechism* (Canterbury, N.H., 1850); Frederick W. Evans, *A Short Treatise on the Second Appearing of Christ in and through the Order of the Female* (Boston, 1853); Frederick

W. Evans, *Tests of Divine Inspiration or the Rudimental Principles by which True and False Revelation in all Eras of the World Can Be Unerringly Discriminated* (New Lebanon, 1853); William Leonard, *A Discourse on the Order and Propriety of Divine Inspiration and Revelation Showing the Necessity Thereof in All Ages to Know the Will of God* (Harvard, 1853); Frederick W. Evans, *Ann Lee, the Founder of the Shakers. A Biography with Memoirs . . . Also a Compendium of the Origin, History, Principles, Rules and Regulations, Government and Doctrines of the United Society of Believers in Christ's Second Appearing* (New Lebanon, 1871).

48. James Holmes, *A Collection of Useful Hints of Farmers, and Many Valuable Recipes* (West Gloucester, 1850). This was followed by *The Farmer's Second Book* (West Gloucester, 1853 [?]) and *The Farmer's Third Book* (West Gloucester, 1856). See also *Improved Shaker Washing Machine . . . , Manufactured and for Sale by the United Society of Shakers at Shaker Village* (Concord, N.H., 1859); *Catalogue of Herbs, Roots, Barks, Powdered Articles . . . Prepared in the United Society* (Portland, Me., 1864); *Circular Concerning the Dress of Believers* (Mount Lebanon, 1886 [?]).

49. See *A Biography of the Life and Tragical Death of Elder Caleb M. Dyer Together with the Poem and Eulogies of His Funeral* (Manchester, N.H., 1863); *Shakers: A Correspondence between Mary F.C. of Mount Holly City and a Sister Shaker Sarah L. of Union Village*, ed. R. W. Pelham (Union Village, Ohio, 1868).

50. See Evans, *A Short Treatise . . . , Tests of Divine Inspiration . . . ,* and *Ann Lee, the Founder of the Shakers. . . .* See also his *Autobiography of a Shaker and Revelation of Apocalypse with an Appendix* (Mount Lebanon, 1869), *Shaker Communism or Tests of Divine Inspiration . . .* (London, 1871), *Elder Evans to Henry George* (Mount Lebanon, 1886), *One Hundred Years of Shaker Life, Centennial of Communism and Peace* (Mount Lebanon, 1874), *A Suggestion of an Exchange of Women for Men Legislators* (Mount Lebanon, 1890), and *Shaker-Russian Correspondence between Count Leo Tolstoi and Elder F.W. Evans* (Mount Lebanon, 1891).

51. See White and Taylor (n. 2), pp. 182 ff.; and on the use of military pensions, pp. 227–28.

52. See above, chap. 3.

53. See below, chap. 6.

54. R. W. Pelham, *A Shaker's Answer to the Oft Repeated Question "What Would Become of the World if All Should Become Shaker"* (Union Village, Ohio, 1868); Frederick W. Evans, *Elder Evans to Henry George* (Mount Lebanon, 1886); Daniel Fraser, "Shaker Support for Henry George," *New York Tribune*, December 23 and 26, 1886; Evans, *Shaker-Russian Correspondence*.

55. Julia Neal, *By Their Fruits. The Story of Shakerism in South Union, Kentucky* (New York, 1947).

56. J. Prudhommeaux in 1904 commented on the disappearance of the custom of saying confession to Elders.

57. Andrews reports that by this time the dancing had become more sedate, without the old turns and whirls, and that the religious services had tended to become mechanical repetitions of ritual formulas, lacking any freshness of inspiration. See Edward D. Andrews, *The Gift to Be Simple* (New York, 1940), p. 157.

58. Ibid., p. 86, n.8; p. 157.

59. Prudhommeaux reported that in 1904 he had asked Elder Daniel at Mount Lebanon if any of the Shakers still practiced spiritualism, and that Daniels had replied, "No, it has stopped completely and, besides, for many years now we have discouraged all such manifestations. There are still a few old fashion Shakers who go into trances and say they are inspired, but we pretend not to notice their foolishness" (J. Prudhommeaux, "Notes de Voyages," written at Mount Lebanon, October 16, 1904).

60. Reported by Julia Neal (see n. 55), p. 260.

61. At South Union, recreation brought them more and more in contact with the outside world. They paid calls in the neighborhood. They attended the circus and sports events. In 1910 they had a telephone installed. See Julia Neal (n. 55), p. 256.

62. "They now receive all sorts of books and magazines, do no more than quote the Bible, and their respect for Mother Ann and her doctrines is largely based on indifference. Books containing the teachings of the glorious founder are deemed sacred, but only in the sense that no one touches them" (Prudhommeaux [see n. 59]).

63. In an 1891 letter to the sisters of North Family, Frederick Evans expressed his satisfaction that all was going well *for the sisters* in respect to numbers and ability to work. The same could not be said of the brothers. Evans sought consolation in the belief that to explain this disproportion in religious organizations there is a general law according to which the number of men in them is always inferior to the number of women. See his *Immortalized Elder Frederick Evans* (Pittsfield, 1893), pp. 114–15.

64. Julia Neal remarks that the religious inspiration had dried up and cites the time when the ministry was called upon to decide whether or not by letting one's beard grow one becomes immune to sore throats. After much discussion it was left up to each individual to decide for himself (Neal [see n. 55], p. 240).

65. "After the Civil War, when shoes and cloth could be purchased more cheaply at a store than produced in the colony, many members decided to do just that, and thus began the disintegration of the sect's firm economic foundation" ("Death of a Sect," *Life* [March 21, 1949], p. 148).

66. Older members accepted the new practice of buying things from the outside, but not without regret for the passing of the frugal forms of their former self-suffcent economy. See Neal (n. 55), p. 263.

67. Alex Kent cites an elder who wrote him saying that they were tired

of trying to maintain their farms by paying outsiders to do the work, something that was absolutely contradictory to the principles of life they had undertaken to uphold. The elder continued his complaint by stating that there had been a decline not only in the number of members but also in the quality of the community's spiritual life ever since they had begun to hire people to work their fields, after being forced to do so because they lacked the members necessary to perform this task themselves. See Alex Kent, "Cooperative Communities in the U.S.," *U.S. Department of Agriculture Bulletin,* vol. 6, no. 35 (July 1901), p. 576.

68. The Shakers had always adopted orphans, but these adoptions seldom produced converts. William Hinds reports that, of the thousands of children placed with the society for one reason or another, few remained after attaining maturity. An elder told him that during his own 49 years with the society they had taken in enough children to make a line half a mile long, and that he had had enough. See William A. Hinds, *American Communities* . . . (Oneida, 1878), p. 57. Daryl Chase points out that of the 144 boys taken in by one society between 1821 and 1864, 102 went back into the world. See Chase (n. 3), p. 120.

69. White and Taylor (see n. 2), p. 389.

70. Chase (see n. 3), pp. 5–6.

71. Ibid.

72. *Life* (see n. 65).

73. See below, sect. III of this chapter.

74. The Antinomian position was implicitly recognized by the Shakers. See n. 24.

75. See above, chaps. 1 and 2.

76. Citing a contemporary observer of revivalist enthusiasm, Daryl Chase describes how the "power of God" was so great that even young and vigorous onlookers fell to the floor as if wounded in battle and howled so loudly that they could be heard from far away. See Chase (n. 3), p. 22.

77. See above, chap. 3.

78. Daryl Chase cites this anecdote taken from I. Stewart, *The History of Free-Will Baptists* (Dover, N.H., 1862).

79. Chase, pp. 24 ff.

80. For descriptions of revivalists' "jerks," taken from letters written by Shaker missionaries in Kentucky, 1805, see ibid., p. 263. See also Neal (n. 55), pp. 13–15, and McNemar, *Kentucky Revival.*

81. See Neal, p. 13.

82. Ibid., p. 15.

83. Ibid., p. 17.

84. Divine revelation was supposed to come directly to each individual and each person was supposed to be capable of understanding spiritual matters for himself, without benefit of written texts or licensed commentators. See ibid., pp. 17–18. This is close to the theme of the Inner Light, so dear to the Quakers, and, before them, to Zwickau's theory of

prophecy. See Leif Eeg-Olofsson, *The Conception of the Inner Light in Robert Barclay's Theology: A Study of Quakerism* (London, 1954).

85. White and Taylor (see n. 2), p. 152.

86. R. E. E. Harkness, "Social Origins of the Millerite Movement" (Ph.D. diss., University of Chicago, 1927).

87. Joseph Smith was personally engaged in real estate speculation and in 1806 had founded a bank of issue, printing money: "The Kirtland Safety Society Bank." The failure of this bank precipitated his flight.

88. E. A. Shannon, *Economic History of the People of the United States* (New York, 1934), pp. 352–53.

89. Chase (see n. 3), p. 151.

90. See William Leonard, *Copy of the Record* . . . and *Lives and Sufferings of Christ*, as well as other texts listed under n. 41.

91. See Paulina Bates, *The Divine Roll and Book from the Lord God* . . . (Canterbury, N.H., 1849): "These two fat volumes are no longer available in the libraries. Wise old Frederick Evans put an end to this chapter of Shaker History." See Prudhommeaux (n. 59).

92. See Chase (n. 3), p. 156.

93. Ibid.

94. Ibid., p. 170.

95. Here is the list as established by Daryl Chase: Union Village (*Wisdom's Paradise*), Mount Lebanon (*Holy Mount*), Watervliet (*Wisdom's Valley*), North Union (*Valley of God's Pleasure*), Whitewater (*Lovely Plain of Tribulation*), Groveland (*Union Branch*), Tyringham (*City of Union*), Hancock (*City of Peace*), Enfield, Connecticut (*City of Love*), Enfield, New Hampshire (*Chosen Vale*), Harvard (*Lovely Vineyard*), Shirley (*Pleasant Garden*), Canterbury (*Holy Ground*), Alfred (*Holy Land*), Sabbathday Lake (*Chosen Land*).

96. Both Daryl Chase and White and Taylor report that Dr. Peebles, who accompanied Evans to England, was an American spiritualist leader. Andrews, however, remarks on the reluctance of the Shakers to recognize spiritualist techniques such as table-tipping and automatic writing. See Andrews (n. 2), p. 175.

97. See Stewart (n. 42).

98. See Green (n. 41); also, *An Interesting Narrative of Our Savior Jesus Christ*, a message from Pontius Pilate (Canterbury, N.H., 1849).

99. See also Leonard (n. 41), a spirit message.

100. See Lafume (n. 41), pp. 4–5.

101. See ibid., pp. 15–16.

102. See ibid., p. 18.

103. See Chase (n. 3), p. 156.

104. See Neal (n. 55), p. 63.

105. White and Taylor (see n. 2), p. 161. They had previously attempted to use tobacco in a ceremony called the "smoking gift," a ritual probably borrowed from the Indians. See Andrews (n. 2), p. 143.

106. Sylvester Graham's "Treatise on Bread and Bread Making" dates from 1837.

107. White and Taylor, p. 161

108. Ibid., p. 216.

109. Ibid.

110. Daryl Chase quotes a manuscript defending Grahamism, in which the writer claimed that a strict vegetarian diet eased the sexual torments of young people so that those "addicted to venereal pollution became harmless as babes" (Chase [n. 3], p. 96).

111. See Ivan Skhoukine, *Le suicide collectif dans le Raskol russe* (Paris, 1903). The wave of suicides, which began around 1660, lasted until the second half of the 19th century.

112. We shall return to discussion of this temptation in chapter 6.

113. The second temptation is reported by White and Taylor (see n. 2), p. 246. They tell how a man appeared at Mount Lebanon "burdened with an important message which he declared had been delivered to him by Mother Ann herself." He was received by Frederick Evans to whom he declared that the founding Mother "wished her people to know that the time for the necessity of the virgin life had expired, and she now wished her followers to marry and give in marriage." To this the elder replied that they were disciples not of Ann Lee but of her principles, and that if she had fallen from her light that is no reason why they should do the same. " 'Well, but Elder,' said the stranger, 'what if Mother Ann should appear to you in person and tell you what she told me?' To this Evans replied, 'We would take her down to the visitors' room and try to convert her.' "

114. H. S. Bender, *La vision anabaptiste* (Montebéliard, 1950), pp. 18–19.

115. *Immortalized Elder Frederick W. Evans*, ed. Anna White (Pittsfield, 1893), p. 111.

116. Ibid., pp. 121–22.

117. Ibid., p. 121.

118. According to an interview reported by Nordhoff, Evans was thinking of something like this, at least for a while. Elder Evans told him that he believed there should be a celibate order in every Protestant community and that its members should earn their own living and not be mendicants. He added that he thought the needs and consciences of every civilized society would be served by making membership in such an order available. See C. Nordhoff, *The Communistic Societies of the U.S.A. . . .* (New York, 1875), p. 159.

119. See above, chap. 3.

120. *Immortalized Frederick Evans* (see n. 115), p. 110.

121. Neal (see n. 55).

122. Melcher (see n. 2), pp. 230 ff.

123. Ibid., pp. 234 ff.

124. Ibid., p. 241.

125. Kent (see n. 67), p. 577.

126. Neal (see n. 55), pp. 263–68.

127. Edward D. Andrews, *Shaker Furniture. The Craftsmanship of an American Communal Sect* (New Haven, 1937).

128. Andrews (see n. 57), p. 144.

129. See William Plumer's correspondence with Miss Lydia Coombs (1782–83), in "The Original Shaker Communities in New England," ed. F. B. Sanborn, *New England Magazine* 22 (1900): 303–09.

130. *Our Revolutionary Forefathers. The Letters of Barbé-Marbois During His Residence in the United States as Secretary of the French Legation (1779–1785)*, trans. Eugene Parker Chase (New York, 1929), pp. 180–84.

131. Fayette Mace, *Familiar Dialogues in Shakerism* (Portland, Me., 1838), pp. 86–88. This account is in large part taken from McNemar, *Kentucky Revival*, pp. 60–62 pass.

132. Theo Schroeder, "Shaker Celibacy and Salacity Psychologically Interpreted," *New York Medical Journal* (June 1, 1921), pp. 800–05. In this article Schroeder cites the following lines of Shaker verse as an indication that they were nude when they danced:

> We dance each like a living spark
> As David danced before the Ark.

The evidence is not decisive. For a justification of ritual dancing, see *Millennial Church*, pp. 85–97.

133. Andrews (see n. 57), pp. 40–41.

134. Ibid., p. 29.

135. Nordhoff (see n. 118), p. 256.

136. Clara Endicott Sears, *Gleanings from Old Shaker Journals* (Boston, 1916), p. 220.

137. E. F. Dow, "Portrait of the Millennial Church of the Shakers," *University of Maine Studies*, vol. 34, 2d ser., no. 19 (August 1930).

138. Melcher (see n. 2), p. 302.

139. A. E. Bestor, *Backwoods Utopias . . . 1663–1829* (Philadelphia, 1950), pp. 235–36. See also, Andrews (n. 2), pp. 290–92.

140. White and Taylor (see n. 2), pass.

141. Frederick Evans, *Shakers. Compendium . . . with Biographies . . .* (New York, 1859), pp. 188–89.

142. *Millennial Church*, p. 84.

143. See below, chap. 6.

144. *Millennial Church*, pp. 75–84.

145. Prudhommeaux (see n. 59), p. 50.

146. *Millennial Church*, p. 84.

147. See above, section on "Second Phase."

148. *Seventh Census, 1850* (Washington, D.C., 1853), p. 5.

149. *Ninth Census, 1870* (Washington, D.C., 1872), p. 521.

150. Hepworth Dixon, *La nouvelle Amérique*, trans. P. Chasles (Paris, 1874), p. 269.

151. Statistical abstract of the *Eleventh Census, 1890*.

152. The 1936 *Religious Bodies* gives the recapitulatory table.
153. Dow (see n. 137), p. 43.
154. Chase (see n. 3), pp. 268–71.

Notes to Chapter Five

1. These are the words of Ann Lee, in *Testimonies,* p. 224.
2. The Shaker explanation of their position is the subject of an exchange of letters between the Shaker, Daniel Offord, and Koresh. *Letter from Daniel Offort with reply by Koresh* (Mount Lebanon, 1892).
3. See above, chap. 2, n. 60.
4. See below, sect. II, "Philosophic Arguments."
5. On the Skoptsy, see Tsakny, *La Russie sectaire* (Paris, 1888), p. 50. On distinctions within the Raskol, see Pierre Pascal, *Avvakum et les débuts du Raskol* (Paris, 1930), pp. 560 ff.; also Conybeare (see chap. 3, n. 49).
6. This is the way to understand the difference between the Raskol and the Skoptsy sect. See Ionel Rapaport, *Introduction à la psychopathologie collective: La secte mystique des Skoptsy* (Paris, 1943), p. 108, n. 111.
7. A Christensen, *L'Iran sous les Sassanides* (Copenhagen–Paris, 1936), p. 311. See also, A. Christensen, *Le règne du roi Kawadh et le communisme Mazdakite* (Copenhagen, 1925).
8. On bundling, see H. R. Stiles, *History of Bundling* (Albany, 1871). For bibliography on Oneida, see J. W. Eaton and S. M. Katz, *Research Guide of Cooperative Group Farming* (New York, 1942), pp. 47–48; also D. D. Egbert and S. Persons, *Socialism and American Life,* vol. 2 (Princeton, 1952). On libertarian thought in anarchist circles, see G. Narast, *Milieux libres: Quelques essais contemporains de vie communiste en France* (Paris, 1908); Jean Maitron, *Histoire du mouvement anarchiste en France (1880–1914)* (Paris, 1952), pp. 355–79.
9. P. Alfaric, *L'évolution intellectuelle de Saint Augustin* (Paris, 1918), 1:140–41.
10. *Millennial Church,* pp. 156–57.
11. J. P. Sartre, *Baudelaire* (Paris, 1947), p. 94.
12. *Testimonies,* p. 14.
13. *Millennial Church,* p. 152.
14. *Testimonies,* p. 33.
15. Ibid., p. 26.
16. Ibid., p. 21.
17. Ibid., p. 20.
18. See above, chap. 2.

19. *Testimonies*, p. 33.

20. *Millennial Church*, pp. 144–45.

21. *Testimonies*, p. 14.

22. Ibid., p. 31. On the baptism in the Spirit see *Millennial Church*, pp. 283–86.

23. *Testimonies*, p. 13.

24. This is a Shaker slogan. Further on we will see other uses made of it.

25. John Dunlavy, *The Manifesto* . . . (Pleasant Hill, Ky., 1818), p. 286.

26. Ibid., p. 312.

27. Daryl Chase, "The Early Shakers" (Ph.D. diss., University of Chicago, 1938), p. 54.

28. Ibid., p. 49.

29. See above, chap. 2, end of sect. III.

30. See below, end of this section.

31. Blaise Pascal, *Pensées*, ed. Brunschwigg and Boutroux, no. 276.

32. See above, chap. 2, sect. I.

33. In his autobiography Frederick Evans confesses that he read the Bible only to find illustrations for his own ideas, and that for many years he paid no attention to the "Revelation of Saint John the Divine."

34. *Testimony*, p. 24.

35. Ibid., pp. 28–29.

36. *Millennial Church*, p. 139.

37. Ezekiel 18:20.

38. *Millennial Church*, pp. 139–40.

39. *Testimony*, p. 25; *Millennial Church*, p. 142.

40. *Millennial Church*, pp. 142–43.

41. See above, chap. 2, sect. III.

42. *Millennial Church*, pp. 143–44.

43. Ibid., p. 144.

44. Ibid., pp. 147–48.

45. Ibid., p. 151

46. Ibid., pp. 152 ff.

47. Ibid., pp. 152–153; *Testimony*, pp. 17–18.

48. George Albert Lomas, *Plain Talks upon Practical Religion* . . . (Albany, 1873), pp. 12–13.

49. *Millennial Church*, pp. 166–67. The same interpretation is found in Dunlavy's *Manifesto* (see n. 25), p. 291. Again, in *Millennial Church*, p. 164: "As well may we talk of a man's traveling both east and west at one and the same time, as of his following Christ in the regeneration, while living in the works of generation."

50. *Millennial Church*, pp. 172–73.

51. See Charles-Henri Nodet, "Position de saint Jérôme en face des problèmes sexuels," in *Etudes carmélitaines: Mystique et continence* (Paris, 1952), pp. 308–56.

52. *Shakers. A Correspondence between Mary F. C*[arr], *of Mount Holly*

City, and a Shaker Sister Sarah L[ucas], *of Union Village*, ed. Richard Pelham (Union Village, Ohio, 1868).

53. Ibid., pp. 8–9.

54. Ibid., p. 17.

55. Ibid., pp. 19–20.

56. Frederick Evans, "Religious Communism," in his *Autobiography of a Shaker* (New York, 1888), pp. 201–02.

57. Frederick Evans gives six reasons for considering the Essenes as pre-Shakers. These will be discussed below, in chap. 7.

58. *Millennial Church*, p. 100.

59. G. Van der Leeuw, "La religion dans son essence et dans ses manifestations," in his *Phénoménologie de la religion* (Paris, 1948), p. 93.

60. Anna White, *The Motherhood of God* (Canaan Four Corners, N.Y., 1903), pp. 3–6.

61. *Millennial Church*, pp. 1–6.

62. To this demonstration of how the family engenders property as we know it, A. G. Hollister adds a demonstration of how property engenders the family as we know it, and particularly, the venal quality of love: "Husbands and wives are bought and sold," money is paid for love, and love is given for money. See A. G. Hollister, *Mission of Aletheian Believers Called Shakers* (Mount Lebanon, 1892–99), pp. 18–19.

63. Evans (see n. 56), pp. 215–16.

64. Hollister, p. 2

65. Richard Pelham, *A Shaker's Answer to the Oft-Repeated Question: "What Would Become of the World if All Should Become Shakers?"* (Union Village, Ohio, 1868). This text was reproduced without the author's name in Giles B. Avery, *Sketches of Shakers and Shakerism. Synopsis of Theology of United Society of Believers in Christ's Second Appearing* (Albany, 1884), pp. 31 ff. Quotations are taken from this edition.

66. See above, chap. 2, sect. III.

67. These premises and conclusions are similar to those of G. Naidenoff, "Histoire sainte de la famille," in *Rythmes du Monde*, no. 3–4 (1949), pp. 134 ff.

68. *A Correspondence* (see n. 52), p. 18.

69. *Testimonies*, p. 233.

70. Ibid.

71. Daniel Fraser, *The Music of the Spheres* (Albany, 1887), pp. 24 ff.

72. See above, chap. 4, sect. III.

73. *Millennial Church*, p. 150.

74. See above, chap. 4, sect. II, "The Third Phase."

75. *Immortalized Elder Frederick Evans* (Pittsfield, 1893), p. 15.

76. Evans (see n. 56), pp. 199–200.

77. See above, chap. 4, sect. II, "The Second Phase."

78. Pelham (see n. 65), p. 32.

79. White (see n. 60), p. 11.

80. A. G. Hollister, *Synopsis of Doctrines Taught by Believers in Christ's Second Appearing* (Mount Lebanon, 1893), pp. 21–22.

81. *Millennial Church*, p. 100. In support the Shakers cite Proverbs 8 and Proverbs 3:17–19.

82. "Many of the Gentiles embraced Christianity by profession. Among these were men eminent for natural wisdom, literary talents, and even learned philosophers. These obtained great influence in the church, and thereby brought in various mysteries pertaining to the religions of the Gentile nations, particularly those in high repute for their wisdom and learning. These were mysteriously blended with the doctrines of Christ and the apostles . . . From this source originated the doctrine of the *Trinity*, or three persons in one God, all in the masculine gender" (*Millennial Church*, p. 201).

83. See above, this chapter, sect. III.

84. "Remember that Jesus was born a Jew, born of a woman and under the law, and that he was a man, not a God" (Evans [see n. 56], p. 208).

85. *Millennial Church*, p. 290; also see above, chap. 3, sect. III, "Feminism."

86. *Testimonies*, pp. 264–65.

87. Ann Lee said: "I have often seen Saint Peter and Saint Paul and conversed with them and with all the apostles; and with Christ Jesus my Lord and my Head: for no man is my head, but Christ Jesus. . . . Christ is my husband" (*Testimonies*, p. 165).

88. "I am married to the Lord Jesus Christ. He is my head and my husband and I have no other. I have walked hand in hand with him in Heaven" (ibid.).

89. "I feel the blood of Christ running through my soul and washing me" (ibid., p. 166).

90. White (see n. 60), pp. 22–23.

91. Dunlavy's *Manifesto* (see n. 25), p. 316.

92. White (see n. 60), p. 22.

93. Ibid., pp. 22–23.

94. Evans (see n. 56), p. 23.

95. Ibid., pp. 197–98.

96. See above, chap. 4, n. 63.

97. *Millennial Church*, pp. 150–51.

98. Ibid., pp. 200–01.

99. Ibid., p. 205.

100. *A Correspondence* (see n. 52), pp. 15–17.

101. *Testimonies*, p. 245.

102. Daniel Rathbun, *A Letter from Daniel Rathbun of Richmond in the County of Berkshire to James Whittaker Chief Elder of the Church Called Shakers* (Springfield, 1785); also, Mary Dyer, *A Portraiture of Shakerism . . .* (Concord, N.H., 1822).

103. *Report of the Examination of Canterbury and Enfield before the New*

Hampshire Legislature at the November Session, 1848 . . . from Notes Taken at the Examination (Concord, N.H., 1849), pp. 35–36.

104. *Report of the Examination* (see n. 103).

105. Joseph Dyer, *A Compendious Narrative, Elucidating the Character, Disposition and Conduct of Mary Dyer from the Time of Her Marriage in 1799, till She Left the Society Called Shakers in 1815 . . . by Her Husband, Joseph Dyer . . .* (Concord, N.H., 1818), p. 84.

106. Fraser, *Music of the Spheres*, p. 24.

Notes to Chapter Six

1. Seth Y. Wells, "Exposition Continued . . . ," in R. R. Hinmann, *The Blue Laws of the New Haven Colony* (Hartford, 1838), p. 274. This is Wells's *Brief Exposition* (Albany, 1834), augmented by a series of notes and included in the Quaker study of Connecticut's intolerant "blue laws." See above, chap. 2, n. 28.

2. See Chart no. 10.

3. Charles Nordhoff, *Communistic Societies of the United States* (New York, 1875), pp. 135–36.

4. Daryl Chase, "The Early Shakers" (Ph.D. diss., University of Chicago, 1938), p. 166.

5. *Millennial Church*, p. 62.

6. Chase, p. 165.

7. Chase describes this in detail.

8. John Cassian, *Collations* 8:5.

9. Anna White and Leila Taylor, *Shakerism, Its Meaning and Message* (Mount Lebanon, 1905), pp. 102–03.

10. See Chart no. 6.

11. Wells's book (see n. 1) went through many editions. Evans's *Compendium* (New York, 1859) was also edited at different times and under various titles.

12. Wells, p. 11; see also, Evans, p. 45.

13. Wells, p. 11.

14. Ibid.

15. For example, see Roxalana Grosvenor, *The Shaker's Covenant* (Boston, 1873).

16. See below, section entitled "Texts of the Covenants."

17. See ibid.

18. On the junior class, see Wells, p. 13; also Evans, p. 48; and *Millennial Church*, pp. 60 ff.

19. On the Church Order, see Wells, p. 15; Evans, p. 48; *Millennial*

Church, p. 58; also the section below entitled "Texts of the Covenants."

20. See above, chap. 5, sect. III.

21. For example, in his letter to Robert Dale Owen: "Has it not been the desire, the constant wish of your big, benevolent heart to gather the people into communities, so that, as the prime object, they might be fed and clothed? Has not this been the mainspring of your life-long labors, to educate the ignorant, to feed the hungry and clothe the naked—to lower the rich and elevate the poor? And have you not sought as an end that which is but the effect of an end? Have not your people hungered more after the fruits of the Kingdom of Heaven than after the Kingdom itself and its righteousness? Is not here the cause of the universal failure of the mere earthly man to form a community, and the true cause of the success of the mere spiritual man, who without possessing a tithe of the external, worldly wisdom and advantages, without even thinking or caring about a community or socialism, has been instinctively drawn into it by laws to him as unseen and unknown as were those which organized and fashioned him in his mother's womb?" This letter to Robert Owen's son is quoted by White and Taylor (see n. 9), p. 304. Owen replied that he would come to New Lebanon and stay there for two months, and that, if things were as had been described, he would become a Shaker. In his *Autobiography* (Mount Lebanon, 1869), Evans makes the semiarrogant, semicrestfallen comment: "I'm still waiting for him to come."

22. Cf. the precedent of Abram Whitrow, below, in chap. 1.

23. A. E. Bestor, *Backwoods Utopias . . . 1663–1829* (Philadelphia, 1950), p. 6, n. 10.

24. J. Prudhommeaux, "Un siècle de communisme expérimental aux Etats-Unis" (unpublished Master's thesis, Leçons au College Libre des Sciences Sociales, 1912), pp. 81 ff.

25. W. A. Hinds, *American Communities* (Chicago, 1908), pp. 100–01. Hinds draws his material from a monograph by E. O. Randall, *History of Zoar Society, a Sociological Study in Communism*, 2d ed. (Columbus, Ohio, 1900).

26. See Prudhommeaux (n. 24); W. R. Perkins, *History of the Amana Society* (Iowa City, 1891); also Bertha M. Shambaugh, *Amana That Was and Amana That Is* (Iowa City, 1932).

27. Michael A. Mikkelsen, *The Bishop Hill Colony; a Religious Communistic Settlement in Henry County, Illinois* (Baltimore, 1892); also Prudhommeaux (see n. 24).

28. Alex Kent, "Cooperative Communities in the United States," *Bulletin of the Department of Labor* (July 1901).

29. The document is attributed to Elder Calvin Harlow and is cited by White and Taylor (see n. 9), p. 301.

30. Ibid., p. 304; see also above, n. 21.

31. George Lomas, *Plain Talks* (Albany, 1873), p. 10.

32. Wells (see n. 1), pp. 289–90.

33. Josiah Warren was the founder of several experimental communities. Among these were: Equity, founded in 1835, in Tuscara County, Ohio, and Utopia, founded in 1847, also in Ohio. The idea of using a unit of work-time as the medium of exchange was proposed by Robert Owen in 1820. Warren put this idea into practice by establishing "Time Stores." These are described by J. H. Noyes in his *History of American Socialisms* (Philadelphia, 1870), p. 95, and by Bestor (see n. 23), pp. 185 and 227.

34. *Millennial Church* (p. 60) affirms that noviate Families "are generally encumbered with children, and often with those who are aged and infirm, besides more or less poor persons who bring in nothing with them and who . . . must have their equal share of support, whether they are able to earn it or not."

35. In the *Testimonies* (p. 210) Mother Ann is reported to have reproached a member for not eating all the meat on his bone: "Take this bone, pick it clean and learn to be prudent."

36. The principal lawsuits were over: property being divided between husband and wife; the return of property to a member leaving the society; taxes in lieu of military service; etc.

37. Nordhoff (see n. 3), p. 161.

38. See above, chap. 5, sect. IV.

39. George Lomas, in *Plain Talks,* explained that, knowing the hundreds of difficulties which confront a True Believer when he is bound by civil law to an unbelieving partner, they could do no more than persuade the husband and wife to arrive at some mutual understanding and thus maintain the faith of the believer either by obtaining written permission for him (or her) to leave the household, or by obtaining an agreement whereby the couple would live together with the same purity of soul and body that the believer would practice in the society. It was always preferable, said Lomas, for the husband and wife to agree that they would live according to Shaker principles (i.e. in a Family). However, when for reasons of business, children, property, etc., the couple had permission to live outside the society, they were made to understand that strict compliance with Shaker beliefs was indispensable if they were to remain members in good standing. Any secret or unconfessed infractions of Shaker practices would lead to their expulsion.

40. See above, chap. 5, sect. IV.

41. *Account of Some of the Proceedings of the Legislature of the State of Kentucky and New Hampshire, 1828 . . . in Relation to the People Called Shakers,* reprinted (New York, 1846).

42. *Report of the Examination of the Shakers at Canterbury and Enfield, before the New Hampshire Legislature at the November Session, 1848: Including the Testimony at Length, Several Extracts from Shaker Publications, the Bill Which Passed the House of Representatives, the Proceedings in the Pillow Case together with the Letter of James W. Spinney* (Concord, N.H., 1849), pp. 38–39.

43. *Investigator, or a Defence of the Order, Government and Economy of the*

United Society Called Shakers against Sundry Charges and Legislative Proceedings (Lexington, Kentucky, 1828).

44. *The Shaker Society Adv-s Gass, Banta, etc.* (n.p., 183?).

45. The title indicates the attitude (see n. 43).

46. Julia Neal, *By Their Fruits. The Story of Shakerism in South Union, Kentucky* (New York, 1947), p. 38.

47. Quoted by Marguerite Melcher in *The Shaker Adventure* (Princeton, 1941), pp. 89–91.

48. Chase (see n. 4), p. 248.

49. Roxalana Grosvenor, *The Shaker Covenant* (*Never Before Published*), *with a Brief Outline of Shaker History* (Boston, 1873). Roxalana Grosvenor testified that she signed the Covenant, 11 July 1834.

50. See above, the "1795 Transcription of the 1788 Oral Covenant."

51. M. R. Mayeaux, "Les biens d'Eglise considérés comme patrimoine des pauvres à travers les conciles occidentaux du XIᵉ siècle," in *Inspiration religieuse et structures temporelles*, a collective work (Paris, 1948), p. 139.

52. "From the point of view of an economically privileged person, if a few men owned the world, their property would look as tainted as the property of someone who owns other people. A society, a nation or even an association composed of all societies existing at a given time, could never own the earth. Men are never more than its users and, like the head of a family, have an obligation to improve it for the use of generations to come" (Karl Marx, *Capital* [Vienna-Berlin, 1932–33], 3:826). See also, the translation into French by Max Rubel, *Pages choisies . . .* (Paris, 1948), p. 294.

53. "The Shaker system cannot become . . . a hospital for incurables . . . nor a nursery . . . nor an asylum for the mentally ill" (A. G. Hollister, *Mission of Alethian Believers* [Mount Lebanon, 1892–99], p. 2).

54. Chase (see n. 4), pp. 137 ff.

55. Paul Passy, "*Liefra,*" *colonie coopérative agricole* (Paris, 1910), p. 6.

56. Frederick Evans, *Autobiography,* reprinted (New York, 1888), pp. 209 ff.

57. See below, sect. III.

58. H. C. Puech, *Le Manichéisme* (Paris, 1949), p. 85: "In every communion, Eucharist or Lord's Supper, we invoke the daily meals of the Elect." See also, ibid., n. 365: "It is nevertheless true that certain Manichaeans tried to set up a parallel between the Christian Eucharist and the purifying effect of the Elect on foods consumed during their ceremonial meal." For a discussion of the transubstantiation which was supposed to occur at such ceremonial meals because of the physical presence of the Elect, see ibid, pp. 90–91.

59. See above, chap. 4, II.

60. *Millennial Church,* p. 287, par. 15.

61. Ibid., pars. 13–14.

62. Ibid., p. 289, par. 21.

63. Ibid., par. 22.

64. This paragraph is a paraphrase of *Millennial Church,* pp. 288–91.

65. For the Quaker practice of silent prayer, see Henry Van Etten, *Le culte quaker d'après les données de la mystique* (Paris, 1945).

66. This list and description is found in J. Maitron, *Histoire du mouvement anarchiste en France* (Paris, 1951), pp. 355 ff.

67. Catalogue in J. W. Eaton and S. M. Katz, *Research Guide on Cooperative Group Farming. A Research Bibliography* . . . (New York, 1942), pp. 35–40.

68. *Millennial Church,* p. 67.

69. Ibid., p. 66.

70. "The first in the Ministry stands as the leading Elder of the Society" (ibid.). See also, Grosvenor, *Shakers' Covenant* (n. 15), Articles 1, 2, and 3.

71. "We are . . . subject to one united, parental and ministerial administration, which has been regularly supported from the first foundation pillars of the Institution . . ." (Grosvenor, *Shaker's Covenant,* Article 1, par. 1. On the "parental order," see above chap. 5.

72. *Millennial Church,* p. 66.

73. White and Taylor (see n. 9), p. 68.

74. Ibid., pp. 69–70.

75. Ibid., p. 70.

76. Ibid., pp. 71–72.

77. Shaker Church Covenant, in *The Shaker* 7 (October-November 1877): 75–76, 85–86; also in *The Manifesto* 19 (January 1889): 3–12.

78. Ibid., Article 1, section 2.

79. Ibid., Article 3.

80. Ibid., Article 5.

81. Ibid., Article 3; see also, Marguerite Melcher (n. 47), pp. 137–43.

82. The Shaker's Covenant, Article 5.

83. Chase (see n. 4), pp. 166–70.

84. See the provisions of the Covenant cited above.

85. Detail reported by Hervey Elkins, *Fifteen Years in the Senior Order of Shakers: A Narration of Facts Concerning that Singular People* (Hanover, 1853). Also cited by Charles Nordhoff (see n. 3), p. 171.

86. See the provisions of the "Junior Covenant" cited above.

87. Elkins, p. 171.

88. Ibid., pp. 174–75; see also, Edward D. Andrews, *The People Called Shakers* (New York, 1953).

89. Nordhoff (see n. 3), pp. 175, 142–44.

90. Ibid., p. 135.

91. Ibid., pp. 135–51.

92. Ibid., pp. 164–65.

93. Bestor (see n. 23), pp. 235–36.

94. Nordhoff, p. 166.

95. According to Nordhoff, the North Family at Mount Lebanon

numbered 60 people, 6 of whom, all women, worked in the kitchen and dining room.

96. Nordhoff, p. 161.

97. Ibid.

98. Ibid., p. 139.

99. On the horse collar, see the well-known work of Lefèvre des Noettes. As for the metal pen, we know that as early as 1790 the Frenchman Thévenot was manufacturing long-lasting pens made of brass to replace the goose quills then in use. In 1803 the Englishman Whise started to use sheet steel to manufacture the first cheap metal pens. But it is quite possible that the Shakers knew nothing of these precedents.

100. The list of these inventions is given by White and Taylor (see n. 9), p. 310; See also Edward D. Andrews, *The Community Industries of the Shakers* (Albany, 1932).

101. G. Friedman, *Ou va le travail humain* (Paris, 1950), pp. 19–39, 79.

102. Nordhoff, p. 161.

103. See below, chap. 7.

104. The Perfects among the Manichaeans neither produced nor prepared their own food: "Gardening, picking, milling, pressing and cooking were sins to be committed by the catechumens, who were the only ones allowed to bring food to the Elect. Using a number of ritual formulas, those receiving the food would begin by cursing the foodbearer and disclaiming all responsibility for the series of crimes committed in preparing the repast, then he would absolve the guilty food-bearer, who was at the same time his benefactor, before accepting and consuming his gift" (Puech [see n. 58], p. 90).

105. W. J. Warner, *The Wesleyan Movement in the Industrial Revolution* (London, 1930), chaps. 5 and 6.

106. *Testimonies*, pp. 209–10.

107. Ibid., p. 208.

108. Ibid.

109. Ibid.

110. *Testimonies*, pp. 215, 212.

111. Ibid p. 210.

112. Ibid., p. 211. Obviously, this should be compared to the well-known analyses of Max Weber and R. H. Tawney.

113. *Testimonies*, pp. 207–21: "Counsel in temporal things: industry, cleanliness, prudence, economy, giving of alms, charity to the poor."

114. Mother Ann said that it is not right to warm ourselves around a fire while others shiver with cold; and, although fire gives us comfort, it it would be sinful to depend solely on it to keep ourselves warm. The Mother's solution was to work so that the power of God would warm her (see *Testimonies*, p. 225). In the third generation of Shakers "industriousness" won out over asceticism and they installed hot-air registers in their Family houses.

115. "Phebe Spencer, being on a visit to the Church, at Watervliet, asked Mother's counsel concerning some superfluities which she and her family had gathered, such as gold beads, jewels, silver buckles, and other ornaments of the kind. Mother Ann answered, 'You may let the moles and bats have them; that is, the children of this world; for they set their hearts upon such things; but, the people of God do not want them'" (*Testimonies*, p. 208).

"She also said, 'You ought to dress yourself in modest apparel, as becomes the people of God, and teach your family to do likewise. You ought to be industrious and prudent, and not live a sumptuous and gluttonous life; but labor for a meek and quiet spirit, and see that your family is kept decent, and regular, in all their going forth, that others may see your good works'" (ibid., p. 208).

"While Mother Ann was at Petersham, in the summer of 1783, she took an opportunity to instruct some of the heads of families, who were there, concerning their temporal economy; and admonished them against some of their costly and extravagant furniture, saying 'Never put on silver spoons, nor table cloths for me; but let your tables be clean enough to eat from without cloths, and if you do not know what to do with them, give them to the poor'" (ibid., p. 211).

116. See the plates in Edward D. Andrews, *Shaker Furniture* (New Haven, 1937).

117. *Testimonies*, p. 207.

118. John Dunlavy, *The Manifesto* . . . (Pleasant Hill, Ky., 1818), pp. 63–64.

119. *Testimonies*, p. 213.

120. See above, chap. 4, n. 67.

121. Nordhoff (see n. 3), pp. 161–62.

122. See above, n. 28; also chap. 4, n. 67.

123. W. Hepworth Dixon, *New America* (London, 1867).

124. *Testimonies*, p. 33.

125. On Francis Wright and the founding of Nashoba, see Bestor (n. 23), p. 219, n. 31.

126. Neal (see n. 46), p. 59.

127. Ibid.,

128. Chase (see n. 4), p. 194.

129. Ibid., p. 195.

130. Manuscript of the Western Reserve Historical Society, reproduced by Chase, p. 194.

131. *Social Gathering, Dialogue between Six Sisters of the North Family of Shakers* (Albany, 1873), p. 7.

132. *Testimonies*, p. 86.

133. Chase (see n. 4).

134. Ibid., p. 189.

135. White and Taylor (see n. 9), pp. 182–83 and 196–99, give two

of these requests. On page 199 they quote E. M. Stanton, the Secretary of War, who recognized the special rights of this religious community, "whose conscientious scrupules abjure war or the payment of commutation fee."

136. Ibid., p. 203.

137. *Affectionately Inscribed to the Memory of Frederick W. Evans*, ed. Anna White (Pittsfield, 1893), p. 107.

138. Daniel Fraser, *The Music of the Spheres* (Albany, 1887), pp. 9–10.

139. Elie Reclus, "Etudes sociologiques: Visite aux Shakers de Mount Lebanon," *Société Nouvelle, 1886* (2ᵉ année), 1:458–470; 2:5–17.

140. *Social Gathering* (see n. 131), p. 13.

Notes to Chapter Seven

1. *Social Gathering, Dialogue between Six Sisters of the North Family of Shakers* (Albany, 1873), p. 16.

2. Ibid., p. 6.

3. See *Millennial Church*, Pt. V, chap. 4. for "A brief illustration of the four general dispensations," see pp. 223 ff.

4. Ibid., p. 189.

5. Ibid., p. 190.

6. See above, chap. 6, section on "The Religion of Shaker Communism."

7. See above, chap. 5, sect. II.

8. *Millennial Church*, pp. 224–25.

9. *Testimony*, pp. 55 ff. Interpreting the text of Leviticus 15:17–18, the *Testimony* says that under Mosaic law in no case could a man and woman copulate without breaking their ties with the rest of the people of Israel in the camp. The act itself severed their connection and exposed them to general opprobrium as impure and outside the camp of their people. They could not be readmitted until they had been purified, since nothing impure was allowed in the camp.

10. I. de Beausobre, *Histoire critique de Manichée et du Manichéisme* (Amsterdam, 1735); also "Dissertation sur les Adamites de Bohême," in J. Lenfant, *Histoire de la guerre des Hussites et du Concile de Basle* (Paris, 1731).

11. E. H. Broadbent, *Le pèlerinage douloureux de l'Eglise fidèle à travers les âges*, trans. (Yverdon, Switzerland, 1938).

12. Frederick Evans, *Autobiography of a Shaker . . .* (New York, 1888), p. 46.

13. Frederick Evans, *Shakers. Compendium of the Origin, History, Principles, Rules and Regulations, Government and Doctrines of the United Society of Believers in Chirst's Second Appearing* (New Lebanon, 1859), p. 75.

14. See above, chap. 6, section on "Religion of Shaker Communism."

15. Evans (see n. 13), pp. 74–75.

16. John Dunlavy, *The Manifesto or a Declaration of the Doctrines and Practice of the Church of Christ* (New York, 1847), p. 324.

17. See above, chap. 5, section on "Ideological Arguments."

18. Evans (see n. 13), p. 70.

19. Frederick Evans, *Who is Ann Lee?* (Mount Lebanon, 1889), pp. 7–9.

20. The book was printed by the Shakers in East Canterbury, N.H., in 1893. It has a preface by Henry Blinn, a Shaker elder who thought the work capable of making the Christian communist order more widely and correctly known to the public.

21. Charles Edson Robinson, *A Concise History of the United Society of Believers Called Shakers* (East Canterbury, N.H., 1893), p. 8.

22. Ibid., pp. 5, 9.

23. Ibid., p. 9.

24. Ibid., pp. 5–6.

25. *Testimony*, p. 182.

26. This line of reasoning is found in Dunlavy's *Manifesto*, pp. 297 ff.

27. This comparison was to their disadvantage when it supported an accusation of popery; it was to their advantage when it defended their socio-economic status.

28. Dunlavy's *Manifesto*, p. 275.

29. Ibid., p. 276. This Shaker perfectionism is just one example of the American perfectionism which was the subject of a careful study by M. E. Gaddis, "Christian Perfectionism in America" (Ph.D. diss., University of Chicago, 1929).

30. Dunlavy's *Manifesto*, p. 276. W. Dirks has outlined a similar analysis: "The bourgeois accepted the world as pagan and installed himself in it after taking certain precautions. He 'reified' Christian renunciation, transforming it into a question of alms and personal sacrifices. He relegated any real renunciation of the world to the religious orders; from this came a fundamental weakening of religious reality, a secularization of the world, and the so-called 'spiritualization' of Christianity which led to apostasy" (Walter Dirks, "Le Marxisme dans une vision chrétienne," *Esprit* [May-June 1948], p. 796).

31. Dunlavy's *Manifesto*, pp. 276, 300. This refusal to take an oath was common among similar dissident groups. The reason for this can be found on page 300 of the *Manifesto*. An oath, Dunlavy explains, is the subjective equivalent of objective coercion such as occurs in carrying out the law or in simply recognizing the law's right to force obedience.

32. This is another familiar dissident theme. Medieval dissidents felt a similar resentment of the mendicant orders. See S. Runciman, *Le Manichéisme mediéval*, trans. (Paris, 1949), p. 116. For the Russian sects, see the resumé of K. K. Grass, *Die russischen Sekten, I. Die Gottesleute oder Chlüsten* (Leipzig, 1907–09), in R. Hertz, "Sectes russes," in his *Melanges de sociologie religieuse* (Paris, 1928), pp. 238–39.

33. Dunlavy's *Manifesto*, p. 276.

34. See above, chap. 6. sect. III.

35. *Testimony*, p. 21.

36. Ibid., pp. 24–25. During the Inquisition the diabolic nature of the Antichrist seems to have become clear. The *Testimony* refers to it as the "mother of all abominations," whose scarlet robe was the blood of the millions of human beings she had persecuted to death.

37. Ibid., p. 319.

38. Ibid., p. 321.

39. Ibid., p. 342.

40. Ibid., p. 216. This can be compared to H. Maisonneuve, *Etudes sur les origines de l'Inquisition* (Paris, 1942). See particularly the study of repressive laws in the Codes of Theodosius and Justinian.

41. *Testimony*, pp. 169–70.

42. Ibid. On the precarious nature of evaluating information about Manichaens until about 1930, see H. C. Puech, *Le Manichéism* (Paris, 1949).

43. A. Guillaumont, "Les Messaliens," in *Etudes carmélitaines: Mystique et continence* (Paris, 1952), pp. 131–38.

44. "As for the horror of blood, the Paulicians were so far from this principle that they had a reputation as warriors ardent in battle and ferocious in slaughter. This is why Byzantium feared them and why she later used them to defend her frontiers" (H. C. Puech, "Bogomilisme et Paulicianisme," in Puech and Vaillant *Le traité contre les Bogomiles de Cosmas-le-Prêtre* [Paris, 1945], p. 317).

45. *Testimony*, p. 215.

46. Ibid., p. 218

47. Ibid., p. 220.

48. Ibid., p. 222.

49. Ibid., p. 220.

50. Ibid., p. 222.

51. Ibid., p. 327.

52. Ibid., pp. 220–21.

53. See above chap. 4, sect. II.

54. *Testimony*, p. 297.

55. Ibid., p. 315.

56. Ibid., p. 255.

57. See above, chap. 5, sect. II.

58. *Testimony*, p. 277.

59. Ibid.

60. Ibid., pp. 294–95.

61. Ibid., p. 326.

62. Ibid., p. 327.

63. Frederick Evans, *Shaker-Russian Correspondence between Count Leo Tolstoi and Elder F. W. Evans* (Mount Lebanon, 1891). See below, this chapter, section on *"Tolstoi's Christianity."*

64. *Testimony*, pp. 333 ff.

65. Ibid., p. 335.

66. Ibid., p. 308 ff.

67. On pages 353–54 of the *Testimony* we learn that when the Friends were accepted as a legal religion they joined forces with "the Beast" and so soon died and were without life.

68. *Testimony*, p. 347.

69. Ibid., p. 357.

70. Ibid.

71. See above, chap. 5, sect. III.

72. See above, this chapter, sect. I.

73. On the other hand, Bethel-Aurora received a visit from W. Weitling, the precursor of European communism. This visit is described in Macdonald's manuscript. For an account of Macdonald's visits to the different American communities, see C. Whittke, *The Utopian Communist* (Baton Rouge, 1950).

74. The bibliography for the different communities is given by J. W. Eaton and S. M. Katz, *Research Guide on Cooperative Group Farming. A Research Bibliography on Rural Cooperative Production and Cooperative Communities* (New York, 1942), pp. 42–67; A. E. Bestor, *Backwoods Utopias* (Philadelphia, 1950), pp. 253–55; also by Donald Drew Egbert and Stow Parsons, *Socialism and American Life* (Princeton, 1952), 2: pass.

75. Bestor (see n. 74), pp. 44–45.

76. *Testimony*, p. 357.

77. See above, chap. 3, sect. II.

78. The name of Busro is spelled in several different ways, according to the text: Busro, Bussro, and Bussrow are the most common.

79. Daryl Chase, "The Early Shakers" (Ph.D. diss., University of Chicago, 1938), p. 203.

80. See above, chap. 6, section on "The Religion of Shaker Communism."

81. Anna White and Leila Taylor, *Shakerism. Its Meaning and Message* (Mount Lebanon, 1905), p. 19.

82. J. A. Bole, *The Harmony Society* (Philadelphia, 1904), pp. 126–27.

83. Chase (see n. 79), p. 205 and n. 2.

84. Ibid., p. 202.

85. Bestor (see n. 74), p. 39, says that it is through the Shakers that the German communal tradition was translated into American terms.

86. See above, chap. 3, sect. II.

87. Daryl Chase who cites the fact refers to a published thesis by J. Geddes, *The United Order among the Mormons* (New York, 1922). On the cooperative aspect of the Mormon experiment see G. H. Bousquet, "Une Théologie économique: L'Eglise Mormone," *Rev. Eco. Pol.* (1938) pp. 106–45.

88. Chase (see n. 79), pp. 208 ff.

89. K. J. Arndt, "The Harmonists and the Mormons," *American-German Review*. vol. 10, no. 5 (June 1944).

90. On this type of Shaker publication see above, chap. 4, sect. I.

91. Evans (see n. 12), p. 88.

92. Ibid.

93. The Oneida sect explained these propositions in two small treatises: *Mutual Criticism* (Oneida, 1876) and *Male Continence* (Oneida, 1877).

94. See Eaton and Katz (n. 74) for complete list.

95. Evans (see n. 12), p. 89.

96. See above, chap. 5, sect. III; also A. G. Hollister, *Mission of Alethian Believers Called Shakers* (Mount Lebanon, 1892), pp. 22–23.

97. In a letter to *The American Socialist* Elder James S. Prescott affirmed that the human race could be physically improved by scientific breeding and careful selection according to the laws of natural reproduction. "This is pretty strong language for a Shaker" was the comment by W. A. Hinds, in his *American Communities*, rev. ed. (Chicago, 1902), pp. 50–51.

98. Hinds, pp. 61–62.

99. J. H. Noyes, *History of American Socialisms* (Philadelphia and London, 1870), p. 595.

100. "Ebenezers" was the name sometimes used for "Amana."

101. R. A. Parker, *A Yankee Saint. John Humphrey Noyes and the Oneida Community* (New York, 1935), p. 158.

102. Bestor (see n. 74), p. 52.

103. The relations between Lane and the Shakers are analyzed in detail by Clara Endicott Sears in *Gleanings from Old Shaker Journals* (Boston, 1916), pp. 263–72.

104. See above, this chap., sect. I, 6.

105. E. Halévy, "Naissance du Méthodisme en Angleterre," *Revue de Paris* (August 1906), pp. 863–64.

106. See above chap. 2, sect. I. Ingham's reply was published in the *Weekly Miscellany* on 4 July 1740.

107. Halévy (see n. 105), p. 863.

108. J. H. Blunt, in *Dictionary of Sects*, points out that the dispute between the Glassites and the Dalites was based on their interpretation of a verse in the Epistle of Timothy, in which the apostle affirms that the priest should have only one wife (*vir unius mulieris*). The Glassites understood this to mean "one wife, once and for all," thus excluding the possibility of remarriage for a minister. The Dalites interpreted the verse to mean "one wife at a time" and allowed their ministers to remarry.

109. Halévy (see n. 105), p. 864.

110. Bestor (see n. 74), p. 95.

111. Evans (see n. 12), p. 25.

112. Bestor, p. 96.

113. John Bellers was a friend of William Penn. His book was published in 1695.

114. W. S. Warder, "A Brief Sketch of the Religious Society of People Called Shakers," dated 1817 and published in *New View of Society. Tracts*

Relative to This Subject, etc. . . . by John Bellers . . . by Robert Owen. . . by W. S. Warder, ed. Robert Owen (London, 1818).

115. Ibid., pp. 5 ff.

116. Ibid.

117. Bestor, p. 106. He refers to MacDonald's diaries of 1824–26 published in *Indiana Historical Society Publications*, vol. 4, n. 2 (Indianapolis, 1942), pp. 184–96.

118. Bestor, pp. 47–48.

119. Ibid., p. 220.

120. Ibid., p. 50, n. 37. On D. Latham, see Chase (n. 79). On Daniel Fraser, see letter reproduced in Evans (n. 13), pp. 123–24.

121. Bestor, p. 203.

122. White and Taylor (see n. 81), p. 159.

123. There is an allusion to this visit in Daniel Fraser's letter cited in Evans' *Autobiography* (see n. 12), p. 124.

124. See above, chap. 5, sect. III.

125. W. Leonard, *A Discourse of the Order and Propriety of Divine Inspiration . . .* (Harvard, 1853), pp. 84–87.

126. R. Ruyer, *L'Utopie et les Utopies* (Paris, 1950), p. 249.

127. M.L. Berneri, *Journey through Utopia* (London, 1950), p. 243.

128. Morris Hillquitt, *History of Socialism in the United States* (New York and London, 1903), pp. 316–18.

129. This letter is quoted in *Immortalized Elder Frederick Evans* (Pittsfield, Mass., 1893), pp. 120–21.

130. Ibid., pp. 122–23.

131. In a 1952 doctoral thesis for the University of Paris, Miss Baumann studies Bellamy's sources carefully. She finds no mention of Shaker influence except when he praises Nordhoff's book as a work of great importance. Through Nordhoff, Bellamy surely knew the monograph by Hervey Elkins.

132. See above, chap. 6, sect. III.

133. Evans reproached Bellamy for permitting the use of tobacco.

134. See above, chap. 6, sect. III.

135. These details and related religious questions are presented in detail in his *Open Letter to Pope Leo XIII,* dated 11 September 1891. A French translation of this letter by Paul E. Passy may be found in his *"Liefna," colonie coopérative agricole* (Paris, 1910).

136. George (see n. 135). p. 29.

137. Eaton and Katz (see n. 75), p. 40, list about ten single tax colonies: Arden, Ardentown, Fairhope, Single tax Corporation, Free Acres, Gilpin Point, Haleidon, Robin Hill, Shakertown, Tahanto, Trapelo, etc.

138. Elder Fraser's letter was dated December 23. It was published in the *New York Tribune* on December 26 as an answer to an article that had appeared in the same newspaper three days earlier under the title "The Catholic Pastoral and Mr. George."

139. Before this date a translation of the *Kreutzer Sonata* had been published in America, and the book was probably in the hands of the elders. Before this, the Shakers had had extended dealings with a Russian consul in New York.

140. The text of Tolstoi's letter is the one given in *Shaker-Russian Correspondence* (Mount Lebanon, 1891) and is taken from the copy in the New York Public Library, The text of Evans's letter follows the version in *Immortalized Frederick W. Evans*, pp. 116–20, which is somewhat more complete than what was published in the *Shaker-Russian Correspondence*.

141. M. J. Bienstock, *Tolstoï et les Doukhobors. Faits historiques réunis et traduis* (Paris, 1902), pp. 208 ff., see also, Henry Lasserre, *The Communities of Tolstoyans* (Toronto, 1944).

142. See above, chap. 6, section on the "Three Types of Families."

143. A theme familiar to Evans. See his *Autobiography* (n. 13), p. 42.

144. Allusion to Evans's gnosticism, a theme which he develops in his autobiography.

145. See Lasserre (n. 142); also Hertz (n. 33), p. 229: "When we talk of Tolstoyism we forget that it is hardly more than a literary transcription for educated people of the thoughts and feelings found in dissident Russian peasants around 1912."

146. Evans died on 6 March 1893.

147. The tendency to spiritualism which so astonished Tolstoi was waning among the Shakers.

148. Tolstoi, *Rayons de l'aube*, Fr. trans. M. J. Bienstock (Paris, 1901), p. 3. Translator's note: The English title of this Tolstoi play is *Light Shines in the Darkness*.

149. *La religion et les religions. Ultimes paroles*, Fr. trans. Halpérine Kaminsky (Paris, 1908), p. 233. This text can be compared with the Shaker idea of evolution in religion and Shaker liberalism in interpreting the Holy Scriptures (see above, this chapter, introductory paragraphs). Also, Cyrus O. Poole, *Spiritualism as Organized by the Shakers* (Mount Lebanon, 1887), p. 11.

150. Lasserre (see n. 141). The citation is from the French translation, p. 29.

151. "Neighborly love is incompatible with oaths, violence, military service and private property" (*Tolstoï et les Doukhobors* [see n. 141], pp. 229–30).

152. This is the subject of the *Kreutzer Sonata*. Tolstoï's personal commentary can be found in *Plaisirs vicieux*, Fr. trans. Halpérine Kaminsky (Paris, 1892), pp. 120–34. Translator's note: *Plaisirs vicieux* is a French anthology of Tolstoi's writings on various vices.

153. Tolstoi, "Marchez, pendant que vous avez la lumiére," Fr. trans. M. J. Bienstock, in *Oeuvres* (Paris, 1903), 26:175–76 (this is the short story known in English as *Walk in the Light*). In his *Plaisirs vicieux* there is also a theme recalling the Shakers: "History shows us humanity pressing for-

ward, ceaselessly and invincibly, from the dawn of time to the present day, moving out of polygamy and polyandry toward a monogamy of incontinence, and then finally toward a continence observed even in marriage."

154. Tolstoi, *Kreutzer Sonata,* concluding remarks by the author.

155. M. I. Markovitch, *Tolstoï et Ghandi* (Paris, 1928), p. 106.

156. Ibid., p. 108.

157. Ibid., see also, Tolstoi's *Plaisirs vicieux,* pass.

158. *Tolstoï et Ghandi,* chap. 5.

159. Ibid., pp. 145 ff.

160. Ghandi wrote Tolstoi for the first time during a stay in London in 1909.

161. Ghandi, *La jeune Inde,* Fr. trans. Hélène Hart (Paris, 1924), pp. 295–98.

162. See above, chap. 2, sect. III; also chap. 5, sect. I.

163. See above, chap. 6, section on "Living Conditions."

164. Shâbuhragân, quoted by Puech in *Le Manichéisme,* p. 59; for account of Manichaeus's voyage to India, see ibid., p. 44.

165. *Tolstoï et Ghandi* (see n. 155).

166. On the subject of similarities between the Khlysti and the early Christian communities or even the Australian aborigines: "It would be useless to explain any striking resemblances by alleging that they represent survivals of ancient Finnish paganism. If the religion of the Australian aborigines, the early Christians and the Russian sect are astonishingly similar in their expressions and practices that is because they all appeared in societies at the same stage of what Durkheim called *effervescence*" (Hertz [see n. 32], p. 248).

Notes to Conclusions

1. See above, chap. 7, sect. I,1.

2. See ibid., 4.

3. See ibid., sect. II, end of 5.

4. Along with the comments of Marcel Mauss, we can cite a letter from Simone Weil, published in the *Cahiers d'Etudes Cathares* (April-June 1949), pp. 4–5. She reproaches the God of the Old Testament on the same grounds as those used by the Shakers in their biblical criticism. And is there not a resonant note of Shakerism in another of her declarations: "I can see no difference except in details of terminology between the Manichaean and the Christian conceptions of the relation between good and evil" (Simone Weil, Letter to S. Petrement, quoted in *Synthèse* [October 1951], p. 180).

5. Memo containing ideas developed at length in M. Meillet, "Trois conférences sur les Gathâ de l'Avesta," *Annales du Musée Guimet* (Paris, 1925).

6. *Anthropologie* (1924), pp. 276 ff.

7. E. G. Leonard (see above, chap. 1, nn. 37, 52, and 56).

8. For presentation of this argument, see chap. 3, sect. III, 4.

9. Engels touched on this question in a series of articles written for the *New Moral World*, November 3, 1843. See "Progress of Social Reform on the Continent," Mega 1, 2, p. 441.

10. B. Nicolaievski and O. Maechen-Helfen, *Karl Marx* (Paris, 1937), pp. 73–74. The authors allude to the influence of communism in the early Christian sects on the organization of secret societies and the leagues, and they point out how much the ideas of Saint-Simon, Owen, and Fourier resemble the ideals of the early Christians.

11. Friedrich Engels, *Anti-Dühring* (Paris, 1931), 1, pp. 201–14. Desroche included a commentary on this passage in his *Signification du Marxisme* (Paris, 1949), pp. 134 ff.

12. Frederich Engels, *Beschreibung der in neuerer Zeit enstandenen und noch bestehenden kommunistischen Anseidlungen* (Description of Recently Founded and Still Extant Communistic Societies), Mega 1, 4, pp. 351–66. This study appeared without the author's name in the February-March issue of *Deutsches Bürgerbuch für* 1845, a collection edited by H. Puttmann. In his letters to the *New Moral World* Engels explained the circumstances of this anonymous publication: "A collection of studies on this subject was published by H. Puttmann of Cologne. *It contained, among other things, an account of the American* communities and of your own establishment in Hampshire which has done so much to dissipate prejudices as to the impracticability of our ideas" (Letter of February 22, in the *New Moral World* [March 8, 1845]; reproduced in Mega 1, 4, p. 343).

In another letter which, like the first, was signed "an old friend of yours in Germany," Engels tells of the first of the meetings held at Elberfeld. He lists the contributions of Hess, Koettingen, et al., "after which Mr. Friedrich Engels, who recently published several pages in your columns on continental communism [see above, 'n. 9], discussed at some length what is practical and advantageous in the communist system. To support his assertions he gave some details on the American communities and on your own establishment at Harmony." The same letter identifies the author of *Beschreibung* . . . : "Dr. Puttmann has published a collection of essays containing an excellent paper by Dr. Hess . . . and an account of the American communities, including the one at Harmony, by Friedrich Engels" (undated letter in the *New Moral World*, May 10, 1845; reproduced in Mega 1, 4, pp. 345–48). For a complete text of this letter translated into French, with commentary, see Henri Desroche and G. Dunstheimer, "Une étude de Friedrich Engels sur les coopératives communautaires du XIXe siècle," *Communauté* (August 1954), pp. 41–62.

13. This is the series of articles mentioned above, n. 9.

14. Engels mentions Skaneateles, Brook Farm, Northampton, and Equality. He seems to hope that these communities will eventually join up with the American workers' movement and set the revolutionary process into motion (*Beschreibung*, p. 361). Actually, Engels is committing a gross generalization in selecting these particular four communities for whom Eaton and Katz as well as A. E. Bestor give the following dates:

Northhampton Association	1842–46
Equality (or Hunt's Colony)	1843–46
Brook Farm	1841–47
Skaneateles Community	1843–46

The article by John Finch, which was Engels's source of information, had appeared in the *New Moral World* during the year 1844; Engels wrote his article in 1845. It so happens that 1844 and 1845 were boom years for the communitarian movement in America, as the dates for the above-mentioned communities attest. But the movement promised more than it produced, and Engels based his hopes on what proved to be only good intentions.

15. A description of this experiment is found on pp. 361–65 of Engels's study.

16. Finch's account of the number of communities is well below the actual number. See chart no. 6.

17. At this point there was a long quote from Finch describing the society at Pleasant Hill, and then another quotation, this one by an English traveler named Pitkeithley, who had visited New Lebanon. The section on the Shakers is followed by descriptions of the Rappites, the Zoarites, and the Owenites at Harmony (*Beschreibung*, pp. 355–65).

18. Ibid., p. 365.

Index